# Handbook
# of
# Aeronautical
# Inspection
# and
# Pre-Purchase

*Aircraft Knowledge*
*12 Steps to Pre-Purchase Inspections*
*Annual Inspection*
*Inspections*
*100-Hour Inspections*
*Special Inspections*
*Maintenance Requirements*
*Mechanic Requirements*
*Alterations*
*Major Repairs*
*Owner Produced Parts*
*Aircraft Imports*                          *By Denny Pollard*

Order this book online at www.trafford.com
or email orders@trafford.com

Most Trafford titles are also available at major online book retailers.

Print information available on the last page.

ISBN: 978-1-4120-5065-4 (sc)
ISBN: 978-1-4122-3288-3 (e)

*Trafford rev. 12/29/2018*

www.trafford.com

**North America & international**
toll-free: 1 888 232 4444 (USA & Canada)
fax: 812 355 4082

# Disclaimer

The information provided in this book is not intended to supercede or supplement the FAA approved engine, airframe, propellers, or appliance maintenance and/or operator's manuals. Those FAA approved manuals must be utilized when performing maintenance and/or operating Type Certificated products. Denny Pollard assumes no liability resulting from the use of the information contained in this book. While every effort is made to ensure accuracy, Denny Pollard makes no representation as to the accuracy of, and cannot accept any legal responsibility for any errors, omissions, miss-statements or mistakes within the pages of this book. In no event Denny Pollard will not be liable to you for any damages (including, without limitation, consequential, incidental or special damages, including lost profits or lost savings), or for illegal acts or actions, arising from the use of the pages in this book. The issues and recommendations discussed in this book do not constitute legal advice. I have made an earnest attempt to provide proper citation to the work of others, but I do apologize if I have failed to provide appropriate credit to anyone for their efforts or ideas. My objective is to alert you to some common issues so that you can avoid or minimize legal trouble.

# Acknowledgments

This book is a collection of information gathered from many sources, including the Federal Aviation Administration, industry, engine manufactures, aircraft, manufactures, personal experiences, and other mechanics. A special thanks goes to Little Flyers, Hanger 16 Airport Road, Kearny, AZ. If it were not for the family-centered business like Little Flyers and dedicated mechanics that take pride in their workmanship the aviation industry, as we know it would not exist.

Additional thanks to Textron Lycoming "Key Reprints" that assist the owner and operator improve their engine's performance and reliability.

# About the Author

Denny Pollard was born in Jerome, Idaho in 1954. He grew up and went to school in Hansen, Idaho. " I never intend to live in Idaho," he says. He currently lives in Northern California.

His aviation career started in the summer of 1964 as he watched the crash of an agriculture airplane in Hansen, Idaho. He heard the sounds, smelled the burning flesh, and watched the pilot burn to death; the thoughts and smell have never left him.

Denny is currently an Airframe and Powerplant (A&P) mechanic and holds an Inspection Authorization (IA). He has cut his knuckles and smashed his fingers bucking rivets and fitting sheet metal on aircraft. He has owned and operated an aviation repair business restoring damaged aircraft to serviceable condition. He has taught for a Part 147 aviation school training mechanics to become technicians on aircraft. He has written and published an aviation newsletter "The Aviator" for several years some of the articles appear in this book.

Denny has always tried to help others and share his knowledge of hard knocks so other will not have to repeat his mistakes. This is how his writings started. Not a schooled writer by trade having done poorly in English he has made a great effort in putting his words down on paper. It has been a life long dream to publish a book and now the dream has come true. "This is indeed a time to savor."

# INTRODUCTION

The airplane purchase process is a long and difficult one for most people, especially first-time airplane buyers. That's because there is a great deal of hard work involved. If you want to be sure that the airplane is worth the purchase price and is in the condition that has been described to you, several essential steps must be taken prior to consummating the deal.

In everyday life, we try to make everything we do as simple and easy as possible. When it comes to buying an airplane, however, there's no easy way out. If you handle your airplane purchase like you might an automobile, you are leaving yourself wide open for problems.

Hearing the horror stories of new owner only after they purchased their first aircraft and knowing how easy it is to protect your investment I decide to write down what I have learned over several years.

Purchasing an aircraft is a process one must go through and not knowing how much it will cost to repair or to replace parts to make the aircraft safe is the unknown. Unlike purchasing your first car you may not of lost much on the investment, but with aircraft costing in the thousands of dollars and annual inspections costing in the hundreds/thousands of dollars. Your pride and joy may become an albatross around your neck.

To prevent your aircraft from becoming an albatross, you can follow my twelve steps for pre-purchase and not end up with a lemon. I have inspected all types of aircraft from the Piper Cub to the Boeing 747 and the process is the same. Start with the records and end up at the taillight.

Are you considering buying an aircraft? Sometimes you may find the right one but it's not in your area. How can you buy with confidence over a long distance or even have the one in your area verified by an expert in the aviation inspection/appraisal field?

When is the proper time to take a close look at the maintenance records of any used aircraft you expect to purchase? A well-kept set of maintenance records, which properly identifies all previously performed maintenance, alterations, and AD compliances, is generally a good indicator of the aircraft condition. This is not always the case, but in any event, before you buy, require the owner to produce the maintenance records for your examination and require correction of any discrepancies found on the aircraft or in the records. Many prospective owners have found it advantageous to have a reliable unbiased maintenance person examine the maintenance records, as well as the aircraft, before negotiations have progressed too far. If the aircraft is purchased, take the time to review and learn the system of the previous owner to ensure compliance and is continuity when you modify or continue that system.

To inspect an aircraft you have to determine if it's fit, in an airworthy condition, and just not safe for flight. To accomplish this you will need a checklist. I have always found using a checklist will save time and you will not miss anything.

Probably the quickest way to get an FAA Inspectors attention in your new aircraft is not having good aircraft records (logbooks). These records are the only way to determine if inspections and maintenance good or bad has been accomplished. In my twelve steps and through out the book you will notice I keep referring to the aircraft records they are really the **GOLDEN BEE BEE** to purchasing a good aircraft.

This book documents the history, experiences and hardships of purchasing aircraft. It describes the difficult and hazardous situations demanding ingenuity, resourcefulness and a lot of difficult hard work. Denny's years of experience in the aviation field demonstrates a lesser-known side of aviation that is from the mechanic's' perspective. This book is the first of its' kind and once started, compels the reader to continue to the last page.

# Table of Contents

# CHAPTER 1

## PRE-PURCHASE INSPECTION

# Pre-Purchase Official Status

Before you buy your next aircraft, have an independent inspection completed by an Airframe and Powerplant mechanic. Whether you are an American or overseas buyer you will be able to buy with confidence with a pre-purchase inspection. With your pre-purchase inspection you should receive an extensive condition report verifying the condition and originality on the aircraft you wish to purchase. The pre-purchase should be able to tell you if the aircraft is currently airworthy, and if the aircraft has been in an accident or been modified.

Along with the detailed report you should receive several photographs, including pictures of the fuselage, engine compartment, and interior and close ups of areas of concern. After the inspection, the mechanic or agent for service should discuss this information with you.

Are you aware the pre-purchase agreement you sign may be the single most important document, among the dozen or so documents sometimes required? And which specific items should you include in your purchase agreement.

Has your aircraft (Or the One That You Are Thinking About Purchasing) been subjected to less than scrupulous inspection and maintenance practices, over the years?

Are you completely confident that all pertinent and repetitive Airworthiness Directives (AD's) have been accomplished?

Is the aircraft in compliance with the requirements of?

1.  Title 14 CFR 91 section 91.207 - Emergency Locator Transmitters.
2.  Title 14CFR 91 section 91.411/413 - Static System/Transponder.
3.  Are all of the required FAA Form 337's in your aircraft records.
4.  Have unauthorized repairs been made to the aircraft.
5.  Have items been installed in your aircraft without the proper documentation.

Sometimes even a very competent pre-purchase inspection does not include a complete inspection of the aircraft records because it is often very time consuming to read them thoroughly. Positively, the most enlightening pre-buy inspection is a good evaluation of the aircraft maintenance records. A complete evaluation will identify the current status of the aircraft as required by 14 CFR 91.417, uncover time frames of no maintenance, or lack of maintenance, identify inaccurate engine cycle tracking as well as aircraft time tracking and reveal aircraft damage history.

A pre-purchase inspection **has no** official status under Title 49 of the Code of Federal Regulations (CFR's). I want to explain the FAA rules, there are 100 titles to the U.S. Code Title 49 is Space and Aeronautics. All the CFR's are in Title 49, title 49 is broke down in parts that start with part 1 Definitions and so on. In each part it is futher broken down to sections. Each section is broken down to subsections such as Title 49, part 91, section 91.7, (.7 is a sub section).

To perform a pre-purchase inspection some minor disassembly is normally accomplished during the inspection. Disassembly of aircraft for inspection is considered maintenance. Any maintenance performed even during a pre-purchase inspection will require a maintenance record entry. Be aware there is nine inspections the FAA will recognize and a pre-purchase inspection is not one of them. More on the required inspections will be covered in Chapter 5 Inspections.

Prospective purchaser is responsible for discovering discrepancies that can only be revealed by in-flight evaluation such as flight characteristics, proper functioning of navigational instrumentation, avionics and autopilot. The purpose of the Pre-purchase Inspection is to protect the interest of the buyer; it is not intended to be an Annual/Airworthiness Inspection.

Unlike an automobile, the continuing costs of maintaining, insuring, storing, operating, and the overhaul or repair of major components can quickly outpace the amount of money that was spent up front for the purchase of your airplane. As there are many models and price ranges available, the purchaser is encouraged to set a range of expectations. The object of the pre-purchase inspection of a used airplane is to preclude the purchase of a "hanger queen." If the seller shows any hesitancy in allowing his or her airplane to be put to a complete pre-purchase inspection, you should back away from the airplane. No one wants to buy someone else's troubles.

I recommend that any potential buyer be extremely suspicious of airplanes advertised with a **"fresh annual"**. Think hard now; if you were selling your airplane, how much would you spend on an annual? Would you insist the mechanic correct every little thing that was wrong? Most of the time this is window dressing on a hanger queen. It's often a sign that should read, " Do Not Buy Me." Besides, you are going to do a pre-purchase that is so thorough, that once you have decided to accept the airplane. You will have the mechanic go ahead and complete an annual inspection because it is already at least 40 to 50% complete anyway, so a "fresh annual" adds no value to the airplane in your eyes.

You're in the market for an aircraft. You're already preapproved for an aircraft loan. You find what looks like the perfect aircraft. Sound just like buying a house, but how can you be sure it doesn't have any hidden defects?

In the past few years, the statutes and courts decisions of most states have changed the old common law rule of caveat emptor (let the buyer beware). Today, the practical rule has become: Seller beware of the buyer, his lawyer and his pre-purchase inspection.

The best way to avoid buying a bad aircraft is to make your purchase offer contingent on your pre-purchase inspection report. After the seller accepts your offer, you can hire an aircraft mechanic/inspector to determine if the seller, his agent for service, or broker has fully disclosed all known defects.

Since maintenance **"know how"** is not transferred with the aircraft, the new operator generally goes through a learning cycle before he is able to rapidly pinpoint the important/critical problem areas of the aircraft. In this respect, identification of known areas where structural and component failure problems have been experienced will help in the preparation of an initial maintenance program by a new operator.

# Pre Purchase Agreement Statement

From time to time a facility or technician is ask to do a pre purchase inspection on an aircraft that a party is possibly going to purchase.

**DO NOT** put your company or your career in jeopardy. It is important that the shop or technician make no recommendations about what to look at on the aircraft and avoid any opinions. Opinions and recommendations have a way of coming back to haunt you. After the sale you or your firm may be included as parties defendant in a lawsuit by an irate buyer seeking a pound of flesh. A pre purchase inspection is simply designed to give a buyer a low cost look at the aircraft. It is not and should not be an airworthiness inspection. If you do a pre-purchase inspection always put a logbook disclaimer as follows:

## Warning Disclaimer

I, we, hereby acknowledge and agree that this pre-purchase inspection is not an airworthiness inspection and is not an inspection defined by the Federal Aviation Regulations. The items inspected are selected at random or at the request of the buyer(s) and/or seller(s), and this shop or mechanic(s) gives no opinion and makes no recommendations with regard to the airworthiness of this aircraft, its engine(s), accessories, and avionics or the accuracy of its records and maintenance history.

Buyer: _____ Date:_____
Inspection Facility and/or Mechanic: _____

# Doing Your Home Work

Doing your homework starts with selecting the right aircraft. There are several ways to do a pre-purchase inspection on used aircraft and whether the method you choose is right for you depends on the outcome. There are many who say that nothing short of a fresh annual inspection is the best way to go, while others do little more than a cursory exam. Just remember a fresh annual may be the worst annual inspection. The aviation community is based on trust and section 43.12 protects us against fraud. If someone approves an aircraft for return to service **WITHOUT** accomplishing the scope and detail of Part 43 Appendix D (Annual Inspection requirements), they may have committed fraud and this is a Federal crime.

One way to protect yourself is have the Airframe and Powerplant (A&P) mechanic who holds an Inspection Authorization (IA) or a Part 145 Repair Station with the proper ratings perform the inspection and provide you with a copy of the check sheet they will use to accomplish the inspection. As the items are accomplished on the check sheet the mechanic should put his mark or better their initials beside the item completed. A sample check sheet is provided in the Appendix section to assist you.

There are several sources to find information about the aircraft you are about to purchase one that will give you some idea of the problems a certain aircraft has. This information can be found in the Aviation Maintenance Alerts, which cover all most every aircraft make and model.

Issued monthly, the Aviation Maintenance Alerts are prepared from information submitted by persons who operate and maintain civil aeronautical products. The Alerts provide a uniform means through which safety and service experience may be interchanged. The intent of this publication is to improve safety and service reliability of aeronautical products. AC 43-16, General Aviation Airworthiness Alerts, contains information that is of assistance to maintenance and inspection personnel in the performance of their duties. These items are developed from submitted FAA Form 8010-4 and articles pertaining to aviation. This publication is made available to the public free of charge by telephoning (405) 954-4171 or by writing to the address below.

FAA Forms 8010-4 provides the FAA and industry with a very essential service record of mechanical difficulties encountered in aircraft operations. Such reports contribute to the correction of conditions or situations which otherwise will continue to prove costly and/or adversely affect the airworthiness of aircraft.

The Flight Standards Service Difficulty Reports (General and Commercial), known as the weekly summary, contains all information obtained from FAA Form 8010-4 and those service difficulties, which were reported by telephone. Reports of a significant nature are highlighted with a "star" border, while reports, which are of an "URGENT AIRWORTHINESS CONCERN," are highlighted with a black and white slashed border. These highly significant items are sometimes obtained from sources other than FAA Form 8010-4. This publication is distributed to Flight Standards District Office (FSDO), Manufacturing Inspection District Offices (MIDO's), and Aircraft Certification Offices (ACO's). This publication is also made available to the public free of charge by telephoning (405) 954-4171 or by writing to:

FAA
Flight Standards Service
ATTN: Safety Data Analysis Section (AFS-643)
P.O. Box 25082
Oklahoma City, OK 73125-5029

You can select make, model and read what mechanic's in the field have found, and what difficulties you may find on the aircraft you want to select for purchase.

Let's assume you have already selected the aircraft by make and model you want to purchase. What should you do next? Remember the FAA is your best friend when purchasing an aircraft. So get the maximum benefit from your taxpayer's dollars when you visit your local FAA District Office (FSDO) and request assistance.

# Step By Step How to Pre-Purchase

I have come up with the 12 steps to a successful pre-purchase if followed step by step it will save you hundreds if not thousands of dollars and headaches. Remember there are two types of inspections aircraft and records. You must determine which one or both you will require to have completed. I suggest both because without one the other cannot be completed correctly.

# Step 1.

Sign a contract with the current owner that will include a pre-purchase inspection. A contract is an agreement made upon the exchange of sufficient consideration, to do or not to do a certain thing. There are three elements of importance to the contact before you sign as follows:

1. Agreement
2. Subject matter
3. Consideration

When these three elements are satisfied, then the contract may be enforceable by the law. The creation of a contract must begin with an offer (agreement). The offer must be valid, contemplate, and communicated to the seller. Make sure and write in the contract what the pre-purchase inspection will cover in detail (Subject matter). Make sure you have the right to cancel at your pleasure the bargain if you find defects the owner will not repair or make whole (Consideration). Insist that a clause be inserted for any latent defects found within a time frame in days or operating hours such as: Excessive oil leaks, low engine compression, maintenance service contracts, and etc. This clause will allow you to back out of the contract and get your money back if the previous owner does not make the aircraft whole by making repairs.

If the owner implies a warranty for certain items or for the whole aircraft make sure it is written in the contract what those items are, for how long, and who will pay to make them whole. In most states they have Civil Codes that will cover implied warranties by the seller. The seller in most cases by the act of offering his aircraft for sale, asserts or represents that his aircraft is merchantable for some special purpose and the buyer relies on that implied assertion or representation. Many aircraft dealers and private individuals will want you to sign a contact that contains **"no express warranty connected with this sale"** be wary of this statement. For example if you tell the seller you plan to use the aircraft to fly from city to city for business. And after the purchase of the aircraft you find the engine is burning excessive amounts of oil. This may be considered a latent defect in most states and may be covered under Civil Codes for implied warranties. Contact an aviation lawyer in your state to find out what your States Civil Codes address.

Before signing any contracts with an individual, used aircraft dealer or aircraft broker take the contract to an **aviation lawyer** and have them include a statement that the aircraft has to be in an **airworthy condition** at the time of the sale. To protect your assets include a statement that all required AD's and inspections items be complied with, owner to provide a list of all life limited parts for the pre-purchase inspection, etc. If you buy a fixer-upper or an as-is aircraft, better know as a hangar queen you still need a contract. Remember if a conflict arises after the sale the contact is the only legal document you will have in a court of law to protect yourself with. You may want to include that the manufacturers owner's manuals, maintenance manuals, service letters and bulletins, and other technical data pertaining to their aircraft be included/provided. These may be available from the previous owner but are not required to be transferred to a new owner. If the service manuals are not available from the previous owner, they usually may be obtained from the aircraft manufacturer. Having an aviation lawyer assist you in writing the contract will be money well spent if a problem arises later. This is no time to trust anyone, no hand shakes, no verbal agreements, no trades, get it in writing from the start.

# Step 2.

Each aircraft will have a data plate attached to the aircraft, as required by part 45. CFR Part 45, Identification and Registration Marking, sets forth the requirement for each aircraft and aircraft engine to be identified by means of a fireproof identification (ID) plate that contains specified identification information. Propellers, propeller blades and hubs must also be identified by ID plates or other approved methods such as stamping, engraving, and etching. The identification information will include the name of the builder, the model designation, the builder's serial number, the type certificate number (if any), production certificate number (if any), and for aircraft engines, the established rating. The Federal Aviation Administration (FAA) uses the identification data to establish conformity to the type design prior to issuing an airworthiness certificate and to establish compatibility with the type design for subsequent repairs and alterations to the product.

The FAA is aware that identification information and ID plates have been altered and switched from one aircraft to another in an apparent effort to avoid the time and expense of establishing that an aircraft conforms to an FAA-approved type design. An example would be removing an ID plate from an aircraft destroyed in an accident and installing it on a similar type aircraft of unknown origin and then applying for an airworthiness certificate on the basis of the data contained on the ID plate. The practice of "building" or "rebuilding" an aircraft and affixing an ID plate, which was previously affixed to another aircraft, is clearly not in the public interest. Accordingly, the FAA amended CFR Section 45.13 to prohibit the removal, change, or placement of identification information on aircraft, aircraft engines, propellers, propeller blades and hubs, and to prohibit the removal or installation of an ID plate without the approval of the FAA Administrator except for persons performing maintenance under CFR Part 43, Maintenance, Preventive Maintenance, Rebuilding and Alteration.

Persons authorized to perform maintenance under the provisions of CFR Part 43 are exempt from the requirement of having to obtain individual approval from the Administrator (FAA) when it is necessary, during certain maintenance operations, to remove or change identification information or to remove an ID plate. Removal of an ID plate would be considered necessary during certain maintenance operations such as caustic cleaning, paint removal, or sandblasting. Removal of an ID plate would also be considered necessary when the structure to which the ID plate is fastened has to be repaired or replaced for maintenance purposes. The changing of identification information would be considered necessary when instructed to do so in compliance with specific maintenance procedures contained in manufacturers' manuals, letters, or bulletins that are incorporated in and made a part of an airworthiness directive. An ID plate removed during maintenance operations must be reinstalled in the original location from which it was removed prior to releasing the product to service.

The Type Certificate Data Sheet (TCDS) number is required to be on the data plate. Write down all the information on the data plate for the airframe, engine and propeller. The Type Certificate Data Sheet (TCDS) is a part of the Type Certificate as required by 14 CFR 21.41. Each aircraft's type certificate data sheet includes approved weight and balance information as well as other operating limitations to ensure the aircraft airworthiness and conformity to its type certificate.

Obtain a copy of the aircraft, propeller, and engine (TCDS) go to the FAA web site or your local IA mechanic. The Make/Model information and all current Type Certificate Data Sheets are now available to you on the FAA web site. FREE. This information is included as a part of AIR's Regulatory and Guidance. It is completely searchable for words or phrases and each TCDS is available in Adobe Acrobat PDF format. To access this information, do the following:

1. Start your browser (Internet Explorer or Netscape)
2. Go to the FAA home page at http://www.faa.gov/avr
3. Click on the link to Regulation and Certification (AVR)
4. Click on the link to Aircraft Certification
5. Click on the link to Regulatory and Guidance Library
6. Choose 'Make Model (TCDS)' and click on GO

**FOR EXAMPLE**: If you need to find some information about a Cessna 421 contained in its TCDS, this is what you do after going through the six steps listed above: click on 'Models by TC Holder'; scroll down to 'Cessna Aircraft Company' and click on the triangle to the left to expand all the Cessna models; scroll down to 421. Click on A7CE (which is the TCDS number associated with the Cessna 421) and you will see the embedded TCDS document in PDF format. Clicking on the embedded document will launch the Adobe Acrobat reader and display the TCDS.

The TCDS will tell you basic weight and balance, flight control rigging, type of engines and propeller combinations that can be installed and a list life limited parts. Think of the TCDS as the Mother of All Data, since this is what each aircraft is manufactured to. Type certificate data sheets are the official specifications of an aircraft, aircraft engine, and propeller issued by the FAA.

# Step 3.

With the aircraft selected take the N-number to your local FSDO and ask a maintenance airworthiness inspector known as an Aviation Safety Inspector (ASI) to run the N-number in their database. Where can you find the Flight Standards District Office (FSDO) closest to you? Answer: http://www.faa.gov/avr/afs/fsdo/index.cfm. You will want to ask if the aircraft has every been in an accident that was reported. A paper copy of this information will not be given to you since it is protected under the Freedom of Information Act, but parts of the record may be explained like accidents, major/minor alterations, and major/minor repairs if reported and who is the current registered owner. This information may in some cases be found on the Internet, but be advised some aviation websites are not current. The FAA website (www.faa.gov) contains the N-numbers of all U.S. registered aircraft and is updated every 24 hours.

# Step 4.

Order a paper copy or CD-ROM for the N-number aircraft you have selected to purchase from the Aircraft Registration Branch. There is one aircraft record per CD which is viewable using Adobe Acrobat Reader. The most current Acrobat Reader will be included on the CD. The Aircraft Registration Branch maintains registration records on individual aircraft and also serves as a repository for airworthiness documents received from FAA field offices.

Aircraft registration records contain documents related to an aircraft's registration history such as applications for aircraft registration, evidence of ownership, security agreements, mechanics liens, lien releases, leases, and lease terminations. The Airworthiness portion of the file contains items such as applications for airworthiness, copies of airworthiness certificates, major repair and alteration reports, and related items. Additional information included will be any FAA Form 337's for Major Repairs and Alterations, if they were submitted. The information in this official record should match with the aircraft records the owner is required to keep. Keep in mind some owners do not or have not sent FAA Form 337 copies to Oklahoma City as required because they think it will affect the selling price of their aircraft. If the records do not match a red flag should go up.

The records for aircraft removed from the U.S. Civil Aircraft Register prior to 1984 are usually paper files, and in most instances have been sent to Federal Storage. These records may be retrieved, and are available on paper only at time of this printing. Copies of aircraft records are available to the public subject to the following fees:

**CD ROM**

$5.00 per CD-ROM – one aircraft record per CD.
*Plus, if required* $3.00 to certify the record is true and complete, generally only required for court cases.

**PAPER**

$2.00 Search Fee charged for each aircraft record requested.
*Plus* $0.25 for photocopy of first page of records on paper, and $0.05 for each successive paper page. An average paper record has 76 pages. *Plus, as appropriate* $2.00 if the record must be recalled from Federal Storage. $3.00 to certify the record is true and complete generally only required for court cases. A billing letter will be sent with the requested aircraft records.

## *NOTE*

*There is no charge for copies provided to government offices for use in official duties.*

**Requests from outside the U.S.** must be in writing and accompanied by a check or money order made payable to the Federal Aviation Administration in U.S. funds sufficient to cover the projected fee. For more information, call the Aircraft Registration Branch at (405)-954-3116.

**Mailing Address:**

> FAA
> Aircraft Registration Branch, AFS-750
> PO Box 25504
> Oklahoma City, OK 7312

There may be other records on file at federal, state, or local agencies that are not recorded with the FAA. Now that you have the FAA Official copy of records they should match the owner set. All the AD's, life limited items, required inspections and maintenance should be recorded in the maintenance records the owner has. A good record search will uncover costly items that may or may not of been completed.

Remember **DO NOT** purchase and aircraft without ordering the aircraft records and checking them. This is one **STEP** you do not want to skip.

# Step 5.

Have a title search performed to assure the aircraft has a clear title. This can be accomplished in Oklahoma City at the registry, which is co-located at the Aircraft Registry. When you contact the registry ask for the title search branch at (405) 954-3116. The object of the title search is to ascertain that there are no liens or other hidden encumbrances against the ownership of the aircraft.

A clear title is a term commonly used by aircraft title search companies to indicate there are no liens (chattel mortgage, security agreement, tax lien, artisan lien, etc.) in the FAA aircraft records. Title searches for the aviation public is not performed by the FAA's Civil Aviation Registry; however, the aircraft records contain all of the ownership and security documents that have been filed with the FAA. The Civil Aviation Registry records acceptable security.

In addition, some states authorize artisan liens (mechanic liens). These also need to be recorded. Check your state's statutes. Federal liens against an owner (drug, repossession, etc.) may not show at all. **Know your seller! See Step 4 order the records.**

Either search the aircraft records yourself, or have it done by an attorney or qualified aircraft title search company. A list of title search companies qualified in aircraft title and records search can be found in Advisory Circular (AC) Form 8050-55, Title Search Companies. This form is available from the Civil Aviation Registry. **CAUTION:** FAA registration cannot be used in any civil proceeding to establish proof of ownership!

# Step 6.

Locate a mechanic and agree on the price or fee for services to be rendered if possible. This may not be possible since no telling where the aircraft inspection may lead or how long the record check may take. In order to perform the inspection, all applicable aircraft, engine, and STC holder's manuals, instructions and service information must be available and utilized. Using the website **www.faa.gov** check airman records and make sure the mechanic you select is really a mechanic. You will want to see their A&P certificate and a picture ID card. Write down the A&P certificate number and address and use the FAA website to check their ratings. More on this subject will be covered later in Inspector Requirements chapter 3. If you have the mechanic's A&P number contact your local Flight Standards District Office (FSDO) and have the FAA run a check to make sure the mechanic is still active. Ask if the A&P mechanic holds an IA certificate, he or she should have a fixed base of operation in the Flight District area where the IA works. Each local FSDO has an IA file on all IA's in their district and can tell you it they are currently active. Again more on this subject will be explained in Chapter 3 Mechanic Requirements.

# Maintenance Contract

Once you have selected the mechanic to perform your pre-purchase inspection your next step is to write a contract outlining exactly what you expect the mechanic duties will be and what you expect to see in writing when they have completed the pre-purchase inspection. This contract should include the complete aircraft maintenance records check, airworthiness directives (AD) compliance list with all AD's complied with, service bulletins complied with, major/minor repairs or alteration performed, service difficulty reports, engine borescope inspection, oil analysis, and a complete list of unairworthy items found during the aircraft inspection. Also, the check sheets the mechanic will follow for the pre-purchase, obtain a copy of it. You will also want a type certificate data sheet (TCDS) for the aircraft you are considering, which can be found at http://www.faa.gov/.

Be advised that a complete maintenance record inspection is very important and may take several hours if not days to complete. The record inspection can save you thousands of dollars if the records are incomplete. As an example Code of Federal Regulation (CFR) section 43.10 Disposition of Life-Limited Aircraft Parts, if they have not been maintained and tracked there may be an addition cost to have them replaced or overhauled. Or if the equipment list is not up-dated reflecting major alterations that were never approved by the FAA, your insurance company may not insure the aircraft because the aircraft does meet it type design based on the airworthiness certificate. See Chapter 4 for more on this subject.

# Step 7.

Arrange with the seller to have the pre-purchase inspection completed at a place of your choosing not the owners if possible. This will include obtaining and signing a hand receipt for all the maintenance records that will be in your possession. Also arrange to have the aircraft test flown before the pre-purchase inspection. This should be included in your contract with the current owner. Have the pilot record all readings on the gauges and any problems while operating the aircraft (See Step 8 for details). Before the flight check for the airworthiness certificate, aircraft registration certificate, current weight and balance note the date and signature, and insure the equipment list is onboard before take off and it's correctness. This can be accomplished as part of the pre-flight inspection.

The scope of the inspection may vary with respect to the model and age of the aircraft, the purchaser's intended use, the desired cost of the inspection and the monetary risk the Buyer is willing to accept.

Be sure to come to a mutual agreement with the prospective aircraft owner/seller and mechanic concerning exactly what work/inspection is to be performed. Misunderstandings usually result from a lack of clear communication, check your contract. Attention to the following details will usually avoid the ill will a later disagreement may generate.

1. Itemize the work to be done so the owner will have a clear understanding of the work to be accomplished.

2. Establish a firm understanding about the cost, or range of cost, anticipated for the job.

3. If an pre-purchase inspection is involved, indicate that certain maintenance is required to perform the inspection, such as:

   a. Removing cowling and fairing, opening inspection plates, etc.
   b. Cleaning the aircraft and engine.
   c. Disassembling wheels and other components to determine their condition.

4. Advise the owner that an inspection involves determination of compliance with aircraft specifications and airworthiness directives (AD's).

5. Agree whether routine servicing is to be included as part of the inspection or if it is to be performed separately. Such servicing is not a part of the inspection, but may be conveniently done while conducting the inspection. Such items might be:

   a. Cleaning spark plugs.
   b. Servicing landing gear shock struts.
   c. Changing oil.
   d. Making minor adjustments.
   e. Servicing brakes.
   f. Dressing nicked propeller blades.
   g. Lubricating where necessary.
   h. Stop-drilling small cracks and minor patching of cowling and baffles.

6. The owner/seller should be made aware that the annual, progressive, or pre-purchase inspection does not include correction of discrepancies or unairworthy items and that such maintenance will be additional to the inspection. A person authorized to perform maintenance if agreed on by the owner and holder of the A&P certificate may accomplish maintenance and repairs simultaneously with the inspection. This method would result in an aircraft that is approved for return to service with the completion of the inspection. A written list of discrepancies and unairworthy items not repaired concurrently with the inspection must/should be made and given to the owner. Record uncorrected discrepancies and unairworthy items in the maintenance records. The owner must make arrangements for correction or deferral of items on the list of discrepancies and unairworthy items with a person authorized to perform maintenance prior to returning the aircraft to service. The holder of the A&P ensures that any item permitted to be inoperative by a MEL or under 14 CFR part 91, section 91.213(d)(2) are properly placarded and any maintenance for deferral has been carried out. Any deferred items are to be included on the list of discrepancies and unairworthy items. The owner should be informed that the aircraft should not be operated until the discrepancies and unairworthy items are corrected or are appropriately deferred. In this case a Special Flight permit may be required to relocate the aircraft.

7. Establish a reasonable time frame to accomplish the inspection.

8. Request the owner/seller/broker to supply the complete aircraft records (airframe, engines, and propellers) for study, review, and entries. Point out that this is necessary to properly conduct a pre-purchase inspection. Make sure and sign a hand receipt for the records.

9. Complete the inspection as soon as practicable. Often, an aircraft will sit around the shops waiting for parts, even though the inspection has actually been completed. In this case, it is advisable to officially report the aircraft unairworthy. (Refer to 14 CFR part 43, section 43.11(a)(5).) When the parts arrive, the repairs can be completed and the aircraft approved for return to service in the usual manner by the person who makes the repairs. The time lapse may represent several weeks, or even months, and things can deteriorate on the aircraft. Also, there is the chance that an AD involving some part of the aircraft may have been issued in the interim. In these cases, it might be unwise to complete the repairs originally intended and sign off the aircraft as "airworthy" without doing another complete inspection.

10. Ask the seller to provide you with a FAA Form 8130-9 Statement of Conformity. Make this part of your contract or part of the pre-purchase inspection. If a seller refuses to sign a Form 8130-9 start looking for another aircraft to purchase. If an aircraft does not pass conformity then it cannot be airworthy.

# Step 8.

Contact the mechanic and arrange to start the pre-purchase inspection by giving the aircraft maintenance records to the mechanic. Read Chapter 3 before selecting a mechanic. Make sure the mechanic signs a hand receipt for the maintenance records, this should be spelled out in you pre-purchase contract with the mechanic. Yes you do need a second contract with the mechanic. Now just be patient let the professionals do their job. The mechanic should use some type of checksheet ask for a copy before signing a contract for services and make it part of the contract. Below is a short list of items your pilot or mechanic should check for to start before a complete inspection is completed. In the Appendix is a detailed list.

Before starting the engine(s) the master switch is turn on and the engine gages' static readings are observed. Quite often you will discover gages that do not return to zero on shut down. During starting the voltmeter is observed for low voltage, which could indicate possible battery or starter problems.

The following items are checked and recorded during taxi and run up:

1. Ignition switch safety check
2. Com/transceiver check
3. Clock/timer/chronometer
4. Hour meter operation
5. Outside air temp
6. Atis identifier/barometric setting
7. Altimeter indicated altitude compared with field elevation
8. Brakes parking brakes
9. Ground steering
10. Wheel balance
11. Oil pressure idle cruise
12. Oil temperature
13. Cylinder head temperature(s)
14. Fuel pressure/flow, idle/cruise
15. Primary alternator/generator (DC & AC)
16. Standby/#2 alternator/generator (DC & AC)
17. Primary/standby voltage regulator
18. Magneto operation/drops
19. Propeller response
20. Vacuum/gyro air pressures, primary/stand-by/#2:
21. Engine controls
22. Throttle, mixture, prop, carburetor heat/alternate air, cowl flap(s), turbo
23. Carburetor air temperature
24. Hydraulic pressure
25. Tach calibration check

26. Exhaust gas temperature(s) Turbine inlet temperature
27. Compressor discharge temperature
28. Static power, max rpm/manifold press/fuel pressure/flow
29. Crankcase pressure, cowl flaps open, closed (at full static power)
30. Idle mixture rise/idle rpm/cut-off
31. Flight director/gyro horizon
32. Horizontal situation indicator/direction gyro
33. Turn coordinator/turn & bank
34. Compass/remote indicating compass
35. De-ice
36. Surface, windshield, prop de-ice
37. Propeller feather/un-feathering

With all the above out of the way and recorded it is time to taxi back to the hanger and start the compression checks if you have reciprocating engines. The above checklist is located in the Appendix section.

# Step 9.

After completion of the pre-purchase inspection make sure your mechanic has made the appropriate maintenance entries for the maintenance he performed such as: Removing and reinstalling the spark plugs, removing and installing inspection panels and cowling. If a mechanic does any removal of inspection panels or cowling they have to make maintenance record entry in accordance with 14 CFR 43.5. This will also protect you incase there is a dispute with the seller if something gets broken or is missing. Take lots of pictures to document what is found, this will prevent a controversy later if it arises.

Although a pre-purchase inspection by its very nature must fall short of a more complete inspection of the aircraft, such as it done on an annual basic to meet Part 91 requirements, a good pre-purchase inspection can be thorough, especially for the less complex aircraft. Remember there is no regulatory basic for a pre-purchase inspection in the CFR's; any unairworthy items found by the mechanic should be on a list given to the owner signed and dated by the mechanic. Make sure the owner is aware of the regulatory requirement that mechanics are required to make maintenance record entries for all maintenance-performed in accordance with CFR 43.5.

As the complexity of the aircraft under consideration increases, so does the amount of time and necessarily the cost required for an equally thorough pre-purchase inspection. But even several hundreds dollars spent at this stage can pay great dividends, should unexpected problems be identified before the purchase is made. Then a decision can be made either to not go forward, or to renegotiate the proposed financial terms to compensate for any repairs that might be immediately, or in the very near future, be necessary.

Require the mechanic to provide you a written inspection report dated, signed, with make, model, serial number, N-number and tach time. This report should contain any unairworthy items found, repairs, alterations, time left on life limited parts, items not accounted for etc. A copy of the unairworthy items should be given to the registered owner. The mechanic has an obligation and requirement to notify the registered owner. The courts have generally held mechanics and manufactures responsible for liable for failure to warn users of known dangerous conditions. Manufacturers usually inform the public by the use of Service Letters and Service Bulletins. Mechanics use maintenance record entries and a letter to the owners informing them of unairworthy items.

With the Pre-purchase inspection results in hand make a list of all items that will be required to be repaired to make the aircraft airworthy. Any item that can be deferred should be noted and the price of repairs should be negotiated with the current owner and included in the contract before taking ownership. **Again make sure to get everything in writing. This is no time to shake hands and make agreements.** The bottom line is to protect yourself and your assets.

# Step 10.

Before taking delivery of the aircraft, make a final inspection in accordance with the pre-purchase agreement you have made with the Seller. Make sure the Airworthiness Certificate, Operating Limitations (if required), Aircraft Data Plate, Weight and Balance data, Aircraft Maintenance Records, and any other required documents are with the aircraft. After the sale of an aircraft the previous owner is required by CFR part 91 to provide the new owner with all the aircraft records. This is the only time they are required to turn over all the records to the new owner.

# Step 11.

Below are the documents you may expect to receive with your new or used aircraft:

1. Bill of sale or conditional sales contract.
2. FAA Form 8100-2, Standard Airworthiness Certificate, or FAA Form 8130-7, Special Airworthiness Certificate, which may include a copy of the Operation Limitations.
3. All maintenance records containing the following information:
    a. The total time in service of the airframe, each engine, and each propeller;
    b. The current status of life-limited parts of each airframe, engine, propeller, rotor, and appliance;
    c. The time since last overhaul of all items installed on the aircraft that are required to be overhauled on a specified time basis;
    d. The identification of the current inspection status of the aircraft, including the time since the last inspection required by the inspection program under which the aircraft and its appliances are maintained;
    e. The current status of applicable Airworthiness Directives (AD's), including for each the method of compliance, the AD number, and the revision date. If the AD involves recurring action, the time and date when the next action is required; and
    f. A copy of current major alterations to each airframe, engine, propeller, rotor, and appliance.
4. Equipment list, and weight and balance data.
5. Appropriate aircraft flight manual and or Operating Limitations
6. What manuals should you receive with the aircraft?
    a. Manufacturers owner's manuals
    b. Maintenance manuals
    c. Service letters and bulletins
    d. Other technical data pertaining to their aircraft.

All of the required records and documentation are provided for the aircraft; i.e., an up-to-date approved flight manual, equipment list, maintenance records, FAA-accepted Instructions for Continued Airworthiness (ICA) and or FAA-acceptance maintenance manual(s) (MM), and any other manuals required by Sections 21.31, 21.50, 23.1529, 25.1529, 27.1529, 29.1529, 33.4, and 35.4. These documents must be in the **English language**.

# Step 12.

Before looking at any aircraft finish reading the rest of this book.

The twelve steps do not have to be followed in order, I suggest after selecting an aircraft take the N-number to you local FSDO first and have the FAA run a check on it as mentioned in Step #3. This may save you from having to accomplish any more steps. Knowledge is power and power will save you money. This knowledge may save your life.

# CHAPTER 2

## AIRCRAFT REQUIREMENTS

# Flight Manual

Airplane Flight Manual (AFM) contains operating procedures and techniques that may be categorized as warnings, cautions, and notes. The AFM provides information to safely operate the airplane under normal, abnormal, and emergency conditions. The AFM contains the operating limitations, operating procedures, and performance information for the airplane. Not all aircraft will have an AFM some will have a Pilot Operating Handbook (POH), but which everyone you are using it is required to be in the aircraft when in operation.

Widespread use of computers has led to the capability of replacing or supplementing parts of the conventional paper AFM with a computerized version. Guidance for FAA approval of computerized AFM information is presented in Appendix 1 of AC. 25.1581. CFR Section 25.1581 requires that FAA-approved information be segregated, identified, and clearly distinguished from each unapproved part of the AFM. Unapproved material should be labeled that it is for guidance information only and must be located in a different section than the approved material. Information that may not be required for operation under the CFR, but is approved by the FAA (e.g., stopping performance with autobrakes) should be placed in the same section as other approved material. Information that is neither required by the CFR nor approved by the FAA (e.g., takeoff or landing performance on runways contaminated by standing water, slush, or snow) should be labeled as guidance information and placed in a different section than any approved material.

Each page of the approved portion should bear the notation, **"FAA Approved,"** a unique date of approval or revision number for that page, the airplane type or model designation, and an appropriate document identification number. For AFM pages produced by an STC applicant, both the STC applicant's name and the airplane type or model designation should appear. Some of the current reversions can be found for the following aircraft:

1. Air Tractor (940) 564-5616
2. American Champion Aircraft Corporation (262) 534-6315
3. Beech aircraft (800) 625-7043 technical support.
4. Boeing aircraft (206) 655-1131 information.
5. Cessna aircraft (316) 517-5800 product support.
6. Cirrus aircraft (800) 279.4322 product support
7. Gulfstream Aerospace Corporation (912) 965-3000.
8. Maule Air (229) 985-2045
9. Mooney aircraft (800) 331-3880 product support.
10. Piper aircraft (561) 567-4361 push 1 for AFM.

When revisions are incorporated, a means of indicating those parts of the information that have been changed should be provided. For example, vertical bars placed in the margin of the revised page may be used for this purpose. Each revised page should be identified in the same manner as the original, with the exception of the new date and revision notation, as applicable.

Any required **weight and balance** information that is not a physical part of the AFM **must be** incorporated by reference in the Limitations Section of the AFM per section 25.1583. The separate weight and balance document and revisions must be FAA-approved using appropriate approval procedures acceptable to the FAA. Be sure and check the Type Certificate Data Sheet for the basic empty and gross weights.

# Equipment List Requirement

An equipment list is a list of items approved by the FAA for installation in a particular aircraft. The list includes the name, part number, weight, and arm of the component. An equipment list is furnished with the aircraft, which specifies all the required equipment, and all equipment approved for installation in the aircraft. The weight and arm of each item is included on the list, and all equipment installed when the aircraft left the factory should be checked.

When an Airframe and Powerplant mechanic adds or removes any item on the equipment list, he or she must change the weight and balance record to indicate the new empty weight and Empty Weight Center of Gravity (EWCG), and the equipment list is revised to show which equipment is actually installed. A comprehensive equipment list, which includes all of the items of equipment, approved for a particular model of aircraft. The POH for each individual aircraft includes an aircraft specific equipment list of the items from this master list. When any item is added to or removed from the aircraft, its weight and arm are determined in the equipment list and used to update the weight and balance record. Information can be found in Aircraft Weight and Balance Handbook FAA-H-8083-1.

An airplane-specific equipment list is provided with each individual airplane at delivery, and is typically inserted at the rear of this Pilot's Operating Handbook.

The comprehensive equipment list provides the following information in column form: In the Item Number column, each item is assigned a coded number. The first two digits of the code represent the assignment of item within the ATA Specification 100 breakdown (Chapter 11 for Placards, Chapter 21 for Air Conditioning, Chapter 77 for Engine Indicating, etc.). These assignments also correspond to the Maintenance Manual chapter breakdown for the airplane. After the first two digits (and hyphen), items receive a unique sequence number (01, 02, 03, etc.). After the sequence number (and hyphen), a suffix letter is assigned to identify equipment as a required item, a standard item or an optional item. Suffix letters are as follows:

-R = required items or equipment for FAA certification
-S = standard equipment items
-O = optional equipment items replacing required or standard items
-A = optional equipment items which are in addition to required or standard items

In the Equipment List Description column, each item is assigned a descriptive name to help identify its function. In the Reference Drawing column, a drawing number is provided which corresponds to the item.

If additional equipment is to be installed, it must be done in accordance with the reference drawing, service bulletin or a separate FAA approval. In the Wt Lbs and Arm Ins columns, information is provided on the weight (in pounds) and arm (in inches).

Addition or removal of equipment included in this list is considered by the FAA to be a **minor** alteration. The weights and arms are included with the items in the equipment list, and these minor alterations can be done and the aircraft approved for return to service by an appropriately rated mechanic. The only documentation required is an entry in the aircraft maintenance records and the appropriate change to the weight and balance record in the POH/AFM.

Any major alteration or repair requires the work to be done by an appropriately rated mechanic or facility. The work must be checked for conformity to FAA-approved data and signed off by a mechanic holding an Inspection Authorization, or by an authorized agent of an appropriately rated FAA-approved repair station. A repair stations record or a FAA Form 337, Major Repair and Alteration must be completed which describes the work. A dated and signed revision to the weight and balance record is made and kept with the maintenance records, and the airplane's new empty weight and empty weight arm or moment index are entered in the POH/AFM.

Weight and balance is of such vital importance that each mechanic maintaining an aircraft must be fully aware of his or her responsibility to provide the pilot with current and accurate information for the actual weight of the aircraft and the location of the center of gravity. The pilot in command has the responsibility to know the weight of the load, CG, maximum allowable gross weight, and CG limits of the aircraft.

The weight and balance report must include an equipment list showing weights and moment arms of all required and optional items of equipment included in the certificated empty weight.

All of the required equipment **must be** properly installed, and there should be no equipment installed that is not included in the equipment list. If such equipment is installed, the weight and balance record must be corrected to indicate it.

# Weight and Balance

Weight and balance data are no longer required to be entered on FAA Form 337. However, it is imperative that weight and balance checks and computations be made very carefully. Since practically every aircraft manufacturer uses a different method of weight and balance control, it would be impossible to provide a universally adaptable method. When revising weight and balance data, these general guidelines should be followed.

1.  The weight and balance data should be kept together in the aircraft records.
2.  When making revisions, use a permanent easily identified method, with full-size sheets of paper large enough to contain complete computations and minimize the possibility of becoming detached or lost.
3.  Each page should be identified with the aircraft by make, model, serial number, and registration number.
4.  The pages should be signed and dated by the person making the revision.
5.  The nature of the weight change should be described.
6.  The old weight and balance data should be marked "superseded" and dated.
7.  A new page should show the date of the old figures it supersedes.
8.  Appropriate fore and/or aft extreme loading conditions should be investigated and the computations shown.
9.  Example loading computations may be helpful.
10. On large aircraft, be careful to distinguish between empty weights and operating weights that may include items, such as commissary supplies, spare parts, lavatory water, etc.
11. On small aircraft, it is often convenient to post a placard in the aircraft indicating the empty weight, useful load, and empty CG, along with example loadings or general instructions, to cover the most likely loading conditions. (Refer to 14 CFR section 91.9(b)(2). AC 120-27, Aircraft Weight and Balance Control, and AC 91-23, Pilot's Weight and Balance Handbook, contain useful information applicable to the functions performed by the holder of an IA on general aviation aircraft.

On General Aviation aircraft there is not a requirement to perform a weight and balance reweigh, this requirement is only for Part 121 and 135 aircraft. Their requirement is every three years to reweigh the aircraft. The reasoning is aircraft tend to get heavier as they get older due to dirt, paint, structural repairs, alterations, and lost tools. I would recommend as part of the purchase contract to include a reweigh to certify the weight and balance. Having the aircraft reweighed is money well spent. The **owner or operator** is responsible for maintaining the equipment list, CG and weight distribution computations, and loading schedules, if necessary.

# Minimum Equipment Lists (MEL's)

The Code of Federal Regulations (CFR's) requires that all aircraft instruments and installed equipment is operative prior to each departure. When the FAA adopted the minimum equipment list (MEL) concept for 14 CFR part 91 operations, this allowed for the first time, operations with inoperative items determined to be nonessential for safe flight. At the same time, it allowed part 91 operators, without a MEL, to defer repairs on nonessential equipment within the guidelines of part 91.

There are two primary methods of deferring maintenance on small, **non-turbine**-powered airplanes operated under part 91. They are the deferral provisions in section 91.213(d) and a FAA-approved MEL.

The aircraft should conform to the aircraft specification or type certificate data sheet (TCDS), any changes by supplemental type certificates (STC) and/or its properly altered condition. When the aircraft does not conform, the aircraft is **"unairworthy."**

When inspecting aircraft operating without a MEL, the rule 14 CFR Part 91, section 91.213(d), allows certain aircraft not having an approved MEL to be flown with inoperative instruments and/or equipment. These aircraft may be presented for annual or progressive inspection with such items previously deferred or may have inoperative instruments and equipment deferred during an inspection. In either case, the holder of an IA is required by 14 CFR Part 43, section 43.13(b) to determine that:

a.  The deferrals are eligible within the guidelines of that rule.

b.  All conditions for deferral are met, including proper recordation in accordance with 14 CFR Part 43, sections 43.9 and 43.11.

c.  Deferral of any item or combination of items will not affect the intended function of any other operable instruments and or equipment, or in any manner constitute a hazard to the aircraft. When these requirements are met, such an aircraft is considered to be in a properly altered condition with regard to those deferred items.

The **owner or operator** is responsible for maintaining the equipment list, CG and weight distribution computations, and loading schedules, if necessary. Be familiar with minimum equipment list for general aviation aircraft. Guidance in this area is provided in AC 91-67, Minimum Equipment Requirements for General Aviation Operations under 14 CFR Part 91.

# Life Limited Parts

Aircraft that have no history of civil certification often-present significant "unknowns" when it comes to such critical safety matters as life-limited parts and aircraft design. Thus, such aircraft often do not have the basis on which to build an aviation safety program that is effective and appropriate to ensure safe operations.

Life limited parts are those parts that have received a specific life limit from an approved FAA document for that aircraft. Some examples of FAA approved documents are the Type Certificate Data Sheets (TCDS), Approved Airplane Flight Manual (AFM), and the FAA Approved Airworthiness Limitations Section of the aircraft maintenance manual and Airworthiness Directives.

Service bulletins are not mandatory by regulation in nature but the life limited parts called out in a service bulletins generally are. Why? Because the type certificate data sheet for the engine references the service bulletin as the source for the life limited parts listing making the replacement times contained in the service bulletin sometimes mandatory. To determine what parts are "Life Limited" for your aircraft it is best to start at the Type Certificate Data Sheet and follow the road signs from there.

The Regulation Part 43.10 refers to the "current status" of life-limited parts. To know the current status of life limited parts on your aircraft you will need to answer the following questions:

*   Which parts on the aircraft is life limited?
*   What are the Serial Numbers/Part Numbers?
*   What are parts Life Limits (This can change periodically)?
*   How much time is left on the life limit?
*   Where to find a list of Life limited parts?

Operation of an aircraft with expired life limited parts is against the regulation (Ref 14 CFR Part 91.403(i) and 91.409(e)). Therefore, you must know the status of each life-limited part to be sure you are not operating out of compliance.

Some life limited parts must be replaced based not upon total time in service but rather based upon total cycles in service. This can be a trap to owner/operators. You see the regulation referring to keeping the current total time (section 91.417((a)(2)(i)) does not refer to the Cycle count or Landing Count. Therefore, keeping track of the Cycles and Landings on your aircraft becomes a requirement by default. When the Life Limited Parts Replacement Requirement calls out replacement of a part at a total cycle count of XYZ, and we don't know the total cycle count, we cannot demonstrate that the part is not past the limit. The situation then mandates tracking of landings and cycles in order to demonstrate compliance.

Life-limited parts may be used for the remaining time left on the part providing the record of time is clearly reflected in the aircraft log books. End of life (time limit) must be reflected in the aircraft log at the time of Standard Airworthiness Certification. Where the military life is less than the civil life, the military life-limit will be used. Where the civil life-limit is less than the military, the civil will be used. In either case the time (life-limit) to be used is that of the lesser time. This can be exceeded only if a new life-limit is established on the type data sheet.

What to look for when it comes to Life Limited Parts:

1. Part identification – part number and serial number.
2. Manufacturer and date of manufacture.
3. Total time-in-service.
4. Current status of life-limited parts.
5. Time since the last overhaul of each part, which is required to be overhauled on a specified time basis.
6. Identification of current inspection status, including time since last required inspection or maintenance performed.
7. Current status of applicable airworthiness directives (AD) and DoD directives (i.e., engineering change, technical order, maintenance work order, etc.), including the date, method, and compliance requirement; if the AD involves recurring action, time and date when the next action is required.
8. A list of current major alterations, repairs or modifications for each part.
9. Date any work was accomplished.
10. Work authentication.

# NOTE

1. *Amendments or extensions are not allowed for life-limited items and/or those designated by AD's unless authorized in FAA-approved revisions.*
2. *Life limited components may not be prorated.*

For example, section 91.417(a)(2)(i), requires the total service time of the airframe, each engine, propeller, and rotor. Compliance to section 91.417(a)(2)(ii) requires a maintenance record of the current status of life-limited parts of each airframe, engine, propeller, rotor, and appliance. All entries should be written in English and not with erasable materials such as lead/carbon pencils.

Manufacturers producing approved aircraft parts should maintain records of serial numbers for "retired" life-limited or other critical parts. In such cases, the owner who mutilates applicable parts is encouraged to provide the original manufacturer with the data plate and/or serial number and final disposition of the part. If you find data plates missing a RED flag should go up. What to look for:

1. Questionable part numbers, fraudulent or suspicious Technical Standard Order or FAA-Parts Manufacturer Approval markings and/or re-identification, stamp-overs or vibro-etching on the data plate.
2. Parts delivered with photocopied or missing maintenance release tags.
3. Parts with a finish that is inconsistent with industry standards (e.g., discoloration, inconsistencies, resurfacing).
4. New parts sold with maintenance release tags reflecting a status other than new.
5. Parts with poor documentation exhibiting incomplete or inconsistent part identity information.

**Life-Limited Parts Status Records**. Requires records for components of the airframe, engine, propellers, rotors, and appliances that are identified to be removed from service when the life-limit has been reached.

1. The current life-limited status of the part is a record indicating the life-limit remaining before the required retirement time of the component is reached. This record must include any modification of the part in accordance with AD's, service bulletins, or product improvements by the manufacturer or applicant.

2. The following are not considered a current life limited status record:

   a. Work orders
   b. Maintenance installation records
   c. Purchase requests
   d. Sales receipts
   e. Manufacturers documentation of original certificate
   f. Other historical data

3. Whenever the current status of life-limited parts records cannot be established or has not been maintained (e.g., a break in current status) and the historical records are not available, the airworthiness of that product cannot be determined and it must be removed from service.

## *NOTE*
### *A serviceable parts tag does not constitute an overhaul record.*

## Overhaul Records

Check the part records and attached work orders for the following:

1. Disassembly data
2. Dimensional check data
3. Replacement parts list
4. Repair data
5. Reassemble/test data
6. Reference to data including overhaul specifications

# Life-Limited Parts II

Present day aircraft and powerplants commonly have life-limited parts installed. These life limits may be referred to as retirement times, service life limitations, parts retirement limitations, retirement life limits, life limitations, or other such terminology and may be expressed in hours, cycles of operation, or calendar time. They are set forth in type certificate data sheets (TCDS), AD's, or the limitations section of FAA-approved airplane or rotorcraft flight manuals. Additionally, instructions for continued airworthiness, which require life-limits be specified, may apply **(See CFR Part 23 Appendix G and Part 27 Appendix A).**

14 CFR Section 91.417(a)(2)(ii). Requires the current status of life-limited parts to be part of the maintenance record. If total time-in-service of the aircraft, engine, propeller, etc., is entered in the record when a life-limited part is installed and the time-in-service of the life-limited part is included, the normal record of time-in-service automatically meets this requirement.

Many components, presently in-service, were put into service before the requirements to keep maintenance records on them. Propellers are probably foremost in this group. In these instances, practicable procedures for compliance with the record requirements must be used. For example, total time-in-service may be derived using the procedures when the records for an aircraft are lost or destroyed. In order to re-construct them, it is necessary to establish the total time-in-service of the airframe. This can be done by reference to other records that reflect the time-in-service; research of records maintained by repair facilities; and reference to records maintained by individual mechanics, etc. When these things have been done and the record is still incomplete, the owner/operator may make a notarized statement in the new record describing the loss and establishing the time-in-service based on the research and the best estimate of time-in-service. Or if records prior to the regulatory requirements are just not available from any source, time-in-service may be kept since last complete overhaul. **Neither of these procedures is acceptable when life-limited parts status is involved or when airworthiness directive (AD) compliance is a factor.** Only the actual record since new may be used in these instances.

A system should be developed that will identify, trace, and maintain the hours on all life-limited components in the airplane. If such a system did not previously exist and the exact life of the component is not known, a life limit will be established based upon airplane records and historical data. The original airplane manufacturer will be significantly involved in establishing these life limits. In addition to these requirements, the reporting of failures, malfunctions, or defects should be accomplished in accordance with Part 21, 21.3, to determine the necessity for corrective action. **Life-limited parts that have reached or exceeded their life limit, or have missing or incomplete records are required to be replaced.**

Critical parts go through numerous specialized processes (shot peening, chemical dips, etc.) during manufacture. The life limits of the parts are based upon the design and the processes they undergo during manufacture.

Purchasers and installers of life-limited critical parts should be careful to assure that parts are approved by original manufacturer or by PMA and that component historical record cards are accurate. If there are questions about the validity of component cards, the original manufacturer often can provide assistance.

An aircraft must be inspected in accordance with an annual inspection program or with one of the inspection programs outlined in 14 CFR section 91.409, in order to maintain a current Airworthiness Certificate. The aircraft may not be operated unless the annual inspection has been performed within the proceeding 12 calendar months. FAA Form 8100-2, Standard Airworthiness Certificate Item 6—Indicates the Airworthiness Certificate is in effect indefinitely if the aircraft is maintained in accordance with 14 CFR parts 21, 43, and 91 and the aircraft is registered in the United States. The **BIG QUESTION** is how does Life Limited Parts play into this.

The A&P who holds an IA certificate have to determine the condition of airframes, airframe systems, and components. Determine that an aircraft is in conformity with FAA Specifications. Determine that applicable Airworthiness Directives have been complied with. Conducts a thorough and detailed inspection of the whole aircraft. All 100-hour and annual inspection paperwork will comply with CFR Part 43 Appendix D. No aircraft will be returned to service following an inspection as outlined above until all discrepancies affecting airworthiness have been corrected. This includes life-limited parts documentation in accordance with CFR 43.10.

Is it the mechanics responsibility to make a list of all life-limited parts and ensure they are within limits? The answer is YES, if during an inspection. Yes, mechanics are required in ensure the aircraft meets all the requirements before approved for return to service. If mechanics can not trace all life limited parts in accordance with section 43.10, mechanics are required to give the owner a list of discrepancies and make a maintenance entry for Unairworthy aircraft in accordance with section 43.11. This will relieve the mechanic of liability and place it on the owner/operator where it belongs.

Remember mechanics (A&P's) **ARE NOT** responsible for the airworthiness of aircraft the owner/operator is. But this does not relieve the mechanic of their duty. A problem cannot be repaired, properly or negligently, if it is not discovered during inspection.

# CHAPTER 3

## MECHANIC REQUIREMENTS

# Inspector Requirements

The person who you select to accomplish your pre-purchase or any inspection/maintenance needs to be a person who is properly certificated and holds an Airframe and Power plant (A&P) certificate. In addition you may want this person to hold an Inspection Authorization (IA) under 14 CFR Part 65 Subpart D. Not all A&P mechanics are created equal and not all A&P's meet the recent experience requirement in accordance with Part 65 section 65.83. This may also hold true for the IA you select.

You should select an A&P who is very familiar with the type, make, and model of aircraft you want to purchase and has several years of experience maintaining them. During the interview phase with the mechanic ask to see their A&P, IA certificates and picture identification. Write down:

1. The certificate number.
2. Their current address.
3. Date of issue.
4. Type of ratings held.

With this information in hand make an appointment with your local Federal Aviation Administration (FAA), Flight Standard District Office (FSDO) Aviation Safety Inspector (ASI). Bring the information obtained from the mechanic you interviewed and ask the FAA inspector to check their data base to insure the mechanic is current in the FAA system and their address is correct. Each FSDO office has an office file on every IA in their district. You are not allowed to review their individual file, but the inspector can answer questions pertaining to the IA's record. You will want to know how long the person selected has held their certificates. Are they actively working full time or part time? Do they have the tools, equipment, and maintenance manuals to perform the inspection? Ask around at the local airport about the A&P or IA and get a good feel for their mechanic ability, knowledge, reputation, and honesty. Some information about all FAA certificated pilots and mechanics is listed on the Internet. This information may or may not be up-dated. So telephone or make an appointment with your local FSDO inspector and ask them to check the airman against the FAA database. Make sure the mechanic you select and paying is watching out for your interests and not someone who may have an interest in the sale of the aircraft.

# Inspection Authorization (IA) History

The Federal Aviation Administration (FAA) initiated the issuance of the inspection authorization (IA) more than 50 years ago. This system of allowing qualified mechanics the privilege of performing certain inspections has served well in the maintenance of the U.S. civil fleet. The attainment of an IA and performance of the duties of that certificate greatly enhance the privileges and responsibilities of the aircraft mechanic. The IA permits the airframe and powerplant (A&P) mechanic to perform a greater variety of maintenance and alterations than any other single maintenance entity.

The determination of airworthiness during an inspection is a serious responsibility. For many general aviation aircraft, the annual inspection could be the only in-depth inspection it receives throughout the year. In view of the wide ranging authority conveyed with the authorization, the test examines a broader field of knowledge than required for the A&P certificate and reflects the emphasis that is placed on the holder of the certificate in perpetuating air safety.

The requirements to obtain an Inspection Authorization (IA) are as follows if an A&P meets the requirements of Title 14 of the Code of Federal Regulations (CFR) section 65.91.

# Inspection Authorization Privileges and Limitations CFR Section 65.95

The holder of an inspection authorization (IA) may perform:

1. Inspect and approve for return to service any aircraft.
2. Inspect and approve for return to service any related part.
3. Inspect and approve for return to service any appliance.

## *NOTE*

*May approve for return after a major repair or major alteration to it in accordance with CFR Part 43, if the work was done in accordance with technical data approved by the Administrator (FAA).*

4. Perform an annual inspection.
5. Perform or supervise a progressive inspection according to section 43.13 and 43.15.
6. When they exercises the privileges of an inspection authorization the holder shall keep it available for inspection by the aircraft owner, the mechanic submitting the aircraft, repair, or alteration for approval (if any), and shall present it upon the request of the Administrator or an authorized representative of the National Transportation Safety Board, or of any Federal, State, or local law enforcement officer.

The holder of an inspection authorization **MAY NOT** exercise the privileges of the authorization if:

1. They change their fixed base of operation without notifying the FAA Flight Standards District Office or International Field Office for the area in which the new base is located, in writing, of the change.
2. Except any aircraft maintained in accordance with a continuous airworthiness program under CFR Part 121.

Each inspection authorization expires on March 31 of each year. However, the holder may exercise the privileges of that authorization only while he holds a currently effective mechanic certificate with both a currently effective airframe rating and a currently effective powerplant rating.

An inspection authorization ceases to be effective whenever any of the following occurs:

1. The authorization is surrendered, suspended, or revoked.
2. The holder no longer has a fixed base of operation.
3. The holder no longer has the equipment, facilities, and inspection data required by section 65.91I(3).

To be eligible for renewal of an inspection authorization for a 1-year period an applicant must present evidence annually, during the month of **March**, at an FAA Flight Standards District Office, or an International Field Office that the applicant still meets the requirements of section 65.91(c)(1) through (4) and must show that:

1. Has performed at least one annual inspection for each 90 days that the applicant held the current authority.
2. Or has performed inspections of at least two major repairs or major alterations for each 90 days that the applicant held the current authority.
3. Or has performed or supervised and approved at least one progressive inspection in accordance with standards prescribed by the Administrator.
4. Or has attended and successfully completed a refresher course, acceptable to the Administrator, of not less than 8 hours of instruction during the 12-month period preceding the application for renewal.

5. Or has passed on oral test by a FAA inspector to determine that the applicant's knowledge of applicable regulations and standards is current.

## *Note*
**If a FAA FSDO Inspector does not sign the IA certificate on FAA Form 8310-5 for the coming year it is not valid.**

# The Responsible of an IA

The basic functions of the holder of an inspection authorization (IA) are set forth in 14 CFR section 65.95. With the exception of aircraft maintained in accordance with a Continuous Airworthiness Program under 14 CFR Parts 121 or 135, an IA may inspect and approve for return to service any aircraft or related part or appliance after a major repair or major alteration. Also, the holder of an IA may perform an annual inspection and he or she may supervise or perform a progressive inspection.

The holder of an IA as required by 14 CFR Part 43.13 determines that the required placards and documents set forth in the aircraft specification or type certificate data sheet are available and current. The aircraft should be reported as being in an unairworthy condition if these placards and documents are not available. Missing, incorrect, or improperly located placards are regarded as an unairworthy item, and the owner or operator should be informed that, under the requirements of 14 CFR Part 91.9, the aircraft may not be operated until they are available.

The holder of an IA should refer to the registration and airworthiness certificates for the owner's name and address; the aircraft make, model, registration, and serial numbers needed for recording purposes. Be sure not to use manufacturers' trade names as they do not always coincide with the actual model designation (Cessna Skylane is CE-182, Piper Seneca III is PA-34-220T, etc.). If registration and airworthiness certificates are not available, the aircraft does not need to be reported in unairworthy condition; however, the owner or operator should be informed that the documents required by 14 CFR Part 91 section 91.203(a)(i)(2)(b), should be in the aircraft and the airworthiness certificate displayed, WHEN THE AIRCRAFT IS OPERATED.

A primary responsibility of the holder of an IA is to determine airworthiness by inspecting repairs or alterations for conformity to approved data, and assuring that the aircraft is in a condition for safe operation. During inspection of major repairs or major alterations, the holder of an IA must also determine that they are compatible with previous repairs and alterations that have been made to the aircraft.

The holder of an IA **must personally** perform all inspections. The Code of Federal Regulations (CFR's) does not provide for delegation of this responsibility. This means doing the AD research and inspection themselves.

The holders of an IA CANNOT approve the data for major repairs or major alterations. He/she may, however, inspect to see that alterations conform to data PREVIOUSLY APPROVED BY THE ADMINISTRATOR (14 CFR Part 65, section 65.95). This means the holder of an IA ensures that approved data is available and is used as the basis for the approval. This availability determination should be made prior to beginning the repair or alteration. If data is unavailable, or if the holder of an IA is unsure of the acceptability of the available data, the local Aviation Safety Inspector (ASI) should be consulted.

# General Privileges and Limitations of an A&P mechanic CFR Section 65.81

A certificated mechanic may:

1. Perform or supervise maintenance or preventive maintenance.
2. Perform or supervise the alteration of an aircraft.
3. Perform or supervise maintenance of appliances.
4. Perform or supervise maintenance of a part, for which he is rated.
5. May perform additional duties in accordance with 14 CFR Part 65.85, 65.87, and 65.95.
6. **MAY NOT** repair or perform major repairs to, and major alterations of:
   a. Propellers
   b. Any repairs to, or alteration of instruments, and.
7. **MAY NOT** supervise the maintenance, preventive maintenance, or alteration of, or approve and return to service,
   a. Any aircraft, appliance, or part thereof, for which he is rated unless he has satisfactorily performed the work concerned at an earlier date:
      1. If he has not so performed that work at an earlier date, they may show his ability to do it by performing it to the satisfaction of:
         a. Administrator (FAA Inspector)
         b. Under the direct supervision of a certificated and appropriately rated mechanic.
         c. Under the direct supervision of a certificated repairman, who has had previous experience in the specific operation concerned.
8. **MAY NOT** exercise the privileges of his certificate and rating unless:

   1. Understand the current instructions of the manufacturer.
   2. Understand the current the maintenance manuals for the specific operation concerned.

The A&P/IA in the course of certifying an aircraft to be airworthy, may be laying their certificates on the line for work of unknown quality, done at unknown times, and in some cases by unknown persons, and at times that may not be known.

### NOTE
*When the holder of an IA approves an aircraft for return to service, he or she will be held responsible for the condition of the aircraft AS OF THE TIME OF APPROVAL.*

# Airframe Authorizations Privileges and Limitations CFR Section 65.85

A certificated mechanic with an airframe rating may perform:

1. Approve and return to service an airframe.
2. Any related part or appliance, after he has performed, supervised, or inspected its maintenance or alteration.
3. May perform the 100-hour inspection required by Part 91 on an airframe or any related part or appliance, and approve and return it to service.

A certificated mechanic with an airframe rating **MAY NOT** perform return to service:

1. Repair or perform major repairs.

2. Major alterations.

# Power plant Authorizations Privileges and Limitations CFR Section 65.87

A certificated mechanic with a powerplant rating may:

1. Approve and return to service a powerplant.
2. Propeller.
3. Any related part or appliance, after he has performed, supervised, or inspected its maintenance or alteration.
4. May perform the 100-hour inspection required by Part 91 on a powerplant or propeller, or any related part, and approve and return it to service.

A certificated mechanic with a powerplant rating **MAY NOT** perform:

1. Major repairs.
2. Major alterations.

# Releasable Airmen Data

In accordance with Section 715 of the Aviation Investment and Reform Act for the 21st Century, the Airmen Certification Branch released a database containing the addresses and pertinent certificate information. For those airmen who have not requested that such information be withheld from public release their addresses and certificates numbers, which may of included social numbers were released. The CD-ROM version of this database is no longer available as of 18 January 2001.

Department of Transportation's Federal Aviation Administration (FAA) will begin issuing new, security-enhanced airman certificates to the nation's 650,000 active pilots and mechanics. FAA Administrator Marion C. Blakey unveiled the new certificate before hundreds of aviation enthusiasts at the Experimental Aircraft Association (EAA) AirVenture 2003.

The new credit card-sized certificates are made from high-quality composite PVC media card stock and incorporate new security features, such as a hologram of the FAA seal. They will replace the existing paper airman certificates, which can be easily damaged. Social Security number will no longer be used for your certificate number. The FAA computer will at random select a certificate number and will assign it to you. This new system is to protect your personal information.

The new certificate's durability and features will further protect pilot and mechanics identities and add one more element of security to our aviation system. No social security number will be used and new numbers will be assigned.

The certificate will be issued to all new and existing airmen as they achieve higher levels or additional ratings. It will replace certificates that have been lost or damaged. The Registry issues approximately 246,000 airman and 70,000 aircraft certificates annually.

The new certificate features graphics of the Wright Brothers, 1902 Wright Glider, 1903 Wright Flyer, Boeing jet aircraft, DOT seal, and a hologram of the FAA seal. The Wright Family Fund provided images of the Wright Brothers.

The FAA's Civil Aviation designed the new certificate. If you desire to have one of the new certificates send a letter to the address below with your certificate number, date of birth, and current address to airman records Oklahoma City. In addition include a $2.00 check or money order payable to the Treasury of the United States.

Remember when you receive your new certificate the issue date will be the current date the Registry issued it. This date does not mean the date you obtain your certificates for the first time.

Federal Aviation Administration
Civil Aviation Registry, AFS-760
P.O. Box 25082
Oklahoma City, OK   73125

# CHAPTER 4

## MAINTENANCE RECORDS

# Entries into the Aircraft Records

Find out if the maintenance records are complete. Missing maintenance records are not necessarily disqualifying. For a pre-purchase inspection in general, missing maintenance records from more than 10 to 20 years ago are not nearly as important as missing maintenance records currently. If there are no maintenance records, there is reason to be suspicious that the airplane was stolen. With any missing maintenance records you must assume that the airplane has some damage history. It will be up to you and your mechanic to find the evidence on the prebuy. Most of the time you won't get access to the maintenance records until the prepurchase inspection, but you can find out whether they are complete or not fairly early on. If the maintenance records are incomplete it may be impossible to prove compliance with some or all Airworthiness Directives (ADs). The assurance of a seller that all ADs have been complied with is worthless, as that airplane is not airworthy unless the maintenance records detail the method of compliance with each and every applicable AD.

The holder of an IA and other maintenance personnel or agencies are required to record maintenance, inspections, or alterations performed or approved in accordance with the requirements of 14 CFR Part 43, sections 43.9 and 43.11. The owner or operator is required by 14 CFR Part 91, section 91.417 to keep maintenance records. The holder of an IA is also required to indicate the total aircraft time in service when a required inspection is done.

# Significance of Maintenance Record Entries

Responsibility for maintenance work performed rests with the person whose signature and certificate number is entered on the appropriate maintenance record and/or forms. The responsibility for annual and progressive inspections and approval for return to service of major repairs or major alterations is assumed by the holder of an IA whose signature and certificate number appears on the appropriate maintenance records.

**Aircraft Logs**. "Logs," as commonly used, is an across-the-board term, which applies to the aircraft maintenance records "books," and to all accompanying records concerning the aircraft. These maintenance records provide a history of maintenance, a control for inspection schedules, data needed to properly accomplish time replacements of components or accessories, and a record of Airworthiness Directive compliance. Like damage history, missing maintenance records also make it more difficult to establish a good feeling about the price of an aircraft that you are considering.

When it comes to aircraft maintenance records what is required by Title 49 of the Code of Federal Regulations?

14 CFR Part 91.417 Explains out what maintenance records are required and how long those records must be kept by the owner/operator.

14 CFR Part 91.417 (a)(2) Explains the permanent records that must be "retained and transferred with the aircraft at the time the aircraft is sold.

14 CFR Part 91.417 (a)(2)(i) Explains the total time in service of the airframe, each engine, and each propeller and each rotor simply involves keeping track of time accumulation.

14 CFR Part 91.417 (a)(2)(ii) Explains about Life limited parts that have received a specific life limit from an approved FAA document.

14 CFR Part 91.417 (a)(2)(iii) Time since overhaul.

14 CFR Part 91.417 (a)(2)(v) Explains proper documentation of AD compliance.

14 CFR Part 91.417(a)(2)(vi) Explains the Form 337's that documents Major Alterations, which need to be retained permanently and transferred with the aircraft.

14 CFR Part 91.417 (a)(1) Explains aircraft records if not superceded by new identical records within the first 12 months following approval for return to service may be discarded.

# Paperwork Review

CFR Part 91.403(a) makes the owner or operator of an aircraft primarily responsible for maintaining an aircraft in an airworthy condition. CFR Part 91.7(b), on the other hand, delineates the responsibility of one who is the Pilot-in-Command. This regulation states, in part, that the Pilot-in-Command is responsible for determining if the aircraft is in a condition for safe flight. It does not state that he must determine if the aircraft is in an airworthy condition. In every aircraft is a required airworthiness certificate and in block 3 of that certificate it states the two conditions that must be met for and aircraft is considered airworthy:

1.  **The aircraft must conform to its type certificate.** Conformity to type design when the aircraft configuration and the components installed are consistent with the drawings, specifications, and other data i.e. STC field approved alterations.
2.  **The aircraft must be in condition for safe operation.** Condition of the aircraft relative to wear and deterioration, i.e. skin corrosion, window delamination/crazing, fluid leaks, tire wear, etc.

## *NOTE*
*If one or both of these conditions are not met, the aircraft would be considered unairworthy.*

Now knowing what the word airworthy means performing a maintenance record inspection is the only way to know if all the required inspections and time change items have been accomplished.

The owner or operator is responsible for all Airworthiness Directives (AD's), Life limited parts, required inspections, maintaining the equipment list, CG and weight distribution computations, and loading schedules if necessary, and the airworthiness of the aircraft.

CFR Part 43.11 contains the requirements for inspection entries. While these requirements are imposed on maintenance personnel, owners and operators should become familiar with them in order to meet their responsibilities under CFR 91.405.

The maintenance record requirements of section 43.11 applies to the 100-hour, annual, and progressive inspections under Part 91; inspection programs under CFR Parts 91 and 125; approved airplane inspection programs under CFR Part 135; and the 100-hour and annual inspections under section 135.411(a)(1).

Appropriately rated mechanics are authorized to conduct these inspections and make the required entries. Particular attention should be given to section 43.11(a)(7) in that it now requires a more specific statement than previously required under section 43.9. The entry, in addition to other items, must identify the inspection program used; identify the portion or segments of the inspection program accomplished; and contain a statement that the inspection was performed in accordance with the instructions and procedures for that program.

Questions continue regarding multiple entries for 100-hour/annual inspections. Neither CFR Part 43 nor CFR Part 91 requires separate records to be kept. CFR Part 43.11, however, requires persons approving or disapproving equipment for return to service, after any required inspection, to make an entry in the record of that equipment. Therefore, when an owner maintains a single record, the entry of the 100-hour or annual inspection is made in that record. If the owner maintains separate records for the airframe, powerplants, and propellers, the entry for the 100-hour inspection is entered in each, while the annual inspection is only required to be entered into the airframe record.

# Discrepancy Lists

Before to October 15, 1982, issuance of discrepancy lists (or lists of defects) to owners or operators was appropriate only in connection with annual inspections under CFR Part 91; inspections under section 135.411(a)(1); inspection programs under part 125; and inspections under CFR Part 91.217. Now, CFR Part 43.11 requires that a person performing any inspection required by CFR Parts 91, 125, or section 135.411(a) (1) prepare a discrepancy list.

When a discrepancy list is provided to an owner or operator, it says in effect, except for these discrepancies, the item inspected is airworthy. It is imperative, therefore, those inspections are complete and that all discrepancies appear in the list. When circumstances dictate that an inspection be terminated before it is completed, the maintenance record should clearly indicate that the inspection was discontinued. The entry should meet all the other requirements of section 43.11. It is no longer a requirement that copies of discrepancy lists be forwarded to the local Flight Standards District Office (FSDO).

Discrepancy lists (or lists of defects) are part of the maintenance record and the owner/operator is responsible to maintain that record in accordance with section 91.417(b)(3). The entry made by maintenance personnel in the maintenance record should reference the discrepancy list when a list is issued.

**Example of a record entry for an annual inspection in which the aircraft was found to be unairworthy.**
March 31, 2004
Total Aircraft Time 1853.00 Hours
Tach Reading 975.80
I certify that this aircraft has been inspected in accordance with an annual inspection and a list of discrepancies and unairworthy items dated March 31, 2004 have been provided for the aircraft owner.

I.B. Good
A&P 123456789 IA

**Example of a discrepancy list to be provided to an aircraft owner when reporting an aircraft with unairworthy items after completing an annual inspection.**
Academy Aviation
Hangar 78
North Field
Anywhere, CA 12345

Mr. John Doe
1234 W. Airplane Ave.
Anywhere, CA 12345

Dear Mr. Owner:

This is to certify that on March 31, 2004, I completed an annual inspection on your aircraft, a Cessna 195B, S/N 1234, N1234, and found the following unairworthy items:

1. Compression in No. 3 cylinder read 30 over 80, which is below the manufacturer's recommended limits.
2. The muffler has a broken baffle plate, which is blocking the engine exhaust outlet.
3. There is 6-inch cracks on bottom of left wing just aft of main landing gear attach point.

I.B. Good
A&P 123456789 IA

# Preventive Maintenance Entries

Private pilots or higher are permitted by Part 43 (Maintenance, Preventive Maintenance, Rebuilding, and Alterations) section 43.3(g) of the Federal Aviation Regulations to only perform "preventive" maintenance on any aircraft owned by or operated by that pilot and not used under Parts 121, 127, 129, and 135.

Pilots, like mechanics, are required to be trained to perform the preventive maintenance tasks before accomplishing the tasks alone.

The performance rules of CFR Part 43.13 apply to each person performing this preventive maintenance. They will use the methods, techniques, and practices prescribed in the **current** manufacturer's manual and instructions for continued airworthiness, or other methods, techniques, and practices acceptable to the Administrator. The individual shall use the tools, equipment, and test apparatus necessary to ensure completion of the work in accordance with accepted industry practices. The work shall be done in such a manner that the aircraft worked on will be at least equal to its original or properly altered condition.

## *NOTE*

*In section 43.13 it states at least equal to its original. Take note it does not say less than or better than the original. In addition you have to have training on what you are repairing, have current manufacture manuals and tooling. This will in some cases require a pilot to have calibrated torque wrench and pressure gages just like A&P mechanics.*

Although maintenance requirements vary for different types of aircraft, experience shows that most aircraft need some type of preventive maintenance every 25 hours or less of flying time and minor maintenance at least every 100 hours.

The holders of mechanic and repairman certificates, persons working under the supervision of these mechanics and repairmen, repair stations certificated under Part 145, and air carriers certificated under Parts 121 and 135, are authorized to perform preventive maintenance. These persons are also authorized to perform other maintenance. Therefore, it is of little consequence to them how a particular function is classified, since they are authorized to perform the function as either preventive maintenance or as other maintenance. Further, the procedures used in approving for return to service and recording are identical.

Since owners/pilots are not authorized to approve work accomplished by others, Section 43.9(a)(3) is not applicable when preventive maintenance is performed by the holder of a pilot's certificate. The holder of the pilot's certificate doing the work is the only person who can sign the approval for return to service.

Each person who performs this preventive maintenance **shall make** an entry in the aircraft maintenance records containing the following information:

1. The date of completion of the preventive maintenance work and aircraft total time-in-service. Total time in service is optional for normal and preventive maintenance.
2. A description of the work performed and identified as preventive maintenance.
3. The name, signature, certificate number, and kind of certificate held.

When the aircraft maintenance records are reviewed you may see an Airframe and Powerplant (A&P) certificate or a pilot certificate (PC) number in the return to service. Both are acceptable provided they follow the guidelines.

CFR Part 1, Section 1.1, defines preventive maintenance as **"simple or minor preservation operations and the replacement of small standard parts not involving complex assembly operations."**

The CFR's list relatively uncomplicated repairs and procedures defined as preventive maintenance. Certificated pilots, excluding student and recreational pilots, may perform preventive maintenance on any aircraft owned or operated by them that are not used in air carrier service. These preventive maintenance operations are listed in 14 CFR Part 43, appendix A, under Preventive Maintenance. Owners and pilots must use good judgment in determining that a specific function may appropriately be classified as preventive maintenance. Reference AC 43-12, Preventive Maintenance.

Preventive maintenance is limited to the following work, provided it does not involve complex assembly operations:

1. Removal, installation, and repair of landing gear tires. If you have to remove the brakes to perform this task you can not perform it.
2. Replacing elastic shock absorber cords on landing gear.
3. Servicing landing gear shock struts by adding oil, air, or both.
4. Servicing landing gear wheel bearings, such as cleaning and greasing.
5. Replacing defective safety wiring or cotter keys. Only is the safety wire is broken.
6. Lubrication not requiring disassembly other than removal of nonstructural items such as cover plates, cowlings, and fairings.
7. Making simple fabric patches not requiring rib stitching or the removal of structural parts or control surfaces. In the case of balloons, the making of small fabric repairs to envelopes (as defined in, and in accordance with, the balloon manufacturers' instructions) not requiring load tape repair or replacement.
8. Replenishing hydraulic fluid in the hydraulic reservoir.
9. Refinishing decorative coating of fuselage, balloon baskets, wings tail group surfaces (excluding balanced control surfaces), fairings, cowlings, landing gear, cabin, or cockpit interior when removal or disassembly of any primary structure or operating system is not required.
10. Applying preservative or protective material to components where no disassembly of any primary structure or operating system is involved and where such coating is not prohibited or is not contrary to good practices.
11. Repairing upholstery and decorative furnishings of the cabin, cockpit, or balloon basket interior when the repairing does not require disassembly of any primary structure or operating system or interfere with an operating system or affect the primary structure of the aircraft.
12. Making small simple repairs to fairings, nonstructural cover plates, cowlings, and small patches and reinforcements not changing the contour so as to interfere with proper airflow.
13. Replacing side windows where that work does not interfere with the structure or any operating system such as controls, electrical equipment, etc.
14. Replacing safety belts. This task may require a torque wrench, which is calibrated.
15. Replacing seats or seat parts with replacement parts approved for the aircraft, not involving disassembly of any primary structure or operating system.
16. Trouble shooting and repairing broken circuits in landing light wiring circuits.
17. Replacing bulbs, reflectors, and lenses of position and landing lights.
18. Replacing wheels and skis where no weight and balance computation is involved.
19. Replacing any cowling not requiring removal of the propeller or disconnection of flight controls.
20. Replacing or cleaning spark plugs and setting of spark plug gap clearance. Will require torque wrench.
21. Replacing any hose connection except hydraulic connections.
22. Replacing prefabricated fuel lines.
23. Cleaning or replacing fuel and oil strainers or filter elements.
24. Replacing and servicing batteries.
25. Cleaning of balloon burner pilot and main nozzles in accordance with the balloon manufacturer's instructions.
26. Replacement or adjustment of nonstructural standard fasteners incidental to operations.

27. The interchange of balloon baskets and burners on envelopes when the basket or burner is designated as interchangeable in the balloon type certificate data and the baskets and burners are specifically designed for quick removal and installation.
28. The installations of anti-misfueling devices to reduce the diameter of fuel tank filler openings provided the specific device has been made a part of the aircraft type certificate data by the aircraft manufacturer, the aircraft manufacturer has provided FAA-approved instructions for installation of the specific device, and installation does not involve the disassembly of the existing tank filler opening.
29. Removing, checking, and replacing magnetic chip detectors. May require a torque wrench.
30. The inspection and maintenance tasks prescribed and specifically identified as preventive maintenance in a primary category aircraft type certificate or supplemental type certificate holder's approved special inspection and preventive maintenance program when accomplished on a primary category aircraft provided:
    a. They are performed by the holder of at least a private pilot certificate issued under part 61 who is the registered owner (including co-owners) of the affected aircraft and who holds a certificate of competency for the affected aircraft (1) issued by a school approved under CFR Part 147.21(e) of this chapter; (2) issued by the holder of the production certificate for that primary category aircraft that has a special training program approved under Part 21.24 of this subchapter; or (3) issued by another entity that has a course approved by the Administrator.
    b. The inspections and maintenance tasks are performed in accordance with instructions contained by the special inspection and preventive maintenance program approved as part of the aircraft's type design or supplemental type design.
31. Removing and replacing self-contained, front instrument panel-mounted navigation and communication devices that employ tray-mounted connectors that connect the unit when the unit is installed into the instrument panel, (excluding automatic flight control systems, transponders, and microwave frequency distance measuring equipment (DME)). The approved unit must be designed to be readily and repeatedly removed and replaced, and pertinent instructions must be provided. Prior to the unit's intended use, and operational check must be performed in accordance with the applicable sections of Part 91 of this chapter.
32. Updating self-contained, front instrument panel-mounted Air Traffic Control (ATC) navigational software databases (excluding those of automatic flight control systems, transponders, and microwave frequency distance measuring equipment (DME)) provided no disassembly of the unit is required and pertinent instructions are provided. Prior to the unit's intended use, an operational check must be performed in accordance with applicable sections of Part 91 of this chapter. Reference (Secs. 313, 601 through 610, and 1102, Federal Aviation Act of 1958 as amended (49 U.S.C. 1354, 1421 through 1430 and 1502); (49 U.S.C. 106(g) (Revised Pub. L. 97-449, Jan. 21, 1983); and 14 CFR 11.45)

# Why Research Logbooks

The maintenance records reliability/correctness and records are the responsibility of the aircraft owner and not the maintenance personnel who do the work or recording. Often owners do not have a working knowledge of what is required by the FAA for Airworthiness or what should be entered in the logbooks. This is an area where logbook research can be helpful.

Research determines that all the FAA requirements are being met, the maintenance personnel are performing quality work and recording it correctly and that no inspections or maintenance pertinent to the aircraft is being overlooked or missed. It is also used to determine the quality of recorded work, if there is any damage history or repairs, and 337's for repairs and alterations. This all reflects on the value and reliability of the aircraft and may indicate future problems or long-term concerns. There is often a pattern of maintenance recorded in the books that precedes future expensive maintenance. See Chapter 23 Alterations and Major Repairs.

# What Is The Cost Of A Record Search

Since the charges are set by the quality of the logbooks, mechanics can tell more with an estimate after the books are received and looked over. The prices vary from $50.00 per logbook for an easy set to $100.00 and up per book for a difficult set. The difficulty of the maintenance records (books) as to legibility and continent determines the cost per book. Several mechanics charge by the hour to perform maintenance record checks. This is because it is very time consuming. So make sure you know if you are paying by the hour or by the maintenance record book.

# When Should You Have Logbooks Researched

The best times to think about maintenance record research are when considering the purchase of an aircraft and when considering selling aircraft. By all means when purchasing an aircraft get a pre-purchase from a shop that is familiar with that type aircraft, but does not do the maintenance on that particular one. Pre-purchases are always very helpful in determining the quality of the aircraft. However, it is wise to have the logbooks evaluated on a periodic basis for long-term owners as a second opinion on the quality of work being received. This helps avoid problems further down the road with maintenance and records.

Some shops and people specialize in piston-powered certified aircraft. Some shops and people specialize in turbine aircraft. Pick a shop or person that's familiar enough with the maintenance practices of the aircraft to provide the quality of service you desire.

# What Do Mechanics Find

Mechanics look for the maintenance history of the airframe, its damage history that is recorded, status of different airframe components determined by the type and model of aircraft. They check the records for tire, brake discs and linings, motors and control cable replacements and their frequency or lack of it. Instrument replacements, vacuum pump and filter replacements are checked on frequency or lack of. Engine components/accessories replacements/overhauls are checked for and correlated as to time between as well as the engine history. Engine history includes cylinder replacements, total time, time since major overhaul, who did the overhaul and when. Status of all pertinent Airworthiness Directives is checked as well as manufacturer's recommendations, time limits and specifications. Also, look for problems that are peculiar to the aircraft model and design and the engine. Record last maintenance on all those items pertinent to aircraft and look for missing inspections slow flight period and unusual periods of downtime, which can be questionable.

# Information For Pre-Purchases

Sometimes even a very professional pre-purchase does not include a complete inspection of the maintenance records because it is often very time consuming to read them thoroughly. A&P's can help you in determining whether an aircraft should be considered for purchase by looking at the maintenance status, damage history and AD's recorded or not recorded in the log books. A&P's can look for things that should be recorded for that particular aircraft model, type and age; these items make the aircraft either more valuable or less reliable purchase. These are items that would determine whether the aircraft was headed toward difficulties, was poorly maintained or was well maintained and appears to be a good purchase.

# How Long Does It Take

The length of time required is determined by the state of the maintenance records themselves. Typewritten/computerized entries are easier to read and therefore take less time to understand. However, most maintenance records entries (particularly older ones) are hand written and some are almost illegible and difficult to decipher and understand. Those take longer and require a greater concentration, greater knowledge of aircraft terminology and the ability to read between the lines. This does not mean that some great maintenance was not accomplished, only that the mechanic himself did the entry and had lost some of his fine motor skills by being a mechanic. Also maintenance records entries can become very faded or water stained and this makes them almost unreadable. It can take from half-hour for easy maintenance records to more than several hours for a difficult book. Determining status sometimes takes more than one reading and constant going back to review.

# How To Research Logbooks

Read them, recording when different items have been accomplished, Airworthiness Directive and Service Bulletin status of airframe, engine and all the accessories. Record engines total time, time since major overhaul, time since top overhaul, cylinder replacements and who the work was accomplished by and when. Check for time intervals on engine accessories, airframe motors and all the manufacturer's recommendations on time limits and servicing for the aircraft and engine. Also check for FAA Form 337s for repair or alteration and damage history to the airframe, propeller or engine. Check for instrument replacement, vacuum pump and filters replacements. Check on tire; brake discs and linings replacement frequency. Also check for the lack of the above records. Each model of aircraft has design weaknesses that are peculiar to it alone and look for recorded work in regard to them.

# What To Look For

Check the following items:

1. Maintenance status on items that have time/calendar limits for both airframe and engine components/accessories.
2. Items that should be inspected/replaced at regular intervals.
3. Unusual replacement of some items.
4. Too many tire changes, brake disc and linings replacements.
5. Lots of instrument work, vacuum pump and filter replacements.
6. Cylinder or accessory changes.
7. Or too few of the above.
8. Times where there has been little flight time.
9. Unusual period of downtime or no flight between inspections.
10. Replacement of hoses. Check for FAA From 8130-3 on all new hoses.
11. What was replaced when the engine was overhauled or replaced, check the work orders.
12. Airworthiness Directives/Service Bulletins.
13. Missing inspections and things that should have been recorded for aircraft integrity.
14. Accident/damage history, parts replacement.
15. Propeller changes/overhaul.
16. Copies of work orders from Part 145 repair stations.

# Accident History

Accident history helps determine the value of aircraft. It also helps determine the aircraft's reliability and the possibility of future or present structural problems that may not be noticed. If accident repairs are not done correctly or to a level in accordance with the manufacture, structural problems can develop through weakening /stressing components/skins or structure. The re-repair of the damage can be extremely expensive and may not provide the stability desired. During the record research you should find maintenance entries for any damage repair work. This may be in the maintenance record, on a FAA Form 337, or work order from a Repair Station.

# Results Written

The results of the research should be written in the form of a report listing the most recent replacements for various items, engine total time, time since overhaul, cylinder replacements, and manufacturer's time before overhaul recommendation. The overhauled and date will also be listed along with a list of when overhauls on accessories and other items should be accomplished. There should be a list of items, replacements or inspection missing if there are any. Whether there was any accident/damage history with when it was repaired, by who and flight time will be listed with whether this might jeopardize the aircraft's reliability or cause future problems. Any questionable entries, time periods, unusual downtimes should be listed. There should also be a list of what might need to be checked and watched in the future.

# How Can You Have A Set of Logbooks Researched

First call an A&P, Repair Station, or FBO to get information. They will need a full copy of all the logbooks. It is not recommended that you send the logs themselves as they might get lost in the process and are irreplaceable. Make sure someone in the company signs a hand receipt for your maintenance records. It is a good practice to have a back up set of records incase something should happen to the originals.

# Aircraft Registration Branch

Where to find your aircraft records with the FAA.

**Telephone:**
Aircraft Registration Information and Assistance     (405) 954-3116 or (866) 762-9434
Special N-Number Information and Assistance     (405) 954-4206 or (866) 762-9434
Note: These information lines are staffed from 7:30 a.m. to 3:45 p.m.

**Mailing Address:**
FAA
Aircraft Registration Branch, AFS-750
PO Box 25504
Oklahoma City, OK 73125

# CHAPTER 5

## INSPECTIONS

# Inspection Requirements

The Code of Federal Regulations (CFRs) require the inspection of all civil aircraft at specific intervals; to assure that the aircraft, condition is equal to its **original or properly altered** condition with regard to aerodynamic function, structural strength, and resistance to vibration.

Inspection interval requirements are established considering the purpose for which the aircraft is used and its operating environment. Some aircraft must be inspected each 100 hours of time in service while others must be inspected only once each 12 calendar months.

The inspection requirements for aircraft, in various types of operation, are stated in sections 91.169, 91.171, or Subpart D of CFR Part 91. The latter prescribes an inspection program for large and turbine-powered multi-engine airplanes (turbojet and turboprop). If you are concerned with the inspection of a large airplane (over 12,500 pounds) or a turbojet or turbopropeller-powered multiengine airplane, you should determine the inspection requirements for that specific airplane.

Code of Federal Regulations provide for the inspection of all civil aircraft at specific intervals, depending generally upon the type of operations in which they are engaged, for the purpose of determining their overall condition. In order to determine the specific inspection requirements and rules for the performance of inspections, reference should be made to the Code of Federal Regulations, which prescribe the requirements for the inspection and maintenance of aircraft in various types of operations.

All civil aircraft must be inspected at certain intervals as provided in the Code of Federal Regulations to determine the aircraft condition.

1. Generally, the inspection interval will depend upon the type of operation in which the aircraft is engaged.
2. Some aircraft must be inspected at least once each 12-calendar month, while inspection is required for others after each 100 hours of flight.
3. An aircraft may also be inspected in accordance with an inspection system set up to provide for total inspection of the aircraft over a calendar or flight-time period.
4. In order to determine the specific inspection requirement and rules regarding inspections, reference should be made to the Code of Federal Regulations, which prescribe the requirements for the inspection of aircraft in various categories of operation.

Each person performing an inspection required by Code of Federal Regulations (CFR) Part 91, 121, 125, or 135, **shall**:

1. Perform the inspection so as to determine whether the aircraft, or portion(s) thereof under inspection, meets all applicable airworthiness requirements.
2. If the inspection is one provided for in CFR Part 121, 125, 135, or CRF 91.409(e), perform the inspection in accordance with the instructions and procedures set forth in the inspection program for the aircraft being inspected.

# Maintenance Record Comparison

Maintenance record comparison is where the mechanic will spend the bulk of there time in the research process to compare what is found on the aircraft and what was written or not written in the maintenance record. If you order the aircraft records from Oklahoma City they should match the comparison check. As you read through the maintenance record and find scheduled items that have been complied with write them down with the tach time, cycle and date.

It is always better to start with the last maintenance record entry and work your way back through the inspections and requirements. You should list all scheduled maintenance such as 25-hour oil changes, 50-hour inspections, 100-hour inspections, special inspections, inspection replacement, lubrications, and AD compliance.

It becomes very important to have a complete AD compliance list to match up to the aircraft records. Some AD's may have been complied with and the AD compliance record may say to see record entry dated on a certain date. This is why it is very important to have all the aircraft records to verify the AD's compliance. I have seen the owner compliance record referring to the airframe logbook and the owner could not locate the record. Without the aircraft record the AD had to be re-accomplished costing several hundred to thousands of dollars. Having an AD compliance list showing the date, how the AD was accomplished, certificate and signature could have saved the owner time and money.

If you find an AD that was not complied with in the maintenance record check the AD compliance records. It may give you the name and certificate number of the person who accomplished it. Some mechanics type the maintenance record on what is commonly called a paste in logbook entry. Sometimes the owner forgets to paste the entry in the maintenance record, but he does not have to as long as he has it available.

Remember the owner does not have to keep their maintenance records in a logbook. Maintenance records can be on single sheets of paper, paste in entries, work order provided by a Part 145 Repair Station and other means. All the Code of Federal Regulation (CFR) requires is the owner maintain them and make them available for inspection. As the old saying goes a mechanic could write the entries on toilet paper and it becomes official paper.

One reason to perform an inspection is to make a list of all of the accessories on the aircraft. Often times IA's and A&P mechanics overlook the accessories AD's, because the owner does not or will not pay for the mechanic's time to research the accessories. The operation rule CFR Part 91 makes it clear the owner/operator is responsible for AD's, but if an inspection is completed and the mechanic approves an aircraft for return to service they are now responsible for not complying with that inspection.

Since the mechanic is making a list of all the accessories now is a good time to make a list of all the Life Limited items. Mechanics are now responsible during inspections to comply with CFR section 43.10 of the rule. This rule requires records for components of the airframe, engine, propellers, rotors, and appliances that are identified to be removed from service when the life-limit has been reached.

The current life-limited status of the part is a record indicating the life-limit remaining before the required retirement time of the component is reached. This record must include any modification of the part in accordance with ADs, service bulletins, or product improvements by the manufacturer or applicant. The following are not considered a current life limited status record:

1. Work orders
2. Maintenance installation records
3. Purchase requests
4. Sales receipts
5. Manufacturers documentation of original certificate
6. Other historical data

Whenever the current status of life-limited parts records cannot be established or has not been maintained (e.g., a break in current status) and the historical records are not available, the airworthiness of that product cannot be determined and it must be removed from service. Life Limits are explained in detail in Chapter 2 under Life Limits.

# Types of Inspections

There are at least **ten types** of inspections that can and should be checked during the record check.

1. Annual Inspection
2. 100-hour Inspection
3. Progressive Inspection
4. 50-hour Inspection
5. Lighting Strike Inspection
6. Corrosion Inspection
7. Hard or Overweight Landing Inspection
8. Severe Turbulence Inspection
9. Required Inspection by an AD
10. Manufactures Inspections

**Annual:** Can only be performed by an Inspection Authorization (IA), manufacture, or a Repair Station with the proper airframe ratings. An annual inspection is only good until the ink dries. The FAA does not hold a mechanic responsible for the continued airworthiness of the aircraft after an inspection for two reasons.

1. CFR Part 91.403(a) states that the owner or operator is primarily responsible for the airworthiness.

2. The FAA realizes it is not fair to hold a mechanic responsible when the aircraft is no longer in the mechanic's care.

When an mechanic signs off an annual and approves the aircraft for return to service by their signature they are stating that they re-inspected every bit of maintenance that was every performed all the way back to the date on the Airworthiness Certificate. This will include:

1. Major repairs
2. Major alterations
3. Service bulletins
4. Supplemental Type Certificate (STC)
5. Field Approvals
6. Every AD and recurrent AD

The IA's are held responsible for performing a complete inspection and for finding things. In addition they can be held responsible for items missed on inspections by the FAA. Reference section 43.11 and 43.15.

**100-hour Inspection:** Can be performed by an Airframe and Powerplant (A&P) or a Repair Station with the proper airframe ratings. Be advised that the scope and detail of a 100-hour inspection is the same as the annual inspection except who can approve it for return to service.

Each person performing an annual or 100-hour inspection shall use a checklist while performing the inspection. The checklist may be of the person's own design, one provided by the manufacturer of the equipment being inspected or one obtained from another source. This checklist must include the scope and detail of the items contained in CFR Part 43 section 43.15(c) and appendix D.

Each person approving a reciprocating-engine-powered aircraft for return to service after an annual or 100-hour inspection **shall**, before that approval, run the aircraft engine or engines to determine satisfactory performance in accordance with the manufacturer's recommendations of:

1. Power output (static and idle r.p.m.).
2. Magnetos.
3. Fuel and oil pressure.
4. Cylinder and oil temperature.
5. All items to be inspected are in CFR Part 43 Appendix D.

Each person approving a turbine-engine-powered aircraft for return to service after an annual, 100-hour, or progressive inspection **shall** before that approval for return to service:

1. Run the aircraft engine or engines to determine satisfactory performance in accordance with the manufacturer's recommendations. Reference section 43.15(c)(2).

**Progressive Inspection:** Can be performed by an Inspection Authorization (IA) or a Repair Station with the proper airframe ratings. At the end of the 12-month Progressive Inspection the IA has the same responsible as the annual for return to service. Reference section 43.11(d).

Each person performing a progressive inspection shall, at the start of a progressive inspection system, inspect the aircraft completely. After this initial inspection, routine and detailed inspections must be conducted as prescribed in the progressive inspection schedule. Routine inspections consist of visual examination or check of the appliances, the aircraft, and its components and systems, insofar as practicable without disassembly. Detailed inspections consist of a thorough examination of the appliances, the aircraft, and its components and a system, with such disassembly as are necessary. For the purposes of this inspection, the overhaul of a component or system is considered to be a detailed inspection.

**Shall** use the tools, equipment, and test apparatus necessary to assure completion of the work in accordance with accepted industry practices. If the manufacturer recommends special equipment or test apparatus, (the mechanic) must use that equipment or apparatus or its equivalent acceptable to the Administrator. See Chapter 22 Tools for the meaning and explanation of equivalent tools. Reference section 43.13.

Before an aircraft can start a Progressive Inspection program the local FSDO must be notified and a copy of the program presented. This will also require a maintenance records entry starting the program.

A progressive inspection is detailed in section 91.409(d). The person authorized in the progressive inspection manual, usually an IA, must perform and supervise. An A&P can do the work, but the **IA has to sign off each of the phases**, (part of supervision) because only the person listed in the manual can sign off the progressive inspection.

**50-Hour Inspection:** Can be performed by an Airframe and Powerplant (A&P) or a Repair Station with the proper airframe ratings. In accordance with the manufactures current maintenance manuals.

**Lighting Strike Inspection:** Can be performed by an Airframe and Powerplant (A&P) or a Repair Station with the proper airframe ratings. In accordance with the manufactures current maintenance manuals.

**Corrosion Inspection:** Can be performed by an Airframe and Powerplant (A&P) or a Repair Station with the proper airframe ratings. In accordance with the manufactures current maintenance manuals.

**Hard or Overweight Landing Inspection:** Can be performed by an Airframe and Powerplant (A&P) or a Repair Station with the proper airframe ratings. May also be called a **Special Inspection.** The stress induced in a structure by a hard or overweight landing depends both on the gross weight at touchdown and the severity of impact (rate of sink). It is difficult to estimate vertical velocity at the time of impact, and whether a landing has been sufficiently severe to result in structural damage. With this in view, a special inspection should be performed after:

1. A landing is made at a weight known to exceed the design landing weight, or
2. A rough landing regardless of the landing weight.
3. Wrinkled wing skin is a sign of an excessive load, which may have been imposed during a landing. Another indication easily detected is fuel leaks and/or fuel stains along riveted seams.
4. Other possible damage locations are spar webs, bulkheads, nacelle skin and attachments, wing and fuselage stringers.

If these areas do not indicate adverse effects, probably no serious damage has occurred. A more extensive inspection and alignment are necessary if damage is noted. Aircraft are designed to absorb the loads imposed during normal operation and accept a certain amount of overload. Excessive loads, however, result in failure or deformation of the structure. This deformation may be slight or prominent, but it is usually visible. In any case, it can be detected and classified by certain appearances peculiar to the type of overload applied. In the majority of cases, loads, which result in deformed parts also, overload the adjacent structure. Because of the possibility of hidden damage, a qualified mechanic, repair station, or the aircraft manufacturer should be called upon to make a detailed inspection when deformation is noted. This is especially true when an aircraft has been in an accident or subjected to suspected overloads on the structure.

Each level of inspection must be clearly defined in the operator/applicant's continuous airworthiness maintenance program. For example, a specific area of the aircraft may require only a visual inspection during pre-flight A and B checks but will require a derailed, X-ray, or Zyglo inspection in the same area for a "C" or "D" check under a progressive inspection program. In accordance with the manufactures current maintenance manuals.

**Severe Turbulence Inspection:** If the combination of gust velocity and airspeed is too severe, the stress induced in structural members can cause damage. May also be called Special Inspections. Inspection should be performed after a flight through severe turbulence as follows:

1. Upper and lower wing surfaces – inspect for excessive buckles or permanent set wrinkles.
2. Spar webs – inspect for buckling, wrinkles, and sheared attachments.
3. Nacelles – Inspect for buckling around nacelle and nacelle skin at the wing leading edge.
4. Fuel leaks – fuel leaks may indicate open rivet seams with broken sealant.
5. Fuselage skins – inspect top and bottom areas for wrinkles, which are probably diagonal.
6. Empennage – inspect surfaces for wrinkles, buckling and/or sheared attachments, and also areas of attachment to fuselage. A more extensive inspection and alignment are necessary if damage is noted.
7. In accordance with the manufactures current maintenance manuals.

**Inspection Required by ADs:** Can be performed by an Airframe and Powerplant (A&P) or a Repair Station with the proper airframe ratings. Take note that Service Bulletins may be required to be completed if referenced in the AD, in accordance with the AD requirements.

**Manufactures Inspections:** Can be performed by an Airframe and Powerplant (A&P) or a Repair Station with the proper airframe ratings. In accordance with the manufactures current maintenance manuals.

**All inspections** must be signed off in accordance with section 43.11, containing the following:

1. Date of inspection.
2. Total Time of aircraft.
3. Brief description of the extent of the inspection.
4. Signature of mechanic.
5. Certificate number of mechanic and rating held.
6. Kind of certificate held by the person approving or disapproving the aircraft or portions there of, for return to service.

## *NOTE*
*Total time can be recorded with hobbs meter, tach, or by each flight time in the logbook.*

Some aircraft have more than one hobbs meter. One starts tracking time as soon as the master switch is turned on. A second may be attached to the main or nose landing gear strut and starts tracking time at extension of the gear and turn off when there is weight on wheels. Total time is defined in CFR Part 1, as the time from the moment the aircraft leaves the surface of the earth to the time it returns to land.

During the record inspection check the Hobbs and Tach meters as they may have been changed and the times are different. When a new meter is installed the previous time is added to the new hobbs meter time to give total time.

# The Fresh Annual

I recommend that any potential buyer be extremely suspicious of airplanes advertised with a **"fresh annual."** Think hard now; if you were selling your airplane, how much would you spend on an annual? Would you insist the mechanic correct every little thing that was wrong? Most of the time this is window dressing on a hangar queen. The for sale sign on the aircraft should read, "Don't buy me." Besides, you are going to do a prebuy that is so thorough, that once you have decided to purchase the airplane, you will have the mechanic go ahead and complete an annual inspection because it is already at least 40 to 60% complete anyway, so a "fresh" annual adds no value to the airplane in your opinion.

Be advised there are requirements in CFR Part 43 section 43.13 that requires mechanics to use the tools, equipment, and test apparatus necessary to assure completion of the work in accordance with accepted industry practices. If special equipment or test apparatus is recommended by the manufacturer involved, he must use that equipment or apparatus or its equivalent acceptable to the Administrator. Be very careful with equivalent tooling the mechanic will be using. Request the mechanic provide you with some sort of documentation showing their tools are equivalent to the manufacturers recommended tools. See Chapter 22 on equivalent tool requirements. You can contact your local FAA FSDO to answer questions about tooling. Also, section 43.15 requires the mechanic to perform the inspection so as to determine whether the aircraft, or portion(s) thereof under inspection, meets all applicable airworthiness requirements.

If the person performing any inspection required by Part 91, 125 or 135.411(a)(1) finds that the aircraft is unairworthy or does not meet the applicable type certificate data, airworthiness directives, or other approved data upon which its airworthiness depends, that persons must give the owner or lessee a signed and dated list of those discrepancies. And don't forget to make a maintenance record entry stating the above.

What this means is during your pre-purchase inspection on an aircraft with a "fresh annual" your mechanic discovers unairworthy items that should have been found during the annual inspection. The mechanic who performed the last annual inspection may be in violation of Part 43. Make sure your pre-purchase mechanic provides you and the current owner with a list of discrepancies along with a maintenance record (logbook) entry for the unairworthy items.

Part 43.12 Maintenance records: Falsification, reproduction, or alteration.
a. No person may make or cause to be made:
  1. Any fraudulent or intentionally false entry in any record or report that is required to be made, kept, or used to show compliance with any requirement under this part;
  2. Any reproduction, for fraudulent purpose, of any record or report under this part; or
  3. Any alteration, for fraudulent purpose, of any record or report under this part.

The unlawful activity for making false entries is to revoke all of an airman's FAA certificates as referenced in FAA Order 2150.3. Under U.S. Code section 44709 of the Act, the Administrator may issue an order amending, modifying, suspending, or revoking, in whole or in part, any certificate issued by the agency if, as a result of a reexamination or any other investigation, the Administrator determines that safety in air commerce or air transportation and the public interest require issuance of the order. Prior to issuing such an order, the FAA must advise the certificate holder of the charges or reasons for the proposed action and, except in the case of an emergency requiring immediate action, provide the certificate holder with an opportunity to respond. Reference 49 U.S.C. App. 142.

# Inspection Meanings

So let's look at the different type of inspections that can be accomplished.

**Condition Report** – Usually accomplished by an agent of a lending institution and is a selected blend of the Casual and the Pre-purchase inspections to determine the current market value.

**Pre-flight Inspection** – A FAA required inspection normally performed by the pilot prior to flight. Standards vary greatly with individual and situation. No disassembly is involved. The scope may be found in the Owner/Pilot manual for that particular aircraft.

**25/50 Hours Inspection** – A non-FAA required inspection usually performed in conjuncture with an oil and filter change whose scope is usually determined by the service facility. Its purpose is to address interim service items and to arrest small discrepancies before they develop into larger ones. Some disassembly is involved to access engine, battery, brakes and various systems reservoirs. Most aircraft manufacturers have 50 hours service requirements in their inspection schedules. Some Airworthiness Directives have 50 or 100 hours requirements.

**100 Hours Inspection** – Only required if the aircraft is for hire or flight instruction. The scope of this detailed inspection is outlined by CFR Part 43 Appendix D or by the manufacturer's inspection guide, which is the same as the annual inspection except who can perform return to service. The inspection may be accomplished and signed off by the aircraft manufacturer, appropriately rated FAA repair station, or a certificated airframe and powerplant mechanic. Not all 100 hours inspections are equal, and in reality many are substantially abbreviated. **NOTE** Airworthiness Directive may have 100 hours requirements.

**Annual Inspection** – The scope and detail are the same as a 100 hours inspection. The inspection may be performed and signed off by the aircraft manufacturer, appropriately rated repair station or an airframe and powerplant mechanic holding a current Inspection Authorization (IA). An annual inspection is a FAA required inspection. A progressive inspection program can satisfy the annual inspection requirements. The depth and integrity of this inspection varies widely with the industry. Considerable disassembly is required. Ideally Airworthiness Directive search and compliance verification should be completed during the inspection.

**Progressive Inspection** – May be used in lieu of a normal Annual/100 hour maintenance program if approved by the local FAA FSDO. It is a blend of 25/50 hour, 100 hour and Annual inspection requirements integrated into closely spaced inspections called events covering detailed inspection of certain limited area(s) in rotation with an overall visual and service inspection of the entire aircraft. All events must be completed within a calendar year to satisfy Annual inspection requirements.

A progressive inspection program may be written for your particular aircraft and mission or selected from manufacturer's publications. The events may be few as 2 covering 100 hours or as many as 16 covering 400 hours of operation. The advantages are more appropriate individual inspection intervals, less down time, spread out maintenance bills, more detailed overall inspection, with small discrepancies repaired before becoming large. The disadvantages may include increased maintenance scheduling, a 10 hours limit on over flight time, reluctance of some shops to administer the program, and the requirement of a recently completed Annual inspection to initiate the program. A simple program could be as follows:

**Event #1** (due at 6 months/50 hours) – detailed inspection Powerplant/Propeller – routine inspection Airframe

**Event #2** (due at 12 months/100 hours) – detailed inspection Airframe – routine inspection Powerplant/Propeller.

**Special Inspections** – inspections that do not coincide with 100 hours/annual inspection intervals. Some are required like 24 months on altimeter/encoder/transponder certifications (if operating in controlled airspace). Others are optional, but generally accepted by the industry like engine major overhaul. An overhaul or new component constitutes a detailed inspection. Typical examples are propeller and governor overhaul, engine accessories overhaul, 500-hour magneto and alternator inspection, oxygen bottle hydrostatic test (ICC regulation), wing bolt inspection/replacement, and inspection of landing gear and flight control trim actuators. A list may be found in the maintenance manual pertaining to your aircraft.

**Static System Tests** – Certain aircraft are required by Section 91.411 to have altimeter and static system tested. These tests are described in Appendix E of Part 43. Equipment, materials, and required tests for test equipment are specified in CFR Part 145. Persons authorized to perform altimeter and static systems tests are identified in section 91.411.

Performance of this test with all static instruments connected will assure that leaks have not been introduced at instrument connections. Use of the following procedures is satisfactory as a means for compliance with the static pressure system proof test and inspection:

1. Visually inspect the ports, plumbing, accessories, and instruments connected to the static system and repair or replace those parts which are defective; e.g., broken "B" nuts, cracked flare sleeves, deteriorated flexible tubing, bad valves, etc. Purge the system, if necessary, to remove foreign matter which may have accumulated in the tubing.
2. Check the static port heater to assure proper operation by noting either ammeter current or that the Pitot tube or static port gets hot to the touch.
3. When an aircraft has more than one static system, test each system separately to assure their independence and to assure that the leak rate for each system is within tolerance.
4. Connect the test equipment directly to the static ports, if practicable. Otherwise, connect to a static system drain or tee connection and seal off the static ports. If the test equipment is connected to the static system at any point other than the static port, it should be made at a point where the connection may be readily inspected for system integrity after the system is returned to its normal configuration. Remove all static port seals after completion of the static system test.
5. For unpressurized airplanes, conduct the static pressure system proof test to the standards prescribed in CFR section 23.1325(b)(2)(i) or section 25.1325(c)(2)(i), as applicable.
6. For pressurized airplanes, conduct the static pressure system proof test to the standards prescribed in CFR section 23.1325(b)(2)(ii) or section 25.1325 (c)(2)(ii), as applicable.

   a. An accurate vacuum gauge referenced to atmospheric pressure and connected to the static pressure system may be used to measure the equivalent cabin differential pressure.
   b. Either the altimeter in the airplane under test or that in the test equipment may be used as a vacuum gauge, provided that barometric pressure is converted to pressure in pounds per square inch (PSI). A convenient formula for this conversion is: inches of mercury PSI = 2.036.

Altimeter tests are performed in accordance with CFR Part 43, Appendix E. If the altimeter test is to be performed with the instrument installed in the airplane, the following guidelines should be observed:

1. The static leak test should be conducted first to assure that there are no static system leaks to influence altimeter indications.
2. Permit the altimeter to stabilize after a flight before performing the test.
3. Use portable test equipment or barometric test equipment is authorized if it is calibrated and the operator has the proper repair station ratings.
4. When vibration is applied to the instrument, assure that it is not of a magnitude, which will mask a sticky altimeter.

**Airworthiness Directives (AD)** Airworthiness Directives **are mandatory**, FAA required inspections or operating limitations usually very detailed, sometimes have optional compliance methods but generally enforce a manufacturer's inspection or maintenance requirement such as a service bulletin. The owner/operator is primarily responsible for AD compliance.

**Service Communiqués** An informational letter from the manufacturer alerting owner(s) of minor problems or of additional services or operational information. It has no regulatory status.

**Service Instructions** A manufacturer's publication with expanded detailed inspection or repair procedures that may be referenced by an Airworthiness Directive.

**Service Bulletins** an important manufacturer's publications relating to improved inspection, maintenance or repair procedures, which often authorize improved parts or material. Compliance with a service bulletin may be required by a particular Airworthiness Directive. Usually compliance with service bulletins will keep your AD exposure very low.

### Emergency Locator Transmitters (ELT)

The ELT must be evaluated in accordance with TSO-C91a, TSO-C126 for 406 MHz ELT's, or later TSO's issued for ELT's. ELT installations must be examined for potential operational problems at least once a year (section 91.207(d)). There have been numerous instances of interaction between ELT and other VHF installations. Antenna location should be as far as possible from other antennas to prevent efficiency losses. Check ELT antenna installations in close proximity to other VHF antennas for suspected interference. Antenna patterns of previously installed VHF antennas could be measured after an ELT installation. Testing of an ELT must be performed within the first 5 minutes of an hour, and only three pulses of the transmitter should be activated. For example, a test could be conducted between 1:00 p.m. and 1:05 p.m., with a maximum of three beeps being heard on a frequency of 121.5 MHz.

A properly certified person or repair station within 12-calendar months must accomplish an inspection of the ELT after the last inspection.

### Inspection of ATC Transponder

All transponders must be tested every 24-calendar months, or during an annual inspection, if requested by the owner. The test must be conducted by an authorized repair facility properly equipped to perform those functions in accordance with CFR 91 section 91.413.

# Aircraft With Discrepancies or Unairworthy Conditions

If the aircraft is not approved for return to service after a required inspection, use the procedures specified in 14 CFR Part 43, section 43.11. This will permit an owner to assume responsibility for having the discrepancies corrected prior to operating the aircraft.

A person who is authorized by 14 CFR Part 43 to do the work can clear the discrepancies. Preventive maintenance items could be cleared by a pilot who owns or operates the aircraft, provided the aircraft is not used under 14 CFR Parts 121, 129, or 135; except that approval may be granted to allow a pilot operating a rotorcraft in a remote area under 14 CFR Part 135 to perform preventive maintenance.

The owner may want the aircraft flown to another location to have repairs completed, in which case the owner should be advised that the issuance of FAA Form 8130-7, Special Flight Permit, is required. This form is commonly called a ferry permit and is detailed in 14 CFR Part 21, section 21.197. The certificate may be obtained in person or by fax at the local FSDO or from a Designated Airworthiness Representative.

If the aircraft is found to be in an unairworthy condition, an entry will be made in the maintenance records that the inspection was completed and a list of unairworthy items was provided to the owner. When a person authorized to perform maintenance corrects all unairworthy items and that person makes an entry in the maintenance record for the correction of those items, the aircraft is approved for return to service.

For those items permitted to be inoperative under CFR Part 91 section 91.213, that person shall:

1. Place a placard, which meets the aircraft's airworthiness certification regulations, on each inoperative instrument and the cockpit control of each item of inoperative equipment, marking it **"Inoperative."**
2. Instruments have to be disabled or removed from the aircraft.
3. Shall add the items to the signed and dated list of discrepancies given to the owner or lessee. Reference Part 91 section 91.405(c).

# Incomplete Annual Inspections

If an annual inspection is not completed, the holder of an IA should:

1. Indicate any discrepancies found in the aircraft records.
2. NOT indicate that an annual inspection was conducted.
3. Indicate the extent of the inspection and all work accomplished in the aircraft records.

Other documents which are often needed but not a part of the airworthiness requirement might be a state registration and if the aircraft is equipped with a transceiver, a Federal Communications Commission radio license. The owner or operator is responsible for maintaining these documents. However, the holder of an IA will be performing an appreciated service by informing the operator of any deficiencies in the display and carriage of these documents.

On aircraft for which no approved flight manual is required, the operating limitations prescribed during original certification and as required by 14 CFR Part 91, section 91.9, must be carried in or be affixed to the aircraft. Range markings on the instruments, placards, and listings are required to be worded and located as specified in the type certificate data sheet.

# Inspection Do's and Don'ts

## DO'S

DO have an assortment of proper tools for the inspection.

DO have an inspection check form and a regular inspection procedure. **STICK TO IT**.

DO remove all inspection plates and cowlings in the area to be inspected.

DO clean all items to be inspected. This is essential in order to clearly see the parts you are inspecting. Inspect before and after cleaning.

DO check all moving parts for proper lubrication and check the "jam" or locking nuts on push-pull controls or adjustment devices for security.

DO familiarize yourself with proper safetying techniques and inspect for proper safetying. Re-safety a part you have unsafetied before inspecting the next item.

DO seek assistance in any questionable area. A certificated mechanic, an approved repair station, or your local FAA inspectors are your prime contacts. Use them.

DO the job right the first time—save a life—it may be your OWN.

# DON'TS

DON'T be hurried—take plenty of time to properly inspect each item. If you don't know what to do next, ASK.

DON'T move the propeller unless the magneto switch reads "OFF," or the ignition system is otherwise rendered inoperative.

DON'T presume an item is airworthy until it has been checked.

DON'T check landing gear by kicking it—raise it off the ground.

DON'T perform any complex inspection or maintenance operation unless a certificated mechanic properly supervises you.

DON'T take the attitude—it can't happen to me.

## Let's review:

1. 14 CFR section 43.9 entries. Any person who maintains, rebuilds, or alters an aircraft, airframe, aircraft engine, propeller, or appliance shall make an entry containing:

   a. A description of the work or some reference to data acceptable to the FAA;
   b. The date the work was completed;
   c. The name of the person who performed the work; and
   d. If the work is approved for return to service, the signature, certificate number, and kind of certificate held by the person approving the aircraft for return to service.

2. 14 CFR section 43.11 entries. When a mechanic approves or disapproves an aircraft for return to service for an annual, 100-hour, or progressive inspection, an entry shall be made including:

   a. Aircraft time in service;
   b. The type of inspection;
   c. The date of inspection;
   d. The signature, certificate number, and kind of certificate held by the person approving or disapproving the aircraft for return to service; and
   e. A signed and dated listing of discrepancies and unairworthy items.

3. 14 CFR section 91.409(e)—Airplanes. Inspection entries for 14 CFR section 91. 409(e). Airplanes (those over 12,500 pounds, turbo jet, or turbopropeller-powered multiengine airplanes) are made according to 14 CFR section 43.9 and they shall include:

   a. The kind of inspection performed;
   b. A statement by the mechanic that it was performed in accordance with the instructions and procedures for the kind of inspection program selected by the owner; and
   c. If the aircraft is not approved for return to service, statement that a signed and dated list of any defects found during the inspection was given to the owner.

4. FAA Form 337, Major Repairs and Major Alterations. A mechanic who performs a major repair or major alteration shall record the work on FAA Form 337 and have the work inspected and approved by a mechanic who holds an Inspection Authorization. A signed copy shall be given to the owner and another copy sent to the local FSDO within 48 hours after the aircraft has been approved for return to service. However, when a certificated repair station does a major repair, the customer's work order may be used and a release given as outlined in 14 CFR Part 43, appendix B.

5. 14 CFR section 91.411—Altimeter and Static Tests. 14 CFR section 91.411 requires that every airplane or helicopter operated in controlled airspace under IFR conditions have each static pressure system, each altimeter, and each automatic pressure altitude reporting system tested and inspected every 24 calendar months. The mechanic shall enter into the records:

   a. A description of the work.
   b. The maximum altitude to which the altimeter was tested.

c.  The date and signature of the person approving the aircraft for return to service.

6.  14 CFR section 91.413—Transponder Tests.  14 CFR section 91.413 requires that anyone operating an Air Traffic Control (ATC) transponder specified in 14 CFR section 91.215(a) have it tested and inspected every 24 calendar months.  The mechanic shall enter into the records per Part 43 section 43.9

a.  A description of the work.
b.  The date and signature of the person approving the airplane for return to service.  The person should hold a Repair Station Certificate with the proper rating.

# Airworthiness Directives (AD's)

The authority for the role of the Federal Aviation Administration (FAA) regarding the promotion of safe flight for civil aircraft may be found generally at Title 49 of the United States Code (USC) Section 44701 et. Seq. (formerly Title VI of the Federal Aviation Act of 1958 and related statutes.)  One of the ways the FAA has implemented its authority is through 14 CFR Part 39, Airworthiness Directives (AD's).  Pursuant to its authority, the FAA issues AD's when an unsafe condition is found to exist in a product (aircraft, aircraft engine, propeller or appliance) of a particular type design.  AD's are used by the FAA to notify aircraft owners and operators of unsafe conditions and to require their correction.  AD's prescribed the conditions and limitations, including inspection, repair or alteration under which the product may continue to be operated.  AD's are authorized under Part 39 and issued in accordance with the public rulemaking procedures of the Administrative Procedure Act, 5 USC 553, and FAA procedures in Part 11.

AD's are published in the Federal Register as amendments to CFR Part 39.  Depending on the urgency, AD's are issued as follows:

**Normally** a notice of proposed rulemaking (NPRM) for an AD is issued and published in the Federal Register when an unsafe condition is believed to exist in a product.  Interested persons are invited to comment on the NPRM by submitting such written data, views, contained in the notice may be changed or withdrawn in light of comments received.  The comment period is usually 30 days.  When the final rule, resulting from the NPRM is adopted, it is published in the Federal Register, printed, and distributed by first class mail to the registered owners of the product(s) affected.

**Emergency AD's.**  AD's of an urgent nature may be adopted without prior notice (without an NPRM) under emergency procedures as immediately adopted rules.  The AD's normally become effective in less than 30 days after publication in the Federal Register and are distributed by first class mail, telegram or other electronic methods to the registered owners and certain known operators of the product affected.  In addition, notification is also provided to special interest groups, other government agencies, and Civil Aviation Authorities of certain foreign countries.

AD's may be issued which apply to aircraft, engines, propellers, or appliances installed on multiple makes or models of aircraft.  When the product can be identified as being installed on a specific make or model aircraft, the AD distributed by first class mail to the registered owners of those aircraft.  However, there are times when such a determination cannot be made, and direct distribution to registered owners is impossible.  For this reason, aircraft owners and operators are urged to subscribe to the Summary of Airworthiness Directives, which contains all previously published AD's, and a biweekly supplemental service.

Each AD contains an applicability statement specifying the product (aircraft, aircraft engine, propeller, or appliance) to which it applies.  Some aircraft owners and operators mistakenly assume that AD's do not apply to aircraft with other than standard airworthiness certificates.  Unless specifically stated, AD's apply to the make and model set forth in the applicability statement regardless of the classification or category of the airworthiness certificate issued for the aircraft.  Type certificate and airworthiness certification information is used to identify the product affected.  Limitations may be placed on applicability by specifying the serial number or number series to which the AD is applicable.  When there is no reference to serial numbers, all serial numbers are affected.

AD's are regulations issued under Part 39. Therefore, no person may operate a product, to which an AD applies, except in accordance with the requirements of that AD. Owners and operators should understand that to "operate" not only means piloting the aircraft, but also causing or authorizing the product to be used for the purpose of air navigation, with or without the right of legal control as owner, lessee, or otherwise. Compliance with emergency AD's can be a problem for operators of leased aircraft because the FAA has no legal requirement for notification of other than registered owners. Therefore, it is important that owner(s) of leased aircraft make the AD information available to the operators leasing their aircraft as expeditiously as possible, otherwise the lessee may not be aware of the AD and safety may be jeopardized.

The belief that AD compliance is only required at the time of a required inspection, e.g., at a 100-hour or annual inspection is not correct. The required compliance time is specified in each AD, and no person may operate the affected product after expiration of that stated compliance time.

In some instances, the AD may authorize flight after the compliance date has passed, provided that a special flight permit is obtained. Special flight authorization may be granted only when the AD specifically permits such operation. Another aspect of compliance times to be emphasized is that not all AD's have a one-time compliance requirement. Repetitive inspections at specified intervals after initial compliance may be required in lieu of or until a permanent solution for the unsafe condition is developed.

The owner or operator of an aircraft is primarily responsible for maintaining that aircraft in an airworthy condition, including compliance with AD's.

This responsibility may be met by ensuring that properly certificated and appropriately rated maintenance person(s) accomplish the requirements of the AD and properly record this action in the appropriate maintenance records. This action must be accomplished within the compliance time specified in the AD or the aircraft may not be operated.

Maintenance persons may also have direct responsibility for AD compliance, aside from the times when AD compliance is the specific work contracted for by the owner or operator. When a 100-hour, annual, progressive, or any other inspection, required under Parts 91, 121, 125, or 135 is accomplished, CFR section 43.15(a) requires the person performing the inspection to determine that all applicable airworthiness requirements are met, including compliance with AD's.

Maintenance persons should note even though an inspection of the complete aircraft is not made, if the inspection conducted is a progressive inspection, determination of AD compliance is required for those portions of the aircraft inspected.

The person accomplishing the AD is required by, CFR section 43.9, to record AD compliance. The entry must include those items specified in CFR section 43.9(a)(1) through (a)(4). The owner or operator is required by CFR Part 91.405 to ensure that maintenance personnel make appropriate entries and, CFR section 91.417, to maintain those records. Owners and operators should note that there is a difference between the records required to be kept by the owner under CFR section 91.417 and those CFR section 43.9 requires maintenance personnel to make. In either case, the owner or operator is responsible for maintaining proper records.

Certain AD's permits pilots to perform checks of some items under specific conditions. AD's allowing this action will include specific direction regarding recording requirements. However, if the AD does not include recording requirements for the pilot, CFR section 43.9 requires persons complying with an AD to make an entry in the maintenance record of that product. CFR section 91.417(a) and (b) requires the owner or operator to keep and retain certain minimum records for a specific time. The person who accomplished the action, the person who returned the aircraft to service, and the status of AD compliance are the items of information required to be kept in those records.

The registered owner or operator of the aircraft is responsible for compliance with AD's applicable to the airframe, engine, propeller, appliances, and parts and components thereof for all aircraft it owns or operates. Maintenance personnel are responsible for determining that all applicable airworthiness requirements are met when they accomplish an **inspection** in accordance with CFR Part 43.

**To perform an AD search of any aircraft there are steps that should be followed in sequence.**

**Step 1.** You will need the entire aircraft maintenance records and equipment list. Check the equipment list against the maintenance records.

**Step 2.** If the lists do not match make a list of all the equipment that is not on the equipment list that has been added to the aircraft. This will involve making a complete inventory of all the items on the aircraft such as: Type of ignition switch, STC equipment installed with and without a FAA form 337 and maintenance entry, different radios, entertainment equipment, seat belts, or type of clock to name a few. To perform this task start at the spinner and end with the white navigation light writing down all the equipment. Take note of the dates and tach, hobbs meter, or total time they were completed.

**Step 3.** To do a complete AD search you will need to make four separate AD lists. One list for the airframe, engine, propeller, and appliances. Under each list you will want to find all the AD's that applies to the equipment. Some of the AD's will not be required, if an AD does not apply it should be recorded and the AD compliance sheet should note the reason why it does not apply such as: Not required by serial number or part number. This process should be applied to all four lists.

Most mechanics will find it very easy to find all the AD's on the airframe, engine, propeller, and appliances and it is straight forward using the make model and serial number on a computer with the proper software or the FAA web site, to perform this task. By selecting the make and model all the AD's will appear on your computer screen and hitting the print key a list is easily printed out.

**Step 4.** The real AD search begins when you start with the appliance research. With the list you have made from your inspection of the aircraft and the equipment list now the real work begins. You will have to look up each item on your list to see if an AD applies. Using the example of seat belts a search revealed AD's were found in the Small aircraft and rotor aircraft (8) documents, Large aircraft (6) documents and under appliances (3) documents. These (17) documents cover all most every make and model aircraft. The person accomplishing the AD is required by, CFR Part 43.9, to record AD compliance as required.

Be careful even if you have seen the same make and model aircraft the AD list will be different on each aircraft, because they are not all equipped the same. Each aircraft will require the same search as stated above because of their uniqueness.

When you are done you should have four (4) separate AD lists. One for the engine, propeller, airframe and appliances.

You should think of an AD search as being all things in the past. This means from the time the aircraft rolled off the assembly line to the current inspection you are now performing, you are held responsible. This will also include any AD that may have been missed in the past during an inspection. Also, this will include major alterations or repairs, which may now require an AD. Be advised there may be an AD issued against an FAA Form 337 in some cases.

# Chapter 6

## INSPECTION GUIDES

# Maintenance Standards And ATA Codes

Maintenance standards are the same if you are keeping or selling the aircraft or if you are the only one that flies the aircraft. There is no conditional airworthiness, such as "I only fly on blue sky days". Some manufactures and mechanics consider some special inspections to be mandatory, such as 500 hour/5 year magneto and alternator inspections, and Lycoming 400 hour valve inspection.

The following criteria should be met to sign off an annual or 100-hour inspection as referenced in CFR Part 43 Appendix D. Using the following criteria and ATA codes provided should give you a good feel for the aircraft and its condition. This list is by no means all conclusive it is only a guide to start. Each make and model aircraft will have different areas that should be inspected, but this guide will certainly let you know if the aircraft is in an safe condition for flight or not.

## NOTE

*Manufacturer's manuals and Airworthiness Directives may supersede the following standards.*

## 0580 PITOT-STATIC/TRANSPONDER CERTIFICATION
Pitot static/encoder/transponder certifications to be current or to be scheduled.

## 1100 PLACARDS/MARKINGS this is a CFR Part 91 requirement. Required placards range
markings and decals must be legible and installed. Reference 14 CFR Part 91section 91.7.

## 2400 ELECTRICAL
Aircraft battery load test is within specification with no case or terminal damage; battery box, drain, vent and cables must be in good condition with protective terminal boots and grommets. Protective boots must be on all exposed electrical terminals. Alternator AC component to less than .12 VAC. Wiring and components must be aircraft approved and in good condition, properly routed, bundled, secured and protected from damage. Voltage regulators/protection relays are within manufacturer's limits.

## 2500 EQUIPMENT/FURNISHINGS
All equipment installed on aircraft is expected be in working order and have reasonable residual service life. Seat belts and shoulder harnesses are in good condition with TSO indent tags. Seat structures and rails are to be in good condition and with proper stops/locks.

ELT battery due date not less than two month away and meet applicable current voltage standards, 'G' switch operational and unit free of corrosion.

## 2700 FLIGHT CONTROLS/SURFACES
All flight control systems to be rigged within specifications. Control surfaces are to meet published free play limits, if not published, the max limit is 2.5% of cord. Repainted flight control surfaces are to have been balanced and documented. Balance control surfaces are reasonably free of distortion/damage; control tips in good condition and secure.

# 3100 INDICATING AND RECORDING

All instrumentation is to work and be in reasonable calibration. The compass is to be readable, full of fluid, and a current readable deviation card displayed. Panel mounted Avionics units are to have overhang support if required. Avionics/panel wiring/plumbing be properly routed, bundled and secured with positive clearance from flight controls; no automotive wiring, terminals, splices, or electrical tape are permitted. Instrument panel shock mounts are to be in good condition.

# 3200 LANDING GEAR

Tires cannot be less than 1/32 treads in any area, not weathered into cord and meet minimum ply rating required. Tubes cannot be creased, wrinkled or over 5 years old when accessed. Tire/wheel assemblies are dynamically balanced at each major inspection and the max weight in ounces should not exceed more than 1/2 wheel diameter. There should not be any cracks, extensive corrosion or distortion on wheel components, dust seals serviceable and wheel bearings free of damage. Brake disc condition must meet manufacturer's minimums; linings have 25% wear remaining; brake hydraulic cylinders dry. Shock disc/cords must meet manufacturer's minimum specifications. Shimmy dampener must be full, with no leakage, functional and securely mounted. Shock struts are to be dry and fully serviced. Landing gear torque links must be in good condition without excess free play. Landing gear retraction system rigging must be within service manual specifications. Gear warning, safety switches, auto extenders must be functional and properly adjusted.

# 3300 LIGHTING

All aircraft lighting must be in working order.

# 3500 OXYGEN SYSTEM

Oxygen bottle hydrostatic test current. Reference AC 43.13 and Part 43 section 43.16.

# 5100 STRUCTURE

Previous structural repairs must be of reasonable quality and in accordance with approved methods and properly documented. Only minor structural deformation, un-repaired damage or light surface corrosion not affecting structural integrity or quality of flight will be accepted.

# 5200 DOORS

Cabin door latches, locks and handles are being in good working order.

# 5600 WINDOWS

Windows and windshields are free of moderate or heavy crazing and extended cracks and vision clear.

# 6000 PROPELLER (S)

Prop blades having excess dressing or damage are to be overhauled, reconditioned, or replaced. Any worn or suspicious prop mounting hardware will be changed. No engine or dye oil leakage is permitted from prop hubs. Spinner and bulkheads must be properly fitted, free of cracks and fiber washers under mounting screws.

# 7000 ENGINE (S)

Engines should be placed on an oil analysis program; filter medium will be checked for metals. Accessible oil pick-up screens are to be inspected. Minimum engine differential compression readings at top of stroke 70/80 bottom 65/80. Direct readings to be within 30% of each other. Engine shock mounts are to be relatively free of delamination, sagging or hardening. Engine cooling baffles seals must be complete, secured, in good condition and properly positioned.

# 7010 COWLING

All cowling fasteners/receptacles mounts latches must be installed and in good working condition. Cowling must be in good repair; cowl flap hinges not worn out and controls serviceable.

## 7800 EXHAUST

Exhaust systems cannot be bulged, knotted or cracked, reasonably gas tight; flame tubes/baffles must be in mufflers if originally equipped. No leaks are permitted in cabin heat exchanger. Mounting hardware brackets, clamps, and gaskets must be in good condition.

# Life Limited Inspections

The FAA clearly states that, "mandatory service bulletins (SB's) issued by manufacturers are to be considered advisory only. Small airplane design approval holders cannot unilaterally impose mandatory compliance with manufacturer's SB's. FAA policy does not permit this approval to be delegated to organizations or individuals." Michael Gallagher, Manager Small Airplane Directorate, 25 April 2001".

To make life limits mandatory the proper document would be the Type Certificate data Sheet (TCDS) not the maintenance manual via a service bulletin. Unless required by the TC, mandatory service bulletins are issued by manufacturers, to protect the manufacturer from tort claims. Is it a good idea to overhaul an engine every 12 years, sure I agree, but a service bulletin is not the way to do it.

Remember life limits are in the maintenance manuals and if you are a Part 121 or 135-certificate holder then the service bulletins are **mandatory**. Under Part 91 they are still a **recommendation** and do not have to be accomplished, but in some cases by not doing them may void any warranty you have on the item. Remember if an AD refers to a service bulletin then that service bulletin is now mandatory even for Part 91 users.

## Some Typical Life Limits
**This checklist is not exhaustive and does not supersede Manufacture's publications!**
### SAMPLE ONLY

| Calendar/ Hourly Life limited Items: | Years | Hours |
|---|---|---|
| **Airframe** | | |
| Gyro air filters, central | 5 | 500 |
| Non-Teflon fuel, oil, and hydraulic hoses | 15 | 3000 |
| Teflon fuel, oil, and hydraulic hoses | 20 | 4000 |
| Seat belt/shoulder harness webbing | 7 | |
| Stabilizer attach bolts | 25 | 6000 |
| Wing bolts | 25 | 6000 |
| | | |
| **Engine** | | |
| Engine shock mounts | 15 | TBO |
| Non-Teflon fuel, oil, and hydraulic hoses | 8 | TBO |
| Teflon fuel, oil, and hydraulic hoses | 15 | TBO |

| Special Inspection Items: | Years | Hours |
|---|---|---|
| Gyro air pump carbon vanes | 6 | 500 |
| Electric hydraulic pump motor | 15 | 500-1500 |
| Electro mechanical gear actuator | 15 | 3000 |
| Gear actuator motor brushes | 2 | 250 |
| Gear motor internal inspection/lubrication | 15 | 3000 |
| Flight control trim actuator(s) | 15 | 4500 |
| Electrical flap actuators/motors | 20 | 4000 |
| Stabilizer mounting bolts torque inspection | 5 | |
| Wing attach bolts torque inspection | 5 | |

| | Years | Hours |
|---|---|---|
| **Propeller** | | |
| Fixed pitch propeller recondition | 6 | 2000 |
| Mounting hardware | 20 | 2000 |
| Constant speed propeller overhaul | 10 | 1500 |
| Prop governor reseal | 15 | 1500 |
| Governor | 5 | 1800 |
| Accumulators | 5 | 1800 |
| | | |
| **Engine** | | |
| Gear drive alternator internal inspection | 5 | 300 |
| Belt driven alternator internal inspection | 5 | 500 |
| Internal magneto inspection | 5 | 500 |
| Valve inspection/dry lash clearance | 15 | TBO |
| Cam/cam follower inspection (TCM engines) | 15 | mid life |
| Bendix fuel injector servo overhauls | 20 | TBO |
| Pressure carburetor overhauls | 20 | TBO |
| Primer nozzles cleaned and spray pattern | 5 | |
| Continental unmetered fuel pressure check | 2 | 400 |
| Diaphragm fuel pumps overhaul | 20 | TBO |
| Internal starter inspection | 5 | mid-life |
| Turbocharger oil inlet check valve(s) | 10 | 1000 |
| Turbocharger oil scavenge check valves(s) | 10 | 1000 |
| Hydraulic wastegate actuator(s) resealing | 10 | 1000 |

## *** NOTE ***

*This is only a guide and should not be considered FAA approved data for life limits. Consult the manufacture recommendations, type certificate data sheets (TCDS), AD's, or the limitations section of FAA-approved airplane or rotorcraft flight manuals.*

# The Pre-Inspection Run-Up

FAA regulations require post-inspection run-ups to verify proper operation of power plant system after inspections, servicing and repairs. When performed at the start of the inspection the pre-inspection run-up becomes a valuable tool in properly administering the annual/100 hour inspection. Properly performed and documented it can help prevent those surprises that seem to manifest them-selves at the end of the inspection process. Reference Part 43 section 43.15(c).

First consideration is for the owner/operator to communicate anything they have experienced outside of normally operating parameters so the technician can be on guard for these problems. You will do well to record the incidences as they happen, a progressive history will give your technician valuable diagnostic clues. Written information help prevent misunderstandings between maintenance and operators.

Over the years operators have developed their own pre-post run-up form, which is a single page of single spaced lines, which document the information they most need without being too cumbersome.

There are several ways to prepare the aircraft for the run-up, one is if there are large or numerous oil leaks clean the engine so as to give the mechanic a chance in finding the source. Following diagnostic equipment is then installed:

1. Accurate voltmeter for additional monitoring of the electrical system.
2. Vacuum gage for those aircraft only having indicator lights.

3. Pressure gage calibrated in inches of water attached with hose to the oil filler neck to measure engine case pressure. (Teledyne Continental Motors TCM SB 89-9).
4. Metered/un-metered fuel gages for TCM fuel injected engines if pressures are in doubt.
5. Hydraulic pressure gage for those aircraft with engine driven pumps and no installed gage.
6. Direct reading oil pressure gage if indications or oil pressure are suspect.
7. Direct reading fuel pressure gage if indications or fuel pressure are suspect.
8. Air conditioning gages.

A hand held photo tach is placed on board to check tach accuracy. Brief inspection of the engine compartment and the aircraft are conducted at this time so as not to cause any damage during the run-up. Before starting the engine(s) the master switch is turn on and the engine gages' static readings are observed. Quite often a mechanic will discover gages that do not return to zero on shut down. During starting the voltmeter is observed for low voltage, which could indicate possible battery or starter problems. A sample pre-inspection checklist is provided in the Appendix section.

# Visual Inspections

Over 80 percent of the inspections on large transport category aircraft are visual inspections. On small transport aircraft the ratio is even greater and on general aviation aircraft, virtually all inspections are visual. Visual inspection is usually the most economical and fastest way to obtain an early assessment of the condition of an aircraft and its components. Most of the defects found on aircraft are found by visual inspections, and the airframe manufacturers and users depend on regular visual inspections to ensure the continued airworthiness of their aircraft. Consequently, it is important that visual inspection methods be understood and properly applied by those responsible for the continued airworthiness of aircraft. Proficiency in visual inspection is crucial to the safe operation of aircraft. Such proficiency is gained from experience, but also by learning the methods developed by others.

Visual inspection is defined as the process of using the eye, alone or in conjunction with various aids, as the sensing mechanism from which judgments may be made about the condition of a unit to be inspected. Visual inspection is used to:

1. Provide an overall assessment of the condition of a structure, component, or system.
2. Provide early detection of defects before they reach critical size.
3. Detect errors in the manufacturing process.
4. Obtain more information about the condition of a component showing evidence of a defect.

In many situations, no reliable alternative exists to visual inspection. Visual procedures are mandated by the FAA for structural inspections to support Supplementary Structural Inspection Documents (SSIDs), Service Bulletins (SBs), and Airworthiness Directives.

Typical airframe defects found in aircraft, which can be detected by visual inspection, can be divided into three types:

1. **Cracks.** Typical surface cracks can be detected by visual inspection. Surface cracks caused by fatigue are an example of skin cracking at fasteners. Sometimes an underlying crack can cause a distortion, which can be detected visually.
2. **Corrosion.** An example of blistering of paint in a fuel cell caused by corrosion. Chipped and loose paint on a wing skin shows internal corrosion.
3. **Disbonding.** It is very difficult to detect disbonding by visual means, since it is usually an internal condition and not likely to show up on the surface of an aircraft. Wherever a bonded surface becomes disbonded, corrosion is likely to occur and may be detected visually.

Other defects, such as system and component wear, accidental damage, environmental damage from long term storage, sunlight, etc., can also be detected visually.

Visual inspection procedures should all contain steps in a logical format. A procedure has four basic parts:

1. A basis for the inspection.
2. Preparatory arrangements.
3. Implementation of the inspection.
4. Evaluation of the results.

Some activities, which represent good practice, may not be specifically called out in the procedures, but should be completed if they are relevant. Examples of such good practice are:

1. **Preliminary Inspection.** A preliminary inspection of the overall general area should be performed for cleanliness, presence of foreign objects, deformed or missing fasteners, security of parts, corrosion, and damage. If the configuration or location of the part conceals the area to be inspected, it is appropriate to use visual aids such as mirror or borescope.

2. **Precleaning.** The areas or surface of parts to be inspected should be cleaned without damaging any surface treatment, which may be present. Contaminants that might hinder the discovery of existing surface indications should be removed. Some cleaning methods may remove indications of damage; care should be used if the cleaning tends to smear or hide possible indications of trouble. Surface coatings may have to be removed at a later time if other NDI techniques are required to verify any indications that are found. Some typical cleaning materials and methods used to prepare parts for visual inspection are detergent cleaners, alkaline cleaners, vapor degreasing, solvent cleaners, mechanical cleaning, paint removers, steam cleaning, and ultrasonic cleaning.

3. **Corrosion Treatment.** Any corrosion found in the preliminary inspection should be removed before starting a close visual inspection of any selected part or area. Manufacturers' handbooks, when available, are a good general guide for treatment of corrosion. Recommendations of AC 43-4, if appropriate, should be used on aircraft for which the manufacturer has not published a recommended corrosion inspection schedule or treatment program. The AC contains a summary of current available data regarding identification and treatment of corrosion on aircraft structure and engine materials. Examples of types of corrosion damage detectable by the visual method are also given.

4. **Use of Visual Aids.** When inspecting the area required, visual aids should be used as necessary. An inspector normally should have available suitable measuring devices: a flashlight and a mirror.

# Record Keeping/Type of Inspection

All defects found should be documented by Maintenance Record entry; written report, squawk sheet, photograph, or videos recording for appropriate evaluation. Depending on the rules governing the facility and person performing the inspection, the report may be limited to simply reporting findings without any rejection or acceptance disposition. The type, location, and approximate size of any defects present should be documented. Based upon the particular inspection process specification (i.e., AD, Service Bulletin, Maintenance Manual requirement, or normal inspection discovery) the mechanic, repairman, or other authorized person should determine the particular acceptance, rework, repair or rejection status of the part or structure being inspected.

The full value of visual inspection can be realized only if records are kept of the conditions found on parts inspected. The size and shape of the finding and its location should be recorded along with other pertinent information, such as rework performed or disposition. The inclusion of some permanent record of a defect on a report makes the report much more complete.

It should be stressed that frequent and effective use of illustrations not only will enhance the effectiveness of the procedure but also is indispensable in communicating to the inspector the nature of the defects to be found. In addition to textual and anecdotal data, the following types of records are commonly used:

1. **Sketches.** The simplest record is a sketch of the part showing the location and extent of the defect. On large areas it may be sufficient to sketch only the critical area.

2. **Photography.** Photographs (still or video recording) of defects can be taken for visual record purposes. Photographs produce a permanent and highly descriptive record since they show both size and location on the part. They are permanent, reproducible, and the required equipment is readily available. It is good practice to include a scale in the photo when practicable as well as some marking for identification. This is particularly necessary if the photograph is likely to become an exhibit involved in litigation.

Visual inspection tasks are divided into four categories relating to their difficulty and degree of effectiveness as follows:

1. Walk around Inspection.
2. General Visual Inspection.
3. Detailed Visual Inspection.
4. Special Detailed Visual Inspection.

**Walk Around.** The walk around inspection is a general check conducted from ground level to detect discrepancies and to determine general condition and security. Most maintenance instructions mandate walk around inspections on a periodic basis. The overall purpose is to serve as a quick check to determine, if detectable inconsistencies exist, which would affect the performance of the aircraft.

**General.** A general inspection is made of an exterior with selected hatches and openings open or an interior, when called for, to detect damage, failure, or irregularity. When a specific problem is suspected, the general inspection is carried out to identify, if possible, the difficulty. General inspections are also routinely used when panels are open for normal maintenance.

Aircraft history should be used to gain information useful in inspecting the aircraft (e.g., are there recurring problems or have there been hard landings). In addition the aircraft should be clean enough for an effective inspection to take place, the necessary tools and equipment should be available (e.g., flashlight, rag, notebook), and other aids, tools, and procedures may be necessary (e.g., inspection of some aircraft is easier if already on jacks, but this is not always necessary).

**Detailed.** A detailed visual inspection is an intensive visual examination of a specific area, system, or assembly to detect damage failure or irregularity. Available inspection aids should be used. Surface preparation and elaborate access procedures may be required.

**Basis for Inspection.** A detailed inspection is called for when a specific problem is suspected and the general inspection dictates additional inspection. Or, if the inspection is otherwise mandated, a detailed visual inspection is carried out to identify, if possible, the difficulty. Detailed inspections are also periodically called for on damage-tolerant aircraft to ensure the airworthiness of the critical structure.

**Preparation for the Inspection.** Tools and equipment will vary, but may include a prism, supplemental lighting, mirror, magnifying glass, flashlight, dye penetrant, notebook, droplight, rolling stool, and standard and specialized hand tools. Also review the SBs, ADs, aircraft history, and accident reports. Other aids such, as knowledge of a specific aircraft and common problems may be essential even if not on the inspection card.

**Special Detailed.** A special detailed inspection is an intensive examination of a specific item, installation, or assembly to detect damage, failure, or irregularity. It is likely to make use of specialized techniques and equipment. Intricate disassembly and cleaning may be required.

**Basis for Inspection.** As systems and structures have become more complex, special inspections using extraordinary techniques and equipment have evolved to ensure airworthiness. These are covered in instructions for special detailed inspections. Special detailed inspections are also periodically called for on damage-tolerant aircraft to ensure the airworthiness of the critical structure.

**Preparation for the Inspection.** Tools and equipment will vary but may include a flashlight, mirror, video borescopes, special aids and tooling, dremel, rolling stool, image enhancement and recording devices, supplemental lighting, magnifying glass, dye penetrant, notebook, and standard and specialized hand tools. Documentation required is specific to the procedures outlined by steps on work cards and maintenance manuals; review of Service Bulletin SBs, AD's, and aircraft history; and reference to the original or referred discrepancy, if any. Another aid is the discrepancy report from the contracting NDI Company.

# Preparation for the Inspection

Tools and equipment will vary, but may include:

1. A prism
2. Supplemental lighting
3. Mirror
4. Magnifying glass
5. Flashlight
6. High intensive light
7. Dye penetrant
8. Notebook
9. Droplight
10. Rolling stool
11. Standard and specialized hand tools
12. Cable tensionometer
13. Propeller protractor
14. Calibrated differential compression tester
15. Mag timing box
16. Borescope

Documentation required is specific to the procedures outlined by steps on work cards or manufactures procedures. Also review the Service Bulletin (SB), AD's, aircraft history, and accident reports. Other aids such, as knowledge of a specific aircraft and common problems may be essential even if not on the inspection card or in the maintenance manual.

It should be emphasized that eye-mirror-flashlight is an indispensable combination for visual inspection. Aircraft structure and components requiring inspection are frequently located beneath skin, cables, tubing, control rods, pumps, and actuators. Therefore, good secondary access by reflection is often essential. Visual inspection aids usually consist of a strong flashlight, a mirror with a ball joint, and a 2-to 5-power simple magnifier. The mirror should be of adequate size (except for very awkward access situations) with reflecting surface free of dirt, cracks, and worn coating; and the swivel joint should be tight enough to maintain its setting. A magnifying mirror may be useful in some situations. A 10-power magnifier is recommended for positive identification of suspected cracks; however, other NDI techniques, such as dye penetrant, magnetic particle, or eddy current can also be used to verify indications. Visual inspection of some areas can only be accomplished with the use of remote viewing devices, such as borescopes and video imaging systems.

Some magnifying devices recommended for use in conducting visual inspections include: hand-held magnifiers with single and multiple lenses jeweler's eye loupes, illuminated magnifiers, pocket/desk type microscopes, toolmaker's microscopes, rigid/flexible borescopes, and video imaging systems. These devices are available with numerous features, such as 1 to 2000 power, self-contained illumination, adjustable variable magnification (zoom), stereo viewing, data storage/transmission; computer generated electronic alignment targets, and measuring capability.

A borescope is a long, tubular, precision optical instrument, with built-in illumination, designed to allow remote visual inspection of internal surfaces, or otherwise inaccessible areas. The tube, which can be rigid or flexible with a wide variety of lengths and diameters, provides the necessary optical connection between the viewing end and an objective lens at the distant, or distal, tip of the borescope. Rigid and flexible borescopes are available in different designs for a variety of standard applications, and manufacturers also provide custom designs for specialized applications.

Borescopes are used in aircraft/engine maintenance programs to reduce or eliminate the need for costly teardowns. Aircraft turbine engines have access ports that are specifically designed for borescopes. Borescopes are also used extensively in a variety of aviation maintenance programs to ensure the airworthiness of difficult-to-reach components. Borescopes typically are used to inspect interiors of hydraulic cylinders and valves for pitting, scoring, porosity, and tool marks; inspect for cracked cylinders in aircraft reciprocating engines; inspect turbojet engine turbine blades and combustion cans; verify the proper placement and fit of seals, bonds, gaskets, and subassemblies in difficult-to-reach areas of aircraft and aeronautical equipment; and assess Foreign Object Damage (FOD) in aircraft, airframe, and powerplants. Borescopes may also be used to locate and retrieve foreign objects in engines and airframes.

# CHAPTER 7

## CIVIL AVIAITON REGISTORY

# Civil Aviation Registry

The Federal Aviation Administration's (FAA's) Civil Aviation Registry is responsible for developing, maintaining, and operating national programs for the registration of United States civil aircraft and certification of airmen.

The Registry's Aircraft Registration Branch (ASF-750) issues approximately 70,000 aircraft registration certificates and processes approximately 225,000 documents affecting title to or interest in aircraft, engines, propellers, and air carrier spare part locations annually. The Registry reserves and assigns all U.S. identification marks (N-Numbers) to U.S. civil aircraft.

The Registry maintains the permanent records of over 320,000 active civil aircraft and provides approximately 700 copies of aircraft records daily for review to users of the Public Documents Room located in the Registry Building at the Mike Monroney Aeronautical Center in Oklahoma City, Oklahoma.

The Registry is responsible for the review, evaluation, and development of any new or amended regulations pertaining to aircraft registration and the recordation of documents contained in the CFR, Parts 47, 49, and petitions for exemptions thereof.

The Registry's Airman Certification Branch (AFS-760) has final authority for the issuance of permanent airmen certificates and provides over 180,000 each year. Of the more than 4.2 million airmen records, approximately 580,000 are considered to be active pilots. Certificates are issued for pilots, flight engineers, flight and ground instructors, aircraft dispatchers, mechanics, repairmen, parachute riggers, control tower operators, and flight navigators.

The Registry assists in programs affecting aviation safety such as the National Aviation Safety Program by providing statistics and aiding in publicizing the safety programs held in the various FAA regions. The Registry also assists law enforcement agencies by providing technical advice and certified copies of records. The Registry represents the FAA in Federal Court hearings as custodian of the official agency records for both aircraft and airmen.

**Civil Aviation Registry Branch Services:**

- Civil Aviation Registry Aircraft Registration Branch (ASF-750)
- Civil Aviation Registry Airman Certification Branch (AFS-760)

# Aircraft Registration

The procedures for aircraft registration and issuance of registration numbers are contained in 14 CFR Part 47, Aircraft Registration. The registration of aircraft is not a function of airworthiness certification; however, U.S. registration is a prerequisite for issuance of an airworthiness certificate. The FAA must ensure that an aircraft presented for airworthiness certification is properly registered (Title 49,U.S.C. 44704I, and section 21.173).

**Proof of Ownership**. The applicant for registration of an aircraft must submit proof of ownership to the FAA Aircraft Registration Branch (AFS-750) that meets the requirements prescribed in Part 47. The Aeronautical Center Form 8050-2, Aircraft Bill of Sale, or its equivalent may be used as proof of ownership. If the applicant did not purchase the aircraft from the last registered owner, the applicant must submit a complete chain of ownership from the last registered owner to the applicant. The purchaser under a contract of conditional sale is considered the owner for the purpose of registration. The contract of conditional sale may be submitted as proof of ownership in lieu of a bill of sale.

The U.S. owner submits to AFS-750 all information required to obtain aircraft registration. Permanent registration will be received via AC Form 8050-3, Certificate of Aircraft Registration. If the U.S. aircraft owner desires to receive a temporary registration prior to receiving the permanent one, a request should also be made at this time for Standard Form 14, Telegraphic Message. This form serves as a temporary Certificate of Aircraft Registration.

An aircraft is eligible for registration in the United States only if it is owned by:

1. An U.S. citizen. A U.S. citizen by definition of 14 CFR section 47.2 can be an individual, or partnership where each individual is a U.S. citizen, or a corporation organized under the laws of the United States, state, territory, or possession of the United States of which the president and at least two-thirds of the board of directors are U.S. citizens and 75 percent of the voting interest is owned or controlled by U.S. citizens;
2. A resident alien;
3. A corporation other than classified as a U.S. citizen, lawfully organized and doing business under the laws of the United States or of any state thereof, if the aircraft is based and used primarily in the United States; or
4. A government entity (federal, state, or local).

The aircraft may not be registered in a foreign country during the period it is registered in the United States.

# Eligible Registrants

If you purchase an aircraft, you must apply for a Certificate of Aircraft Registration from the Civil Aviation Registry before it may be operated. Do not depend on a bank, Loan Company, aircraft dealer, or anyone else to submit the application for registration. Do it yourself (in the name of the owner, not in the name of the bank or other mortgage holder).

You can help make sure your aircraft is properly registered by verifying that the aircraft description entered on the Aircraft Registration Application and Aircraft Bill of Sale (or equivalent) is identical to the data inscribed on the aircraft manufacturer's data plate. The manufacturer permanently affixes the data plate to the aircraft fuselage. This quick and simple check should help avoid delays in the issuance of the AC Form 8050-3, Certificate of Aircraft Registration.

You should immediately submit evidence of ownership, an AC Form 8050-1, Aircraft Registration Application, and a $5 registration fee at the time of this printing to:

> Federal Aviation Administration
> Civil Aviation Registry, AFS-750
> Mike Monroney Aeronautical Center
> P.O. Box 25504
> Oklahoma City, OK 73125

Fees required for aircraft registration may be paid by check or money order made payable to the Treasury of the United States.

A bill of sale form that meets the FAA's requirements for evidence of ownership is AC Form 8050-2, Aircraft Bill of Sale, which may be obtained from the nearest FSDO. The form includes an information and instruction sheet. If a conditional sales contract is the evidence of ownership, an additional $5 fee is required for recording. For FAA registration, the bill of sale need not be notarized.

The Aircraft Registration Application includes an information and instruction sheet. Submit the white and green copies to the Civil Aviation Registry; keep the pink copy in your aircraft as evidence of application for registration until you receive your Certificate of Aircraft Registration, AC Form 8050-3. The pink copy is good for 90 days and is legal only in the United States. If you plan to operate the aircraft outside the United States, you need to contact the Civil Aviation Registry at (866) 762-9434 and receive temporary authority by fax. Registration certificates are issued to the person whose name is on the application.

If there is a break in the chain of ownership of the aircraft (i.e., if it is not being purchased from the last registered owner), you are required to submit conveyances to complete the chain of ownership through all intervening owners, including yourself, to the Civil Aviation Registry.

The aircraft owner may also use the Aircraft Registration Application to report a change of address. The FAA issues a revised certificate at no charge. If the certificate is lost, destroyed, or mutilated, a replacement certificate may be obtained at the written request of the holder. Send the request and $2 (check or money order payable to the Treasury of the United States) to:

Federal Aviation Administration
Civil Aviation Registry, AFS-750
P.O. Box 25504
Oklahoma City, OK 73125

The request should describe the aircraft by make, model, serial number, and registration number. If operation of the aircraft is necessary before receipt of the duplicate certificate, the Civil Aviation Registry may, if requested, send temporary authority by fax. Include in your request your full address; fax number, and a telephone number where you can be reached.

A Certificate of Aircraft Registration should be in the aircraft before an Airworthiness Certificate can be issued. Some of the conditions under which the Certificate of Aircraft Registration becomes invalid, as described in 14 CFR section 47.41 are:

1. The aircraft becomes registered under the laws of a foreign country;
2. The registration of the aircraft is canceled at the written request of the holder of the certificate;
3. The aircraft is totally destroyed or scrapped;
4. The holder of the certificate loses his or her U.S. citizenship or status as a resident alien without becoming a U.S. citizen;
5. The ownership of the aircraft is transferred; or
6. Thirty days have elapsed since the death of the holder of the certificate.

When an aircraft is sold, destroyed, or scrapped, the owner shall notify the FAA by filling in the back of the Certificate of Aircraft Registration and mailing it to AFS-750.

Use of an original Aircraft Registration Application, AC Form 8050-1, is required. Photocopies and computer-generated copies of this form are not acceptable for the registration of aircraft. Aircraft Registration Applications may be obtained from the Aircraft Registration Branch or your local FAA Flight Standards District Office (FSDO). The applicant's physical location or physical address must also be shown on the application if a post office box (PO box) is entered as the mailing address.

# Register An Amateur-Built Aircraft

AC Form 8050-88, Identification Number Assignment and Registration of Amateur-Built Aircraft, is used by the Civil Aviation Registry to notify you of action taken on your application for registration of amateur-built aircraft. The reverse side of AC Form 8050-88 is an Affidavit of Ownership for Amateur-Built Aircraft. Complete the reverse side of AC Form 8050-88 when applying for registration of an amateur-built aircraft. You may designate an aircraft serial number of your choice at this time. This becomes the official serial number. Submit AC Form 8050-88 along with AC Form 8050-1 to register your aircraft. If you have not reserved a special N-Number, the Civil Aviation Registry automatically assigns an N-Number at this time. An experimental checklist is provided the Appendix section.

# Surplus Military Aircraft

Certain surplus military aircraft are not eligible for FAA certification in the STANDARD, RESTRICTED, or LIMITED classifications. Since no civil aircraft may be flown unless certificated, you should discuss this with a FAA Aviation Safety Inspector (ASI) at your local FAA Flight Standard District Office, who can advise you of eligible aircraft certification procedures before your buy. An additional source for advice on amateur-built and surplus military aircraft is the Experimental Aircraft Association (EAA), located in Oshkosh, Wisconsin, (414) 426-4800.

# Replace Registration Certificate

If a certificate of registration is lost, mutilated, or destroyed, the holder of such a certificate must apply to the Aircraft Registration Branch for a duplicate. A check or money orders made payable to the United States Treasury in the amount of $2 (U.S. Funds) must accompany the request. If the owner has applied for a duplicate and has paid the fee, the owner may request a temporary certificate. The FAA Aircraft Registration Branch issues the temporary certificate. Please include return FAX number with your request.

# Change Address

A change of address may be made by mailing the address, aircraft registration number, make, model and serial number, including the original signature of the registered owner to the FAA Aircraft Registration Branch. If the address indicated is listed as a Post Office Box, General Delivery, Rural Route, or Star Route, please provide directions or a map for locating your residence.

A post office box is not acceptable as a residence address. A residence address must be furnished; however, if you wish a post office box -preferred mailing address, you may furnish both. If your residence address is listed as General Delivery, Rural Route, or Star Route, you must provide directions, or a diagram, for locating the residence attested by your signature. A new certificate is not required when updating your address and will not be issued automatically. To make a change of address you will need a change of address form, submit AC Form 8060-55. This form is available from the FAA web site under certification of people or at your local Flight Standard District Office (FSDO). The forms from the FAA web site are in Adobe's Acrobat format and require the Acrobat Reader, which is available at no charge from Adobe Systems, Incorporated. This utility works with Microsoft Windows 3.x/95/98/ME/NT/2000/XP, IBM OS/2, DOS, the Macintosh, and UNIX. The Acrobat Reader allows you to view and print the forms after you download them to your machine. However, you will first need to download and install the appropriate Adobe Acrobat Reader.

# Airworthiness Certificate

An Airworthiness Certificate is issued by the FAA only after the aircraft has been inspected and it is found that it meets the requirements of Title 14 of the Code Federal Regulations (14 CFR) and is in a condition for safe operation. Under any circumstances, the aircraft must meet the requirements of the original type certificate. The certificate must be displayed in the aircraft so that it is legible to passengers or crew whenever the aircraft is operated. The Airworthiness Certificate may be transferred with the aircraft except when it is sold to a foreign purchaser.

The Standard Airworthiness Certificate is issued for aircraft type certificated in the normal, utility, acrobatic, and transport categories or for manned free balloons. An explanation of each item in the certificate follows:

Item 1.  Nationality—The "N" indicates the aircraft is of United States registry. Registration Marks the number, in this case 12345, is the registration number assigned to the aircraft.

Item 2.  Indicates the make and model of the aircraft.

Item 3.  Indicates the serial number assigned to the aircraft, as noted on the aircraft data plate.

Item 4.  Indicates that the aircraft, in this case, must be operated in accordance with the limitations specified for the "NORMAL" category.

Item 5.  Indicates the aircraft has been found to conform to its type certificate and is considered in condition for safe operation at the time of inspection and issuance of the certificate. Any exemptions from the applicable airworthiness standards are briefly noted here and the exemption numbers given. The word "NONE" is entered if no exemption exists.

Item 6.  Indicates the Airworthiness Certificate is in effect indefinitely if the aircraft is maintained in accordance with 14 CFR Parts 21, 43, and 91 and the aircraft are registered in the United States. Also included are the date the certificate was issued and the signature and office identification of the FAA representative.

In purchasing an aircraft classed as other than Standard, it is suggested that the local FSDO be contacted for an explanation of the pertinent airworthiness requirements and the limitations of such a certificate.

The FAA initially determines that the aircraft is in a condition for safe operation and conforms to type design, then issues an Airworthiness Certificate. A Standard Airworthiness Certificate remains in effect as long as the aircraft receives the required maintenance and is properly registered in the United States. Flight safety relies in part on the condition of the aircraft, which may be determined on inspection by mechanics, approved repair stations, or manufacturers who meet specific requirements of 14 CFR Part 43.

If the Airworthiness Certificate in the aircraft is unreadable or damaged take it to the FSDO for a replacement it is **FREE** and only takes a few minutes to replace in most cases. If you have lost your certificate make an appointment with a FAA Inspector ASI and bring all your aircraft records with you. Based on your records a new certificate will be issued.

# Special Airworthiness

The Special Airworthiness Certificate (Ferry Permit) is issued for all aircraft certificated in other than the Standard classifications (Experimental, Restricted, Limited, and Provisional). The may require operation limitations.

Once the FAA has determined that the aircraft is eligible for a special airworthiness certificate, the FAA will:

1. Issue a Special Airworthiness Certificate, FAA Form 8130-7, with the appropriate operating limitations.

2. Make an aircraft log book entry that the aircraft has been found to meet the requirements for the requested certificate, and that FAA Form 8130-7 has been issued.

3. Complete sections V and VIII of the Application for Airworthiness Certificate, FAA Form 8130-7.

The below Operating Limitations are a part of the Special Flight Permit issued to aircraft. Flight crewmembers must be properly certificated and rated in accordance with 14 CFR Part 61.

1. The flight described above shall be made under VFR/VMC day conditions only, (unless the additional limitation below authorizes differently). The flight shall be made by the most direct and expeditious route consistent with the aircraft operating limitations and weather.
2. Occupancy of the aircraft is limited to the pilot, essential flight crew required to operate the aircraft and its equipment and personal baggage.
3. Flight over congested areas is prohibited, and takeoffs and landings shall be conducted to avoid congested areas in the vicinity of any of the airports used in conjunction with this authorization. Flight over a foreign country must have special permission from that country.
4. Prior to flight, the aircraft must be inspected by a certificated mechanic or repair station to determine the aircraft is safe for the intended flight. The result of that inspection will be entered in the permanent aircraft records with the following similarly worded statement: **"This aircraft has been inspected and has been found safe for the intended flight in accordance with Special Flight Permit dated ____."**
5. Operation of this aircraft is subject to the approval of the registered owner. The aircraft must display U.S. registration identification marks and have a registration certificate issued to its owner on board. This permit is valid for one flight only (Direct) with necessary fuel stops.
6. Any Airworthiness Directive pertinent to this make and model of aircraft that requires compliance must be complied with before the ferry flight is initiated unless the AD specifies that the aircraft can be ferried to a location where the requirements of that specific AD can be accomplished.

The FAA Inspector may add additional limitations as required to the above list as need to assure safety of the aircraft and flight.

# FQA Airworthiness Certification

**What is an airworthiness certificate?**

An airworthiness certificate is a FAA authorization to operate an aircraft.

**Who may apply for an airworthiness certificate?**

A registered owner or owner's agent may apply for an airworthiness certificate.

**Are there different types of airworthiness certificates?**

There are two types of FAA airworthiness certificates: FAA Form 8100-2, Standard Airworthiness Certificate, and FAA Form 8130-7, Special Airworthiness Certificate. 14 CFR section 21.175 defines the two types.

**Where do I obtain information regarding airworthiness certification processes?**

The following steps define the process for obtaining a standard or special airworthiness certificate.
**Standard airworthiness certificate process:**
- Step 1. Register the aircraft.
- Step 2. Submit the formal application.

- Step 3. Determine aircraft eligibility.
- Step 4. Issue standard airworthiness certificate.

**Special airworthiness certificate process:**
- Step 1. Register the aircraft.
- Step 2. Submit the formal application.
- Step 3. Determine aircraft eligibility.
- Step 4. Issue Special airworthiness certificate.

**I am buying a used aircraft that currently has a FAA Form 8100-2, Standard Airworthiness Certificate. Is the existing airworthiness certificate transferable, or must I apply for reissue of a new airworthiness certificate?**

The existing standard airworthiness certificate is transferable (14 CFR section 21.179), however, the aircraft must first be registered by the new owner, still conform to its approved type design, and be in a condition for safe operation.

**Who is authorized to issue FAA airworthiness certificates?**

Only FAA Aviation Safety Inspectors and authorized Representatives of the Administrator (i.e., Designees), as defined in 14 CFR part 183, Representatives of the Administrator may issue airworthiness certificates.

**Can the FAA revoke an airworthiness certificate?**

If the aircraft no longer meets its approved design and/or is in an unairworthy condition, the FAA may revoke the existing airworthiness certificate in any category (14 CFR section 21.181).

**Does the FAA have any information regarding the definition of the term airworthy?**

FAA Order 8130.2, Airworthiness Certification of Aircraft and Related Products, Chapter 1, provides an interpretation of this term. To be airworthy an aircraft must conform to its type certificate as well as be in a condition for safe operation. A word of caution is necessary, however, if this concept of airworthiness is to be applied effectively in enforcement cases. Where the evidence clearly demonstrates that the aircraft is not in a condition for safe operation, the NTSB will undoubtedly sustain a finding that the aircraft was unairworthy.

# Special Registration Number (N-number)

An U.S. identification number of your choice may be reserved, if available. This number may not exceed five characters in addition to the prefix letter "N." All five characters may be numbers (N11111) or four numbers and one suffix letter (N1000A), or one to three numbers and/or two suffix letters (N100AA) may be used.

Special N-Number requests must be submitted in writing. Written Requests should include at least five (5) N-Numbers of choice listed in order of preference. The request should also include a name, mailing address, phone number, signature, and, if appropriate, title of the requester. Requests for special N-Numbers along with a check or money order made payable to the United States Treasury in the amount of $10 (U.S. Funds) should be submitted to the Aircraft Registration Branch. If your request is approved, you are notified that the number has been reserved for 1 year. You are also informed that this reservation may be extended on a yearly basis for a $10 renewal fee.

When you are ready to place the number on your aircraft, you should request permission by forwarding a complete description of the aircraft to the Civil Aviation Registry. Permission to place the special number on your aircraft is given on AC Form 8050-64, Assignment of Special Registration Numbers. When the number is placed on your aircraft, sign and return the original to the Civil Aviation Registry within 5 days.

The duplicate of AC Form 8050-64, together with your Airworthiness Certificate, should be presented to an Aviation Safety Inspector (ASI) within 10 days from placing the new registration number on your aircraft. The inspector will issue a revised Airworthiness Certificate showing the new registration number. The old registration certificate and the duplicate AC Form 8050-64 should be carried in the aircraft until the new registration certificate is received. Reference 14 CFR section 91.203(a)(1).

Telephone (866) 762-9434 for registration and for N number information. State registration of aircraft is required in approximately 60 percent of the states. Check for your state's requirement.

# Aircraft Data Plates

Aircraft data plates from destroyed aircraft present a unique problem, because entire aircraft have been rebuilt around a recovered and resold data plate. There is no legal basis for an inspector or investigator to retain the data plate from a destroyed aircraft. However, the inspector or investigator will remove the data plate with the permission of the owner or insurance company, deface or destroy the plate, and then return it to the owner or the insurance company. Disfiguring the data plate will eliminate its future usefulness and resale value. Lastly, the FAA Inspector may asked for the data plate and advise AFS-750 in Oklahoma City that the aircraft was destroyed.

All aircraft data plates shall include the following information:

1. Builder's name.
2. Model designation.
3. Builder's serial number.
4. Type certificate number, if any.
5. Production certificate number, if any.
6. For aircraft engines, the established rating.

The identification plate for aircraft must be secured in such a manner that it will not likely be defaced or removed during normal service, or lost or destroyed in an accident. The data plate must be fire proof and marked by etching, stamping, engraving, or other approved method of fireproofing.

On aircraft manufactured before March 7, 1988, the identification plate may be secured at an accessible exterior or interior location near an entrance, if the model designation and builder's serial number are also displayed on the aircraft fuselage exterior. You may see taped to and hand written on the left fuselage section under the elevator. Reference can be found in CFR Part 45.

## Identification of critical components

A part for which a replacement time, inspection interval, or related procedure is specified in the Airworthiness Limitations section of a manufacturer's maintenance manual or Instructions for Continued Airworthiness shall permanently and legibly mark that component with a part number (or equivalent) and a serial number (or equivalent). This is usually on a data plate attached to the part with the following data: permanently and legibly mark the part with:

1. The letters "FAA-PMA".
2. The name, trademarks, or symbol of the holder of the Parts Manufacturer Approval.
3. The part number.
4. The name and model designation of each type certificated product on which the part is eligible for installation.

If a part is too small or that it is otherwise impractical to mark a part with any of the information required by CFR 45.15, a tag attached to the part or its container must include the information that could not be marked on the part.

# Imported Aircraft

What is an import airworthiness approval? This approval is required for airworthiness certification of aircraft, engines, propellers, materials, parts, and appliances imported into the United States from any country that has a bilateral agreement with the United States. This approval certifies that products conform to their FAA type certificates and are in a condition for safe operation.

How you can obtain an import airworthiness approval? Persons, as defined in 14 CFR Part 1, importing aircraft, engines, propellers, materials, parts, and appliances into the United States from a country that has a bilateral agreement with the United States must ensure that each item is accompanied by an export airworthiness approval issued by the Civil Aviation Authority of the country of manufacture. The import airworthiness approval process and corresponding documentation varies from country to country. Contact your local FAA Flight Standard District Office (FSDO) or Manufacturing Inspection Distinct Office (MIDO) to obtain specific requirements for your situation. A import checklist is provided in the Appendix section.

You can find information in the following:

1. 14 CFR Part 21, subpart H, Airworthiness Certificates.
2. 14 CFR Part 21, subpart N, Approval of Engines, Propellers, Materials, Parts, and Appliances: Import.
3. FAA Order 8130.2, Airworthiness Certification of Aircraft and Related Products.
4. FAA Advisory Circular 21-23, Airworthiness Certification of Civil Aircraft, Engines, Propellers and Related Products Imported to the United States.

# Registering a Import Aircraft

To register an imported aircraft, include a statement by the official having jurisdiction over the National Aircraft Registry of the foreign country of export indicating that registration has ended or that the aircraft was never registered. Include the Bill of Sale, signed in ink, from the foreign seller to the U. S. applicant/owner. Also include the completed Aircraft Registration Application, FAA Form 8050-1, and a check or money order made payable to the United States Treasury in the amount of $5 (U.S. Funds). Imports are worked on a priority basis. Please indicate **"Import"** in **RED** ink on the envelope and the request.

Use of an original Aircraft Registration Application, AC Form 8050-1, is required. Photocopies and computer-generated copies of this form are not acceptable for the registration of aircraft. Aircraft Registration Applications may be obtained from the Aircraft Registration Branch or your local FAA Flight Standard District Office. The applicant's physical location or physical address must also be shown on the application if a post office box (PO box) is entered as the mailing address.

# CHAPTER 8

## ENGINES

# Engine Inspections

For most aircraft, two notable items are the engine and the propeller. Mostly because an engine in most cases is rated at 2,000 hours between overhauls (TBO), never assume that it will reach that point. A manufacturer's suggested time between overhauls TBO is made with very tight parameters assumed. Such TBO generally assumes that the aircraft will fly at least 300 hours per year, and will be further subjected to meticulous routine maintenance. This may or in most cases may not be the case.

Treat any airplane with a "fresh engine overhaul" as if the engine is high time. You are much better off buying an airplane with a run-out engine and having it overhauled where and how you want it done. It is impossible on a prepurchase inspection to tell how well an engine overhaul was performed. In a nutshell, the cost of a good engine overhaul exceeds the boost it gives to the selling price of the airplane. That's a given. Assume the overhaul is worthless when negotiating. My rule of thumb is not to consider an overhaul worth its salt unless the engine has at least 200 hours on it since the overhaul, the owner can produce oil analysis records (talk with the analysis company) and the compression is at or close to new-overhaul tolerances.

Very few things hurt an aircraft more than years of idleness. So if you are looking at a particular aircraft that has had only 500 or 600 hours on its engine since the previous overhaul, and that engine has a manufacture TBO of 2,000 hours, be wary if the last overhaul was accomplished 10 years ago. One of the most destructive factors affecting engine life is corrosion that result from lack of use. Just like exposed steel corrodes more so do the "innards" of an engine, particularly when the aircraft is not routinely flown for at least an hour. Running the engine up for 20 minutes once in awhile is the worst thing you can do to an engine. The practice of ground running as a substitute for regular use of the aircraft is unacceptable. Ground running does not provide adequate cooling for the cylinders. In addition, ground running introduces water and acids into the lubrication system, which can cause substantial damage over time to cylinders and other engine components such as camshafts.

Turning the propeller by hand is not recommended as this wipes off the residual oil. Light rust signatures, which have not pitted the cylinder wall, or rust indications above the top ring travel area, are not usually cause for concern. Severe rust will pit the barrel wall and can damage rings. Such damage will usually be evident by low differential compression checks and high oil consumption. Improperly maintained and low-usage aircraft are the most susceptible to premature cylinder service issues.

The owner may be reluctant to overhaul an engine that is running well and is in good health despite the fact that it has reached its TBO. Under such circumstances, he has the option to continue operating the engine on 100-hour increments for so long as the engine remains in satisfactory health, and that a Certificated A&P mechanic also verifies state of health in the engine's logbook. However keep in mind that such operation involves some guesswork as you are now past the number of hours of known experience. Also, the rate of wear increases with wear. This means that the wear rate will be much faster on an engine past 1500 hours as compared to 800 to 1200 hours. Consequently running well past the recommended TBO could result in a much more expensive overhaul than if it had been overhauled at the recommended TBO. One item to note is how much oil consumption is there. A wore out engine burns more oil. Check to see if the seller has tracked oil consumption, this will tell the mechanic allot of information. (Lycoming Key Reprints)

# What Type Of Overhauls Are Their And What Do They Mean

**Overhaul** 14 CFR Part 43 section 43.2(a) clearly states to be overhauled it has to be disassembled, cleaned, inspected, repaired as necessary, and reassembled; and tested in accordance with approve standards. This is the cheap to get by overhaul or minimum standard. You get what you paid for so to speak.

**Rebuilt** in 14 CFR Part 43 section 43.2(b) states it has to be disassembled, cleaned, inspected, repaired as necessary, and reassembled; and tested to the same tolerances and **limits as a new** item using either new parts or used parts that conform to **new part tolerances and limits** or to approved oversized or undersized dimensions. This is what you want to see in the engine maintenance records, rebuilt just like new.

**Top Overhaul** is not a complete overhaul in any since of the meaning. It only reconditions the cylinder jugs and does nothing for the parts inside the case halves. It does not extend the life of the TBO and during a rebuilt they may not meet the requirement of new tolerances or limits. In some cases top overhauls put a greater load on the old worn crankshaft and bearings causing greater wear on these parts.

Manufactures are frequently asked the question should my engine have a top overhaul at some point between major overhauls? Lycoming reply to that question is top overhauls should only be done when needed on the diagnosis of a competent mechanic. It is unfortunate that people spend money needlessly on a top overhaul.

If the new, rebuilt, or overhauled engine starts its TBO cycle with new cylinders and is treated to proper operation, good maintenance, and frequent flight, it should reach the recommended TBO without a top overhaul along the way. An overhauled engine that has reconditioned cylinders is not necessarily a candidate for a top overhaul, but it is very likely that it will require cylinder replacement before the recommended TBO is reached.

# Engine Overhaul Terminology and Standards

TBO time draws near and you need to decide on a course of action. You call around, talk to your maintenance facility, and find that you are totally confused because you don't understand or know the definitions of many of the terms used by the people that you have been talking to. New limits, Service limits, Remanufactured, Rebuilt, New, Used, Overhauled, like new, OEM, Aftermarket, what does it all mean?

Lets look at and define the terms that are approved to be used by the FAA.

**NEW ENGINE** is an engine that has been manufactured from all new parts and tested by a FAA approved manufacturer. The engine will have no operating history except for test cell time when received. No FAA approved manufacturer can approve another entity to manufacture or assemble a new engine.

**NEW LIMITS** are the FAA approved fits and tolerances that a new engine is manufactured to. This may be accomplished using standard or approved undersized and oversized tolerances.

**SERVICE LIMITS** are the FAA approved allowable wear fits and tolerances that a new limit part may deteriorate to and still are a useable component. This may also be accomplished using standard and approved undersized and oversized tolerances.

**REMANUFACTURE** the general term remanufacture has no specific meaning in the CFRs. A new engine is a product that is manufactured from raw materials. These raw materials are made into parts and accessories that conform to specifications for the issuance of an engine type certificate. The term "remanufactured" as used by most engine manufacturers and overhaul facilities, means that an engine has been overhauled to the standards required to zero time it in accordance with section 91.421. As outlined in section 91.421, only the manufacturer or an agency approved by the manufacturer can grant zero time to an engine (Part 21).

**OVERHAULED ENGINE** is an engine, which has been disassembled, cleaned, inspected, repaired as necessary and tested using FAA approved procedures. The engine may be overhauled to NEW LIMITS or SERVICE LIMITS and still be considered a FAA approved OVERHAUL. The engine's previous operating history is maintained and it is returned to you with zero time since major overhaul and a total time since new that is the same as before the overhaul (Part 43.2(b).

**REBUILT ENGINE** is an engine that has been OVERHAULED using new and used parts to NEW LIMITS by the manufacturer or an entity approved by the manufacturer. At the current time neither Teledyne Continental nor Textron Lycoming approve any other entity to rebuild engines for them. The engine's previous operating history is eradicated and it comes to you with zero hours total time in service, even though the engine may have had used components installed that have many hours of previous operating history. Textron Lycoming uses the term Remanufactured in their advertising and commercial media to describe their factory rebuilt engines. Although this term has no official definition in the eyes of the FAA, when used by the Textron Lycoming and only when used by Textron Lycoming the term Remanufactured should be considered the same as the term rebuilt (Part 43.2(a).

When an engine is OVERHAULED or REBUILT the new parts that are used during the repair process can come from a variety of sources. An Original Equipment Manufacture (OEM) part is a new part that is manufactured by the original engine manufacturer to stringent FAA standards. An AFTERMARKET part is a new part that is manufactured by someone other than the original engine manufacturer that meets or exceeds the same stringent FAA guidelines as a new OEM part.

The person or entity using them defines any other terms used to describe the work performed during an engine overhaul. They have no official meaning and often times are very misleading. Terms like **"overhauled to factory specs or tolerances"**, **"rebuilt equivalent"**, **"overhauled to like new condition"** and **"remanufactured to factory fits and limits"** and any other terminology that isn't defined above needs to be investigated as to what those terms actually mean. You will probably find that advertisements and log entries that use undefined terminology are not really delivering what you think you are getting. There are specific requirements by the FAA for the use of the terms **OVERHAULED** and **REBUILT** in an engine's maintenance records. If these requirements are not met it is illegal to use the terms. Any terms other than those listed have no meaning in the eyes of the FAA and should not be accepted by you in your engine logbooks.

**ENGINE OVERHAUL FACILITIES** Engine overhaul facilities can include the manufacturer, or a manufacturer's approved agency, large and small FAA certificated repair stations, and engine shops that perform custom overhauls or individual certificated powerplant mechanics. The services offered by these facilities vary. However, regardless of the type or size of the facility, all are required to comply with section 43.13(a) and 43.13(b). In this regard, it is the responsibility of the owner to assure that proper entries are made in the engine records refer to 14 CFR Part 91 sections 91.405.

Engine overhaul facilities are required by section 43.9 to make appropriate entries in the engine records of maintenance that was performed on the engine. The owner should insure that the engine overhaul facility references the tolerances used (new or serviceable) to accomplish the engine overhaul.

Now that we understand all the terms, let's put it all in a nutshell. Only the manufacturer can currently produce a new or rebuilt engine. Both new and rebuilt engines are made to new limits. A new engine will have all new O.E.M. parts. A rebuilt engine can be produced using a combination of used and new O.E.M. parts. An overhauled engine can be done to new limits or to service limits or a combination of the two using used parts and new O.E.M or new aftermarket parts. An overhauled engine comes to you with its previous operating history intact and zero hours since major overhaul. A new or rebuilt engine comes to you with no previous operating history and zero hours time in service, even though, in the case of a rebuilt engine, some of the parts used may have a previous operating history. Understanding these terms and the regulations that apply to them may make the decisions that you have to make, at TBO time, a little easier.

# Engine Inspection

The pre-purchase inspection should assist in identifying problems with cylinders in service. The points of the engine pre-purchase inspection are:

1. Cylinder differential compression check and trend monitoring.
2. Cylinder borescope inspection, as required.
3. Oil consumption trend monitoring.
4. Oil analysis trend monitoring if available.
5. Baffle condition inspection, correct position, and proper contact with cowl.
6. Induction system examination.
7. Cowling inspection and cowl flap operation check.
8. Ignition system inspection.
9. Verification of accuracy of engine gages.
10. Flight test.

In order to perform the inspection, all applicable aircraft, engine, and STC holder's manuals, instructions and service information must be available and utilized. It is important to note that differential compression checks are used to identify cylinder leakage rates and the source of the leakage. This check cannot be directly related to engine horsepower. Engine testing has shown that certification horsepower ratings will continue to be delivered even when all cylinders are at or below the minimum allowable calibrated compression reading as established by the master orifice tool.

**Borescope** inspection of the cylinder walls are performed to assess the condition of the hone pattern and identify abnormal wear patters, which can contribute to low differential compression reading or increased oil consumption.

**If oil consumption** is more than one quart every three hours of operation or if the oil consumption trend has changed substantially, conduct the differential compression and borescope examination. Aircraft piston engines continuously wear over their service life. One indication of the rate of wear, or indication of the need for inspection or service, is found in oil consumption trends. Every owner/operator should maintain formal records on oil consumption in the aircraft maintenance records. Engines require a certain level of oil consumption to assure proper lubrication of the cylinder walls and rings. Oil consumption trends are excellent indicators of cylinder bore and ring condition.

**Baffle condition** investigations into cylinder service life issues found that maintenance of cylinder and oil cooling systems (incorrect and improperly fitting baffles) are factors in premature cylinder removals. To understand the importance of this cooling control, note that approximately one third of the energy of the fuel used is transferred as heat to the structure cylinder head, barrel, crankcase, etc. and oil. The amount of heat energy that must be removed by the cooling air is approximately equal to the horsepower that is driving the propeller.

The baffles and deflectors normally are inspected during the regular engine inspection, but they should be checked whenever the cowling is removed for any purpose. Checks should be made for cracks, dents, or loose hold-down studs. Cracks or dents, if severe enough, would necessitate repair or removal and replacement of these units. However, a crack that has just started can be stop-drilled, and dents can be straightened, permitting further service from these baffles and deflectors.

**Cowl Flap Installation and Adjustment** during cowl flap installation, adjustments are made to assure the correct "open and close" tolerances of the cowl flaps. This tolerance is of the utmost importance. If the cowl flap is permitted to open too far, the air exiting from the engine section is increased in velocity, thus permitting too great a cooling of the cylinders. Also, if the cowl flaps are not adjusted to open the desired amount, the cylinder head temperature will be higher than allowable limits under certain operating conditions. For each engine installation the cowl flaps are set for tolerances that will permit them to open and close a correct amount, keeping the cylinder head temperature within allowable limits.

**Engine gage** verification of accuracy of the tachometer and manifold pressure gage required for fuel system setup, verify that the fuel flow, cylinder head temperature (CHT) and exhaust gases temperature (EGT) gages are providing accurate indications. Aircraft gage calibration errors can be particularly harmful for high horsepower engines. Gages must be re-marked for modified (STC) engines.

# Engine Visual Inspection

1.  Check the engine mount, vibration isolation mounts, and attach points before each flight.

### NOTE
*If slippage marks are painted across the bolt heads', engine mount, and fuselage at the time the mount bolts are torqued, a break in the paint will give advance warning the mount is coming loose. (Red nail polish works adequately or torque seal.)*

2.  Check all hose clamps for tightness.
3.  Check for fuel and oil leaks.
4.  Check air filter for condition and attachment.
5.  Ensure that all spark plugs are the correct ones, properly torqued. Check that the ignition wires, caps, and plug cap restraints on inverted engines are secured and safetied. Ensure that the kill switch, if applicable, is within easy reach and works as advertised.
6.  Check that the carburetor and the throttle cable are secured and both operate freely from idle stop to full power stop.
7.  Check carburetor boots for cracks that will suck air and may create a lean mixture, high CHT and EGT, and possible engine failure.

# Engine Sudden Stoppage

What is a prop strike? Is it a sudden engine stoppage regardless of the cause? Is it an occasion when a prop blade strikes a foreign object and the engine continues to run? Is it hitting a rock or other loose object with a prop blade while operating on a runway or taxiway? Is it when something or someone impacts a prop blade when the engine isn't running? Is it a bird hitting the propeller?

The only pertinent FAA definition that I have been able to find is in Advisory Circular 43.13. It defines a sudden engine stoppage as; stopping an engine in one revolution or less for any reason, be it from propeller impact or from an engine failure of some sort. Engine manufacturers have service literature that explains the desired course of action after accidental propeller damage and, in the case of Teledyne Continental, defines what their interpretation of a propeller strike is.

Teledyne Continental (TCM) Service Bulletin 96-11, in a nutshell, says that if a propeller must be removed from the aircraft to be repaired following a propeller blade impact of any sort or if the engine physically lost R.P.M.'s from the incident, then the engine has experienced a propeller strike and it should be removed from service and completely disassembled and thoroughly inspected for damage from the incident.

Textron Lycoming, in their Service Bulletin 533, takes the approach that the safest procedure is to take the engine apart for inspection following any incident involving propeller blade damage. However, they have the caveat that the inspecting mechanic may override that position and return the engine to service without disassembly and inspection if they feel that it is the prudent and responsible thing to do.

Textron Lycoming has also published Service Bulletin 475B which requires, in the event that the engine has experienced a propeller strike, inspection and possible rework of the accessory gear train as well as the rear of the engine's crankshaft. Compliance with this service bulletin is mandatory in the eyes of the FAA by A.D. 91-14-22, if and only if, the engine has experienced a sudden engine stoppage not a propeller strike. It should be noted that to comply with A.D. note 91-14-22, the engine does not need to be completely disassembled and that access to the accessory gear train can be accomplished, in most cases, with the engine still installed in the aircraft.

What this all boils down to is that in the case of any accidental damage to a propeller installed on a aircraft operating under Part 91 of the CFR's, it is up to the inspecting technician to determine if the engine should continue in service without total disassembly and inspection. A Textron Lycoming engine, that is being operated on a Part 91 aircraft, that had a sudden engine stoppage, not a propeller strike, must comply with A.D. note 91-14-22 and Service Bulletin 475B at a minimum.

Teledyne Continental powered aircraft operating under Part 135 of the CFR's, have to comply with all manufacturers service bulletins, would have to comply with Service Bulletin 96-11 requiring total disassembly and inspection after any incident that required removal of the propeller for repairs or if the engine physically lost R.P.M.'s during the incident. An aircraft, operating under the same regulations, that is powered by a Textron Lycoming engine, would have to comply with Service Bulletin 475B after a propeller strike of any kind and would also have to comply with A.D. 91-14-22 if the propeller strike was deemed a sudden engine stoppage. On these Textron Lycoming powered aircraft, it is the responsibility of the inspecting technician to determine if the engine should be removed from service for disassembly and inspection.

There may be other additional requirements mandated by insurance policies or engine manufacturer and or over hauler's warranties. Either may require additional inspection requirements but neither may negate the inspections required by the CFR's. Never allow an insurance adjuster to dictate the inspection requirements after an incident. Always rely on the inspecting technician, applicable service data and the CFR's to dictate how thorough an inspection is necessary to continue the engine in service.

After the extent of the inspection has been determined, it is important, as with any major repairs that are accomplished on your aircraft, to find out exactly what is included in the estimate to repair your engine following a prop strike. Are the minimum legal requirements being met? Is the engine going to be completely disassembled and inspected? What other services or inspections are being performed at the same time as the inspection? If the engine is being disassembled does the estimate include testing after reassembly? Are any of the engine's accessories inspected and if so to what extent? Are there any hidden costs? After finding out the answer to these questions, it's time to discuss with your insurance company what they will pay for and what they won't, before it's a big surprise after the inspection has been completed. Many insurance companies will not pay for any inspection requirements unless damage from the incident is found during that inspection. Others will pay for all costs for the inspection and for any parts needed due to the incident. Still others will only pay for the labor to do the job and will not pay for any parts.

Your record inspection should uncover if a propeller strike has happened. If one has and is not documented the owner may be negligent. Negligent only if the owner does not disclose a propeller strike before the sale and you find out after you purchase the aircraft.

# Engine Mounts

The engine mounts refer to the aircraft structure for mounting the engine and not the mount pads or attachment points, which are integral parts of the engine. Some engine mounts are heat-treated and may not be repaired by welding unless normalized and reheat-treated to their previous strength values. When cracks or inferior welds are found in such units, replacement or repair by the manufacturer or authorized repair facility is necessary. Nonheat-treated engine mounts may be repaired by welding if the work is performed in accordance with the manufacturer's instructions and is done by a person authorized in CFR 43. Examine the entire engine mount structure with a magnifying glass, especially at welds. Look for evidence of cracks or failure and inferior welds. Ensure that all attachment bolts are tight and properly safetied.

Structural Substantiation by Analysis. CFR Section 23.307 allows compliance with strength and deformation requirements by structural analysis if the structure conforms to those for which experience has shown the methods employed to be reliable. The procedures for structural analysis would generally be as follows:

1.  Determine the total weight and center of gravity (c.g.) of the engine installation including accessories and propeller.

2.  Determine the effect of the proposed engine installation on the airplane's weight-c.g. envelope as defined on the Type Certificate Data Sheet (TCDS) or Aircraft Specification, or by any Supplemental Type Certificates (STC's) that may have modified it. To minimize certification work, it is advisable to keep this envelope within the existing approved limits. If the weight-c.g. envelope is expanded beyond its existing approved limits in order to accomplish the proposed engine installation all sections of Part 23 of the CFR applicable to performance, flight characteristics, and structural loads should be reviewed for possible effects. Compliance with sections 23.21 through 23.31, which address load distribution and weight limits, must be shown.

3.  Determine the limit flight load factors required for maneuvering, gust encounters, and side loads (14 CFR 23 sections 23.337, 23.341, and 23.363) for the category (normal, utility, or acrobatic) in which the airplane is certificated. Also, determine the limit landing load factors and angular accelerations required by section 23.471 through 23.479 and section 23.521, if seaplane certification is desired), and from these determine the limit load factors acting at the engine installation c.g. under the landing conditions. Note that gust loads acting on engine mounts and their supporting structure at the design minimum weight are generally greater than those experienced at the design maximum weight.

Certain engine installations, particularly those mounted on wings, may experience high flight limit load factors due to the effect of angular accelerations added to linear accelerations under unsymmetrical flight conditions. In cases where the engine installation c.g. is unusually far from the airplane c.g., and in cases where the engines are mounted on the wings, limit flight load factors acting at the engine installation c.g. should be determined for the unsymmetrical flight conditions (section 23.347 through 23.351) and for conditions involving angular accelerations due to unbalanced components of tail load (section 23.423 through 23.443).

Airplanes having wing-mounted engines when high-lift devices are deployed may experience large wing torsional loads. The limit flight load factors required by section 23.345 should, therefore, be determined for airplanes with engines mounted on the wings.

Structural Substantiation by Load Test. Determine the critical limit and ultimate loads from the procedure above. Except where specified otherwise by the applicable section of Part 23 of the CFR itself, each ultimate load will be **1.5 times** the corresponding limit load (reference section 23.303). Each structural element or assembly tested must be able to support limit loads without detrimental permanent deformation, and must be able to support ultimate loads for three seconds without failure. For guidance in determining whether a structural failure has occurred in questionable or marginal test cases, see AC 23-6, "Interpretation of Failure for Static Structural Test Programs." Dynamic tests are acceptable if it is proven that they accurately simulate the design load conditions (reference section 23.307). If a structure has been tested beyond limit load and has any detrimental permanent deformation, it should be clearly and permanently identified to prevent its use as a flight article.

# Engine-Mount Repairs

All welding on an engine mount must be of the highest quality, since vibration tends to accentuate any minor defect. Engine-mount members should preferably be repaired by using a larger diameter replacement tube, telescoped over the stub of the original member, and using fishmouth and rosette welds. However, 30-degree scarf welds in place of the fishmouth welds will be considered acceptable for engine-mount repair work.

Repaired engine mounts must be checked for accurate alignment. When tubes are used to replace bent or damaged ones, the original alignment of the structure must be maintained. When drawings are not available, this can be done by measuring the distance between points of corresponding members that have not been distorted.

If all members are out of alignment, reject the engine mount and replace with one supplied by the manufacturer or one, which was built to conform to the manufacturer's drawings. The method of checking the alignment of the fuselage or nacelle points should be requested from the manufacturer.

Repair minor damage, such as a crack adjacent to an engine-attachment lug, by rewelding the ring and extending a gusset or a mounting lug past the damaged area. Engine-mount rings, which are extensively damaged, must not be repaired, unless the method of repair is specifically approved by the FAA, or the repair is accomplished in accordance with FAA-approved instructions.

If the manufacturer stress relieved the engine mount after welding it, the engine mount should be re-stress relieved after the weld repairs are made.

Check the airframe maintenance records for any repairs or Form 337's. If the mounts have been repaired they should have a maintenance record entry. If when inspecting the mounts and notice any corrosion pitting on any of the tubes this is a sign of trouble. Take note if the aircraft you are purchasing has a turbo their mounts are very prone to having severe pitting corrosion and very expensive to repair or replace.

# Engine Baffle Seals

The baffling installed on the engine of today is the result of considerable study. Special wrap around baffles now guide the cooling air completely around the cylinder heads and barrels. Other baffles channel cooling air into oil radiators and cooling ducts for varicose accessories. Rubber seal are provided along the cowling edged of the baffling. These seals are very important since they provide the necessary airtight seal between the baffling and cowling. Therefore every baffle and its seal must be in its proper position and in good working condition, or satisfactory cooling will not result.

The cooling air piles up inside the cowling and then is channeled around the cylinders. Cooling air is also entering the accessory section to provide the necessary cooling for engine driven accessories. The air in the topside of the cowling is actually under pressure and it is this pressure that forces it to take the desired routes provided by the baffling. You do not have to be a rocket scientist to realize that in such an installation, cooling air simple wouldn't take the desired routes if it were not for this air pressure. Where does this air pressure come from? There are two sources we depend on; ram air from forward movement or flight, and the propeller during ground operations.

Excessive ground run-up, especially in the area of high power can cause damage to pressure cooled engines. The worst thing about such abuse is that it produces accumulative type damage. The damage is seldom great enough to show up right at the moment of abuse, instead it goes by undetected, but it accumulates with more abuse and finally it shows up way down the road in the form of broken piston rings, scored pistons or cylinder or perhaps a premature overhaul. This is one reason to always face the engine into the wind when running up it helps.

Investigations into cylinder service life issues found that maintenance of cylinder and oil-cooling systems (Incorrect and improperly fitting baffles) were factors in premature cylinder removals. To understand the importance of this cooling control, note that approximately one third of the energy of the fuel used is transferred as heat to the structure (cylinder head, barrel, crankcase, etc.) and oil. **The amount of heat energy that must be removed by the cooling air is approximately equal to the horsepower that is driving the**

**propeller.** This is why failure of the cooling baffles to perform efficiently can lead to rapid and significant deterioration of the cylinders and other engine components.

**Baffle Condition Inspection:**

1. Check baffle for condition, correct position, and proper contact with cowl. The front upper cowl baffle seal is most critical, especially at the in board and outboard corners.
2. Repair or replace worn or distorted baffles with FAA approved parts and materials only.
3. Check and adjust inter-cylinder baffles to ensure a tight fit.
4. Seal holes and cracks that would allow cooling airflow to be wasted. This may be accomplished by applying a non-corrosive silicone adhesive/sealant. Consult the aircraft manufacture for application instructions.
5. Check the integrity of all cooling ducts, heater ducts, etc. and repair as necessary.
6. Visually inspect the engine baffle seals for proper positioning by using a light and looking in air inlets and access doors to ensure that forward seals and lower aft seals are all facing forward and not blown back.
7. Inspect the existing baffle seals through the front of the cowl to ensure existing seals are of sufficient length to provide at least 1-inch of contact with upper and lower cowls when properly positioned.

The Piper Aircraft Corporation has one AD 93-23-13, to prevent improper sealing of the baffles seals to the engine cowling, which could result in high engine operating temperatures. Piper Kit 764 093 includes the entire baffle assembly consisting of both baffles and correct material for the baffle seals and repair.

This AD allows the use of Brown Aircraft Supply Engine Baffle Material for certain Piper make/model aircraft only. Take note; that this material may be thicker that the original and not as flexible allowing pressure air to pass over it. This will directly effect the cooling of the engine. If you want to put Browns material on any other aircraft not called out in the AD you will be required to file a Form 337 for a major alteration to be approved by your local FAA FSDO before installation.

Take note; if you use baffle seal material other than called out by the manufacture, it is a major alteration. Seals that have an inspection interval or a related procedure specified in a product's airworthiness limitations or instructions for continued airworthiness. The FAA Inspectors will review the applicant's FAA Form 337, Major Repair and Alteration, or other forms acceptable to the Administrator, to ensure that the performance rules (general), as stated in Title 14 of the Code of Federal Regulations (14 CFR) Part 43, section 43.13, have been incorporated into the applicant's airworthiness program based on the owner/operator's type of operation. Many alterations are actually major design changes and may require a STC. Previously unapproved major changes to structural strength, reliability, and operational characteristics affect the airworthiness of the product and therefore require engineering approval. Typical major alterations in this category include: Any change to manifolding, engine cowling, and or baffling that may adversely affect the flow of cooling air. Reference FAA Order 8300.10 Vol. 2, chapter 1.

Cylinder head temperature should be maintained by regulating the cooling air differential pressure at the start of each fuel mixture control run in such a manner that the peak temperature reached by the hottest cylinder during leaning will be not more than 10F below the maximum specified engine limit. The temperature of all other cylinder heads should be maintained within 50F of the hottest cylinder.

# Hard Facts About Engine Break In

Most people seem to operate on the philosophy that they can best get their money's worth from any mechanical device by treating it with great care. This is probably true, but in many cases it is necessary to interpret what great care really means. This is particularly applicable when considering the break-in of a modern, reciprocating aircraft engine. Aircraft owners frequently ask about the proper procedures for run-in of a new or rebuilt engine so they can carefully complete the required steps. Many of these recommended break-in procedures also apply to engines, which have been overhauled, or had a cylinder replaced.

The first careful consideration for engine run-in is the oil to be used. If you have a Lycoming engine use the latest revision of Textron Lycoming Service Instruction 1014 for this information. The basic rule, which applies to most normally aspirated Lycoming piston engines, is simple; use straight mineral oil of the proper viscosity for the first fifty hours or until oil consumption stabilizes. Then switch to ashless dispersant (AD) oil.

The exceptions to the basic rule above are the O-320-H and the O/LO-360-E series. These engines may be operated using either straight mineral oil or ashless dispersant oil, however, if the engine is delivered with ashless dispersant oil installed, it must remain on ashless dispersant oil. The Textron Lycoming oil additive P/N LW-16702 must be added to the O-320-H and O/LO-360-E engines at airframe installation, and every 50 hours thereafter or at every oil change. FAA-approved lubricating oil that contains, in the proper amount, an oil additive equivalent to LW-16702 will meet the requirements for the additive as stated in Lycoming Service Instruction No. 1014M. All Lycoming turbocharged engines must be broken in with ashless dispersant oil only.

When taking delivery of a new aircraft, there is another point, which must be emphasized. Some aircraft manufacturers add approved preservative lubricating oil to protect new engines from rust and corrosion at the time the aircraft leaves the factory. This preservative oil must be removed by the end of the first 25 hours of operation. Each new or rebuilt engine is given a production test run at the factory before the engine is delivered to an aircraft manufacturer or other customer. After installation in the aircraft, the engine is run again during the test flights. These test runs will insure that the engine is operating normally and will provide an opportunity to locate small oil leaks or other minor discrepancies. In addition, these test runs do the initial seating of the piston rings. The rest of the break-in is the responsibility of the pilot who flies the aircraft during the next 50 hours.

A new, rebuilt, or overhauled engine should receive the same start, warm-up, and preflight checks as any other engine. There are some aircraft owners and pilots who would prefer to use low power settings for cruise during the break-in period. This is not recommended. A good break-in requires that the piston rings expand sufficiently to seat with the cylinder walls during the engine break-in period. This seating of the ring with the cylinder wall will only occur when pressures inside the cylinder are great enough to cause expansion of the piston rings. Pressures in the cylinder only become great enough for a good break-in when power settings above 65% are used.

Full power for takeoff and climb during the break-in period is not harmful; it is beneficial, although engine temperatures should be monitored closely to insure that overheating does not occur. Cruise power settings above 65%, and preferably in the 70% to 75% of rated power range should be used to achieve a good engine break-in. It should be remembered that if the new or rebuilt engine were normally aspirated (nonturbocharged), it would be necessary to cruise at the lower altitudes to obtain the required cruise power levels. Density altitudes in excess of 8000 feet (5000 feet is recommended) will not allow the engine to develop sufficient cruise power for a good break-in.

For those who still think that running the engine hard during break-in falls into the category of cruel and unusual punishment, there is one more argument for high power settings during engine break-in. The use of low power settings does not expand the piston rings enough, and a film of oil is left on the cylinder walls. The high temperatures in the combustion chamber will oxidize this oil film so that it creates a condition commonly known as glazing of the cylinder walls. When this happens, the ring break-in process stops, and excessive oil consumption frequently occurs. The bad news is that removing the cylinders and rehoning the walls can only correct extensive glazing. This is expensive, and it is an expense that can be avoided by proper break in procedures.

To summarize, there are just a few items to remember about engine break-in:

1. If preservative oil has been added by the aircraft manufacturer, drain it not later than the first 25 hours of operation.
2. Follow the engine manufacturers recommendation regarding the oil to be used for break-in and the period between changes.
3. Run the engine at high cruise power levels for best piston ring/cylinder wall mating.

4. Continue break in operation for 50 hours or until oil consumption stabilizes. These simple procedures should eliminate the possibility of cylinder wall glazing and should prepare the engine for a long and satisfactory service life. (Reference Textron Lycoming Key Reprints)

# Metal In Screen And Filters

Because the failure to look for metal in the screens and filter, or ignoring what is found, can lead to catastrophic engine failure, what is the proper action to be taken when metal shows up in the oil screen or oil filter cartridge.

## General Information

1. DON'T PANIC because of small amounts of shiny flakes or small amounts of short hair-like bits of magnetic material. Experience has shown that engines are sometimes pulled unnecessarily.
2. DON'T PANIC if it's a low time engine. A few bits of metal left from manufacturing are not too uncommon in the oil screen or filter on new, rebuilt, or overhauled engines.
3. DON'T PANIC. Again if it's a low-time engine, it may be a replacement for one that had previously suffered a structural failure. The metal may have just been dislodged from some hiding place in the oil cooler, oil lines or oil tank.
4. Item 3 brings up the importance of properly cleaning all items transferred from a failed engine to a replacement engine. On dry sump engines, don't overlook cleaning of the oil tank. Oil coolers and oil lines should be cleaned by a proven method, or replaced.
5. In some rare cases where the pleated cylindrical type oil screen is used, the screen itself may be making metal. Closely inspect the end of the internal relief valve ball. If the ball is deformed, this may be the culprit. Replace the screen assembly.
6. In cases where metal shows up in the filter of a **factory engine that is under warranty**, and its origin is unknown, the metal may be forwarded to the manufacture for inspection. In all cases, the factory Product Support Department should be called before the material is shipped.

**EXAMPLES:**

1. Several pieces of shiny flake-like, nonmagnetic, or several short hair-like pieces of magnetic material — place aircraft back in service and again check oil screen or filter in 25 hours.
2. As in Item 1, but larger amount, such as 45-60 small pieces — clean screen, drain oil, and refill. Run engine on ground for 20-30 minutes. Inspect screen. If clean, fly aircraft for 1 to 2 hours and again inspect screen. If clean, inspect screen after 10 hours of flight time.

## NOTE

*In cases one and two, we are determining whether the small amount of metal was a "one shot and done deal" (not entirely uncommon).*

3. Chunks of metal ranging in size of broken lead pencil point or greater. Remove suction (sump) screen as large pieces of metal may have fallen into the sump. In any event, ground aircraft and conduct investigation. A mixture of magnetic and nonmagnetic material in this case often times means valve or ring and piston failure. Removing bottom spark plugs usually reveals the offending cylinder.
4. Nonmagnetic plating averaging approximately 1/16" in diameter may have copperish tint. Quantity found — ¼ teaspoonful or more; ground aircraft and investigate. If origin can't be determined and this is a factory engine (not a field overhaul) that is under warranty, mail metal to Lycoming factory for analysis, attention Product Support.
5. Same as Item 4, but may be slightly larger in size and minus copperish tint. On direct drive engines, propeller action may be impaired. Ground aircraft. If origin can't be determined and it is a factory engine under warranty, mail material to the manufacturer, attention Product Support.
6. Nonmagnetic metal brass or copperish colored. Resembles coarse sand in consistency. Quantity of ¼ teaspoonful or more — ground aircraft. If origin can't be determined and it is a factory engine under warranty, mail metal to the manufacturer, attention Product Support.

7. Anytime metal is found in the amount of ½ teaspoonful or more, it is usually grounds for engine removal. An exception should be where problem is confined to one cylinder assembly (rings, valves, piston, cylinder). In this case, if the entire engine does not appear to be contaminated, the offending cylinder assembly kit may be replaced. After corrective action is completed, conduct the routine ground running and screen inspection as previously described in Item 2.

8. If any single or several pieces of metal larger than previously mentioned are found, magnetic or nonmagnetic, ground aircraft. If this is a factory engine under warranty, and origin of the metal contamination cannot be determined, a call may be made to the manufacturer Product Support Department. A good description of the metal may result in placing its origin. When phoning the manufacturer or when returning metal removed from engines, supply the complete engine model designation, serial number, history of engine, oil temperatures, oil pressures, and any odd behavior of the engine on the ground or during flight.

## NOTE

*Metal samples for analysis can only by accepted if the engine from which the sample is taken is a new, rebuilt, or overhauled engine from the factory and it is still under warranty. Engines overhauled by other facilities may have parts that cannot be identified by analysis at the manufacturer.*

As an important postscript to "Suggestions if Metal is found in the Screens or Filter," factory personnel have become concerned over unnecessary engine removals because metal was found in a replacement engine after a prior malfunctioning engine was removed. These unfortunate engine removals were largely caused by maintenance personnel failing to thoroughly flush and clean all aircraft oil system components. Because of the difficulty of removing contamination from oil coolers, it is strongly suggested that new oil cooler be used with the replacement engine when an engine is removed because it failed. As a reminder that it is essential to remove metal contamination from the oil system, the factory Product Support Department now sends the following tag with every service engine leaving our factory:

## IMPORTANT

Before installing a replacement engine, all aircraft oil system components, oil coolers, lines and supply tanks, where used, must be thoroughly cleaned for contamination. Manufactures will not be held responsible for contamination to this newly installed engine. (Reference Textron Lycoming Key Reprints)

# Nose Seal Leak

Perhaps the first step in discussing this subject is to first get the terminology correct. The latest revision of Lycoming Service Instruction No. 1324 calls it a Crankshaft Oil Seal. Although almost everyone knows exactly what you are talking about when the term Nose Seal is used, correct terminology can be important. Should this seal leak immediately after installation, it is possible that the seal was damaged during the installation process, but a poor fit between the crankcase and seal or the crankshaft and seal could also be responsible for the leak.

Before installation of a crankshaft oil seal, it is important to check the recess into which it fits for proper size. Excessive wear, which enlarges the crankcase, bore for any reason may cause the crankshaft oil seal to leak. An undersize crankshaft could result in the same poor fit and a leak. This is usually caused by a rusty or pitted surface, which has been polished excessively. Lycoming Service Instruction No. 1111 specifies the maximum undersize grind or polish which is allowable for the removal of rust or pits. It also prescribes the procedures for replating the crankshaft flange and seal area. Measurement of both the crankshaft and the crankcase to insure that they meet Table of Limit tolerances should be standard maintenance procedure before installation of a crankshaft oil seal.

To avoid damage during installation, it is important to follow the instructions provided in the latest revision of the engine manufacture manual and service instructions for Lycoming engines use Lycoming Service Instruction No. 1324. This instruction gives information on the two types of seals, which may be used in

Lycoming direct drive engines, the part numbers of both the standard and the oversized seals, and the method of installing both types of seal.

When a leak at the crankshaft oil seal develops after many hours of normal operation, it is usually the result of other problems. The experienced Field Service Engineers at Lycoming indicate that a restricted breather or an oil slinger clearance that is too tight frequently causes a leaking crankshaft oil seal. The leak might also be caused by a propeller defect, which places an abnormal side load on the crankshaft oil seal.

To avoid the problem of oil leakage at the crankshaft oil seal because of an engine breather restriction, examination of the breather tube to determine its condition is an excellent idea. If the tube is in good condition, also remember that the engine expels moisture through the tube. Under freezing conditions there is some possibility that the moisture may freeze at the end of the tube and ice will build up until the tube is completely restricted. Should this happen, pressure may build up in the crankcase until something gives — usually the Crankshaft Oil Seal.

Since the airframe manufacturers know this is a possibility, and since they design with the intention of preventing engine-related problems of this kind, some means of preventing freeze-up of the crankcase breather is usually a part of the aircraft design. The breather tube may be insulated, it may be designed so the end is located in a hot area, it may be equipped with an electric heater, or it may incorporate a hole, notch, or slot, which is often called a "whistle slot." Because of its simplicity, the whistle slot is often used and is located in a warm area near the engine where it will not freeze. Aircraft operators should know which method of preventing freeze-up is used and then insure that the configuration is maintained as specified by the airframe manufacturer.

Should leakage at the crankshaft oil seal occur as a result of oil slinger clearance, which is too tight, checking for excessive end clearance can initially identify the problem. This can be done with a dial indicator. Remove the prop and then push the prop flange to the extreme aft position and zero the indicator. Then pull the prop flange full forward and read the travel on the indicator. Compare this figure with the limits listed in the Table of Limits for the appropriate engine model.

Should the end clearance exceed the limits specified, the oil slinger clearance should then be checked. On Lycoming engines first, remove the old nose seal and clean the work area. Again, push the crankshaft to the rear of the engine. Insert a .002-inch feeler gage about 3/16-inch wide between the oil slinger on the crankshaft and the crankcase. Again, pull the crankshaft forward. If the .002-inch feeler gage is pinched tight, the required .002- to .007-inch clearance has been exceeded. Lack of appropriate clearance is the result of excessive wear on the crankcase thrust face, which will allow oil to be pumped out past the crankcase oil seal.

Overhaul time is usually when the crankcase thrust face might receive needed repair. Should the crankcase oil seal be leaking excessively, it may simply mean that overhaul time has arrived early. Fortunately this is something, which does not happen very often.

Crankcases with worn or damaged thrust face areas can be repaired by reworking the thrust face area to permit installation of new thrust bearing washers. These bearings are available as repair items. Thrust bearing washers may be reused if they do not show wear and if their thickness is sufficient to maintain compliance with the crankshaft and crankcase end clearance specifications in the Lycoming Table of Limits.

Instructions for repairing the crankcase thrust face are found in the latest revision of Lycoming Service Instruction No. 1354. This repair should bring the oil slinger clearance back into tolerance and should cure the leaking crankcase oil seal, which would also have been replaced during the reassembly of the engine. (Reference Textron Lycoming Key Reprints)

# Engine Hoses

As airplanes and engines attain age, there appears to be a need to reemphasize the inspection or replacement of engine hoses or lines carrying fuel, oil, or hydraulic fluid. The hose manufacturers definitely recommend regular inspection and replacement of all such hoses at engine overhaul even though they look good.

Age limit of rubber-steel or fiber banded hose has generally been established at four years. This limit of four years is generally considered to be "shelf" life. All hose manufactured for aircraft use is marked indicating the quarter year in which it was manufactured. The listing "4Q92" means the hose was manufactured in the fourth quarter of 1992. Maintenance personnel should not use hoses with a high "shelf" life age.

To eliminate relatively short "shelf" life limits, Textron Lycoming has phased in Teflon hoses with silicone coated fire sleeves. These are the only hoses, which are available for field replacement, and they will be found on engines shipped from the factory

Service Instruction No. 1274 lists the fuel and oil hoses used by Textron Lycoming. It also explains how the numbering system defines hose size. This instruction should be used as a reference anytime hoses are to be replaced. Textron Lycoming Service Bulletin No. 509 must also be complied with if rubber hose is used to carry low-lead aviation gasoline. Aeroquip, the manufacturer of hose used by Textron Lycoming, has recorded several failures of 601-type rubber hose. Although it is satisfactory for other purposes, this hose appears to be adversely affected by low-lead aviation gasoline. 601-type rubber hose used for low-lead aviation gasoline is to be replaced after no more than two years of use. Aeroquip and Textron Lycoming recommend that rubber hose be replaced with Teflon hose. Teflon hose is normally unaffected by many of the operating variables that contribute to rubber hose degradation. See chapter 19 under hoses for more on this subject. (Reference Textron Lycoming Key Reprints)

# Cylinder Base Nut Tightening

The need to constantly stress the correct cylinder base nut tightening procedure seems apparent. Operators in the field are occasionally having engine problems and malfunctioning after reinstalling cylinders, and not tightening the cylinder base nuts correctly. The latter tends to cause crankshaft bearing shifting, crankcase fretting or broken cylinder studs, and possible engine failure.

In order to properly reinstall cylinders; consult Textron Lycoming Service Instruction No. 1029. If you do not have a Lycoming engine then consult the engine manufacture for your engine.

Maintenance people should ensure that torque wrenches have been correctly calibrated before accomplishing cylinder base nut tightening. After reinstalling cylinders, a ground run of the engine should be accomplished as outlined in the Engine Operator's Manual," followed by a shutdown and inspection. Then the engine should be test flown normally, and following the flight, a good inspection of the engine should be made before returning the aircraft to routine use. Tightening engine hardware (nuts) should be accomplished every 100 hour or annual inspection. (Reference Textron Lycoming Key Reprints)

# Tip From The Hangar

**These are some of the more common questions asked at the Lycoming service hanger:**

**Question** — Do manufacture new, rebuilt, or overhauled engines require a break-in period that consists of cruise at low power settings?

**Answer** — Definitely not. Fly them as you would a high time engine. In fact, so-called "slow" flying may have harmful effects. The rings may not seat properly resulting in higher than normal oil consumption.

**Question** — At what rate of oil consumption does continued operation of the engine become a hazard?

**Answer** — Generally speaking, when the oil consumption reaches one quart per hour, corrective action should be taken. However, maximum permissible for each particular engine is listed in the engine operator's manual.

**Question** — What are the dangers of operating an engine with high oil consumption?

**Answer** — When excessive amounts of oil get past the rings, there is danger of the ring sticking or breaking with a dramatic rise in oil consumption. Then oil soaked carbon forms at a fast rate. At the same time, the presence of oil in the combustion chamber has the effect of lowering the octane rating of the fuel. Operating temperatures go up. We have now set up conditions inviting detonation and or preignition.

**Question** — If I can't get aviation fuel, may I use automotive fuel if octane rating is equal or higher?

**Answer** — No. As an engine manufacturer, even the use of automotive fuel where an STC has been issued is considered risky and is not recommended. There are 4 or 5 good reasons and all are important. They can be summed up in three words – potential engine failure.

**Question** — What is the most common cause of premature engine wear?

**Answer** — Dirt in the air entering the engine through the carburetor or injector due to worn-out air filter, torn induction hoses or broken air boxes, and then being carried through the engine by the oil.

**Question** — Does the spacer between the propeller and the engine serve any purpose other than streamlining the nacelle?

**Answer** — Yes. In many cases, moving the propeller forward, which increases the clearance between propeller and cowl increases propeller efficiency and reduces nacelle vibration.

**Question** — In some cases, we note a minor discrepancy between the engine operator's manual and the airplane Pilot's Operating Handbook. Which one should be followed?

**Answer** — The airframe Pilot's Operating Handbook. For various reasons, after the engine is installed in the airframe, operational techniques may be altered or certain restrictions may be placed on the engine. A simple example would be a placard restricting continuous operation in a certain RPM range.

**Question** — I fly an aircraft equipped with a fixed pitch propeller. During cruise I'm told to keep increasing the RPM as my cruising altitude is increased. Since I fly pretty high, in order to hold 65% power, I find the RPM is mostly at 2550 to 2600. Won't this high RPM reduce the engine life?

**Answer** — No. The higher RPM won't harm the engine or reduce service life. Remember that you are increasing the RPM only to hold the same power you had at a lower altitude at say, 2350 RPM.

**Question** — Is there really any difference between good automotive oil and aviation oil?

**Answer** — Yes indeed there is! Don't ever use automotive oil in your aircraft engine. These oils are now blended for use with unleaded fuels, and the additives in auto oil cause problems in an aircraft engine that operates at much higher temperatures than the automobile engine. Engine manufactures have encountered engines with holes burned in pistons due to the use of automotive oils that have an ash deposit causing preignition. It seems awfully hard to convince people who have had great success with the oil used in their car that it may not be used in their aircraft engine.

**NOTE** –It might be well to mention that I can't think of a quicker way to void your engine warranty than by using anything other than the recommended and FAA approved aviation fuels and oils.

**Question** — What are some common causes of excessive oil consumption other than the burning of oil due to high engine time?

**Answer** — Building up of crankcase pressure due to "blow-by" caused by ring wear may result in oil being blown out of the breather. The same thing can result from broken piston rings. Oil may be pumped overboard due to a faulty vacuum pump or faulty automotive type fuel pump.

**Question** — My dealer advised me to use straight mineral oil in my new engine until it's "broken in." How do I know when it's "broken in"?

**Answer** — When oil consumption has stabilized. Example: After continued checking of oil consumption you have determined the engine is consistently using one quart in a known number of hours. This period should not exceed 50 hours of operation.

**Question** — I have problems with lead fouling of spark plugs. What can I, as a pilot, do about it?

**Answer** — Several things. See that you have the correct spark plugs that are recommended by the engine manufacturer's charts, not oddballs recommended by some well-meaning friend. Avoid prolonged idling on the ground. Avoid power off descents. Lean out at cruise; even on short cross-country flights. Rotate plugs from bottom to top every 50 hours — or 25 if necessary. (Reference Little Flyers).

# Engine Ground Test

1. Face the aircraft into the wind.
2. Start the engine and observe the oil pressure gage. If adequate pressure is not indicated within 30 seconds shut the engine down and determine the cause. Operate the engine at 1000 RPM until the oil temperature has stabilized or reached 140 F. After warm up, the oil pressure should not be less than the minimum pressure specified in the applicable operator's manual.
3. Check magneto drop-off as described in the latest edition of the maintenance manual and Service Instruction such as Lycoming Service Instructions No. 1132.
4. Continue operation at 1000/1200 rpm for 15 minutes. Insure that cylinder head temperature, oil temperature and oil pressure is within the limits specified in the operator's manual. Shut the engine down and allow it to cool if necessary to complete this portion of the test. If any malfunction is noted, determine the cause and make the necessary correction before continuing with this test.
5. Start the engine again and monitor oil pressure. Increase engine speed to 1500 rpm for a 5-minute period. Cycle propeller pitch and perform feathering check as applicable per airframe manufacturer's recommendation.
6. Run engine to full-static, airframe-recommended power for a period of no more than 10 seconds.
7. After operating the engine at full power, allow it to cool down moderately. Check idle mixture adjustment prior to shutdown.
8. Inspect the engine for oil leaks.
9. Remove the oil suction screen and the oil pressure screen or oil filter to determine any contamination. If no contamination is evident, the aircraft is ready for flight-testing.

## *NOTE*

*Compile a log of all-pertinent data accumulated during both the ground testing and flight-testing.*

The purpose for engine break-in is to set the piston rings and stabilize the oil consumption. There is no difference or greater difficulty in seating the piston rings of a top overhauled engine versus a complete engine overhaul.

*NOTE*

*The maximum allowable oil consumption limits for all Textron Lycoming aircraft engines can be determined by using the following formula:* $.006 \times BHP \times 4 / 7.4 = Qt/Hr.$

# High Time Cylinders/Repairs

The aluminum alloy cylinder heads used on air-cooled aircraft engines are subject to high stresses while operating. In addition, they are heated and cooled with each engine start up and shut down. Over long periods of operation, these stresses can lead to fatigue and eventually the cylinder head may develop cracks.

Lycoming metallurgists argue that welding of cracks in aluminum cylinder heads is not likely to meet with long-term success. Therefore, an overhauled cylinder has little chance of being as serviceable as a new cylinder. Even if there were no cracks at the time of overhaul, metal fatigue is still a factor to be considered. But how? There is no record of time in use required for a cylinder assembly. An overhauled cylinder could have 4000, 6000, or 8000 hours or more when it is put on an overhauled engine. Even a cylinder from your own engine with only one trip to TBO may not make it to TBO a second time.

As a result of the scenario outlined above, Lycoming has for many years' recommended new cylinders when engines are overhauled. To practice what is being preached, Lycoming uses new cylinders on all engines shipped from the factory at Williamsport, including factory overhauls. It is less expensive to install new cylinders during the overhaul as compared to having the engine torn down once or twice for cylinder replacement before it reaches the recommended TBO as an overhauled engine. The added reliability must also be considered. (Reference Textron Lycoming Key Reprints)

# Low-Time Engine May Not Mean Quality and Value

Engine information is usually provided as hours of operation since new or from some major maintenance event. For example, 700 TTSN would indicate that this aircraft and engine have been flown for 700 hours since new from the factory. Other, but not all, engine related abbreviations include SMOH (hours since major overhaul, SPOH (hours since prop overhaul), STOH (hours since top overhaul), and SFRM (hours since factory rebuild). Assuming that the recommended TBO of the engine being considered is 1800 or 2000 hours, it would appear that hours of use in the 400 to 800-hour range would automatically make this engine a very valuable commodity. Unfortunately this is not always true, and therefore an advertisement like those discussed earlier may state numbers and facts, which are absolutely correct, but still misleading.

Consider a situation, which occurred recently. A Lycoming IO-360 engine with less than 700 hours since new was reported to be using oil at the rate of two-thirds quart per hour and losing oil pressure during flight. On closer examination, it was determined that deterioration and wear had caused metal contamination throughout the engine. An engine overhaul was necessary and it included replacement of items such as the camshaft, oil pump gears, and pistons. Why should an engine with less than 700 hours since new be in this sad state?

It should be apparent that the number of hours the engine has operated is only part of the story. We need to know all the facts if we are to understand what may have happened to this normally reliable engine, and also if we are to determine the value of a low-time engine in a pre-owned airplane.

The engine with metal contamination and less than 700 hours of operation had been installed brand new from the factory – MORE THAN 12 YEARS before. The engine logbook shows that during the first 10 years of service this engine had averaged less than four hours of flight time each month. Chances are excellent that there were some months when the engine was not flown at all.

Textron Lycoming Service Instruction No. 1009 states that the recommended TBO is based on the use of genuine Lycoming parts, average experience in operation, and continuous service. Continuous service assumes that the aircraft will not be out of service for any extended period of time. If an engine is to be out of service for longer than 30 days, it should be preserved as specified in Textron Lycoming Service Letter No. L180. Service Instruction No. 1009 also states that because of the variations in operation and maintenance, there can be no assurance that an individual operator will achieve the recommended TBO.

The point of this discussion is simple. A low-time engine may not add value to an aircraft, and the buyer should be aware of all factors, which may affect the condition and value of the engine. An engine, which is not flown frequently, is subject to deterioration as a result of not being used. When the engine does not achieve flight-operating temperatures on a regular basis, the moisture and acids that form as a result of combustion and condensation are not vaporized and eliminated through the exhaust and crankcase breather. As moisture and acids collect in the engine, they contribute to the formation of rust on the cylinder walls, camshaft, and tappets.

As the engine is run after rust has formed, the rust becomes a very fine abrasive causing internal engine wear, particularly to the camshaft and tappets. As these components wear, they make more metal which attacks the softer metals in the engine. Piston pin plugs are examples of parts that may wear rapidly when rust becomes an abrasive inside the engine. This wear could eventually lead to failure.

The infrequently flown engine is just one example of a low-time engine not meeting the expectations of a buyer or new owner. The term zero SMOH is always enticing since it indicates the engine has been overhauled, has zero hours since overhaul, and now may be expected to fly happily on through a full manufacturer recommended TBO. This will happen in some cases, but in others, there will not be a chance of this happening. It depends on the quality of the overhaul.

Textron Lycoming Service Bulletin No. 240 recommends parts to be replaced at overhaul regardless of the apparent condition of the old parts. The number of these new parts used in the engine at overhaul will probably determine the possibilities of achieving a full TBO. Consider that most overhauler's install reconditioned cylinders on the engines they overhaul. These cylinders are not traceable. There is no requirement to maintain a record of their previous history. They may have only 2000 hours of operation, but they could just as easily have 5000, 7000, or more hours of operation. Those cylinders may have been cracked and repaired by welding a procedure that Lycoming metallurgists do not recommend because the strength of a repaired cylinder head may be significantly less than that of a new head. There is no requirement to let a prospective engine buyer know if cylinders have been welded, and this cannot be determined even by close examination. The possibility of finding a reconditioned cylinder with cracks after a few hundred hours of operation is very real. Should this happen, it will be a costly experience.

The lesson to be learned here is a very old one "Buyer Beware." Whether you are looking at those "Aircraft for Sale" advertisements or looking for a replacement engine for an aircraft you already own, consider carefully what you are about to buy. What do you really know about the engine other than the low-time number? How much validity does that number really have? What questions can you ask which may help you to insure that this engine will meet your expectations?

Perhaps simply rereading the paragraphs you have just read may help you to formulate questions you want answered before taking the plunge. In the case of a low-time engine with a history of infrequent flight, borescope examination of the cylinders and an inspection of cam and tappet surfaces by a competent and knowledgeable A&P mechanic would be a very wise move. Always remember that low numbers in the hours of operation records do not guarantee reaching TBO with many long hours of trouble free operation. The buyer must investigate every detail of engine history as closely as possible, and be satisfied that the product does have the value, which the low hours of operation number suggests. (Reference Key Reprints Textron Lycoming dated 1996)

# Newly Overhauled Engine

Treat any airplane with a "fresh engine overhaul" as if the engine is high time. You are much, much better off buying an airplane with a run-out engine and having it overhauled where and how you want it done. It is impossible on a prepurchase inspection to tell how well an engine overhaul was performed. In a nutshell, the cost of a good engine overhaul exceeds the boost it gives to the selling price of the airplane. That's a given. Act accordingly.

Only a fool will put more money into the airplane than he or she expects to get out of at the sale. Assume the overhaul is worthless when negotiating. My rule of thumb is not to consider an overhaul worth its salt unless the engine has at least 200 hours on it since the overhaul, the owner can produce oil analysis records (talk with the analysis company) and the compression is at or close to new-overhaul tolerances.

# Fuel Systems

Many problems with lightweight aircraft engines can be directly traced to the type of fuel used. Many states allow automotive fuels to be sold containing 10 percent alcohol without requiring a label stating so. Alcohol can cause serious problems in aircraft engines so first ensure that the fuel source is a reliable one. Check to see if the aircraft you want to purchase has an STC to use automotive fuel.

**Test for Alcohol in Automotive Fuel.** Take a thin glass jar, mark it one inch from the bottom of the jar with tape or indelible ink, and fill the jar with water up to that mark. Fill the jar to the top with a sample of the fuel to be tested. There is a clear separation between the water and the fuel. Put the lid on the jar and shake. Let it settle for about a minute and check. If the "water" line is now above the first mark, the fuel has alcohol in it. Try another source for fuel and do another test.

## Fuel Primer System

Perform a careful inspection of fuel primer bulbs fitted in suction lines because they deteriorate over time and are a possible source of air leaks, resulting in a lean mixture. Primer bulbs with plastic one-way valves have been known to break loose and completely block the fuel in the fuel line. Positioning the fuel line so the fuel flows upward through the primer bulb will help minimize the possibility of this problem occurring. A permanently fitted fuel pressure gage is recommended because it can check fuel system operation during engine break-in and fuel flow during extreme angles of attack.

## Filters, Fuel Lines, and Throttles Inspection

Finger screens in fuel tanks should be checked every 10 hours for debris or varnish build up from fuel. Nylon mesh fuel filters are preferred with 2 cycle engines. Paper element filters should be avoided because they may severely and invisibly restrict the fuel flow. This is due to a reaction between water and oil detergents. The fuel filter should be distinctly located, between the fuel pump and the carburetors, to facilitate pre-flight inspection and avoid the possibility of air leaks on the suction side.

Check plastic fuel lines for age hardness, discoloration, and over all condition. Fuel line attach points should be checked before each flight. Always clamp a fuel line at the inlet and outlet. A slip-on line might slip off in flight. Leave a little slack in the fuel lines to minimize cracking from vibration.

## Fuel Markings

Code of Federal Regulations Part 23, Section 23.1557I(1), requires that aircraft fuel filler openings be marked to show the word "FUEL" and the minimum fuel grade or designation for the engines. In order that these markings retain their effectiveness, regulations also require that they be kept fresh and clean. It follows, therefore, that frequent washing and occasional painting will be necessary to retain clear legibility.

## Fuel Tank Inspection

Inspect fuel tanks and filler caps for proper alignment, security of attachment, and evidence of leaks. Be certain that vents and vent lines are free from obstructions. Examine fuel lines and connections for leaks, cracks, chafing, and security of attachment. Ensure that overflow and drain lines are not kinked or broken, and that they extend beyond the aircraft skin line (overboard).

Fuel systems incorporate fuel tank sumps and sediment bowls to trap water that could pass through the fuel lines to the engine. Periodically drain fuel from the tank sumps and the sediment bowl, and examine for water or other contamination. Replace and safety drain plugs.

Tests have shown that, in some cases, relatively large quantities of fuel must be drained before an indication of water is noted. Determine the characteristics of your aircraft and drain accordingly. The carburetor, fuel lines, and tank sumps should be drained, if an abnormal amount of water is detected in the main fuel strainers.

## Microbiological Fuel Contamination and Corrosion

Micro-organic growth thrives in turbine fuel and appears as a soapy, slippery slime on the inside surfaces of fuel storage tanks. Microorganisms of bacteria and fungi multiply rapidly and may cause serious corrosion in aircraft fuel tanks, as well as clog fuel filters, screens, and control units. Therefore, turbine fuel storage tanks should be checked frequently for the presence of slime or micro-organic growth. If found, the tank should be cleaned thoroughly to assure removal of the micro-organic growth and prevent further contamination.

Microbiological contamination in turbine fuel is caused by bacteria and fungi, which feed on the constituents of the turbine fuel. The result is sludge, or mat deposit, which has been found in some aircraft fuel tanks and is often loosely, referred to as green slime. However, some deposits have been found in various shades of grey, brown, red, and white. If allowed to develop and grow in the aircraft fuel tanks, microbiological contamination can cause a myriad of problems not the least of which is severe aluminum alloy corrosion in the aircraft integral fuel tanks.

# CHAPTER 9

## PROPELLERS

# Propeller Introduction

Propellers, before the propeller is inspected it should be cleaned with a solution of mild soap and water to remove dirt, grass stains, etc. Propellers should be inspected for pitting (none allowed), nicks, cracks (none allowed), and corrosion, especially on the leading edge and face (none allowed). A four-power magnifying glass will aid in these inspections. The propeller should be inspected in accordance with the propeller manual and the propeller Type Certificate Data Sheet. All AD's should be signed off in the propeller or airframe maintenance records.

For aircraft equipped with adjustable propellers the inspection becomes very serious. There are several very expensive AD's that affect the blade shoulders, grooves, hubs, and retaining hardware. The maintenance record check will identify these as being complied with or not. If no record can be found then assume the AD's have not been complied with. Now we are talking major money for repairs. Be aware if the aircraft has been operated by a Part 135 or Part 121 air carrier their propellers are required to be overhaul at certain intervals as recommended by the manufacture. Under Part 91 that same propeller does not have to be overhauled. Also, if you overhaul the engine you should overhaul the propeller at the same time. This is not required, but is good maintenance practices.

The reason to overhaul both at the same time is most propellers use engine oil to adjust pitch on the blades. All the sludge in the engine, metal from bearing, bushing, and water end up in the hub of the propellers. If you change out the engine without at least having the propeller hub cleaned all the old sludge end up back in the engine or vice verse. Engine and propeller rebuilders and manufactures know this and will not warranty their products if this happens.

Aircraft maintenance personnel should adhere to the following procedures during propeller inspections:

1. Airworthiness Directives (AD's), propeller manufacturers' manuals, service letters, and bulletins specify methods and limits for blade maintenance, inspection, repair, and removal from service. When a manufacturer's data specifies that major repairs to a specific model blade or other propeller components be permitted, those repairs may be accomplished only by an appropriately certificated and rated propeller repair facility. All other propeller blade maintenance and minor repairs, such as removal of minor nicks, scratches, small areas of surface corrosion, and minor ice control boot repairs, can be accomplished only by an FAA-certificated mechanic using the practices and techniques specified by the propeller manufacturer's service data.

2. FAA data on propeller failures indicates that the majority of blade failures occur in the blade tip region, usually within several inches from the tip. However, a blade failure can occur along any portion of a blade including the midblade, shank, and hub, particularly when nicks, scratches, corrosion, and cracks are present. Therefore, during propeller inspection and routine maintenance, it is important that the entire blade be inspected.

3. Corrosion may be present on propeller blades in varying amounts. Prior to performing any inspection process, maintenance personnel should examine the specific type and extent of the corrosion and become familiar with the propeller manufacturer's recommended corrosion removal limitations and practices.

4. Corrosion, other than small areas (**6 square inches or less**) of light surface type corrosion, may require propeller removal and reconditioning by a qualified propeller repair facility. When intergranular corrosion is present, the repair can be properly accomplished only by an appropriately certificated propeller repair facility. Corrosion pitting under propeller blade decals should be removed as described in the propeller manufacturer's service bulletins and applicable AD's.

5. Unauthorized straightening of blades following ground strikes or other damage can create conditions that lead to immediate blade failure. Careful inspection of the leading edges and the flat face portion of the blade may sometimes detect these unapproved repairs. Any deviation of the flat portion such as bows or kinks may indicate unauthorized straightening of the blade. Sighting along the leading edge of a propeller blade for any signs of bending can provide evidence of unapproved blade straightening. Blades should be examined for any discoloration that would indicate unauthorized heating. Blades that have been heated for any repair must be rejected, since only cold straightening is authorized. All blades showing evidence of unapproved repairs should be rejected. When bent propellers are shipped to an approved repair facility for inspection and repair, the propeller should never be straightened by field service personnel to facilitate shipping, as this procedure can conceal damage. Propeller tip damage will sometimes lead maintenance personnel to consider removing damaged material from the blade tips. However, propellers are often "tuned" to the aircraft engine and airframe resonant frequency by being manufactured with a particular diameter to minimize vibration. Unless the manufacturer specifically permits shortening of the blades on a particular propeller, any shortening of the blades will probably create an unairworthy condition. When conditions indicate, inspect blade tips for evidence of shortening and, if necessary, the propeller diameter should be measured to determine if it has been changed by an unauthorized repair.

6. Accurate propeller tracking requires chocking the aircraft in a stationary position and ensuring that the engine crankshaft is tight against the thrust bearing. A blade-tracking datum can be made simply by placing a block on the ground in front of the aircraft in the propeller arc. Raise the block as required to obtain a clearance between the blade tip (prop blade vertical) and datum block not exceeding 1/4-inch. Scribe a line on the block next to the blade tip position. Pull all the blades past the scribed datum. No blade should deviate more than 1/16-inch from the plane of rotation as defined by the scribe mark. When inspecting the propeller track, blades should be gently rocked to detect any possible looseness. Propeller blades exhibiting any looseness or out-of-track conditions exceeding 1/16-inch should not be returned to service without inspection/repair by an appropriately rated propeller repair facility.

The following list is a general guideline for areas that may be defective.

1. Areas requiring plating may only be painted. It is acceptable to paint over plating.
2. Attachment bolts for external counterweights should be inspected for multiple holes. All hardware is required to be replaced at overhaul. More than one bolt hole for safetying may indicate prior service.
3. Possible improper "shot peening" of the outer radius of each blade. Some propeller blades may have been sanded smooth or not properly "peened" in the outer area. The size of the "peening" media was incorrect and may be detected by the course texture of the "peened" surface, which should be uniform in the coverage area.
4. Any questionable items concerning these conditions should be investigated and evaluated by a qualified and appropriately rated propeller repair station.

# Two Blades or Three

Some of the current aircraft are available with a choice of a standard two-blade or optional three-blade propeller. Since the three-blade option can cost an additional $1000 plus or more per engine, and weight 18-20 pounds extra it would be worthwhile to know what you're really getting for the investment.

A three bladed propeller gets you better ground clearance, less noise, and less vibration. The improved ground clearance is achieved because a three-blade propeller can do its job with fewer diameters that it's two-blade counterpart. The shorter blades also have slower tip speeds, which cuts down the noise. This is a high-priority item now, due to environment whack's, building their homes next to airports, which caused regulations, and as a result, some new aircraft have three-blade propellers as standard equipment.

With shorter blades to work with, the designer of a twin can mount the engines closer to the fuselage, reducing the effect of adverse yaw in an engine-out situation. However, this benefit can be accompanied by increased cabin noise. Then there's the matter of "thump," caused by the propeller slipstream beating against the airplane. A three-bladed propeller creates more thumps, but each thump has less impact.

# Propeller Hubs

## Fixed Pitch

Inspection procedures require removal of the propeller spinner for examination of the prop hub area.
1. Cracks may be present in the hub area between or adjacent to bolt holes and along the hub pilot bore.
2. Cracks in these areas cannot be repaired and require immediate scrapping of the propeller.

Propeller attach bolts should be examined for looseness or an unsafetied or cracked condition.
1. Cracked or broken bolts are usually the result of overtorquing.
2. Correct torquing procedures require all bolt threads to be dry, clean, and free of any lubrication prior to torquing.

## Controllable Pitch

Complete inspection/servicing requires the removal of the spinner for examination and servicing of the propeller hub and blade clamp area. All inspection and servicing of the pitch control mechanism should follow the recommendations of the propeller, engine, and airframe manufacturer. All propeller AD's and manufacturers' service bulletins must be checked for compliance.

The hub, blade clamps, and pitch change mechanisms should be inspected for corrosion from all sources, including rain, snow, and bird droppings that may have entered through spinner openings. Examine the hub area for oil and grease leaks, missing lubricaps, and leaking or missing zerk fittings. When servicing the propeller thrust bearings through zerk fittings in the blade clamps, the rear zerk fitting on each clamp must be removed to avoid extruding grease past the bearing grease seal and damaging the seal. Lubricaps should then be pressed over the ends of all zerk fittings.

Propeller domes should be checked for leaks both at the seals and on the fill valve (if so equipped). The dome valve may be leak-tested by applying soapy water over the fill valve end. Domes should be serviced only with nitrogen or dry air in accordance with the manufacturer's recommendations. When propeller domes are inspected and found filled with oil, the propeller should be removed and inspected/repaired by an appropriately rated repair facility.

Fiber block pitch-change mechanisms should be inspected for deterioration, fit, and the security of the pitch-clamp forks.

Certain models of full-feathering propellers utilize spring-loaded pins to retain the feathered blade position. Spring and pin units should be cleaned, inspected, and relubricated as per the manufacturer's recommendations and applicable AD's.

Pitch change counterweights on blade clamps should be inspected for security, safety, and to ensure that adequate counterweight clearance exists within the spinner.

# Propeller Balancing

Propellers can become imbalanced for a variety of reasons. There have been a number of instances where the process of moving an aircraft by pushing or pulling on the propeller blades has moved the blades to an out-of-track condition, creating an imbalance. Propeller damage, however, remains the major contributor to propeller imbalance. Unauthorized or improper repair of propeller spinners has also been identified as a cause of propeller imbalance. Propellers can be balanced by two methods: static balancing and dynamic balancing.

**Static Balancing**. Only removing the propellers and evaluating the vertical and horizontal balance on a special fixture can properly statically balance propellers. Propeller static balancing should be accomplished only by a properly certificated and rated propeller repair facility.

**Dynamic Balancing.** Certain models of propellers may be dynamically balanced in place on the aircraft. When applicable, the aircraft maintenance manual will describe the specific procedures for adding dynamic balance weights. These are usually installed on the propeller spinner backing plate using specialized dynamic-balancing equipment to determine exact weight balance values. Unless the aircraft maintenance manual authorizes dynamic balancing for a specific model, propeller balancing should be limited to static balancing.

# Propeller Vibration

Vibration is the source of many malfunctions and defects that occur throughout the life of the aircraft. Not only will vibration affect parts that are loose or poorly installed, but it will also accelerate wear and cause the ultimate failure of others. There are two types of vibration in aircraft operation low frequency and high frequency.

**Low Frequency** (usually noticeable vibration). A malfunctioning powerplant or propeller, worn engine mounting pads, looseness of the aircraft structure, or improper rigging, usually causes low frequency vibration. The problem causing vibration should be corrected as soon as discovered since it will cause abnormal wear between moving parts of the aircraft and may induce failure in any number of other aircraft parts.

**High Frequency** (less noticeable vibration). High frequency vibration is caused by inherent vibration characteristics of the rotating masses in the engine and propeller. It can also be caused by aerodynamic forces acting through the propeller or by engine firing impulses. Special instruments usually chart high frequency vibrations at the time the aircraft is type-certificated by the FAA. When harmful vibration frequencies are found, placards are installed indicating the engine operating ranges, which must be avoided.

**Factors of Vibration Damage.** The factors of vibration damage can be grouped into three categories: fatigue, excessive clearance, and poor installation. These points should be considered when inspecting for the effects of vibration.

**Fatigue.** Fatigue is the weakening and/or eventual failure of a member due to the cumulative effects of repetitive loads, which cause a change in the molecular structure of the part. Fatigue itself cannot be detected or measured while it is taking place except, possibly, under laboratory conditions. Its effects are usually made known by the ultimate failure of a part. The best prevention against fatigue damage is to maintain a smoothly running powerplant. In addition, control excessive or abnormal looseness in other components of the aircraft by good maintenance practices, particularly engine mounting pads, which are designed to isolate and absorb vibration.

With the above in mind, it is easily understood why the various components must be properly mounted and secured to resist the damaging effects of vibration. Copper lines are especially susceptible to fatigue and become hard and brittle when subjected to vibration. The lines should be periodically replaced or removed and annealed to restore the original softness.

**Excessive Clearance**. Excessive clearances accelerate the wear rates of all components in which they exist and can contribute to the initiation of flutter. Flutter is an aerodynamic function, wherein oscillating high loads are imposed on the affected movable surfaces and can result in rapid fatigue failure of critical areas, such as control surface hinge fittings and attachments. Wear rates are extremely high during flutter. It is very important to maintain clearance within the limit established by the manufacturer.

# Tachometer Inspection

Due to the exceptionally high stresses that may be generated by particular propeller/engine combinations at certain engine revolutions per minute (RPM), many propeller and aircraft manufacturers have established areas of RPM restrictions and other restrictions on maximum RPM for some models. Some RPM limits have never exceed values as close as 3 percent of the maximum RPM permitted, and a slow-running tachometer can cause an engine to run past the maximum RPM limits. Since there are no post-manufacture accuracy requirements for engine tachometers, tachometer inaccuracy could be a direct cause of propeller failure, excessive vibration, or unscheduled maintenance. Tachometer accuracy should always be checked during normal maintenance intervals or sooner if indicators such as excessive vibration or aircraft performance changes might indicate inaccurate RPM readings.

# Propeller Records

Maintenance records are a required part of a system of aircraft maintenance. Propeller maintenance recordkeeping responsibility is ultimately assigned to the owner/operator in accordance with 14 CFR Part 91 section 91.405. Section 43.11 requires that a record of total time in service be maintained for each propeller. In some cases, lack of records may require recompliance with a particular propeller AD. Propeller logbooks are available from various sources, including the propeller manufacturer.

# Numbers of Blades

It is not unusual to observe that aircraft powered by piston or turboprop engines often feature different numbers of propeller blades—ranging from two or three on many light general aviation aircraft to four or more. Research shows eight is the maximum ever used on large transport planes. The reason for this is most often related to the power produced by the engine in question—more powerful engines require more propeller blades.

So why is it that a more powerful engine would need more propeller blades? To understand this problem, we need to realize that a propeller must be tailored to the specific needs of an engine. The job of the propeller is to "absorb" the power produced by the engine and transmits that power to the airflow passing through the propeller disk. Thus, energy is added to the air to speed it up and generate a thrust force on the propeller blades. If the propeller and engine are not properly matched depending on the power of the engine, both become inefficient and performance suffers.

As engine power increases, the aircraft designer has a limited number of options to design a propeller capable of efficiently absorbing that greater power:

1. **Increase the blade angle (or the pitch) of the propeller blades**. In so doing, the angle of attack of the blades increases allowing the blades to impart greater energy to the airflow.
2. **Increase the diameter of the propeller disk; i.e. make the blades longer**. The blades will therefore transfer more energy by affecting a larger volume of air.
3. **Increase the revolutions per minute of the propeller**. The same amount of energy is transferred to the air but in a shorter time.

4. **Increase the camber (or curvature) of the blade airfoil.** A propeller blade is composed of airfoil shapes just like a wing is. Increasing the camber of a propeller blade creates a greater thrust force just like increasing the camber of a wing creates a greater lift force.

5. **Increase the chord (or width) of the propeller blades.**

6. **Increase the number of blades.** Although we have discussed a number of possible solutions, many of these options create more problems than they solve.

7. **Blade angle:** The pitch of the blade is set by the angle that optimizes the aerodynamic efficiency of the blade. If we change the angle, we lose one kind of efficiency in order to gain another making this a very unattractive alternative.

8. **Blade length:** While increasing tip speed is a significant issue (see the next point), size constraints are usually the greatest problem with this option. As the propeller size increases, the landing gear become longer to avoid scraping the blade tips on the runway, and this change has a knock-on effect on a number of structural and weight issues.

9. **Revolutions per minute:** For the same propeller diameter, the blade tips travel faster and faster as the rotational speed increases. Eventually, the blade tips become supersonic where shock waves form, drag increases substantially, and efficiency plummets.

10. **Airfoil camber:** The blade airfoils are chosen for optimum aerodynamic efficiency. By changing sections, we again sacrifice one kind of efficiency for another. Increasing camber may also result in problems with the blade structure.

This leaves us with the final two options, increasing the blade chord or the number of blades. Both result in increasing the **solidity** of the propeller disk. Solidity simply refers to the area of the propeller disk that is occupied by solid components (the blades) versus that area open to the airflow. As solidity increases, a propeller can transfer more power to the air.

While increasing the blade chord is the easier option, it is less efficient because we decrease the aspect ratio of the blades resulting in some loss of aerodynamic efficiency. Thus, increasing the number of blades is the most attractive approach. As the power of engines increased over the years, aircraft designers adopted increasingly more propeller blades. Once they ran out of room on the propeller hub, designers adopted twin contra-rotating propellers on the same engine, such as those used on the Tu-95, which feature a total of eight blades per engine.

# Propeller Spinners/Repairs

Many aircraft are operating with propeller spinners that have been repaired due to cracks and/or enlarged screw attachment holes. These repairs consist of welding and/or installation of patches and are not authorized by most manufacturers. In cases of enlarged attachment holes, many operators are installing "fender" washers (large OD with small ID) to cover up the enlarged hole.

Most aircraft and propeller manufacturers do not approve this practice because an out-of-balance condition may result. An out-of-balance condition may ultimately lead to disintegration of the spinner and a serious compromise of safety. For the reasons previously given, the following manufacturers have issued their policy on propeller spinner repair:

**BEECHCRAFT**: No repairs are allowed that will affect balance.

**CESSNA**: Repairs are allowed provided the spinner is only cracked. Should the spinner have a piece of metal missing, no repairs are allowed. Caution should be exercised to assure that the spinner is not a McCauley manufactured spinner.

**PIPER:** There are no authorized repairs whatsoever.

**HARTZELL:** No modification or repairs are to be made. This is to include "patches" and doublers of any type. The only known exception to this policy is repairs performed on PA 31 series aircraft propeller spinners by the holder of a Supplemental Type Certificate (STC) located in Tucker, Georgia. Also, it should be noted that propeller installations might not always use a Hartzell spinner. A Piper product, for example, may have a Piper spinner installed. It is recommended that the spinner manufacturer be determined before replacement of the spinner. Service Letter HC-SL-61-91 any repairs will require a Field Approval from the FAA.

**McCAULEY**: There are no authorized repairs whatsoever. Service Letter 1992-12C the part must be replaced. There are no repairs permitted on any McCauley spinner, spinner front support, or spinner bulkhead. The following can be used as a guideline to determine airworthiness:

1. Scratches and minor dents no repairs required.
2. Cracks spinner must be replaced.

The maximum allowable depth for wear inside spinners shell due to from support contact is 0.015 inch. No rework is necessary. Any spinner shell showing wear indications beyond this limit must be replaced

**SENSENICH**: Policy is to reference the aircraft maintenance manuals.

Operators should bear in mind that any unauthorized repair renders the aircraft unairworthy in accordance with the 14 CFR part 43 section 43.13.

Spinner assemblies should be inspected during installation in accordance with the propeller or aircraft manufacturer's guidelines. Inspect spinners and backplates for warping, cracks, looseness, missing parts, fasteners, improper repairs, or unauthorized modifications (including addition of balance weights). Any repair of a spinner must be carefully evaluated prior to return to service, since a repair that adds weight to a spinner can create imbalance. Unauthorized or improper repair of propeller spinners has also been identified as a cause of propeller imbalance.

Having said all the above there is one exception to the rule, which is certified Repair Stations working under Part 145, that have developed process specification, which have been accepted by the FAA. This will allow certain repair stations with an limited rating to repair some spinners by a welding process, which is on the repair station Operating Limitation of the Operation Specifications. Be advised before you send your spinner off to a shop to be welded I would suggest you have that Repair Station send you a copy of their ratings showing that they can and are allowed by the FAA to weld your spinner and approve it for return to service.

# Spinner Chrome plating

Chrome plating spinners is strongly discouraged by most spinner manufactures. After time the chrome will start to peel off and the chrome plating can lead to spinner fatigue cracking. In most cases chrome plating will void any warranty. Any chrome plating will require a Field Approval from the FAA.

On several aircraft models the spinner bulkhead is not shaped to the spinners and consequently becomes stressed after installing the mounting screws. Almost all of the cracks go through the nut plate rivet holes and continue forward. Apart from the potential danger of flying debris, it has become a costly endeavor for the operator.

Although vibration due to unbalance may have caused some spinner bulkhead failures, I believe most spinner problems are due to the following practices while the airplane is on the ground:

1. Airplanes are moved by using the propeller as a tow bar. Side loads are exerted on the spinner to change direction during movement. Remedy: use tow bar when moving airplane.

2. Pulling down on the spinner checks nose gear strut extension. Remedy: exert downward pressure on both propeller blades outboard of the spinner.

# Spinner Maintenance Record Entries

Federal Aviation Regulation (CFR) Part 43 section 43.9 states in pertinent parts as follows: "Each person who performs maintenance on an aircraft shall make an entry in the maintenance record of that equipment containing the following information: a description of the work, the date of completion of the work, and the name of the person performing the work." Some recent examples of possible violations of this rule have been brought to the attention of the FAA. Often aircraft mechanics are being employed to perform maintenance on aircraft at the request of owners. This maintenance included the removal of propeller spinners, tail cones, and access panels from the aircraft in order that the agency could inspect the aircraft internally. In most cases this "maintenance" is performed without the required entries being made in the aircraft records. Even removing spinners and access plates is considered maintenance.

The mechanic performing maintenance/inspection is responsible for making the record entry for the work he/she performed, and would be in violation of the CFR Part 43 section 43.5 and 43.9 if the record entry were not completed.

# Propeller Polishing Blades

One question I keep getting, can I polish my propeller blades? **Yes and No**. Polishing the blades removes the protective paint, anodize layer, and encourages corrosion. The warranty may also be voided. Having paint on your propeller is a certification rule under Part 21.

You every wonder why an FAA Inspector stops in front of your aircraft and you get ramped check? It may be the shinny propeller that says; come look at me.

I know having a polished propeller is nice to look at and makes your aircraft stand out. However, it is not in the best interest of the people on the ground not knowing if you propeller has pitting corrosion caused by the polishing. CFR A35.3 explains the manufacture has to provide data to the extent necessary for maintenance or preventive maintenance. For aircraft with a Part 23 or CAR-3 (Airworthiness Standards) Part 23 section 23.609 states each part of the structure must be suitable protected against deterioration or loss of strength in service due to weathering, corrosion, and abrasion.

The rule states the manufacture must provide data to inspect and maintain the propeller and removing the paint on the back or face of a propeller is contrary to the manufactures data. In McCauley propeller Standard Practices Manual SPM100-1, it clearly states to paint hubs to prevent corrosion using Sherwin Williams's products per table 602. If the hubs have been alodined, it must be painted. It futher states to paint the camber side of blade from shank to tip with one tack coat followed by wet coat(s) of flat black paint or gray paint, per appropriate paint scheme. Paint the face side flat black unless otherwise specified.

Tip stripes indicated on paint scheme are to be painted on the camber side only unless otherwise specified.

If you use a dry film paint thickness on constant speed and full feathering propeller blades should be a minimum of 3 mils thick, and on turbine propellers a minimum of 6 mils thick.

McCauley has a large **WARNING** note: This information is not to be used to polish blades of different model number or blades not originally marked with a "P". McCauley made certain blades [X]-09HX-[X]-[X][X] EP blades that can be polished only. If you do not have one of these blades on your aircraft it may have to be painted. None of these blades are fixed pitch; sorry guys paint your blades.

Hamilton Standard repair manual calls out for corrosion treatment (alodine) and paint. So if you send your propeller to a repair station for overhaul or repairs is may come back with the approved paint. In the Service Manual section 5 Service Inspection, Maintenance, and Lubrication paragraph 3. Maintenance(c)(3) Aluminum Alloy Blades- states: "In special cases where a high polish is desired, a responsible party may authorize the use of a good grade of metal polish, provided that upon completion of the polishing all traces of polish are immediately removed and the blades cleaned and coated with a thin film of clean engine oil." In addition this manual calls out certain inspections requirements if you elect to polish your blades.

If you have Hamilton Standard Constant Speed 2B20 propeller such as installed on many Cessna CE-195 aircraft you may be allowed to have a polished propeller. However, you have to have the current maintenance manual that explains the Instructions for Continued Airworthiness (ICA). Without the manual how would you know what maintenance to perform (corrosion preventive) and how often to perform it?

The bottom line here is if the aircraft has a polished propeller installed there should be a maintenance record entry in the propeller logbook or airframe logbook indicating maintenance performed in accordance with the ICA and referenced to the maintenance manual data. If you do not see any propeller maintenance records entries explaining the shinny propeller it should be removed and sent to a propeller repair station for inspection.

If you have a shinny propeller installed on your aircraft and have no documentation allowing it during an 100-hour or annual inspection the aircraft **CAN NOT** be approved for return to service in an airworthy condition by maintenance personnel. If an A&P/IA does approve your propeller for return to service without the proper documentation they are putting their certificates at risk. So please don't put a mechanic in a position to sign off an undocumented propeller installation and repair it is their livelihood we are talking about here.

The proper way is for the mechanic to sign off the inspection and note the aircraft is UNAIRWORTHY due to the propeller not meeting the requirements of Part 21. When the propeller finish is restored by a proper certificated propeller repair station and reinstalled on the aircraft an A&P will clear the unairworthy condition and approve the aircraft for return to service only for the work performed of reinstalling the propeller.

As a side note if an owner/operator operates the aircraft and is ramped inspected by a FAA Inspector every flight is a violation unless they can prove the shinny propeller is legally installed. The FAA will check the pilots flight logs for the number of flight times $1,100.00 per flight. Having your aircraft look good may cost you in the end more than it's worth.

Maintenance records are a required part of a system of aircraft maintenance. Propeller maintenance record keeping responsibility is ultimately assigned to the owner/operator in accordance with FAR Part 91. In some cases, owner and maintenance personnel will not make an record entry. This is contrary to FAR Part 43.5, even preventive maintenance such as filing out nicks requires an record entry. Remember if you have a shinny propeller it will require preventive maintenance and it is required to be logged in the maintenance record. Not performing a preventive maintenance record entry will void the airworthiness of your shinny propeller.

# CHAPTER 10

## LANDING GEAR

# Landing Gear System Inspection

Because of the stresses and pressures acting on the landing gear, inspection, servicing, and other maintenance becomes a continuous process. The most important job in the maintenance of the aircraft landing gear system is thorough, accurate inspections. To properly perform the inspections, all surfaces should be cleaned to ensure that no trouble spots go undetected.

It will be necessary to inspect:

1.  Shock struts.
2.  Shimmy dampers.
3.  Wheels, wheel bearings, tires, and brakes if possible rotate the wheels and listen for smoothness.
4.  During this inspection, check for the presence of installed ground safety locks.
5.  Check landing gear position indicators, lights, and warning horns for operation.
6.  Check emergency control handles and systems for proper position and condition.
7.  Inspect landing gear wheels for cleanliness, corrosion, and cracks.
8.  Check wheel tie bolts for looseness.
9.  Examine anti-skid wiring for deterioration.
10. Check tires for wear cuts, deterioration, presence of grease or oil, alignment of slippage marks, and proper inflation.
11. Inspect the landing gear mechanism for condition, operation, and proper adjustment.
12. Lubricate the landing gear, including the nose wheel steering.
13. Check steering system cables for wear, broken strands, alignment, and safetying; inspect landing gear shock struts for such conditions as cracks, corrosion, breaks, and security.
14. Where applicable, check the brake clearances.
15. Inspect wheels for damage and cracks. A bent or distorted wheel flange generally indicates that it is cracked or broken.
16. Inspect bolts for condition and security of attachment; check the condition of wheel bearings. With the wheel installed on the axle, check excessive side play by moving the wheel back and forth against the thrust washer and adjusting nut.
17. Perform a close visual inspection of the main landing gear for cracks in the vicinity of welds. Examine attachment fittings for condition and elongation of bolt holes.
18. Landing gear that retracts into the wing, nacelle, or fuselage structure should be cleaned and checked frequently for defects and proper operation. Particular attention should be given to locking mechanisms, drag struts, shock strut, stops, linkages, and alignment. Be sure the shock strut is properly inflated and the piston is clean and oiled.
19. Examine fairing doors for satisfactory operation, proper rigging, and for loose or broken hinges.

Nickel and chromium platings are used extensively as protective and wear resistant coatings over high strength steel parts (landing gear journals, shock strut pistons, etc.). Chromium and nickel plate provides protection by forming a somewhat impervious physical coat over the underlying base metal. When breaks occur in the surface, the protection is destroyed.

The amount of reworking that can be performed on chromium and nickel-plated components are limited. This is due to the critical requirements to which such components are subjected.

The rework should consist of light buffing to remove corrosion products and produce the required smoothness. This is permissible, provided the buffing does not take the plating below the minimum allowable thickness.

Wrinkled fabric or metal skin detected in the area of the attachment firings should be referred to a qualified mechanic or repair station for detailed inspection and analysis.

Spring steel shock absorbers require little maintenance. Check for cracks in the fuselage attachment brackets and the axle attachment area. Inspect the strut in the step attachment area.

Excessive play between fittings may be detected more readily if the wheel is off the ground and the landing gear shaken vigorously in a fore and aft direction, as well as up and down. If noticeable clearance is detected at any of the attachment points, the bolts should be removed and inspected for wear or distortion. Defective bolts should be replaced immediately and distorted bushings and fittings repaired or replaced as recommended by the manufacturer. Since there will be considerable movement at the' bearing surface, it is essential that they be inspected carefully and lubricated properly at frequent intervals.

Inspect shock struts for cracks, bowing, and security of attachment. Check braces and fittings for general condition and possible defects.

**Inspect the nose wheel assembly** for general condition and security of attachment. Examine linkage, trusses, and members for evidence of undue wear or distortion. Ensure that all bolts, studs, and nuts are secure with no indication of excessive wear and that they are properly safetied. If a shimmy damper is installed, ensure that it is operating satisfactorily and that the steering mechanism is properly rigged.

# Landing Gear Retracting

When new or retread tires are installed, a landing gear retraction test should be performed to check for proper clearance. Improper tire size may cause the gear to hang up in the wheel well. Check main gear, nose gear, or tail gear uplock and downlock mechanisms for general condition and proper operation. Refer to the manufacturer's service instructions for proper lubrication of retractable landing gear.

Inspect the power sources and the retracting mechanism of the main gear, nose gear or tail gear for general condition, defects, and security of attachment. Determine that actuating cylinders, sprockets, universals, chains, and drive gears are in good condition and within the manufacturer's tolerance. Clean and lubricate using cleaning fluids and lubricants recommended by the manufacturer of the aircraft.

Inspect the aircraft structure to which the landing gear is attached for distortion, cracks, and general condition. Be sure that all bolts and rivets are intact and secure.

Check the grease fittings and ensure grease will pass through the fitting. The FAA has issued an Airworthiness Alert for improper manufactured fittings that are not drilled properly. This prevents the grease from lubricating the required parts.

# Landing Gear Shock Absorbers

Regardless of the type of landing gear installed, a shock absorbing mechanism is provided to absorb the landing loads. Aircraft manufacturers use a number of different shock absorbing devices.

When shock cords are employed, inspect for general condition, cleanliness, stretching, and fraying. Shock cords must be kept free of gasoline and oil, both of which deteriorate rubber products. Follow the manufacturer recommendations regarding life limits of the replacement of shock cords.

Perform a close visual inspection of the main landing gear for cracks in the vicinity of welds. Examine attachment fittings for condition and elongation of boltholes.

Spring steel shock absorbers require little maintenance. Check for cracks in the fuselage attachment brackets and the axle attachment area. Inspect the strut in the step attachment area.

Excessive play between fittings may be detected more readily if the wheel is off the ground and the landing gear shaken vigorously in a fore and aft direction, as well as up and down. If noticeable clearance is detected at any of the attachment points, the bolts should be removed and inspected for wear or distortion. Defective bolts should be replaced immediately and distorted bushings and fittings repaired or replaced as recommended by the manufacturer. Since there will be considerable movement at the bearing surface, it is essential that they be inspected carefully and lubricated properly at frequent intervals.

Inspect shock struts for cracks, bowing, and security of attachment. Check braces and fittings for general condition and possible defects.

Inspect the nose wheel assembly for general condition and security of attachment. Examine linkage, trusses, and members for evidence of undue wear or distortion. Ensure that all bolts, studs, and nuts are secure with no indication of excessive wear and that they are properly safetied. If a shimmy damper is installed, ensure that it is operating satisfactorily and that the steering mechanism is properly rigged.

Inspect oleo-type shock absorbers for cleanliness, leaks, cracks, and possible bottoming of the pistons. Check all bearings, bolts, and fittings for condition, lubrication, and proper safetying.

Following the manufacturer's instructions when replenishing fluid and air pressure charge in the shock Absorber. Steerable tail wheels should be inspected for:

1. Bearing adjustment.
2. Lubrication.
3. Clearance, and range of operation.
4. Check for proper steering action and security of attachment.

Various types of lubricants are required to lubricate points of friction and wear on the landing gear. These lubricants are applied by hand, an oil can or a pressure-type grease gun. Before using the pressure-type grease gun, wipe the lubrication fittings clean of old grease and dust accumulations, because dust and sand mixed with a lubricant produce a very destructive abrasive compound. As each fitting is lubricated, the excess lubricant on the fitting and any that is squeezed out of the assembly should be wiped off. Wipe the piston rods of all exposed actuating cylinders; clean them frequently, particularly prior to operation, to prevent damage to seals and polished surfaces.

## *Note*

**If you are going to jack the aircraft cut two pieces of aluminum a least 12 inches square and place grease between them. Place the plates under each main gear; this will prevent damage to the gear while jacking and down jacking. The wheels will slide on the plates not putting pressure on the airframe or attaching landing gear. Since the grease is between the plates it will not get on the tires or wheels.**

# Wheel and Brake Inspection Points

When mechanical brakes are installed, examine the cables for condition. Worn or frayed cables should be replaced. Check pulleys for ease of turning, alignment, and proper attachment. Check pedals and actuating arms for proper operation. Check friction components for condition.

When hydraulic brakes are installed, inspect fluid lines for detects. Check the system for leakage around wheels, master cylinders, and connections. Inspect for deterioration and security of flexible tubing. Check brake fluid level in the reservoir. A low fluid level may indicate a leak somewhere in the system, requiting a more thorough inspection of the brake system. Always use the type of brake fluid recommended by the aircraft manufacturer. If the brakes pedal wheels feel "spongy" when pressed, it may indicate air in the brake system or other abnormality. Such as the brake hose expanding. Further inspection and corrective action is warranted.

Equipment installations in the wheel well areas probably absorb more punishment than any other portion of an aircraft because they are exposed to moisture of flying debris during take-offs and landings, and when the aircraft is parked they are exposed to atmospheric moisture. After an airplane has entered service, it is difficult to maintain protective paint film on landing gears, equipment installations, and wheel well surfaces because the many complicated shapes, assemblies, and fittings in these areas obscure other surfaces. Items that should receive special attention during wheel well inspections are:

1. Magnesium wheels (especially the areas around the bolt heads, lugs, and wheel webs).
2. Portions or rigid tubing obscured by clamps and identification tapes.
3. Exposed electrical equipment.
4. Crevices between ribs, stiffeners, and lower skin surfaces, which can serve as water or debris entrapment areas.

Corrosion control in wheel well areas may best be attained by frequent cleaning, lubrication, and paint touch-up and judicious use of wheel covers.

Worn brakes come from the use of brakes for steering purposes and should be avoided, since this will cause slower acceleration of the airplane's speed, lengthen the takeoff distance, and possibly result in severe swerving. Brakes should be used to correct for turns or swerves only when the rudder is inadequate. Brakes should be used as lightly as practicable while taxiing to prevent undue wear and heating of the brakes and wheels, and possible loss of ground control. When brakes are used repeatedly or constantly, they tend to heat to the point that they may either lock or fail completely.

When beginning to taxi, the brakes should be tested immediately for proper operation. This is done by first applying power to start the airplane moving slowly forward, then retarding the throttle and simultaneously applying pressure smoothly to both brakes. If braking action is unsatisfactory, the engine should be shut down immediately.

# Tires

Few tire explosions, as opposed to tire burst or tire failure, have occurred in service. The failure mechanism of a tire explosion is thought to be brought about by overhearing of the tire or brake or combinations of these. The heat causes hydrocarbon gasses to be generated inside the tire from overheated rubber (around 50°F) or hydrocarbon contaminants (grease, oil, hydraulic fluid, etc.). These hydrocarbon gasses mix with the high-pressure air and ignite. The use of nitrogen to fill and maintain the tire pressure will prevent the explosive mixture from forming. Moreover, evidence exists that tires inflated with air have shortened service life because the air diffusing into the carcass degrades its inner-ply adhesion. Nitrogen is also a deterrent to wheel corrosion.

Aircraft tires lose air from diffusion into the carcass. Diffusion should not exceed 5 PSI per day. Tires exceeding this rate represent a hazard and should be removed from service.

A FAA-certificated repair station rated for retreading of high-speed aircraft tires should carefully inspect a tire removed from service. Procedures for recording tire servicing should be established to assist in improved maintenance. The history of a tire is important to the retreader in establishing the degree of airworthiness of that tire. Accordingly, tire service records should be readily available to the retreader and should be forwarded when the tire is returned for retreading.

High temperatures are a threat to tire airworthiness. During their life, tires are subjected to stresses, which cause elevated temperatures. Analysis has shown that continued exposure to temperatures as low as 220°F (104°C) can shorten the service life of a tire. Hence, care should be taken to avoid conditions, which will result in tire temperature buildup. The following should be considered in determining whether tires have been exposed to excessive temperatures:

1. Over deflection of tires is caused by underinflation or overload. A tire located adjacent to a failed tire on the same bogie should be removed for inspection by a qualified repair station.

2. Variations in outside diameter (OD) of dual tires can cause excessive load to be transferred to the larger OD tire. Outside diameters of dual tires should, therefore, be matched in accordance with the manufacture recommendations.

Tire wear has an important bearing on judging the type of previous service and whether removal is necessary. Tires worn abnormally can reveal overinflation, underinflation, landing gear or wheel problems, and sometimes, problems with an adjacent tire on the same bogie.

Cuts from foreign object damage (FOD) should be carefully observed. Any damage exceeding approved removal criteria should be noted and the tire removed.

## *Note*
*Do not probe cuts or embedded foreign object damage when the tire is inflated.*

Tread rubber reversion, skid marks, and many other evidences of damage each have unique characteristic patterns usually described in the care and maintenance manuals which the FAA requires tire manufacturers to provide. These can be of great assistance in determining the airworthiness of a tire.

Cuts, cracks, bulges, etc., should be marked with crayon or chalk before deflation, since they may disappear when the tire is deflated.

Evidence of brake heat such as bubbles and discoloration can sometimes be found in the bead area of a mounted tire; however, it is usually necessary to remove the tire to find evidence of such damage. Any tire believed to have been exposed to excessive brake heat should be removed and examined in the bead seat area for evidence of cracking and rubber reversion. If a question exists, the tire should be removed from service and inspected.

Tires on aircraft normally used over long taxi distances or at high gross weights, or a combination of these conditions, are susceptible to shortened service life from heat buildup. If these conditions are excessive, tire failure, thermal fuseplug release, or tire burst may occur during, after takeoff, or during a rejected takeoff.

# Wheels Inspection

Inspect wheels for damage and cracks. A bent or distorted wheel flange generally indicates that it is cracked or broken. Inspect bolts for condition and security of attachment; check the condition of wheel bearings. With the wheel installed on the axle, check excessive side play by moving the wheel back and forth against the thrust washer and adjusting nut. When properly adjusted, safety the retaining nut.

On some make and models the wheels require an NDI inspection before being returned to service. This inspection is usually an eddy current inspection. Personnel in a wheel shop should remove tires from the wheel assembly, disassemble the wheel, clean the parts and bearings using a solvent dip tank or aqueous parts washer, repack the bearings, reassemble the wheel, and install new tires on the wheels, if required. The Wheel and Tire shop may have a media blaster to remove paint and corrosion from wheels prior to inspecting. If wheels are stripped of paint in the wheel and tire shop, they should have all the corrosion removed before for painting.

# Aircraft Wheel Bearings

Everyone knows that proper care and an inspection are essential to maintain wheels, brakes, and ensures long service lives for these components. However, as careful as we are, sometimes-important things are overlooked. One of the most-neglected aircraft parts is the wheel bearing.

As simple and as maintenance-free as they seem, wheel bearings are subject to some of the greatest stresses applied to any aircraft part. They support the entire weight of the aircraft, often several thousand pounds, on a surface area of just a few square inches. Along with these stresses, wheel bearings face such enemies as moisture, dust and lack of proper lubrication.

When an aircraft mechanic thinks of wheel bearings, he normally envisions only one half of the system. Actually, the bearing system is made up of a bearing cone (what most people think of) and a bearing cup. Each of these is subject to the same stresses and dangers, and should be treated with the same care.

When installing new bearings, care should be taken in lubrication. Combining the proper grease and proper packing technique will extend the service life of the bearing.

Most airframe and wheel manufacturers call for either MIL-G-81322, (matching Mobil 28 or Aeroshell 22) or MIL-G-3545 (matching Aeroshell 5). Although packing can be done by hand, it is best performed by mechanical means. Always pack the bearing cone from the wide (outboard) side, making sure that all voids inside the cone are filled. Also, make sure that a generous amount of grease is applied to the roller surfaces on the outside of the cone. If a wheel is to be stored without having the bearing cones installed, a light coat of grease should be applied to the entire surface of the bearing cup to prevent rust and corrosion.

After a bearing cone or cup has been installed, it should be inspected at least as often as the wheel with which it is installed. This generally means that it should be inspected at every tire change and after any high energy-braking event. Also, after washing the aircraft the landing gear in particular, check to be sure that the bearing grease has not been washed out during the cleaning process.

One thing to remember is that often when high-pressure washing, water will find its way into the bearing cavities of wheel assemblies, intermingling with bearing grease. If left in place, the water will cause corrosion on both the bearing cone and cup, which will then require replacement. Thus, great care should be taken in these circumstances. It is usually sufficient to use a damp rag to remove excess dirt and grime from the outside of the wheel.

When inspecting your bearings, degrease them thoroughly with clean solvent, and dry them with filtered compressed air, making sure that they do not spin when drying. Spinning bearings at a high speed poses two dangers. First, spinning without lubrication can damage the bearing, and second, if a bearing is subject to unusually high speeds, it can potentially come apart, causing personal injury.

Take the bearings to a clean, well-lit area for inspection. Examine the cage. Is it in good shape? Has it been bent in places? If it is in any way bent or otherwise damaged, the bearing should be scrapped. Next, look at the roller surfaces. Examine them very closely for corrosion, etching, scratches and heat damage. A good rule of thumb is if the damage can be felt with a fingernail, the bearing should be scrapped.

After completing the inspection, repack the bearing cone with the approved grease, and put it into its original wrapping, if possible, or an airtight plastic bag for storage. Otherwise, install it on the wheel and use protective coverings.

# Bearings Classes

## PRECISION CLASSES

Precision ball bearings are manufactured to tolerance standards set by the Bearing Engineers Committee (BEC) of the American Bearing Manufacturers Association (ABMA). These standards have been accepted by the American National Standards Institute (ANSI) and conform essentially to equivalent standards of the International Organizational for Standardization (ISO).

ABEC standards defined tolerances for several major bearing dimensions and characteristics. They are divided into mounting dimensions (bore, O.D. and width) and bearing geometry. General-purpose, spindle size ball bearings are manufactured to precision classes ABEC 1, ABEC 3, ABEC 5, ABEC 7, and ABEC 9. The ascending numbers indicate increasingly stricter tolerances and additional requirements.

Instrument bearings are produced in comparable classes, with added refinements designated by suffixes: ABEC 3P, ABEC 5P, ABEC 7P, and ABEC 9P, ABEC 5T, and ABEC 7T.

**While ABEC classes are very helpful in categorizing bearing precision, they are not all-inclusive. It should be noted ABEC standards do not include functional testing of assembled bearings, yet this measure can be extremely important.**

**Sizes:** Bearings are sized in both inch and metric dimensions. They are categorized as either instrument or spindles types. This distinctions is primary size-related but is sometimes application-related.

**Configurations:** Most manufactures use deep groove and angular contact (separable and nonseparable) bearings, some of which are available with flanged outer rings. Flanged bearings are especially useful in through-bored housing. The inboard side of the flange provides an accurate positioning surface for bearing alignment, eliminating a need for housing shoulders or shoulder rings.

**Deep Groove Bearing Design:** Deep groove instrument bearings have full shoulders on both sides of the raceways of the inner and outer rings. They can accept radial loads; thrust loads in either direction, or a combination of loads.

**Axial Play:** Axial play, also called endplay, is the maximum possible movement, parallel to the bearing axis, of the inner ring in relation to the outer ring. It is measured under a light reversing axial load. Endplay is a function of radial internal clearance, thus the nominal endplay values. Endplay will increase when a thrust load is imposed, due to axial yield. If this is objectionable, axial shimming or axial preloading can reduce the endplay. **Endplay is not a design specification.**

**Angular Contact Bearing Design:** Angular contact instrument bearings have one ring shoulder partiality or totally removed. This allows a larger ball complement than found in comparable deep groove, bearings, hence a greater load capacity. Speed capability is also greater. Angular contact bearings support thrust loads or combinations or radial and thrust loads. They cannot accept radial loads only – a thrust load of sufficient magnitude must be present. An individual angular contact bearing can be thrust-loaded in only one direction; this load may be a working load or a preload.

**Contact Angle:** Contact angle refers to the nominal angle between the ball-to-race contact line and a plane through the ball centers, perpendicular to the bearing axis. It may be expressed in terms of zero load or applied thrust load.

# Ball and Ring Materials

Selection of a material for bearing ring and balls is strongly influenced by availability. Standard bearing materials have been established. For special materials, availability should be determined and these additional factors considered during the selection process:

1. Hardness
2. Material cleanliness
3. Fatigue resistance
4. Workability
5. Dimensional stability
6. Corrosion resistance
7. Wear resistance
8. Temperature resistance

The three predominant ball and ring materials used by most manufactures are AISE 440C, SAE 52100 and AISI M50.

ASIE 440C stainless steel is the standard material for instrument bearings. It is optional for spindle and turbine bearings. This is a hardenable, corrosion-resistance steel with adequate fatigue resistance, good load-carrying capacity, and excellent stability and wears resistance. Operating temperature range is –400 degree F to 300 degree F for instrument bearings, -400 degree F to 400 degree F for spindle and turbine bearings. Applicable specifications include Federal Standard 66, QQ-S-763 and AMS 5630.

SAE 52100 chrome steel is the standard material for spindle and turbine bearings. It is also available in some instrument sizes, and may be preferable when fatigue life, static capacity and torque's is critical. This material has excellent capacity, fatigue, resistance and stability. Operating temperature limit is 400 degree F when used in spindle and turbine bearings. Applicable specifications include Federal Standard 66, QQ-S-763 and AMS 6491.

# Ceramic Hybrids

Use of ceramic (silicon nitride) balls in place of steel balls can radically improve bearing performance several ways. Because ceramic balls are 50% lighter than steel balls, and because their surface finish is almost perfectly smooth, they exhibit vibration levels two to seven times lower than conventional steel ball bearings.

Ceramic hybrids bearings also run at significantly lower operating temperatures, and can allow running speeds to increase by as much as 40% to 50%. Bearings with ceramic balls have been proven to last up to five times longer than conventional steel ball bearings. Lower operating temperatures help extend lubricant life.

Because of the unique properties of silicone nitride, ceramic balls drastically reduce the predominant cause of surface wear in conventional bearings (metal rings/metal balls). In conventional bearings, microscopic surface aspirates on balls and races will "cold weld" or sticks together even under normal lubrication and load conditions. As the bearing rotates, the microscopic cold welds break, producing roughness and eventually, worn contact surfaces. This "stickpull" characteristic is known as adhesive wear. Since ceramic balls will not cold weld to steel rings, wear is dramatically reduced. Because wear particles generated by adhesive wear are not present in ceramic hybrids, lubricant life is also prolonged. The saving in reduced maintenance cost alone can be significant.

# Bearing Cages

The basic purpose of a cage is to maintain uniform ball spacing, but it can also be designed to reduce torque and minimize heat build-up. Cage loading is normal light but various acceleration and centrifugal forces may develop and impose cage loading. Cages are piloted (guided) by the balls or one of the rings. Typically, low to moderate speed cages are ball-piloted. Most high-speed cages have machined surfaces and are piloted by the land or either the inner or outer ring. The different type cages are: Snap-in, Two-Piece Ribbon, Two piece stamped ribbons (W), One-piece side entry snap in fiber reinforced phenolic, Phenolic/aluminum laminate, Nylon with spherical ball pockets, and bronze to name a few.

# Internal Ball Parameters

The principal internal design parameters for a ball bearing are the ball complement (number and size of balls), internal clearances (radial play, axial play, and contact angle), and raceway curvature.

The number and size of the balls are generally selected to give maximum capacity in the available space. In some specialized cases, the ball complement may be chosen on a basic of minimum torque, speed considerations or rigidity.

# Radial Internal Clearance

Commonly referred to as radial play, this is the maximum possible movement, perpendicular to the bearing axis, of the inner ring in relation to the outer ring. Radial internal clearance is measured under a light reversing radial load and corrected to zero loads, to establish radial play values. The presence and magnitude of redial play are vital factors in bearing performance.

Without sufficient radial play, interference fit (press fits) and normal expansion of components cannot be accommodated, causing binding and early failure. Radial internal clearance of the mounted bearing has a profound effect on the contact angle, which in turn influence bearing capacity, life and other performance characteristics. Proper internal clearance will provide a suitable contact angle to support thrust loads or to meet exacting requirements of elastic yield.

# Bearing Yield

Axial yield is the axial deflection between inner and outer rings after endplay is removed and working load or preload is applied. It results from elastic deformation of balls and raceway under thrust loading.

# Bearing Preloading

Preloading is the removal of internal clearance in a bearing by applying a permanent thrust load to it. Preloading:

1. Eliminates radial and axial play.
2. Increases system rigidity.
3. Reduces nonrepetitive run out.

4. Lessens the difference in contact angles between the balls and both inner and outer rings at very high speeds.
5. Prevents ball skidding under very high acceleration.

# Preloading Techniques

Bearing should be preloaded as lightly as is necessary to achieve the desired results. This avoids excessive heat generation, which reduces speed capability and bearing life. There are three basic methods of preloading:

1. Springs
2. Axial adjustment
3. Duplex bearings

# Bearing Lubrication

Adequate lubrication is essential to the successful performance of anti-friction bearings. Increased speeds, higher temperatures, improved accuracy and reliability requirements result in the need for closer attention to lubrication selection. Lubrication type and quantity have a marked effect on functional properties and service life of each application. Properly selected lubricants:

1. Reduce friction by providing a viscous hydrodynamic film of sufficient strength to support the load and separate the balls from the raceways, preventing metal-to-metal contact.
2. Minimize cage wear by reducing sliding friction in cage pockets and land surfaces.
3. Prevent oxidation/corrosion of rolling elements.
4. Acts as a barrier to contaminants.
5. Serve as a heat transfer agent in some cases, conducting heat away from the bearing.

Lubricants are available in three basic forms:

1. Fluid lubricants (oils).
2. Greases solid to semisolid products consisting of oil and a thickening agent.
3. Dry lubricants, including films. Dry film lubrication is usually limited to moderate speed and very light loading conditions.

# Lubrication Practices

Factory prelubrication of bearing is highly recommended, since the correct quantity of applied lubricant can be as important as the correct type of lubricant. This is especially true of greases, where an excess can cause high torque, overheating and if the speed is high enough-rapid bearing failure. The factory will usually if not always use filtered grease to the appropriate bearing surface. Grease filter sizes range from about 10 to 40 microns depending on grease variables such as thickener and additive particle size.

# Lubricant Selection

Selection of lubricant and method of lubrication are generally governed by the operating conditions and limitations of the system. Three of the most significant factors in selecting a lubricant are:

1. Viscosity of the lubricant at operating temperature.

2. Maximum and minimum allowable operating temperatures.
3. Operating speed.

The primary advantage of grease over oil is that bearings can be prelubricated with grease, eliminating the need for an external lubrication system. This grease is often adequate for the service life of the application, especially in extra-wide series bearings, which have greater than usual grease capacity. It should be noted; grease can be expected to increase the initial bearing torque and may exhibit a slightly higher running torque.

# Bearing Service Life

The useful life of a ball bearing has historically been considered to be limited by the onset of fatigue or spalling of the raceways and balls, assuming that the bearing was properly selected and mounted, effectively lubricated and protected against contaminants.

When a bearing no longer fulfills minimum performance requirements in such categories as torque, vibration or elastic yield, its service life may be effectively ended. Lubrication can be an important factor influencing service life. Many bearings are prelubricated by the bearing manufacturer with an appropriate quantity of lubricant. They will reach the end of their useful life when the lubricant migrates away from the bearing parts, oxidizes or suffers some other degradation. At that point, the lubricant is no longer effective and surface distress of the operating surfaces, rather that fatigue, is the cause of failure. Bearing life is thus very dependent upon characteristics of specific lubricants, operating temperature and atmospheric environment.

Performance of a bearing may be affected by vibration arising from exposure to external vibration or from self-generated frequencies.

Bearing that are subjected to external vibration along with other adverse conditions can fail or degrade in modes known as false brinelling, wear oxidation or corrosion fretting. Such problems arise when loaded bearings operate without sufficient lubrication at very low speeds, oscillating or even stationary. When vibrations are added, surface oxidation and selective wear result from minute vibratory movement and limited rolling action in the ball-to-raceway contact areas. The condition can be relieved by properly designed isolation supports and adequate lubrication.

When dealing with bearing or handling them cleanliness cannot be overstressed. Even microscopic particles of dirt can kill a bearing fast. Consider every kind of foreign matter a potential enemy of bearing performance.

**Work area,** begins with a clean workbench. Having a painted workbench is not desirable as wood surface because it can chip, flake or rust. Under no circumstances should food or drink be consumed on or near work surfaces. Smoking should not be allowed in the room where bearings are being replaced.

**Proper Tools,** to facilitate bearing removal and replacement. Tools require include spanners, drifts, gages and gage blocks, and bearing pullers.

# Dos and Don'ts

### Do's
1. Open packages with scissors, handle only with clean, and dry hands or gloves.
2. Protect unwrapped bearings in by keeping them covered at all times.
3. Align highpoint mark on ring 180 degree from high point of shaft.
4. Use an induction heater for assembly (or arbor press for interference fits).
5. Use clean, burr free tools that are not plated, painted or rusted.
6. Use tweezers to install miniature and instrument bearings.
7. Keep mounting arrangements and blueprints on file for future reference.

## Don'ts

1. Don't open bearing pouch until ready to assemble components.
2. Don't wash new bearings. They are factory cleaned and lubricated.
3. Don't wipe parts dry with a rag, or lint could be introduced into the bearing.
4. Don't spin bearing with compressed air. Internal damage could result.
5. Don't use a hammer or screwdriver to install bearings. **Never drop bearings.**
6. Don't over lubricate or mix different lubricants families.
7. Don't smoke, eat or drink while handling or installing bearings.

For technical information about bearing you can contact the Barden Precision Bearing Company, Danbury, CT. at www.bardenbearing.com.

# Grease

This section is to ensure that mechanics and operators are aware of the potential adverse effects of grease mixing or of substituting the original equipment manufacturer (OEM) specified grease with grease that may not be approved by the OEM or reference Military Specifications (MILSPEC).

## *NOTE*

*The MILSPEC is an U.S. military material specification that defines the requirements for a material and is approved after a process of testing and review. Requirements that are defined for grease MILSPEC categories include, in part, viscosity, temperature range, and corrosion protection. A part's function and exposure determine which grease MILSPEC category is appropriate due to such factors as loads, friction, extreme temperatures, and water and other contaminants.*

Many factors can affect grease compatibility. The product base(s), thickener(s), or any product in the additive package may alter the performance and/or properties of the grease. If the greases are incompatible, these interactions may result in a grease mixture that no longer meets the original specifications. Compatibility testing consists of mixing two greases in varied proportions to ascertain whether the new chemical combination degrades the original properties of the two greases separately. Boeing issued a Service Letter in August 1993, which stated "some incompatibility may exist between MIL-G-23827 greases that are thickened with clay and those that are thickened with lithium soap".

## *NOTE*

*Grease types specified by an OEM or a MILSPEC does not imply grease compatibility with regards to mixing greases. An OEM or MILSPEC may specify several types of grease, which may contain either a clay or lithium soap thickener. Mixing two types of grease listed by the OEM or MILSPEC may have adverse effects caused by an incompatible mixture.*

Based on the design parameters of an aircraft system, the manufacturer may specify the use of a specific type and brand of grease, or they may specify that MILSPEC grease be used. In the latter case, it may be considered that the use of specific grease listed in the Qualified Parts List (QPL) of that specification is acceptable for that application.

Removal "purging" of the old grease from the component when substituting grease products ("purging" consists of replacing a minimum of 90 percent of the old grease).

## *NOTE*

*The term "substituting" as used above also includes a change of grease type or brand from that specified in the maintenance manual or on the QPL of the MILSPEC for the specific application.*

Have you ever thought much about the lubricants used on our airplanes? Piper did. The Piper Inspection Report, Lubrication Chart, provides a list of the materials that are necessary to meet the maintenance requirements of Short Wing Piper aircraft. Unfortunately, one tube of grease cannot meet the needs of all the moving parts on our airplanes. The Piper service manual will provide information and recommendations concerning the different products, what they are used for. Reference Piper Service Bulletin 1044.

# AeroShell Grease

### AeroShell Grease 5
Wheel bearing and engine accessory grease.
Microgel® thickened mineral oil base.
Combines high load-carrying ability with excellent resistance to water and high temperatures. It inhibited against corrosion and oxidation, and has a useful temperature range of -23°C to + 177°C. Used primarily in aircraft wheel bearings and engine accessories operating at high speeds and relatively high temperatures.

### AeroShell Grease 6
General Purpose airframe grease.
Microgel® thickened mineral oil base.
Inhibited against corrosion and oxidation, it features outstanding low temperature torque properties and resistance to water. Useful temperature range of -40°C to +121°C. Used primarily in plain and anti-friction bearings on general aviation aircraft and as a propeller grease.

### AeroShell Grease 7
Advanced multipurpose airframe grease.
Corrosion inhibited and fortified to resist oxidation, it combines excellent load-carrying capacity with a useful temperature range of -73°C to + 149°C. Recommended for highly loaded gears and actuator screw mechanisms, as well as for instrument and general airframe lubrication.

### AeroShell Grease 14
Leading multipurpose helicopter grease.
Calcium soap thickened mineral oil base.
Inhibited against corrosion and oxidation, it is compounded with special anti-rust additives, and gives outstanding protection against fretting and moisture corrosion. Useful temperature range is -54°C to +93°C. Approved by all leading helicopter manufacturers. Recommended for most helicopter main and tail rotor bearings; widely used as a general-purpose helicopter grease.

### AeroShell Grease 15
Extreme temperature ball and roller bearing grease.
Inhibited against corrosion and oxidation, it possesses excellent high temperature and mechanical stability properties, low evaporation rate and superior resistance to water washout. Intended for lightly loaded ball and roller bearings over a temperature range of -73°C to +232°C. Recommended for continuous high temperature service, e.g. in turbine engine controls, and for low temperature applications where low torque properties are required.

### AeroShell Grease 17
Extreme Pressure variant of AeroShell Grease 7.
AeroShell Grease 7 with 5% molybdenum disulphide.
Recommended as general-purpose airframe grease, particularly for heavily loaded sliding steel surfaces where protection against seizure and corrosion is desired, e.g. bogie pivot pins on jet aircraft landing assemblies. It also provides outstanding anti-friction bearing lubrication. Useful temperature range is -73°C to +149°C.

**AeroShell Grease 22**
Versatile multipurpose grease.
Microgel® thickened, synthetic hydrocarbon oil base.
Corrosion inhibited and fortified against oxidation, it has excellent anti-wear properties, load-carrying capacity and water resistance, plus a wide useful temperature range of -65°C to +240°C. Recommended for aircraft wheel bearings, engine accessories and airframe lubrication, and for anti-friction bearings operating at high speeds and at high or low temperatures

# Aircraft Radial Tires

The aircraft radial tire is similar in construction to the radial tires you can use on your automobile. The reinforcement cords are used in a radial direction straight around the tire carcass from one bead to the other. (Bias tires have their plies at an oblique angle relative to the axis of rotation). A typical construction consists of a two or four-ply carcass of nylon cords fastened by a single round-wire bead-bundle on each side, two or four-ply belt of nylon cords, and a steel protection ply beneath the tread.

Laboratory testing showed that the radial tires exceeded dynamic qualification requirements and ran cooler than standard bias ply tires. Wright Laboratory (WL) (formerly AFWAL)-TM-87-205/FIVMA technical memo documents cornering tests that showed that turning side force was lower for the radial tire. To date, all of the radial tires flight qualified and demonstrated on U.S. Air Force aircraft were designed as direct replacements for current bias ply tires. These radial tires meet the same performance requirements, fit the same wheel rims, are the same size, and operate at the same inflation pressures as the bias ply tires they replace.

**Benefits/Drawbacks** Compared to bias tires, radial tires offer an increase in tread life of 16 percent. Radials offer less than a three percent reduction in weight. Reliability is expected to increase because of the tire's cooler operating temperature, increased resistance to tread-cut growth and groove cracking, and increased puncture resistance. Because the radial tires have less rolling resistance, they generate less heat.

The radial's reduced operating temperature, in a short duty-cycle environment, significantly increases the aircraft radial tire's load carrying capability. Both Goodyear and Michelin tires were tested to the **Federal Aviation Administration (FAA) TSO C62C** specification overload requirements of 1.5 times their normal load capacity. Michelin has extended these tests with the Airbus A300 aircraft radial tires to include two takeoff and landing cycles at 2.0 times the tire's load capacity.

The tests also showed that the radial tire produced good overall pilot feel and smoother landings, are considerably lighter and easier to handle and mount, and compatible with the anti-skid system. The average wear-per-landing was comparable to the bias tires.

There are a number of drawbacks or concerns that need to be addressed. In the retrofit situation, there may be some compatibility problems between the radial tire and the aircraft's wheel, brake/antiskid, and strut. These potential incompatibilities stem from the different wheel design criteria and variances in tire stiffness for radials and bias ply tires. In a retrofit application, it will be necessary to conduct verification tests to ensure wheel life. Radial tires that are designed to replace existing bias ply tires in form; fit and function may not be able to be optimized to take full advantage of their operational capabilities. For new aircraft wheel designs, you can optimize the design to realize the advantage radial tires offer. In the durability arena, tread design and size need to be optimized to take advantage of the radial tire's operational capability. There may be some operational concerns of mixing radial tires and bias tires on the same landing gear on the same aircraft.

# Non-Destructive Inspection

The Non-Destructive Inspection (NDI) Shop inspects various aircraft parts to ensure their integrity and functionality. On some aircraft when a wheel is removed and disassembled it may require a NDI inspection be completed before reassembly.

## Dye Penetrant Test

This test consists of passing the component through a dye penetrant line. The component is first submerged in a dye penetrant bath (oil-based), allowed to drip dry, and then rinsed with water. Then the component is submerged in a dye penetrant remover bath (emulsifier) and subsequently rinsed with water. The component is then submerged in a developer bath (water-based). Finally, the component is dried and viewed under a black light, which identifies abnormalities such as cracks in the non-ferrous metal component.

## Magnetic Particle Test

The component to be inspected is immersed in a mineral oil solution containing magnetic particles, and a magnetic field is applied to the component. The magnetic particles in the fluid align themselves to identify abnormalities in the ferrous metal component. The part is then rinsed with a mineral oil solution not containing magnetic particles.

## X-Ray Test

This test consists of taking an x-ray photograph of a component, developing the film, and viewing the resulting image to identify component abnormalities X-ray photography is also used to certify welders, but this can be accomplished using a local x-ray processor if desired.

## OAP Test

An oil sample (approximately 10 cc) is collected from an engine source in a small sample bottle and injected into an OAP analyzer. The system determines the concentration of metals in the oil sample. Following analysis, the OAP analyzer is cleaned. Excess sample material and equipment cleaners are collected as wastes. Empty sample bottles are disposed of as ordinary trash.

# CHAPTER 11

## ELECTRICAL

# Electrical Systems

The term "electrical system" means those parts of the aircraft that generate, distribute, and use electrical energy, including their support and attachments. The satisfactory performance of an aircraft is dependent upon the continued reliability of the electrical system. Damaged wiring or equipment in an aircraft, regardless of how minor it may appear to be, cannot be tolerated. Reliability of the system is proportional to the amount of maintenance received and the knowledge of those who perform such maintenance. It is, therefore, important that maintenance be accomplished using the best techniques and practices to minimize the possibility of failure.

A list of suggested problems to look for and checks to be performed are:

1. Damaged, discolored, or overheated equipment, connections, wiring, and installations.
2. Excessive heat or discoloration at high current carrying connections.
3. Misalignment of electrically driven equipment.
4. Poor electrical bonding (broken, disconnected or corroded bonding strap) and grounding, including evidence of corrosion.
5. Dirty equipment and connections.
6. Improper, broken, inadequately supported wiring and conduit, loose connections of terminals, and loose ferrules.
7. Poor mechanical or cold solder joints.
8. Condition of circuit breaker and fuses.
9. Insufficient clearance between exposed current carrying parts and ground or poor insulation of exposed terminals.
10. Broken or missing safety wire, broken bundle lacing, cotter pins, etc.
11. Operational check of electrically operated equipment such as motors, inverters, generators, batteries, lights, protective devices, etc.
12. Ensure that ventilation and cooling air passages are clear and unobstructed.
13. Voltage checks of electrical system with portable precision voltmeter.
14. Condition of electric lamps.
15. Missing safety shields on exposed high-voltage terminals (i.e., 115/200V ac).

All electrical wires must be provided with some means of circuit protection. Electrical wire should be protected with circuit breakers or fuses located as close as possible to the electrical power source bus. Normally, the manufacturer of electrical equipment will specify the fuse or breaker to be used when installing the respective equipment, or SAE publication, ARP 1199, may be referred to for recommended practices.

# Clamping

Use clamps meeting Specification MS-21919 or plastic cable straps in accessible areas if correctly applied must support wires and wire bundles. Clamps and other primary support devices must be constructed of materials that are compatible with their installation and environment, in terms of temperature, fluid resistance, exposure to ultraviolet (UV) light, and wire bundle mechanical loads. They should be spaced at intervals not exceeding **24 inches**. Clamps on wire bundles should be selected so that they have a snug fit without pinching wires.

# Automobile Alternator

Since an alternator is but one class of generator, approval of alternator installations in light aircraft have been made by the FAA under the rules in CFR Part 23 and 27, which deal with generator systems. It has been found that certain types of alternators (which are apparently used in a number of automotive applications) obtain their field excitation from the battery. When field excitation is obtained this way, there is the danger that; if the alternator were turned off in flight, subsequent loss of discharge of the battery would result in loss of the alternator as well. If you have one of these in your Type Certificated aircraft you need to make sure the proper marking and placards are in place per 14 CFR Part 23 section 23.1541(a)(2).

# Electrical Loads

When installing equipment which consumes electrical power in an aircraft, it should be determined that the total electrical load can be safely controlled or managed within the rated limits of the affected components of the aircraft's electrical power supply system. Addition of most electrical utilization equipment is a major alteration and requires appropriate FAA approval. The electrical load analysis must be prepared in general accordance with good engineering practices. Additionally, an addendum to the flight manual is generally required.

Before any aircraft electrical load is increased, the new total electrical load (previous maximum load plus added load) must be checked to determine if the design levels are being exceeded. Where necessary, wires, wire bundles, and circuit protective devices having the correct ratings should be added or replaced.

The generator or alternator output ratings and limits prescribed by the manufacturer must be checked against the electrical loads that can be imposed on the affected generator or alternator by installed equipment. When electrical load calculations show that the total continuous electrical load can exceed **80 percent** output load limits of the generator or alternator, steps must be taken to reduce the electrical load or increase the generating capacity of the charging system.

The **use of placards** is recommended to inform the pilot and/or crewmembers of the combination(s) of loads that may be connected to each power source. Installation of warning lights can be installed that will be triggered if the battery bus voltage drops below 13 volts on a 14 volt system or 26 volts on a 28 volt system.

# Determination of Electrical Load

Any one or a combination of several acceptable methods, techniques, or practices may determine the connected load of an aircraft's electrical system. However, those with a need to know the status of a particular aircraft's electrical system should have available accurate and up-to-date data concerning the capacity of the installed electrical power source(s) and the load(s) imposed by installed electrical power-consuming devices. Such data should provide a true picture of the status of the electrical system. New or additional electrical devices should not be installed in an aircraft, nor the capacity changed of any power source, until the status of the electrical system in the aircraft has been determined accurately and found not to adversely affect the integrity of the electrical system.

# Determination of Circuit Breaker Ratings

Circuit protection devices must be sized to supply open circuit capability. A circuit breaker must be rated so that it will open before the current rating of the wire attached to it is exceeded, or before the cumulative rating of all loads connected to it are exceeded, whichever is lowest. A circuit breaker must always open before any component downstream can overheat and generate smoke or fire. Wires must be sized to carry continuous current in excess of the circuit protective device rating, including its time-current characteristics, and to avoid excessive voltage drop.

# Aircraft Electrical Wiring

Wires must be sized so that they: have sufficient mechanical strength to allow for service conditions; do not exceed allowable voltage drop levels; are protected by system circuit protection devices; and meet circuit current carrying requirements.

All wire used on aircraft must have its type identification imprinted along its length. It is common practice to follow this part number with the five-digit/letter C.A.G.E. code identifying the wire manufacturer. Existing installed wire that needs replacement can thereby be identified as to its performance capabilities, and the inadvertent use of a lower performance and unsuitable replacement wire avoided. In addition to the type identification imprinted by the original wire manufacturer, aircraft wire also contains its unique circuit identification coding that is put on at the time of harness assembly. This means NO telephone or house wires are allowed in aircraft. Only wire, specifically designed for airborne use, must be installed in aircraft.

Most aircraft wire designs are to specifications that require manufacturers to pass rigorous testing of wires before being added to a Qualified Products List (QPL) and being permitted to produce the wire. Aircraft manufacturers who maintain their own wire specifications invariably exercise close control on their approved sources. Such military or original equipment manufacturer (OEM) wire used on aircraft should only have originated from these defined wire mills. Aircraft wire from other unauthorized firms, and fraudulently marked with the specified identification, must be regarded as "unapproved wire," and usually will be of inferior quality with little or no process control testing. Efforts must be taken to ensure obtaining authentic, fully tested aircraft wire.

The use of wire sizes smaller than #20, particular attention should be given to the mechanical strength and installation handling of these wires, e.g., vibration, flexing, and termination. Wire containing less than 19 strands must not be used. As a general practice, wires smaller than size #20 should be provided with additional clamps and be grouped with at least three other wires. They should also have additional support at terminations, such as connector grommets, strain relief clamps, shrinkable sleeving, or telescoping bushings. They should not be used in applications where they will be subjected to excessive vibration, repeated bending, or frequent disconnection from screw termination.

The voltage drop in the main power wires from the generation source or the battery to the bus should not exceed 2 percent of the regulated voltage when the generator is carrying rated current or the battery is being discharged at the 5-minute rate. Reference AC 43.13-1B Chapter 11.

Since electrical wire may be installed in areas where inspection is infrequent over extended periods of time, it is necessary to give special consideration to heat-aging characteristics in the selection of wire. Resistance to heat is of primary importance in the selection of wire for aircraft use, as it is the basic factor in wire rating. Where wire may be required to operate at higher temperatures due either to high ambient temperatures, high-current loading, or a combination of the two, selection should be made on the basis of satisfactory performance under the most severe operating conditions.

Determining a wiring system's current carrying capacity begins with determining the maximum current that a given-sized wire can carry without exceeding the allowable temperature difference (wire rating minus ambient

ÞC). When wires are bundled into harnesses, the current derived for a single wire must be reduced. The amount of current derating is a function of the number of wires in the bundle and the percentage of the total wire bundle capacity that is being used. Since heat loss from the bundle is reduced with increased altitude, the amount of current should be de-rated.

### Correct Wire Size

To select the correct size of electrical wire, two major requirements must be met:

1. The wire size should be sufficient to prevent an excessive voltage drop while carrying the required current over the required distance.
2. The size should be sufficient to prevent overheating of the wire carrying the required current.

To meet the two above requirements, the following must be known:

1. The wire length in feet.
2. The number of amperes of current to be carried.
3. The allowable voltage drop permitted.
4. The required continuous or intermittent current.
5. The estimated or measured conductor temperature.
6. Is the wire to be installed in conduit and/or bundle.
7. Is the wire to be installed as a single wire in free air.

# Wiring Substitutions

In the repair and modification of existing aircraft when replacement wire is required, the maintenance manual for that aircraft must first be reviewed to determine if the original aircraft manufacturer (OAM) has approved any substitution. If not, then the OAM must be contacted for an acceptable replacement. If you make a wire substitution of wires in the eyes of the FAA is considered an alteration and will require a FAA field approval if it is not called out in the manufacture maintenance manual.

# Wire Specifications

Murphy sets his first trap at the bench stock board before we even get to the aircraft. Generally, the type of wire to be installed is specified in tech data. However, in many cases, tech data guidance is lacking, and one must choose the type of wire to be installed. Remember: Choosing the correct wire for an aircraft system is not simply a matter of selecting the proper voltage rating or wire size.

Over the years, manufacturers have developed many types of wire designed to operate in a variety of functions and environments. Some are resistant to fluids, such as fuel or hydraulic fluid, while others are designed to operate at extremely high temperatures.

Strict standards known as military specifications or "MIL SPECS," developed by the various branches of the armed forces, dictates the different qualities of aircraft wire to us. To choose the correct wire, when the Technical Order (T.O.) does not already specify one, is a simple matter of selecting the MIL SPEC with the desired characteristics. For example: MIL-W-22759C specifies a wire with fluoropolymer insulation, which is resistant to fluids and suitable for use around fuel and hydraulic systems. MIL-W-25038 has a fire-resistant glass or asbestos insulator and is used in high-temperature environments such as engine bays or near bleed air ducts. It will endure temperatures of up to 400°C (750°F) for periods totaling up to 100 hours.

The Defense Department publishes thousands of MIL SPECs. A complete edition alone could fill several shelves in a publication library. Fortunately, aircraft wiring MIL SPECs are also contained in T.O. 1-1A-14, "Aircraft Electric and Electronic Wiring," which can be found in most Air Force T.O. libraries. For those that do not have access to an Air Force reference library you are allowed to use AC 43.13 under wiring and MIL-Specifications.

# CHAPTER 12

## PAINT

## What Does New Paint Hide

If the airplane was recently repainted, the reason was probably to sell it. Have your mechanic look closely to see if it was done to cover up corrosion. Figure the paint job will last about half the time a good one will, and that you'll be looking at paint chipping, cracking and peeling in the first year. Unless the airplane has been on the market for over a year, don't put much stock in a paint job that is under a year old. You may even want to call the paint shop and find what was charged for the job versus what is the rate for a top-quality job. Ask around and find out the reputation of the paint shop.

## Paint Environment vs. Corrosion

New airplanes enter service with no corrosion. Inspection after a few years of service will reveal that most airplanes continue to have a good appearance and are relatively corrosion-free. Some airplanes however, will show evidence of extensive corrosion necessitating skin or structural repair.

The extent of corrosive attack on an airplane is directly related to the environment in which the airplane operates and the corrosion prevention and cleanup measures taken by the owner/operator. In a dry climate, corrosion usually progresses very slowly. If the same airplane is moved from a dry climate to a warm, wet climate with salt water nearby, light corrosion, if untreated, may become severe within a matter of months. Industrial gases in the air also cause corrosion. Corrosion caused by salt air and industrial gases is similar in appearance.

Temperature and atmospheric changes, which occur during the course of each flight, contribute to corrosion. For example, an airplane may take off from an airport where temperature and humidity are high, climb through rain and industrially polluted air, cruise at subfreezing temperatures, and land at another airport where the climate is again hot and humid. During descent, moisture condenses and airborne salts accumulate on airplane skin, in structural cavities such as flap wells, and on other structural surfaces, which may already be contaminated by residue from engine exhaust gases, leakage from fluid and waste systems, and runway soils. These contaminants either directly chemically attach to the metal or absorb and retain moisture and thereby provide an excellent environment for corrosion.

Corrosion is most often thought of as a slow process of material deterioration, taking place over a significant period of time (examples being general corrosion, pitting, exfoliation, etc.). Other forms of corrosion degradation can occur very quickly, in days or even hours, with catastrophic results. These forms (such as stress corrosion cracking, environmental embrittlement, and corrosion fatigue) depend on both the chemical and mechanical aspects of the environment and can cause catastrophic structural failure without warning.

Corrosion is a natural phenomenon, which attacks metal by chemical or electrochemical action and converts it into a metallic compound, such as an oxide, hydroxide, or sulfate. Corrosion is to be distinguished from erosion, which is primarily destruction by mechanical action. The corrosion occurs because of the tendency for metals to return to their natural state. Noble metals, such as gold and platinum, do not corrode since they are chemically uncombined in their natural state. Four conditions must exist before corrosion can occur:

1.  Presence of a metal that will corrode (anode).
2.  Presence of a dissimilar conductive material (cathode), which has fewer tendencies to corrode.

3. Presence of a conductive liquid (electrolyte).
4. Electrical contact between the anode and cathode (usually metal-to-metal contact, or a fastener.

Stop any one of the four and you can break the cycle that corrosion requires. During your pre-purchase inspection special attention should be paid to known areas on aircraft where problems exist.

All corrosive attack begins on the surface of the metal. The corrosion process involves two chemical changes. The metal that is attacked or oxidized undergoes an anodic change, with the corrosive agent being reduced and undergoing a cathodic change. The tendency of most metals to corrode creates one of the major problems in the maintenance of the aircraft, particularly in areas where adverse environmental or weather conditions exist.

# Corrosion Prone Areas

Exfoliation is most prone to occur in wrought products such as extrusions, thick sheet, thin plate and certain die-forged shapes, which have a thin, highly elongated platelet type grain structure. This is in contrast with other wrought products and cast products that tend to have an equiaxed grain structure. Take note that wing spars are in this group, especially twin-engine aircraft where exhaust gases are blown over or under the wing.

**Exhaust Trail Areas.** Both jet and reciprocating engine exhaust gas deposits are very corrosive. Inspection and maintenance of exhaust trail areas should be inspected very closely in these areas. Inspection should also include the removal of fairings and access plates located in the exhaust gas path.

1. Gaps, seams, hinges, and fairings are some of the exhaust trail areas where deposits may be trapped and not reached by normal cleaning methods.

2. Exhaust deposit buildup on the upper and lower wing, aft fuselage, and in the horizontal tail surfaces will be considerably slower and sometimes completely absent from certain aircraft models.

High gloss spot cleaner conforming to MIL-C-85570, Type III, is recommended for cleaning exhaust track areas of high gloss paint systems. This material contains solvents, detergents, and suspended abrasive matter to remove soil by wearing away the surface that holds it.

Steam cleaning is not recommended for general use on aircraft. It erodes paint, crazes plastic, debonds adhesives, damages electrical insulation, and drives lubrication out of bearings.

Paint coatings can mask the initial stages of corrosion. Since corrosion products occupy more volume than the original metal, paint surfaces should be inspected often for irregularities such as blisters, flakes, chips, and lumps.

The primary objective of any paint system is to protect exposed surfaces against corrosion and other forms of deterioration. Operational uses for particular paint schemes include:

1. High visibility requirements.
2. Identification markings.
3. Abrasion protection.
4. Specialty coatings (i.e., walkway coatings).

The paint system on aircraft consists of a primer coat and a topcoat. The primer promotes adhesion and contains corrosion inhibitors. The topcoat provides durability to the paint system, including weather and chemical resistance, along with the coloring necessary for operational requirements.

Some aircraft surfaces (teflon-filled, rain erosion, walkways, etc.) require specialized coatings to satisfy service exposure and operational needs. For these surfaces, refer to the specific manufacturer's maintenance manual for the aircraft in question.

The Environmental Protection Agency, as well as certain local air pollution control districts, has implemented rules which limit the volatile organic content (VOC), or solvent content, of paints applied to aircraft and ground support equipment. It is the responsibility of the user to insure that these rules are understood and obeyed. **FAILURE TO COMPLY WITH CURRENT RULES CAN RESULT IN LARGE FINES.**

Much of the effectiveness of a paint finish and its adherence depend on careful preparation of the surface prior to touch up and repair.

1.  Aged paint surfaces must be scuff sanded to ensure adhesion of overcoated, freshly applied paint. Sanding requires a complete roughening of the paint surface and can be accomplished by hand sanding or with the use of power tools.

2.  For final preparation, ensure that surfaces to be painted are free of corrosion, have been prepared and the surrounding paint leathered, have been cleaned, and have been conversion coated. Replace any seam sealants when necessary. Mask areas as required preventing overspray.

Spray application for touchup, overcoat and total repaint:

1.  Primers should be thinned with the applicable thinner as required and recommended by the paint manufacturer, stirred, and applied in even coats. Primer thickness varies for each type primer but generally the total dry film thickness is 0.6 to 0.9 mils (0.0006 to 0.0009 inch). You should be able to see through this film thickness. Allow primer to air dry prior to topcoat application in accordance with the paint manufacturer's recommendations. Normally topcoat application should occur within 24 hours after primer application.

2.  Topcoats should be thinned with the applicable thinner as required and recommended by the paint manufacturer, stirred, and applied in even coats. Topcoat thickness varies for each topcoat but generally the total dry film thickness is 1.5 to 2.0 mils (0.0015 to 0.002 inch). Allow the topcoat to air dry in accordance with the paint manufacturer's instructions.

    a.  Teflon-filled (antichafe) coatings should be applied over a primer in accordance with the manufacturer's instructions.

Walkway compounds should be applied over a primer in accordance with the manufacturer's instructions.

Coated metal surfaces should not be polished for esthetic purposes. Buffing would remove the protective coating and a brightly polished surface is normally not as corrosion resistant as a nonpolished surface unless it is protected by wax, paint, etc. A bare skin sheet polished to a mirror finish is more resistant than a bare mill finished sheet when both are given regular maintenance.

# Surface Treatment Testing

The most common types of surface treatment for metals used in aircraft construction are: chemical conversion coatings, phosphate treatments for steels, and chromate treatments for aluminum. Other surface treatments include lacquer and chromate films. The identification of these surface treatments may be accomplished by the following procedures:

1.  **Phosphate treatment.** The presence of a phosphate treatment on steel, zinc, cadmium, or aluminum can be confirmed by placing a drop of 20 percent nitric acid ($HNO3$) on the surface and following this with two drops of ammonium molybdate solution. If the metal surface has had a phosphate treatment, a yellow precipitate will form.

2.  **Chromate treatment.** Surface chromate treatments on zinc, cadmium, aluminum, or magnesium are highly colored and are indicative of the application of these treatments. However, a bleached chromate treatment may have been applied and then coated with lacquer to mask any residual

iridescence for the sake of appearance. If so, visual detection of the chromate is impossible. To test for lacquer, proceed as directed in paragraph 3. It should be noted that the bleaching process used in a bleached chromate treatment lowers the corrosion resistance provided by the chromate film.

3. **Lacquer finish**. To test for lacquer, place a drop of concentrated sulfuric acid on the surface. If lacquer is present, the spot will rapidly turn brown with no effervescence. If lacquer is not present, the spot will not turn brown. If the metal is zinc, there will be no rapid effervescence. If the metal is cadmium, there will be no reaction.

4. **Chromate film**. To detect a chromate film on zinc and cadmium, place a drop of 5 percent aqueous solution of lead acetate on the surface. If the metal has been treated, the surface will show no discoloration for 10 seconds. If there is no surface treatment, an immediate dark spot will appear.

# Corrosion Damage and Rework Limits

Corrosion evaluation will be required after general inspection and cleaning to determine the nature and extent of repair or rework. Local blending of corroded areas may be required to determine the total extent of the corrosion problem. Corrosion damage classifications are defined as follows:

1. **Light corrosion**. Characterized by discoloration or pitting to a depth of approximately 0.001 inch maximum. Light, hand sanding or a minimum of chemical treatment normally removes this type of damage.

2. **Moderate corrosion**. Appears similar to light corrosion except there may be some blisters or evidence of scaling and flaking. Pitting depths may be as deep as 0.010 inch. This type of damage is normally removed by extensive mechanical sanding.

3. **Severe corrosion**. General appearance may be similar to moderate corrosion with severe blistering exfoliation and scaling or flaking. Pitting depths will be deeper than 0.010 inch. Extensive mechanical sanding or grinding normally removes this type of damage. Severe corrosion damage beyond the limits of the aircraft structural repair manual will require FAA-approved engineering authorization and may include the following typical corrosion repairs: trimming out of cracked and corroded areas or spot facing of fastener locations.

Determine degree of corrosion damage (light, moderate, or severe) with a depth dial gauge, straight edge, or a molding compound. The depth of corrosion cannot be measured until all the corrosion is removed. Before measurements are made, visually determine if corrosion is in an area, which has previously been reworked. If corrosion is in the recess of a faired or blended area, measure damage to include the material, which has previously been removed. The following method outlines the process for taking measurements with the depth gauge.

1. Remove loose corrosion products, if present.
2. Position depth gauges and determine the measurement reading.

## NOTE
*The base of the depth gauge should be flat against the undamaged surface on each side of the corrosion. When taking measurements on concave or convex surfaces, place the base perpendicular to the radius of the surface.*

3. Take several additional depth readings.
4. Select deepest reading as being the depth of the corrosion damage.

Measurement of the depth of blended pits (material removed) can be made using a depth dial gauge. If the depth dial gauge will not work, clay impressions, liquid rubber, or other similar means, which will give accurate results, may be used to determine material removed. In the event that material removal limits have been exceeded, the area or part should be repaired or replaced. If a replacement or repair criterion is not contained in the repair manual, contact the manufacturer or the FAA.

Special emphasis is directed to the effect of too many extra coats of paint on balanced control surfaces. Mechanics must avoid adding additional coats of paint in excess of what the manufacturer originally applied. If available consult the aircraft manufacturer's instructions relative to finishing and balance of control surfaces.

## *NOTE*
*It is a sure sign if the attaching hardware is painted (bolts and nuts) the flight control surface may have not been rebalanced.*

# Aircraft Paint

When an aircraft is initially certificated, its empty weight and EWCG are determined and recorded in the weight and balance record. Weight and balance is of such vital importance that each Aviation Maintenance Technician (AMT) maintaining an aircraft must be fully aware of his or her responsibility to provide the pilot with current and accurate information for the actual weight of the aircraft and the location of the center of gravity. This is why when an aircraft is repainted a new weight and balance is required, paint has weight and may change the CG. An example is a Boeing 747-400; its external paint can weight between 800 and 1,000 pounds. So if the tail section were repainted it would affect the weight and balance. Reference 14 CFR Part 43 Appendix A (a)(xi). Take note when **any flight control** rudder, aileron, or elevator is repainted it **must** be rebalanced to prevent flutter.

Aircraft finishes can be separated into three general classes: (1) protective, (2) appearance, and (3) decorative. Internal and unexposed are finished to protect them from deterioration. All exposed parts and surfaces are finished to provide protection and to present a pleasing appearance. Decorative finishing includes trim striping, the painting of emblems, the application of decals, and identification numbers and letters.

A good intact paint finish is one of the most effective barriers available for placement between metal surfaces and corrosive media. Touching up the existing paint finish and keeping it in good condition will eliminate most general corrosion problems. When a paint surface has deteriorated badly, it is best to strip and repaint the entire panel rather than attempt to touchup the area. Touchup materials should be the same as the original finish. Check the maintenance manual for the type of paint approve for your aircraft, color is your option.

It should be noted, however, that under section 601 of the Federal Aviation Act of 1958, as amended, (49 U.S.C. 1421), the FAA has the authority to issue minimum standards governing aircraft materials as may be required in the **interest of safety** and to issue reasonable regulations found necessary to provide adequately for safety in air commerce. Typical standards issued by the FAA that relate to aircraft materials, including paint, are contained in 14 CFR sections 23.603, 23.609, 25.603 and 25.609 of the Federal Aviation. In addition, the Code of Federal Regulations contains standards relating to the maintenance of aircraft. The term "maintenance" is defined in section 1.1 of the Code of Federal Regulations (14 CFR Part 1.1) to include preservation of aircraft parts. The painting of aircraft parts in certain cases could be considered to be maintenance, and as such, the requirements of section 43.13 of the Code of Federal Regulations (14 CFR 43.13) and, with respect to repair stations, the requirements of sections 145.109 and 145.217 would be applicable to the materials used in those painting operations.

I have seen aircraft painted with house paint using a roller. Latex house paint is unacceptable for aircraft and should not be used.

# Paint and N-numbers

Under the provisions of the Federal Aviation Act of 1958 and implementing CFR, except as provided in CFR Part 21 section 21.182(b)(2), a civil aircraft must be registered and identified before it may be operated in the United States. Federal Aviation Regulations Part 45 contains provisions concerning display and description of nationality and registration marks on U.S. aircraft. Section 21.182 of the CFR, requires each applicant for an airworthiness certificate to show that the aircraft is identified as required in CFR section 45.11. Part 45 of the CFR sets forth the requirements for display of nationality and registration marks; display of special airworthiness classification marks; identification plates for aircraft, aircraft engines, propellers; and identification of certain replacement and critical aircraft parts and components

Appropriate nationality and registration marks ("N" numbers) must be displayed on the aircraft before a U.S. airworthiness certificate in any category may be issued. Aircraft nationality and registration marking requirements are contained in 14 CFR Part 45, Subpart C.

It is unacceptable to place any emblem, symbol, or decoration between the "N" and the registration number, or between any of the letters or numbers in the registration number. Company names, trademarks, decorations, etc., that are placed on areas of the aircraft other than those prescribed for nationality and registration marks should be evaluated by the local Federal Aviation Administration (FAA) inspector to determine whether they impede or degrade legibility of the required nationality and registration marks.

**Ornamentation** Section 45.21(c)(2),. This section prohibits the use of ornamentation. Shading, when it facilitates the reading of the nationality and registration marks, is not considered to be ornamentation. Similarly, a border around each character is not considered to be ornamentation, but it is considered to be a part of the character for the purposes of FAR sections 45.29(d) and (e).

**Legibility** Section 45.21(c)(3) and 45.21(c)(4). Ornamentation and color contrast may affect the legibility of the nationality and registration marks. For example, nationality and registration marks may contrast in color with the background but still may not be legible if the background is highly decorated in some manner, such as checkering. One means of determining that required nationality and registration marks are legible would be the ability to clearly distinguish 12-inch marks without optical aid (e.g., binoculars, etc.) from a distance of 500 feet, in a horizontal line, perpendicular to the side of the aircraft during daylight hours. Any questions in this area should be resolved on an individual basis through consultation with the local FAA inspector.

**Repainting aircraft nationality and registration marks**. Federal Aviation Regulations Part 45, Subpart C, was amended effective November 2, 1981, (Amendment 45-13), to require the display of 12-inch high nationality and registration marks on aircraft in place of the smaller 2-inch and 3-inch numbers previously allowed. This was based on a determination that the 2-inch and 3-inch marks were too difficult to see. To preclude an undue burden on the aircraft owner/operators, CFR 45 section 45.29 permits owners of certain aircraft to continue to display the smaller nationality and registration marks until such time as the aircraft is repainted or the nationality and registration marks are repainted, restored, or changed. Section 45.29 of the CFR also excludes certain other aircraft from the 12-inch height requirement. Additional information can be found in AC 45-2.

On an aircraft displaying 2-inch marks before November 1, 1981, and on aircraft manufactured between November 2, 1981, and January 1, 1983, you may display those marks until the aircraft **is repainted or the marks are repainted, restored, or changed**. Once the aircraft is repainted or the marks are repainted, restored, or changed, the N-number **must be 12 inches high**.

# CHAPTER 13

## RADOMES

# Radomes Introduction

A radome is a covering whose primary purpose is to protect a radar antenna from the elements. It is a part of the airframe and therefore, should have certain physical as well as electrical properties. Physically, a radome should be strong enough to withstand the air loads that it will encounter and it should be contoured to minimize drag. These properties vary with the shape, design speed, and size of the airplane on which it is to be installed. Electrically, a radome should permit the passage of the radar's transmitted signals and return echoes with minimum distortion and absorption. In order to do this; it should have a certain electrical thickness. The electrical thickness of a radome is related to the physical thickness, operating frequency, and the types of material and construction used. This relationship is defined by a number of complex mathematical equations, which are of interest only to radome design engineers. These equations show that, for given physical properties, a radome should have a certain electrical thickness for a certain narrow range of operating frequencies. This is the reason why C-band radomes will not give optimum performance with X-band radars and vice versa. Also, a very small variation in physical thickness may cause a sizable variation in electrical thickness. Radar efficiency, definition, and accuracy of display depend upon a clear, nondistorted, reflection-free antenna view through the radome. Consequently, a radome should be precisely built for optimum performance.

# Radome Characteristics

There are two general types of radomes, the "thin wall" and "sandwich" types. Thin wall radomes are considered to be thin relative to the wavelength of the radar. They are generally useful when the radar frequency is low enough to permit a skin thickness, which will satisfy the structural requirements. Sandwich radomes consist of two or more plastic skins separated by a dielectric core. The core may consist of honeycomb plastic sections, hollow flutes, or foam plastic. The dielectric and separation of the skins will depend upon the wavelength of the radar frequency or frequencies.

# Radome Damage

Damages to sandwich parts are divided into groups or classes according to the severity and possible effect upon the structure of the aircraft and upon electrical efficiency. Damages are classified in three basic classes:

1. Class I repair--scars, scratches, or erosion affecting the outer ply only.

2. Class II repairs--punctures, delaminations, contamination's, or fractures in one facing only, possibly accompanied by damage to the core.

3. Class III repairs--damage extending completely through the sandwich affecting both the facings and the core.

Probably the most frequent damage to radomes is holes in the structure caused by static discharges. These can be large holes that are readily apparent or small pinholes that are almost imperceptible. Any hole, regardless of size, can cause major damage to a radome since moisture can enter the radome wall and cause internal delamination. If the moisture freezes, more serious damage may occur. If enough moisture collects, the radiation pattern will be distorted and the transmitted signals and return echoes seriously attenuated. Ram air through a hole can delaminate and break the inner surface of the radome and result in separation of the skins or faces of the material from the core, weakening the radome structure. Other types of damage are characterized as dents and scratches caused by impact with stones and birds and improper handling of the radome when it is removed for maintenance of the radar antenna. This type of damage is easily found by inspection.

High performance radar radomes are very precisely constructed and sometimes the slightest change in their physical characteristics, such as excessive layers of paint, can adversely affect radar system performance. All repairs to radomes, no matter how minor, should return the radome to its original or properly altered condition, both electrically and structurally. The performance of proper maintenance to precision radomes requires special knowledge and techniques and the use of proper tools and materials. An improper minor repair can eventually lead to an expensive major repair. A radome having undergone major repairs should be tested to ascertain that its electrical properties have not been impaired. The testing of radomes requires test equipment that usually is found only in repair facilities specializing in radome maintenance. Even minor repairs may affect one or all of the following:

1.  **Transmissivity.** Which is the ability of a radome to pass radar energy through it.

2.  **Reflection.** Which is the return or reflection of the outgoing radar energy from the radome back into the antenna and waveguide system.

3.  **Diffraction.** Which is the bending of the radar energy as it passes through the radome. These electrical properties, when altered by improper repair, may cause loss of signal, distortion and displacement of targets, and can clutter the display to obscure the target. Poor radome electrical performance can produce numerous problems, which may appear to be symptoms of deficiencies in other units of the radar system. The following are examples of improper repair:

    1.  Use of wrong materials - not compatible with original radome materials.
    2.  Patches of different thickness.
    3.  Poor fabrication techniques.
    4.  Nonvoid-free patches.
    5.  Repairs overlapping.
    6.  Holes plugged with resin, screws, metal, wood, and plastic plugs.
    7.  Cuts or cracks simply coated with resin.
    8.  Tape (including electrical tape) over hole or crack and covered with resin.
    9.  Oversize patches.
    10. Too much or too little resin.
    11. Exterior coatings - too many coats, too thick, uneven thickness - metallic base paints.
    12. Filled honeycomb cells.
    13. Repairs made without removing moisture or moisture contamination from inside of radome wall.
    14. Abrupt changes in cross-sectional areas.
    15. Patches projecting above outside contour lines.
    16. Improper cure.
    17. Wrong size cells or density of honeycomb.
    18. Excessive overlap in honeycomb joints.
    19. Poor bonding of skin to core.
    20. Gaps in honeycomb core.

# Radome Inspection

Inspection of aircraft having weather radar installations should include a visual check of the radome surface for signs of surface damage, holes, cracks, chipping, and peeling of paint, etc. Attach fittings and fastenings, neoprene erosion caps, and lightening strips, when installed should also be inspected.

Pay attention to spray paint on any radome it will change the electrical properties. If a radome requires painting it should be sent to the OEM or Repair Station that can strip, repair, and repaint the radome.

Both the physical and electrical properties of radomes should be given careful consideration during repair operations. These properties are carefully controlled during manufacture and should not be altered by improper repairs.

# CHAPTER 14

## FLAMMABILITY CERTIFICATION

# Flammability Certification of Fabric

General flammability requirements for certain structure, electric cables and associated equipment, crew and passenger compartment materials, and cargo compartment materials are addressed in CFR Part 23 and Civil Air Regulations (CAR) Part 3. However, specific acceptable criteria for demonstrating compliance with the fire protection requirements are not specified. Further, Flight Standards Service Release No. 453, which was used in certifying CAR Part 3 airplanes, was cancelled and never replaced with comparable material. Advisory Circular 23-2 incorporates the pertinent sections of Flight Standards Service Release No. 453, Federal Test Method Standard No. 191A, SAE Aerospace Standard (AS) 1055B, and SAE Aerospace Information Report (AIR) 1377A.

Aircraft modifiers will continue to be misled if they do not adhere to FAA Advisory Circular 20-62, Policy for Eligibility and Identification of Approved Aeronautical Replacement Parts. This quality applies not only to fabric, but also to any other replacement part being installed in aircraft. It is, and has been, a common practice of many fabric distributors/contractors to state that their fabric meets, passes, and is certified to section 25.853(b-3) regardless of the fact that they did not hold the required FAA approval and did not perform the tests on the actual rolls of fabric being sold for aircraft use. Therefore, the modifiers may be in violation of CFR Part 43.

All material used for aircraft interiors should come with a certification stating that it meets the required standards of the CFR as stated previously. If the material cannot be positively identified to meet these certification requirements, then it should not be used for aircraft interiors. Transport category aircraft have a more stringent requirement for burn certification as stated in sections 25.853, 25.855, and appendix F.

Aircraft owners and operators should be aware of the requirements stated demand a positive identification of the material installed in their aircraft along with a copy of the certification to be included in the maintenance records. Although section 91.403 makes the owner or operator primarily responsible for the airworthiness of the aircraft, it is also the responsibility of all maintenance personnel to comply with the requirements of CFR Part 43 to assure that the owner/operator is in compliance with section 91.403 before approving the aircraft for return to service.

If you cannot find burn certifications and a maintenance entry, the material may be unairworthy and should be noted on the 100 hour/annual or pre-purchase inspection.

A Malfunction or Defect Report received from a repair station certified for burn tests brought to The FAA's attention the need for clarification of the requirements. The summarized report follows.

During the rebuilding of a Piper PA-18 Super Cub, it was determined that a new headliner was required. After receipt of the new headliner from a popular aviation supplier, the burn certification on the material could not be verified.

The manufacturer provided a statement that "the material was manufactured to meet or exceed the flame and mildew specifications of 14 CFR Part 25 Section 25.853(b)."

First of all, any authorized statement of material burn certification must come from a FAA burn-certified repair station operating under 14 CFR Part 145 or another FAA-approved source, such as a manufacturer under a TSO or PMA. The Operation Specifications of a burn-certified repair station must contain a "Limited Rating for Specialized Services," the specific service authorized, and the specifications to be used. A burn certification must include the name and certificate number of the repair station or other FAA-approved source that performed the required tests. Traceability of approved testing must be maintained all the way to the end product, in this case the headliner. The aircraft certification basis should always be checked to determine which regulations apply to a particular airplane, rotorcraft, engine, propeller, or aeronautical product. Either Part 23, 25, 27 or CAR 3, 4, etc.

The second point concerning this report is that Part 25 deals with the "Airworthiness Standards: Transport Category Airplanes." Obviously, this regulation does not apply to a Piper PA 18 airplane. Part 23 is entitled "Airworthiness Standards: Normal, Utility, Acrobatic, and Commuter Category Airplanes." This regulation does apply to a large number of general aviation type airplanes. However, it does not apply to the PA 18. It should be mentioned that both of these regulations contain very rigorous requirements for certification of materials used in airplane interiors and are more stringent than the requirements for this airplane. The Piper PA 18 airplane was originally certificated under "Civil Air Regulations 3" (CAR 3). CAR 3 is contained in the "Civil Aeronautics Manual 3" (CAM 3). Therefore, the requirements for airplane interiors found in CAM 3, Section 3.388 apply to the Piper PA 18 airplane. FAA-approved materials, which meet or exceed the requirements found in CAM 3, would be acceptable for the PA 18. The requirements of CAM 3 state that if smoking is to be permitted, the material used must be flame-resistant; if smoking is not to be permitted, then a "No Smoking" placard must be installed, and the material used must be flash-resistant.

The aircraft certification basis should always be checked to determine which regulations apply to a particular airplane, rotorcraft, engine, propeller, or aeronautical product.

# Flammable Materials in Aircraft

Manufacturers of aircraft provide a plastic or paper covering for use during final assembly, inspection, and readying of the aircraft for delivery. The intent is to keep the carpeting and upholstery clean. All crew and passenger compartment interior materials must be flash or flame resistant to meet airworthiness certificate requirements. Make sure you have the burn certification for any new interior or seat covers.

# Civil Air Regulation, CAR-3 Aircraft Interior

The requirement for an interior of a CAR-3 aircraft that is used only in 14 CFR, Part 91 operations, where smoking is not permitted, is that the materials shall be flash-resistant. (Reference CAR-3.388.)

For compartments in CAR-3 aircraft where smoking is permitted, the wall and ceiling linings, the covering of all upholstering, floors, and furnishings shall be flame-resistant. Such compartments should be equipped with an adequate number of self-contained ashtrays. All other compartments shall be placarded against smoking. (Refer to CAR Part 3.388.)

If fabric is bought in bulk to refurbish the interior, seats, and ceiling liners for a CAR-3 aircraft used in Part 91 operations, a manufacturer's statement, declaring that the material meets the American Society for Testing and Materials (ASTM) or similar national standard for either flash resistance or flame resistance, would be acceptable, but only for a CAR-3 aircraft installation. (Refer to 14 CFR Part 43, section 43.13(a)). A manufacturer's statement is acceptable due to neither the Civil Aeronautics Administration (CAA) nor the Federal Aviation Administration (FAA) having published an FAA fire standard for either flash or flame resistance for interior materials for CAR-3 aircraft. Since the FAA would accept and recognize a national standard, the mechanic would reference the manufacturer's statement and the national standard that the material meets in the aircraft's maintenance records.

If an annual inspection is performed on a CAR-3 aircraft with a new interior and there is no mention of a manufacturer's statement that the fabric is flash or flame resistant as applicable, the possibility exists that the fabric is an unapproved part. The mechanic should take the necessary steps to ensure that the fabric meets or exceeds the ASTM or national standards. (Refer to 14 CFR Part 23, appendix F.)

If an FAA-approved STC interior kit is installed in a CAR-3 aircraft, and the material and fabric in the kit are PMA or TSO approved, the mechanic should include the STC number in block 8 of FAA Form 337. It is recommended that for all CAR-3 interiors to use only fabric and materials that meet the more stringent requirements of Part 23, appendix F.

The aircraft certification basis should always be checked to determine which regulations apply to a particular airplane, rotorcraft, engine, propeller, or aeronautical product.

# Flammability Tests

One method, but not the only method, for showing compliance for components requiring certification by flammability tests is considered acceptable for demonstrating compliance with regulations for flash-resistant materials (Reference 14 CFR Part 23 section 23.853(a)).

1.  The apparatus should be similar to the one that is defined in Section 4.1 through 4.9, Method 5906 of Federal Test Method Standard No. 191A. The minimum flame temperature measured by a calibrated thermocouple pyrometer in the center of the flame should be 1550°F.
2.  Three specimens, approximately 4 1/2 inches by 12 1/2 inches, with the long dimension parallel to the warp direction of the cloth, should be tested for each sample unit. It has been found that the pattern of some cloth may cause the cloth to be more hazardous in one direction than in the other, in which case the long dimension of the specimen should be parallel to the more hazardous direction.
3.  The specimens should be conditioned to a temperature of 65°F to 75°F and at 45 to 55 percent relative humidity until moisture equilibrium is reached, or for 24 hours, before testing. Only one specimen should be removed from the conditioning environment at a time and immediately subjected to the flame test.
4.  For plain cloth and rigid materials, the procedure described below should be followed.
    a.  Insert the specimen into the holder with the surface that will be exposed, when installed in the airplane, facing down. It should be clamped such that a 2-inch wide center strip is exposed with a 1/2-inch clearance between the holder and each end of the specimen.
    b.  Adjust the burner to give a flame height of 1 1/2 inches.
    c.  Slide the specimen holder into the cabinet into the test position so that the end of the specimen is 3/4 inch above the top of the burner and the specimen then ignited. Approximately 1 1/2 inches of the specimen should be burned before the timing device is started. The timing should be stopped at least 1 inch before the burning front reaches the end of the specimen.
    d.  Determine the average burn rate of the three specimens, using the time required to travel along a minimum of 10 inches of each specimen. If the specimens do not support combustion after the ignition flame is applied for 15 seconds, if the average burn rate of the three specimens does not exceed 20 inches per minute, or if the flame extinguishes itself and subsequent burning without a flame does not extend into the undamaged areas, the material is acceptable.
5.  For napped or tufted cloth, the procedure below should be followed.
    a.  Comb the cloth twice against the nap or tufting so that the nap or tufting is uniformly raised.
    b.  Use a stop to prevent a flash from traveling across the underside of the cloth and igniting the other end of the specimen before the flash has traveled across the upper surface if the cloth is double-napped

The following flammability test is considered acceptable for demonstrating compliance with regulations for flame-resistant materials, except for electrical wire (Reference sections 23.787(d), 23.853(a), 23.1385(e)).

1. The same apparatus, size of specimens and procedures as specified in paragraph a (1) through a (5) above for testing flash-resistant materials should also be used for testing flame-resistant materials, except for the following:

   a. Determine the average burn rate of the three specimens, using the time required to travel along a minimum of 10 inches of each specimen. If the specimens do not support combustion after the ignition flame is applied for 15 seconds, if the average burn rate of the three specimens does not exceed 4 inches per minute, or if the flame extinguishes itself and subsequent burning without a flame does not extend into the undamaged areas, the material is acceptable.

For information on burn certification contact:

Skandia, Inc.
5002 N. Hwy 251
Davis Junction, IL  61020         Telephone (815) 393-4600

## *NOTE*

*ASTM publication D1682 has been discontinued but is still referred to in some Aerospace Material Specification (AMS). The grab test method previously listed in ASTM D1682, sections 1 through 16, has been superseded by ASTM publication D5034. The strip testing method (most commonly used in aircraft) previously listed in ASTM D1682, sections 17 through 21, has been superseded by ASTM publication D5035.*

# Fabric Cloth

**STRENGTH CRITERIA FOR AIRCRAFT FABRIC.** Minimum performance standards for new intermediate-grade fabric are specified in TSO-C14b, which references AMS 3804C. Minimum performance standards for new Grade A fabric are specified in TSO-C15d, which references AMS 3806D.

The condition of the fabric covering must be determined on every 100-hour and annual inspection, because the strength of the fabric is a definite factor in the airworthiness of an airplane. Fabric is considered to be airworthy until it deteriorates to a breaking strength less than 70 percent of the strength of new fabric required for the aircraft. For example, if grade-A cotton is used on an airplane that requires only intermediate fabric, it can deteriorate to 46 pounds per inch width (70 percent of the strength of intermediate fabric) before it must be replaced.

Fabric installed on aircraft with a wing loading less than 9 lb. per square foot (psf), and a Vne less than 160 mph, will be considered unairworthy when the breaking strength has deteriorated below 46 lb. per inch width, regardless of the fabric grade. Fabric installed on aircraft with a wing loading of 9 lb. per square foot and over, or a VNE of 160 mph and over, will be considered unairworthy when the breaking strength has deteriorated below 56 lb. per inch width.

Fabric installed on a glider or sailplane with a wing loading of 8 lb. per square foot and less, and a VNE of 135 mph or less, will be considered unairworthy when the fabric breaking strength has deteriorated below 35 lb. per inch width, regardless of the fabric grade.

# Fabric Testing

Mechanical devices used to test fabric by pressing against or piercing the finished fabric are not FAA approved and are used at the discretion of the mechanic to base an opinion on the general fabric condition. Punch test accuracy will depend on the individual device calibration, total coating thickness, brittleness, and types of coatings and fabric. Mechanical devices are not applicable to glass fiber fabric that will easily shear and indicate a very low reading regardless of the true breaking strength. If the fabric tests in the lower breaking strength range with the mechanical punch tester or if the overall fabric cover conditions are poor, then more accurate field tests may be made. Cut a 1-1/4-inch wide by 4-inch long sample from a top exposed surface, remove all coatings and ravel the edges to a 1-inch width. Clamp each end between suitable clamps with one clamp anchored to a support structure while a load is applied by adding sand in a suitable container suspended a few inches above the floor. If the breaking strength is still in question, a sample should be sent to a qualified testing laboratory and breaking strength tests made in accordance with American Society of Testing Materials (ASTM) publication D5035.

# CHAPTER 15

## AIR-CONDITIONING

# Air-Conditioning Refrigerant Conversions

This subject affects all aircraft and helicopters with CFC-12 (R-12) Vapor Cycle air-conditioning systems. The information is provided to advise all owners, operators, and maintenance entities of proper standards for converting CFC-12 Vapor Cycle Systems to refrigerants approved by the FAA and the Environmental Protection Agency (EPA).

In 1994, the EPA established the "Significant New Alternative [Refrigerant] Policy" (SNAP) Program to review alternatives to ozone-depleting substances like CFC-12. Under the authority of the 1990 Clean Air Act (CAA), the EPA examines new substitutes for their ozone depleting, global warming, flammability, and toxicity characteristics. The EPA has determined that several refrigerants are acceptable for use as CFC-12 replacements, subject to certain use conditions. The EPA provides information about the current crop of refrigerants and their characteristics and details for their use.

Many companies use the term "drop-in" to mean that a substitute refrigerant will perform identically to CFC-12, that no modifications need to be made to the system, and that the alternative can be used alone or mixed with CFC-12. However, the EPA believes the term confuses and obscures several important regulatory and technical points. First, charging one refrigerant into a system before extracting the old refrigerant is a violation of the SNAP use conditions and is, therefore, illegal. Second, law, such as hoses and compressor shutoff switches, may require certain components. If these components are not present, they must be installed. Third, it is impossible to test a refrigerant in the thousands of air-conditioning systems in existence to demonstrate identical performance. In addition, system performance is greatly affected by outside temperature, humidity, usage conditions, etc., and it is impossible to ensure equal performance under all of these conditions. Finally, it is very difficult to demonstrate that system components will last as long as they would have if CFC-12 were used. For all of these reasons, the EPA does not use the term "drop-in" to describe any alternative refrigerant.

Recommended modifications to any Vapor Cycle System should, at a minimum, meet the regulatory requirements under the CLEAN AIR ACT Amendments (CFR Title VI - Section 608). The Society of Automotive Engineers (SAE) provides guidelines for air-conditioning refrigerant retrofit in their publication J1661.

Under the SNAP rule, each new refrigerant must be used in accordance with approved conditions. If you choose to use an alternative, make sure the service shop meets the appropriate requirements and that it has dedicated recovery equipment for blends or recovery/recycling equipment for HFC-134A.

Conversion of Vapor Cycle Systems is considered a major alteration to the aircraft Type design and conversions may be accomplished using the Supplemental Type Certificate or an FAA Field Approval process.

Most Original Equipment Manufacturer's (OEM) chose R-134A to be the long-term replacement for R-12 in air-conditioning systems, both in new aircraft and in retrofit applications. At this time, however, wide-scale performance testing has not been performed on vehicles retrofitted to these blend refrigerants. Should you have questions about retrofitting to an alternative refrigerant, consult the refrigerant's manufacturer and/or the several EPA publications. One such EPA publication you may want to review is titled "Choosing and Using Alternative Refrigerants in Motor Vehicle Air Conditioning," which is available on the Internet at: hhtp://www.epa.gov/doc/ozone/title6/sna[/macssubs.

During the pre-purchase inspection to prevent trim system malfunction caused by contact between the freon air inlet duct and electrical wiring, which could result in loss of control of the airplane, accomplish the following:

1. Inspect the baggage compartment for stringer or air cycle machine (ACM) by-pass duct damage (cracks, frays, nicks, dents, etc.) in accordance with manufactures manual and service bulletins.

2. If fasteners used to secure the compressor condenser unit mounting rails to the baggage floor interfere with the control cables, replace mounting hardware, prior to further flight.

3. Check the turbine air discharge duct or water separator outlet duct from disconnecting from the cold air unit turbine or from the water separator, resulting in the loss of air supply to maintain adequate cabin pressure on bootstrap systems.

4. Inspect for degradation of the structural capability of the airplane fuselage and sudden loss of cabin pressure due to corrosion of the airplane fuselage structure where the air conditions unit/system is mounted.

5. Inspect overheating of fans and consequent failure of the electromagnetic interference (EMI) filter capacitors, which could result in emission of toxic smoke and fumes throughout the airplane, and consequent adverse effects on flight crew and passengers.

6. Perform a visual inspection of all insulation blankets that have been repaired or changed insure they are secured and on leakage have occurred.

7. Inspect all hose connections and condition of hoses for dry rot and leakage. If the fitting feels oily the system should be check for correct freon level and fitting cleaned.

# CHAPTER 16

## AIRCRAFT REPLACEMENT PARTS

# Replacement Parts

The FAA continues to receive reports of replacement parts being offered for sale as aircraft quality when the quality and origin of the parts are unknown or questionable. Such parts may be advertised or presented as "unused," "like new," or "remanufactured." These imply that the quality of the parts is equal to an acceptable part. Purchasers of these parts may not be aware of the potential hazards involved with replacement parts for which acceptability for installation on a type-certificated product has not been established.

The performance rules for replacement of parts and materials used in the maintenance, preventive maintenance, and alteration of aircraft that have (or have had) a U.S. airworthiness certificate, and components thereof, are specified in 14 CFR Parts 43 sections 43.13. These rules require that the installer of a part use methods, techniques, and practices acceptable to the FAA. Additionally, the installer of a part must accomplish the work in such a manner and use materials of such quality, that the product or appliance worked on **will be at least equal to its original not greater than** or properly altered condition with respect to the qualities affecting airworthiness.

The continued airworthiness of an aircraft, which includes the replacement of parts, is the responsibility of the owner/operator, as specified in 14 CFR Parts 91, 119, 121, 125, and 135, sections 91.403, 121.363, 125.243, and 135.413. These rules require that the installer determine that a part is acceptable for installation on a product or component prior to returning that product or component to service with the part installed. Those rules also require that the installation of a part must be accomplished in accordance with data approved by the FAA, if the installation constitutes a major repair or alteration.

As part of determining whether installation of a part conforms with all applicable regulations, the installer should establish that the part was manufactured under a production approval pursuant to Part 21, that an originally acceptable part has been maintained in accordance with Part 43, or that the part is otherwise acceptable for installation (e.g., has been found to conform to data approved by the FAA).

Acceptable replacement parts should be identified using one of the following methods:

**Airworthiness Approval Tag**. FAA Form 8130-3, Airworthiness Approval Tag, identifies a part or group of parts for export approval and conformity determination from production approval holders. It also serves as approval for return to service after maintenance or alteration by an authorized Part 145 Repair Station, or a U.S. Air Carrier having an approved Continuous Airworthiness Maintenance Program under Part 135.

**Foreign Manufactured Replacement Parts**. New foreign manufactured parts for use on U.S. type-certificated products may be imported when there is a bilateral airworthiness agreement between the country of manufacture and the United States and the part meets the requirements under section 21.502.

**Used parts** may be identified by the records required for approval for return to service as set forth in section 43.9. FAA Form 8130-3 may be used for this purpose if the requirements of section 43.9 are contained in or attached to the form and approved for return to service by a U.S. FAA-certificated repair station or U.S. air carrier under the requirement of their Continuous Airworthiness Maintenance Program. There is no set format or form required for a maintenance or alteration record. However, the data or information used to identify a part must be traceable to a person authorized to perform and approve for return to service maintenance and alteration under Part 43. The records must contain as a minimum those data that set forth in section 43.9.

The use of an authorization tag (Yellow Tag) does not approve the installation of a part on a type-certificated product. Additional substantiated authorization for compliance with Part 43 and the FAA-approved data for major repairs and alterations may be required for installation on a type-certificated product.

If the part has been rebuilt, overhauled, inspected, modified, or repaired, the records should include a maintenance release, return to service tag, repaired parts tag or similar documentation from a FAA-certificated person. Documentation describing the maintenance performed and parts replaced must be made for the part (i.e., FAA Form 8130-3 or FAA Repair Station work order). (Reference 14 CFR 43 section 43.9 and Appendix B).

The records should include information, either directly or by reference, to support documentation that may be helpful to the user or installer in making a final determination, as to the airworthiness and eligibility of the part. Listed are examples of information that should be obtained, as applicable:

1. AD status.
2. Compliance or noncompliance with service bulletins.
3. Life/cycle limited parts status (i.e., time, time since overhaul, cycles, history) should be substantiated. If the part is serialized and life-limited, then both operational time and/or cycles (where applicable) must be indicated. Historical records that clearly establish and substantiate time and cycles must be provided as evidence.
4. Shelf-life data, including manufacturing date or cure date.
5. Return to service date.
6. Shortages applicable to assemblies or kits.
7. Import or export certification documents.
8. The name of the person who removed the part.
9. FAA Form 337, Major Repair or Alteration.
10. Maintenance Manual standards used for performing maintenance.

# Eligibility of Parts

How to determining the quality, eligibility and traceability of aeronautical parts and materials intended for installation on U.S. type-certificated products.

The continued airworthiness of an aircraft, which includes the replacement of parts, is the responsibility of the owner/operator, as specified in 14 CFR Parts 91, 119, 121, 125, and 135, sections 91.403, 121.363, 125.243, and 135.413. These rules require that the installer determine that a part is acceptable for installation on a product or component prior to returning that product or component to service with the part installed. Those rules also require that the installation of a part must be accomplished in accordance with data approved by the FAA, if the installation constitutes a major repair or alteration.

The manufacturer of the part should be identified; if not identified it may be difficult to prove that the part is acceptable for installation on a type-certificated product.

In addition to unapproved parts, used or repaired parts may be offered for sale as "like new," "near new," and "remanufactured." Such terms do not aid the purchaser in positively determining whether the part is acceptable for installation on a type-certificated product and do not constitute the legal serviceability and condition of aircraft parts.

**It is the installer's responsibility to ensure airworthiness**. Aircraft parts distributors, aircraft supply companies or aircraft electronic parts distributors, unless they are a Parts Approval Holder (PAH), cannot certify the airworthiness of the parts they advertise and/or sell; therefore, it is the installer's responsibility to request documentation establishing traceability to a PAH.

# FAA-Approved Parts

Many unapproved parts may, at first glance look like an approved part. However, close inspection of the information on the container is needed to determine if in fact the part does comply with the CFR requirements. For example, look on the container for a product such as fabric adhesive and find the PMA part number, STC number, batch number, and shelf life. Then compare what you find with the requirements of section 21.305. Just because a container has the word "FAA/PMA" is not enough. The CFR require more detail. Attention to all details to see that a product complies with the CFR is how consumers can be assured of a safe product that will do the job intended. The four questions you should asked about parts are:

1. What is an approved part?
2. How can approved parts be produced?
3. What is a suspected unapproved part?
4. How do you determine the status of parts?

# Approved Parts

Under 14 CFR Part 21, section 21.305, parts, which were produced under an FAA-approved production system and conform to FAA-approved data, may be approved under the following:

"Approved parts" are identified as parts, which have met one of the following requirements:

1. Produced in accordance with a Parts Manufacturer Approval (PMA) issued under Part 21, Subpart K.

2. Produced in accordance with a Technical Standard Order Authorization (TSOA) issued by the Administrator under Part 21, Subpart O.

3. Produced during the Type Certificate (TC) application process under Part 21, Subpart B, or the Supplemental Type Certificate (STC) application process under Part 21, Subpart E, prior to the issuance of the certificate; subsequently determined to conform to the approved TC or STC data (Reference to CFR 23 section 21.303 (b)(1)).

4. Produced under a TC without a separate production authorization, and an Approved Production Inspection System (APIS) in accordance with Part 21, Subpart F.

5. Produced under a Production Certificate (PC) (including by a licensee if produced under PC authority), in accordance with Part 21, Subpart G.

## NOTE

*The term "licensing agreement" refers to Part 21.133(a)(2) which allows any person to apply for a Production Certificate (PC) if they hold or have rights to the benefit of a Type Certificate (TC) from the owner of the TC. The term "licensing agreement" does not imply or infer that a PC holder may grant production approval to any party on behalf of the FAA. Authority granted by a PC holder to a supplier to ship parts directly to a customer of the PC holder is not considered to be a licensing agreement.*

6. Produced in accordance with an approval under a bilateral airworthiness agreement under Part 21, Subpart N.

7. Approved in any other manner acceptable to the Administrator section 21.305(d).

## NOTE

*Parts, which have been maintained, rebuilt, altered, or overhauled, and approved for return to service in accordance with Parts 43 and/or 145, are considered to be "approved parts." Parts, which have been inspected and/or tested by persons authorized to determine conformity to FAA-approved design data, may also be found to be acceptable for installation. Military surplus parts (defined as parts which have been originally released as surplus by the military, even if subsequently resold by manufacturers, owners/operators, repair facilities, or any other suppliers of parts) may fall under this condition. AC 20-62, Eligibility, Quality, and Identification of Aeronautical Replacement Parts should be referred to for information regarding eligibility and traceability of replacement parts.*

8. Produced as standard parts that conform to established industry or U.S. specifications (nut and bolts).

## NOTE

*Standard parts are not required to be produced under a FAA Approved Production Inspection System; therefore it is incumbent upon the installer (and the producer) to determine that the part conforms. The part must be identified as part of the approved type design or found to be acceptable for installation under part 43. Refer to AC 20-62, for additional guidance on this matter.*

9. Produced by an owner or operator for the purpose of maintaining or altering his or her own product.

10. Manufactured by a repair station or other authorized person during alteration in accordance with an STC or Field Approval (which is not for sale as a separate part), in accordance with Part 43 and Order 8000.50, Repair Station Production of Replacement or Modification Parts.

11. Fabricated by a qualified person in the course of a repair for the purpose of returning a TC product to service (which is not for sale as a separate part) under Part 43.

## NOTE

*In summary, "approved parts" are those which are produced in accordance with the means outlined in Part 21, maintained in accordance with Parts 43, 91, and meet applicable design standards.*

# Acceptable Parts

The following parts may be found to be acceptable for installation on a type-certificated product:

1. Standard parts (such as nuts and bolts) conforming to an established industry or U.S. specification.
2. Parts produced by an owner or operator for maintaining or altering their own product and which are shown to conform to FAA-approved data.
3. Parts for which inspections and tests have been accomplished by appropriately certificated persons authorized to determine conformity to FAA-approved design data.

**Class I Product**
A complete aircraft, aircraft engine, or propeller that has been type-certificated in accordance with the applicable regulations, and for which Federal Aviation Specifications or TC data sheets have been issued.

**Class II Product**
A major component of a Class I product (e.g., wings, fuselages, empennage assemblies, landing gears, power transmissions, or control surfaces, etc.), the failure of which would jeopardize the safety of a Class I product; or any part, material, or appliance, approved and manufactured under the Technical Standard Order (TSO) system in the "C" series.

**Class III Product**
Any part or component that is not a Class I or Class II product, including standard parts. Class III products are considered to be parts.

**New Part**

A product, accessory, parts, or material that has no operating times or cycles.

# NOTE

*There could be time/cycles on a newly type-certificated product (e.g., use of a manufacturer's test cell or certification requirements).*

**Surplus Part**

Describes a product, assembly, part, or material that has been released as surplus by the military, manufacturers, owners/operators, repair facilities, or any other parts supplier. These products should show traceability to a FAA-approved manufacturing procedure.

Many materials, parts, appliances, and components that have been released as surplus by the military service or by manufacturers may originate from obsolete or overstocked items. Parts obtained from surplus sources may be used, provided it is established that they meet the standards to which they were manufactured, interchangeability with the original part can be established, and they are in compliance with all applicable AD's. Such items, although advertised as remanufactured," "high quality," "like new," "unused," or "looks good," should be carefully evaluated before they are purchased. The storage time, storage conditions, or shelf life of surplus parts and materials are not usually known.

**Overhauled Part**

Describes an airframe, aircraft engine, propeller, appliance, or component part using methods, techniques, and practices acceptable to the Administrator, which has undergone the following:

1.  Has been disassembled, cleaned, inspected, repaired when necessary, and reassembled to the extent possible.

2.  Has been tested in accordance with approved standards and technical data, or current standards and technical data acceptable to the Administrator (i.e., manufacturer's data), which have been developed and documented by the holder of one of the following:
    a.  Type Certificate (TC).
    b.  Supplemental Type Certificate (STC), or material, part, process, or appliance approval under section 21.305.
    c.  Part Manufacture Approval (PMA).

**Rebuilt Part**

Describes an aircraft, airframe, aircraft engine, propeller, or appliance, using new or used parts that conform to new part tolerances and limits or to approved oversized or undersized dimensions that has undergone the following:

1.  Has been disassembled, cleaned, inspected, repaired as necessary and reassembled to the extent possible.

2.  Has been tested to the same tolerances and limits as a new item.

**The certification may be verified on a form similar to the FAA Form 8130-3 (i.e., Joint Aviation Authority (JAA), JAA Form One)**, used by European member countries of the JAA with which the U.S. has a bilateral airworthiness agreement. The JAA is an organization of European member nations that has the responsibility to develop JAA regulations and policy. The procedures and the countries, with which the U.S. has bilateral airworthiness agreements and the condition of the agreements, are contained in AC 21-23.

**FAA TSO Markings**

TSOA is issued under section 21.607, subpart O. A TSOA must be permanently and legibly marked with the following:

1. Name and address of the manufacturer.
2. The name, type, part number, or model designation of the article.
3. The serial number or the date of manufacture of the article or both.
4. The applicable TSO number.

### FAA-PMA Symbol
A FAA-PMA is issued under section 21.303. Each PMA part should be marked with the letters, "FAA-PMA," in accordance with 14 CFR Part 45, section 45.15:

1. The name.
2. Trademark, or symbol.
3. Part number.
4. Name and model designation of each certificated product on which the part is eligible for installation.

## NOTE

*Parts that are too small or otherwise impractical to be marked may, as an alternative, be marked showing the above information on an attached tag or labeled container. If the marking on the tag is too extensive to be practical, the tag attached to a part or container may refer to a readily available manual or catalog for part eligibility information. Under a licensing agreement, when the applicant has been given the right to use the TC holder's design, which includes the part number, and a replacement part is produced under that agreement, the part number may be identical to that of the TC holder, provided that the PMA holder includes the letters, "FAA-PMA," and the PMA holder's identification symbol is on the part. In all other cases, the PMA holder's part number must be different from that of the TC holder.*

Shipping Ticket, Invoice, or Other Production Approval Holder's (PAH) Documents or Markings. These may provide evidence that a part was produced by a manufacturer holding a FAA-approved manufacturing process.

### Direct Ship Authority
In order for U.S. manufactured parts, with "direct ship" authority to be recognized as being produced under a manufacturer's FAA production approval. The manufacturer must specifically authorize the shipping supplier, in writing, and must establish procedures to ensure that the shipped parts conform to the approved design and are in condition for safe operation. A statement to the supplier from the certificate holder authorizing direct shipment and date of authorization should be included on the shipping ticket, invoice, or other transfer document. It should contain a declaration that the individual part was produced under a production certificate.

### Maintenance Release Document.
A release, signed by an appropriately certificated person, qualified for the relevant function that signifies that the item has been returned to service, after a maintenance or test function has been completed. This type of documentation could be in the form of a repair station tag, containing adequate information (section 43.9), work order, FAA Form 337, FAA Form 8130-3, or a maintenance record entry, which must include an appropriate description of the maintenance work performed, including the recording requirements of section 43.9 and Appendix B.

## NOTE

*When a noncertificated person certifies that they are shipping the correct part ordered, the only thing they are stating is that the part number agrees with the purchase order, not the status of FAA acceptability of the part.*

### Unusual Part Circumstances
If a particular part was obtained from any of the following, then it should be so identified by some type of documentation (i.e., maintenance record entries, removal entries, overhaul records).

1. Noncertificated aircraft (aircraft without airworthiness certificate, i.e., public use, non-U.S., and military surplus aircraft).

2. Aircraft, aircraft engines, propellers or appliances subjected to extreme stress, sudden stoppage, heat, major failure or accident.
3. Salvaged aircraft or aircraft components.

# Standard Part

A part manufactured in complete compliance with an established industry or U.S. government specification which includes design, manufacturing, test and acceptance criteria, and uniform identification requirements; or for a type of part which the Administrator has found demonstrates conformity based solely on meeting performance criteria, is in complete compliance with an established industry or U.S. Government specification which contains performance criteria, test and acceptance criteria, and uniform identification requirements. The specification must include all information necessary to produce and conform the part, and be published so that any party may manufacture the part. Examples include, but are not limited to, National Aerospace Standards (NAS), Army-Navy Aeronautical Standard (AN), Society of Automotive Engineers (SAE), SAE Sematec, Joint Electron Device Engineering Council, Joint Electron Tube Engineering Council, and American National Standards Institute (ANSI).

## NOTE

*Criteria for acceptable established industry or U.S. Government specifications differs for parts which must meet specifications which include design, manufacturing, test and acceptance criteria, and uniform identification requirements; and for parts (which the Administrator finds demonstrates conformity based solely on meeting performance criteria) which must meet established industry or U.S. Government specifications which contain test and acceptance criteria, and uniform identification requirements. The organizations listed may publish one or both types of specifications.*

The FAA will publicize determinations of parts, which (the Administrator finds) demonstrate conformity based solely on meeting performance criteria. A determination has been made for discreet electrical and electronic components, as published in the Federal Register on January 31, 1997.

# Unapproved Part

A part that does not meet the requirements of an "approved part" refer to definition of "Approved Parts".

This term also includes parts, which have been improperly returned to service (contrary to Parts 43 or 145), and/or parts, which may fall under one or more of the following categories:

1. Parts shipped directly to the user by a manufacturer, supplier, or distributor, where the parts were not produced under the authority of and in accordance with an FAA production approval for the part, such as production overruns where the parts did not pass through an approved quality system.

## NOTE

*This includes parts shipped to an end user by a PAH's supplier who does not have direct ship authority from the Part Authority Holder (PAH).*

2. New parts, which have passed through a Production Approval Holder's (PAH) quality system, which, are found not to conform to the approved design/data.

## NOTE

*Parts damaged due to shipping or warranty issues are not required to be reported as Suspected Unapproved Part (SUP).*

3. Parts that have been maintained, rebuilt, altered, overhauled, or approved for return to service by persons or facilities not authorized to perform such services under Parts 43 and/or 145.

4. Parts that have been maintained, rebuilt, altered, overhauled, or approved for return to service, which are subsequently found not to conform to approved data.

## NOTE

*This would include parts produced by an owner/operator for the purpose of maintaining or altering their own product, which have been approved for return to service, and found not to conform to approved data.*

*This does not include parts currently in the inspection or repair process, such as, parts removed for maintenance. Parts in this status may be considered not acceptable for installation.*

5. Counterfeit parts.

# Detection of Unapproved Parts

The airworthiness of aeronautical products would be in question if the design and quality of the parts are unknown. Positive identification of unapproved parts can be difficult if the parts display characteristics similar to that of an "approved part." The following guidelines offer a means by which "approved parts" (and their sources) may be assessed.

## Procurement Process

A procedure to ensure the procurement of "approved" parts should be established prior to purchasing parts and material for installation in TC products. This procedure should include the following as a minimum:

1. Methods of identifying distributors and or suppliers who have a documentation system, and receiving inspection system which ensures the traceability of their parts to an FAA-approved source.

2. Methods of screening unfamiliar distributors and/or suppliers to determine if the parts present a potential risk of being "unapproved." The following are situations which may raise questions:

   a. A quoted or advertised price, which is significantly lower than the price quoted by other distributors and/or suppliers of the same part.
   b. A delivery schedule, which is significantly shorter than that of other distributors and/or suppliers (when the stock of a like item is exhausted).
   c. Sales quotes or discussions from unidentified distributors, which create the perception that, an unlimited supply of parts, components, or material are available to the end user.
   d. A distributor and/or supplier's inability to provide substantiating documentation that the part was produced pursuant to an FAA approval or inspected, repaired, overhauled, preserved or altered in accordance with the CFR.

## NOTE

*To assist in alleviating issues regarding "lack of documentation" and improve "traceability," the FAA published AC 00-56, Voluntary Industry Distributor Accreditation Program. The AC describes a system for the voluntary accreditation of civil aircraft parts distributors on the basis of voluntary industry oversight, and provides information that may be used for developing accreditation programs. Purchasers conducting business with participants in this program should not be discouraged from implementing their own procurement and acceptance procedures (as outlined in AC 00-56). The Airline Suppliers Association maintains a listing of participants in the voluntary program on the Internet at the following address: http://www.airlinesuppliers.com.*

## Acceptance procedures

Procedures should include a means of identifying Suspected Unapproved Part (SUP) during the receiving inspection and prevent their acceptance. Suggested areas to be addressed include the following:

1. Confirm the packaging of the part identifies the supplier or distributor, and is free from alteration or damage.

2. Verify that the actual part and delivery receipt reflect the same information as the purchase order regarding part number, serial number, and historical information (if applicable).

3. Verify that the identification on the part has not been tampered with (e.g., serial number stamped over, label or part/serial numbers improper or missing, vibro-etch or serial numbers located at other than the normal location).

4. Ensure that the shelf life and/or life limit has not expired, if applicable.

5. Conduct a visual inspection of the part and supporting documents to the extent necessary to determine if the part is traceable to a FAA-approved source. For detailed guidelines on the identification of replacement parts, refer to AC 20-62. The following are examples of positive forms of identification:

   a. FAA Form 8130-3, Airworthiness Approval Tag.
   b. Joint Aviation Authorities (JAA) Form One.
   c. Maintenance records or release document with approval for return to service.
   d. FAA TSO markings.
   e. FAA PMA markings.
   f. Shipping ticket/invoice from PAH.
   g. Direct ship authority letter from PAH.

6. Evaluate any visible irregularities (e.g., altered or unusual surface, absence of required plating, evidence of prior usage, scratches, new paint over old, attempted exterior repair, pitting or corrosion).

7. Conduct random sampling of standard hardware packaged in large quantities in a manner, which corresponds to the type, and quantity of the parts.

8. Segregate parts of questionable nature and attempt to resolve issues regarding questionable status of part (e.g., obtain necessary documentation if inadvertently not provided, or determine if irregularities are a result of shipping damage and handle accordingly).

# Supplier Evaluations

Part 21 requires the quality control system of a PAH to provide a means of determining that supplier-produced components (e.g., materials, parts, and subassemblies) or services (e.g., processes, calibration, etc.), conform to FAA-approved design data, and are in a condition for safe operation. Detailed information and guidance on this subject can be found in AC 21-20, Supplier Surveillance Procedures.

# Aircraft Instruments

Instruments advertised as "high quality," "looks good," or "remanufactured" or that were acquired from aircraft involved in an accident should not be put in service unless they are inspected, tested, and/or overhauled as necessary, by an appropriately rated FAA-certificated repair station, and the installer establishes that (for the aircraft in which) the instrument installed will comply with the applicable regulations. You should have a FAA form 8130-3 with each instrument either from the manufacture when new or from a repair station if it was overhauled with a return to service statement on it.

## *NOTE*

*Instruments are highly susceptible to hidden damage caused by rough handling or improper storage conditions; therefore, instruments that have been sitting on a shelf for a period that cannot be established, should be tested by an appropriately rated FAA-certificated person.*

The approval for return to service after maintenance of aircraft, engines, propellers, appliances, and materials and parts thereof, is the responsibility of the person who performs the maintenance and who signs the record for approval for return to service. The owner/operator is responsible for the continued airworthiness of the aircraft. To ensure continued safety in civil aviation, it is essential that appropriate data be used when inspecting, testing, and determining the acceptability of all parts and materials. Particular caution should be exercised when the origin of parts, materials, and appliances cannot be established or when their origin is in doubt.

# Owner Produced Parts

Does the owner have to manufacture a part themselves or herself, in order for the part to be considered an "owner produced" part?

**Answer:** No. An owner would be considered a producer of a part if the **owner participated** in controlling the design, manufacture, or quality of the part. The FAA would look at many factors in determining whether a person participated in controlling the design, manufacture, or quality of a part. The following would tend to indicate that a person produced a part:

1. The owner provided the manufacturer with design or performance data from which to manufacture the part. This may occur, for instance, where a person provided a part to the manufacturer and asked that the part be duplicated.

2. The owner provided the manufacturer with materials from which to manufacture the part.

3. The owner provided the manufacturer with fabrication processes or assembly methods to be used in the manufacture of the part.

4. The owner provided the manufacturer with quality control procedures to be used in the manufacture of the part.

5. The owner supervised the manufacturer of the part.

As noted above, prior to Amendment 21-41, CFR 21 section 21.303(a) prohibited each person producing a replacement or modification part for sale for installation on a type certificated product from doing so without holding a PMA. In Amendment 21-41, the FAA amended section 21.303(a) to allow a PMA holder to contract with a subcontractor or supplier to manufacture a modification or replacement part under the holder's PMA. In that amendment, the FAA recognized that a modification or replacement part can conform to the approved design data and be 'safe for installation on a type certificated product, as long as the part is produced under an approved fabrication inspection system (FIS).

Amendment 21-41 did not specifically address who "should have held the PMA" where the part was produced in the absence of a PMA. However, any interpretation of section 21.303(a) should be consistent with the focus .in that amendment on the establishment and maintenance of the PIS; therefore, the FAA submit that 21.303(a) creates liability for production of a modification or replacement part for sale for installation on a type certificated product for each person who:

1.  Participates in controlling the design, manufacture, or quality of the part.

2.  And does so with the intent that the part be sold for installation on a type-certificated product.

## NOTE
***The FAA would not construe the ordering of a part, standing alone, as participating in controlling the design, manufacture, or quality of a part.***

If it were concluded that the mechanic produced the part for the purpose of effectuating the repair, the question would remain whether the mechanic would be in violation of section 21.303(a). In the eyes of the FAA that mechanic would not be in violation of Part 21 section 21.303(a), because, the mechanic did not produce the part **for sale** for installation on a type-certificated product.

Here are two examples or owner produced parts: Replacement of spars is a major repair. Spars may be replaced by new parts made by the manufacturer or the holder of a Parts Manufacturer Approval (PMA) for that part. Owner-produced spars may be installed providing they are made from a manufacturer-approved drawing. Also, a spar may be made by reference to an existing spar providing sufficient evidence is presented to verify that the existing spar is an original part, and that all materials and dimensions can be determined. The dimensions and type of wood used are critical to the structural strength of the aircraft. Care should be taken that any replacement spars accurately match the manufacturer's original design.

Ribs may be replaced by new parts made by the manufacturer or the holder of a PMA for that part. Owner-produced ribs may be installed providing they are made from a manufacturer-approved drawing or by reference to an existing original rib. A rib may be made by reference to an existing rib providing sufficient evidence is presented to verify that the existing rib is an original part and that all materials and dimensions can be determined. The contour of the rib is important to the safe flying qualities of the aircraft, and care should be taken that any replacement ribs accurately match the manufacturer's original design.

Let's examine the rules governing the general privileges and limitations of a maintenance technician or certificated mechanic as stated in section 65.81, and the rule governing a repair station's privileges of certificates CFR 145. Under both rules a technician or repair station may perform maintenance, preventative maintenance, and alterations on an aircraft, or appliances for which he is rated. Nowhere in either rule does it say that the maintenance technician or repair station can produce new parts! However, the maintenance regulations allow the manufacture of parts for repair (see number 11 in next question).

A maintenance tech (A&P) or repair station can make patch plates, reinforcement splices, and incorporate them into the repair of a part. But again, a maintenance technician cannot make a brand new part for sale. So who can make a brand new part?

FAA Advisory Circular 21-29, Detecting And Reporting Suspected Unapproved Parts, states that there are eleven ways that a new part can be made. They are:

1.  Parts Manufacturer Approval (PMA)

2.  Technical Standard Order (TSO)

3.  Type Certificate (TC) or Supplemental Type Certificate (STC)

4.  TC with an Approved Production Inspection System (APIS)

5.  Production Certificate (PC)

6.  Bilateral Agreement

7. Any method acceptable to the Administrator.

8. Standard Parts (nuts and bolts)

9. Owner Produced Parts

10. Parts produced per STC instructions as part of an STC modification.

11. Fabricated by a qualified person in the course of a repair for the purpose of returning a TC product to service (which is not for sale as a separate part) under Part 43.

# Chapter 17

## CABIN-COCKPIT INSPECTION

# General Inspection

Inspect cabin and cockpit for general condition, cleanliness, and presence of loose articles, which might interfere with the controls or other systems. Using a flashlight, inspect below and behind the instrument panel for loose or chafing wires instrument line leaks, and any other defect. Check operation of controls for possible interference, full travel, abnormal wear, or other defects.

### Aircraft Placards

Some Pre-March 1, 1979, aircraft such as small airplanes under 6000 lb., do not have FAA approved manuals and require placards only. As a result, alterations to these aircraft may require a FAA Approved Supplemental Airplane (Rotorcraft, etc.) Flight Manual. These aircraft may have an Owner's Manual or some other form of non-FAA approved document that may supplement. The placards for these aircraft are found in most cases on the Type Certificate Data Sheet.

### Airplane Flight Manual (AFM)

When you inspect any aircraft you should look for the approved AFM. On the front page of most manuals you purchase it may come without the N-number and serial number this is so the owner can write in his/her numbers. To find out if the revision date is current check the Type Certificate Data Sheet or contact the aircraft manufacture. Some TCDS will have the current date listed.

Provisions for approval of and revisions to the AFM are as follows:

1. Each page of the approved portion should bear the notation, "FAA Approved" a unique date of approval or revision number for that page, the airplane type or model designation, and an appropriate document identification number. For AFM pages produced by an STC applicant, both the STC applicant's name and the airplane type or model designation should appear.

2. All AFMs, revisions, appendices, and supplements requiring FAA approval must be submitted using approval procedures acceptable to the FAA. A log of currently approved pages in the AFM should be furnished by the applicant in each copy of the manual. A location should be provided on the log for the approval signature and the approval date. Alternatively, a specific approval page can be furnished for the approval signature, the approval date, and the current revision status.

3. When revisions are incorporated, a means of indicating those parts of the information that have been changed should be provided. For example, vertical bars placed in the margin of the revised page may be used for this purpose. Each revised page should be identified in the same manner as the original, with the exception of the new date and revision notation, as applicable.

4. Appendices and supplements should be incorporated in the AFM in a separate section appropriately identified at the end of the basic manual. Supplements should normally follow appendices. Format, page identification, organization, and other details should be the same as that of the basic manual.

5. Appendices and supplements may be developed by the TC holder, STC applicant, or the operator, and should be submitted to the FAA for approval. Usually, the TC holder writes appendices to the AFM, and

an STC applicant or operator supplements the AFM. However, an STC applicant may elect to produce a completely new AFM.

6. It may be necessary to provide a greater amount of descriptive and procedural information in appendices and supplements than that appearing in the basic AFM, if the appendix or supplement is the only source for this information.

7. For airplanes manufactured in the U.S. for foreign operators, appendices and supplements containing the information required by the Foreign Civil Airworthiness Authority (FCAA) may be incorporated into an FAA-approved AFM.

# System Inspections

### Fire Warning
Examine the fire warning and detecting system for security of attachment and general condition. Ensure that wires connecting the sensing devices and the indicating instrument show no evidence of chafing or deterioration.

### Fire Extinguisher
Inspection and maintenance of fire extinguishers should be in accordance with the manufacturer's instructions attached to the extinguisher unit. Ensure that the extinguisher is fully charged. Inspect for general condition and security of attachment and hydrostatic test inspection. Some extinguisher bottles require a weight check in accordance with the manufactures procedures. This may be required as a Special Inspection.

### Cabin Heating
Inspect the cabin heating and ventilating system for leakage and condition of units, lines, and fittings. Check system operation by moving the controls to make certain they function properly.

### Fuel Selector
Check fuel selector valves for leaks, freedom of movement, positive detents, smooth operation, security of mounting, and placards. A person authorized in CFR 43 should correct any defects noted immediately.

### Engine Primer
Check engine primer assembly for leaks and operation. Inspect the entire fuel system for general condition, mounting, and freedom from leaks.

### Electric Bundles Instrument Panel
Inspect electric wire bundles for general, condition, chafing, and routing. Examine connections at terminals, junction boxes, cannon plugs, and clips for looseness and defects. Check condition of circuit breakers, fuses, switches, voltage regulators, and reverse current relays.

### Fuse Clips
Fuse clips (including spares) must be free from corrosion and hold fuses securely, yet permit easy removal. Replace burned out fuses with fuses of proper type and capacity. Replace any fuses used from the supply of spare fuses.

### Hydraulic Reservoir
Inspect the hydraulic system reservoir for general condition, security of attachment, and proper fluid level. Examine the pressure accumulator for defects. Check pumps for security of mounting and condition. Inspect bypass valves and relief valves for leaks. Ensure that lines are properly secured and free from leaks, dents, kinks, cracks or chafing. Check hydraulic brake master cylinder for fluid level and leaks.

# Instruments

Inspect all instruments for security of attachment, cleanliness, legibility of dial markings, security of glass dial covers, proper markings, and general appearance. The magnetic compass should be checked regularly for proper fluid level and accuracy.

## Note

*To service a compass requires a Certified Repair Station with the appropriate rating. This is beyond the limitations of A&P mechanics.*

Check instrument panel indicating and warning lights for operation, condition, and security. Replace inoperative indicator bulbs. Vacuum lines that show signs of deterioration should be replaced. Inspect the instrument panel for freedom of movement and the shock mounts for signs of deterioration. If the instrument panel is equipped with shock mounts, the panel should not come in contact with any part of the aircraft structure, line, or component, rigidly attached to the aircraft structure.

# Inoperative Instruments

Within certain guidelines, the pilot in command may defer repairs to nonessential inoperative instruments, and/or equipment while continuing to operate an aircraft (Reference to 14 CFR section 91.213).

If the determination is made, for the aircraft without minimum equipment list (MEL), that instruments or equipment can have repairs deferred; the operative instrument or item of equipment must be deactivated or removed.

When inoperative instruments or items of equipment are removed, a certificated and appropriately rated maintenance person shall perform that task. The cockpit control of the affected device shall be placarded and the discrepancy recorded in the aircraft's maintenance records in accordance with 14 CFR Part 43 section 43.9.

If instruments or items of equipment are deactivated and the deactivation involves maintenance, it must be accomplished and **recorded** in accordance with 14 CFR Part 43. Deactivated instruments or equipment **_must_** be placarded **"inoperative."** Reference AC 91-67

**New Regulatory Requirements**. The amendment to CFR Parts 43 and 91 provides a regulatory basis for the operation of aircraft with inoperative instruments and equipment. Operators conduct these operations within a framework of a controlled program of maintenance inspections, repairs, and parts replacement. However, operators must exercise good judgment and have, at each required inspection, any inoperative instrument or equipment repaired or inspected or the maintenance deferred, as appropriate. If an owner does not want specific inoperative equipment repaired, then the maintenance person must check each item to see if it conforms to the requirements of section 91.213(d). The operator and maintenance personnel should also assess how permanent removal of the item could affect safe operation of the aircraft.

## NOTE

*When the aircraft is due for inspection 100 hour or Annual in accordance with the CFR, the operator should have all inoperative items repaired or replaced. Reference section 91.405(C).*

## Definitions for Inoperative Instruments

1. **Deferred Maintenance** is the postponement of the repair or replacement of an item of equipment or an instrument.

2. **Equipment List** is an inventory of equipment installed by the manufacturer or operator on a particular aircraft.

3. **Deactivation** means to make a piece of equipment or an instrument unusable to the pilot/crew by preventing its operation.

4. **Inoperative** means that a system and/or component has malfunctioned to the extent that it does not accomplish its intended purpose and/or is not consistently functioning normally within its approved operating limits or tolerances.

5. **Aircraft Flight Manual (AFM).** The AFM is the source document for operational limitations and performance for an aircraft. The term AFM can apply to either an airplane flight manual or a rotorcraft flight manual. FAA requires an AFM for type certification. The responsible FAA Aircraft Certification Office (ACO) approves an AFM.

6. **Aircraft Maintenance Manual (AMM).** The AMM is the source document for maintenance procedures for an aircraft. The term AMM can apply to either an airplane maintenance manual or a rotorcraft maintenance manual. FAA requires the AMM for type certification.

7. **Placard** is a decal or label with letters at least 1/8-inch high. The operator or mechanic must place the placard on or near inoperative equipment or instruments so that it is visible to the pilot or flight crew and alerts them to the inoperative equipment.

8. **Placarding** can be as simple as writing the word **"inoperative"** on a piece of masking tape and attaching it to the inoperative equipment or to its cockpit control. Placarding is essential since it reminds the pilot that the equipment is inoperative. It also ensures that future flight crews and maintenance personnel are aware of the discrepancy.

9. **MEL Authorization**. The MEL applies only to a particular aircraft make, model, serial number, and registration number. Also, it applies only to the operator who received the authorization.

**Inoperative Items Before Flight.** During a preflight inspection for a VFR-day flight, the pilot discovers a navigation light is inoperative.

1. The pilot checks the aircraft's MEL to determine under what, if any, flight conditions the aircraft could be operated without operator navigation lights. The MEL indicates that the aircraft may be operated during daylight hours without operable navigation lights.
2. The pilot checks the procedures document and deactivate the navigation lights by pulling the correct circuit breaker and having it collared by an appropriately certificated person.
3. The pilot places a placard, which indicates that the lights are inoperative near the navigation light control.
4. The pilot examines the conditions of the proposed flight and determines that the flight can be conducted safely without navigation lights.

The CFR require that all equipment installed on an aircraft in compliance with the airworthiness standards and operating rules be operative. The **FAA-approved MMEL** includes those items of equipment and other items, which the FAA finds, may be inoperative and yet maintain an acceptable level of safety. Obviously, the MMEL does not contain required items such as wings, flaps, rudders, etc.

# Digital Clock Installation

The development of the digital clock is the result of advanced technology and that technology is likely to produce different kinds of timing devices in the future. To promote safety, the regulations should be sufficiently flexible to permit the use of more advanced timing devices that are equivalent to sweep-second hand clocks. Inquiries from the aviation community and manufacturers have indicated a need for information concerning approval and installation of digital clocks on certificated aircraft.

Digital clocks may be approved as specified in section 91.205 (FAA-approved equivalents) for installation in certificated aircraft in place of clocks with sweep-second hands, required by section 91.205(d)(6), if the digital clocks provide the following:

1.  A display of hours, minutes, and seconds. The displays may all appear simultaneously or may be individually selected.

2.  When minutes and seconds are selected by a switching action, the switching action should not reset either the real time or the lapsed time.

In addition, the following features would be desirable:

1.  A test function on each clock for testing the operations of all light emitting diodes or incandescent bar lights.

2.  A power failure indicator to display the fault until the indicator has been manually reset in the event of a power failure or power interruption of more than five seconds.

The installation should be accomplished in accordance with **AC 43.13**, Acceptable Methods, Techniques and Practices, Aircraft Alterations. In addition, the clock and airframe manufacturer's instructions should be consulted. The clock function switch position identification and the digital readout should be readable in all lighting conditions from the pilot's normal position. Digital clock installations should be free from hazards in themselves and in their methods of operations and should not affect the response or accuracy of any installed equipment. Reference AC 20-94 for guidance.

# Seat Belts

Minimum strength criteria for safety belt installations have changed through the years. The evolution of minimum strength specifications for small airplanes, beginning with the first Department of Commerce "Aeronautics Bulletin" (Bulletin 7-A) to specify minimum safety belt strength, to the Civil Aeronautics Board "Civil Air Regulations" (CAR), through the Federal Aviation Administration "Code of Federal Regulations" (CFR). The minimum strength criteria for any particular airplane in service depends on the certification basis of the airplane.

A determination of design loads for combined shoulder harness and safety belt installations in civil aircraft has been a long-standing issue. Part of the issue has been resolved by the issuance of TSO-C114. Formerly, there was no aviation standard for shoulder harness systems in civil aircraft. Consequently, commercial production shoulder harness systems usually have the same rated strength as the minimum specified for the safety belt. Shoulder harness attachment points designed into aircraft by manufacturers generally follow the same practice.

The CFR's specify that the restraint strength capacity be sufficient to restrain a 170-pound occupant exposed to the ultimate inertia forces. In the assessment of a combined shoulder harness-safety belt restraint system, a forward static test load distribution of 40 percent to the shoulder harness and 60 percent to the safety belt has been an acceptable combined static test load distribution. In addition, the safety belt alone should be able to carry 100 percent of the total ultimate static test forward load. The 1.33-fitting factor for the attachments in small aircraft type certificated after November 1, 1949 should be used.

## Qualification of installation

The CFR's permit three methods of qualifying a shoulder harness-safety belt system installed in an aircraft after production. These methods are static test, stress analysis, or a combination of stress analysis and static test. Unless original design data are available for the existing airframe, qualification by stress analysis should be based on conservative assumptions (elongation, deformation, stress concentration, load distribution) because of the unknowns that may be involved with the original structural integrity at attachment points. Static testing to ultimate loads in an operational aircraft is undesirable because there is a high risk of permanent airframe damage in some aircraft; however, static testing in a conforming fuselage or cabin section of the same make and model aircraft is an acceptable alternative. The static strength substantiation for restraint system installations is discussed in AC 23-4, Static Strength Substantiation of Attachment Points for Occupant Restraint System Installations.

## What to Look For

Safety belts and shoulder harnesses that show evidence of cuts or fraying should be removed and replaced with approved-type belts. Inspect all safety belts and shoulder harnesses for excessive exposure to the deteriorating effects of sunrays, acid and dirt. Make certain the latching devices are in good condition and operating satisfactorily. Ensure that all fittings and attachment parts are secure and in good condition.

When new nylon webbing is installed, it will be flexed by pulling it across or around a metal bar approximately 1/4 inch in diameter. This action is accomplished by holding each end of the new webbing and pulling it in a beck and forth motion. This will assist in making the webbing pliable by breaking down the finishing glaze on the fabric is broken down to such an extent that the belt or harness can be readily adjusted. The flexing procedure will be accomplished on both sides of the webbing. Make sure the data tag is attached to the belt. The data tag will in most cases be sewed on the belt.

## Note
*Do not mix and match different manufactures belts. Each belt manufacture tests their belts to there process specifications and approved standards.*

**Daily inspection.** Perform the daily inspection using the following procedures:

Check seat belt shoulder harness, restraint harness inertia reel strap webbing for:

1. Deterioration resulting from contact with foreign matter (i.e. acid, petroleum base products, strong caustic soap) shall be cause for removal from service. Surface mold or mildew may be removed by washing. If no deterioration is evident after washing, webbing shall be considered serviceable.

2. Cuts of the webbing caused by a shape-edge instrument of object that severs the vertical of horizontal yarns of the webbing shall be reasons for removal.

3. Broken stitches identified by missing, skipped, torn or ruptured threads in the stitch pattern. Stitching may be repaired and will not be caused for rejection.

4. Fraying of the exterior surface of the webbing causing separation of rupture of yarns sufficient to obscure the identity of any yarn exceeding 20 percent of the with or 2 inches in length, shall render the webbing unserviceable. Fuzzing of the exterior surface caused by broken individual filament in the yarns is not cause for rejection.

## NOTE
*Fuzzing of the exterior surface caused by broken individual filaments in the yarns is not cause for rejection. DO NOT use an open flame to remove any fuzzing.*

5. Discoloration of webbing caused by contact with strong caustic soaps, or acid shall be reason for removal form service. Webbing discoloration resulting from contact with metal articles and hardware is not cause for removal.

## NOTE

*Webbing discolored or soiled by grease, oil, aviation fuels and hydraulic fluid should be cleaned. Fading of webbing by subjection to sunlight is an unreliable indicator of deterioration and shall not be cause alone for webbing rejection.*

## NOTE

*Surface mold or mildew may be removed by washing. If no deterioration is evident after washing, webbing shall be considered serviceable.*

6. Any metal restraint hardware which is corroded or defective in operation shall be inspected for operational use and replaced if found to be substandard or excessively damaged. Missing or unserviceable adjuster webbing retarder springs and loose or missing bolts will be replaces.

7. Check buckles mechanisms for ease of locking and releasing. When locked, the latch should not have a tendency to release inadvertently, nor should it be excessively difficult to release.

8. Pilot/copilot type belts, check for freedom of movement of the link within the mated hook and guide bar. The link shall not bind in any position (i.e. pivot and hook tip) within its operation limits.

9. Inertia reels, check for damage, security, positive locking and unlocking, manual lock-unlock control for proper operation.

10. Examine restraint system attaching points to aircraft. Check for loose bolts, deformity, and corrosion or sharp and jagged edges which may damage webbing.

Cleaning of personnel restraint equipment should be accomplished when webbing is soiled using the following procedures:

## CAUTION

*Do not use bleach. Bleach may cause webbing to deteriorate.*

## NOTE

*No cleaning is authorized to inertial reel webbing strap.*

1. Prepare a concentrated soap and hot water solution, using laundry soap chips, Federal Specification P-S-1792, or equivalent. Cool the solution to approximately 120 degree F (49 decree C), prior to application.

2. Dampen an approved clean brush, with the soap solution and rub lightly over the affected surface area.

3. Rinse the webbing thoroughly with clear, lukewarm water.

4. Place webbing in open air to a drying room to dry.

## NOTE

*Belts utilized in aircraft conducting salt-water pick-up training should be washed in fresh water and corrosion preventive compound (MIL-C-81309) should be applied to metal components.*

# Retrofit Shoulder Harness

A retrofit shoulder harness installation in a small airplane may receive approval by Supplemental Type Certificate (STC), Field Approval, or as a minor change. An STC is the most rigorous means of approval and offers the highest assurance the installation meets all the airworthiness regulations.

A Field Approval is a suitable method of approval for a shoulder harness installation that needs little or no engineering. Shoulder harness installations may receive approval as a minor change in certain cases. In such cases, the FAA certified mechanic who installs the shoulder harness records it as a minor change by making an entry in the maintenance log of the airplane.

The FAA does not encourage the approval of retrofit shoulder harness installations as minor changes. The preferred methods of approval are STC or Field Approval. However, the FAA should not forbid the approval of a retrofit shoulder harness installation as a minor change in:

1. The front seats of those small airplanes manufactured before July 19, 1978, and in other seats of those small airplanes manufactured before December 13, 1986.

A retrofit shoulder harness installation may receive approval as a minor change in these small airplanes if:

1. The installation requires no change of the structure (such as welding or drilling holes).

2. The certification basis of the airplane is 14 CFR Part 23 before Amendment 23-20, Part 3 of the Civil Air Regulations, or a predecessor regulation.

In addition, a minor change installation should follow the guidance for hardware, restraint angles, and attachment locations provided in:

1. Static Strength Substantiation of Attachment Points for Occupant Restraint System Installations.

Installations approved, as a minor change may not provide the occupant with the protection required by regulation (Civil Air Regulation (CAR) 3.386 or 14 CFR Part 23 section 23.0561). However, a properly installed retrofit shoulder harness installation is a safety improvement over occupant restraint by seat belt alone.

Basically, if the aircraft has the hard-points factory installed and the approved shoulder harness system can be installed without modification of the airframe, it would be a minor change.

Some existing aircraft will already have shoulder harness attachment points, often called "hard points", which were installed during production. As an alternative, it is fortunate to be able to attach shoulder belts to reasonably rigid structure where only a doubler may be needed to replace the material removed for fastener holes. Most often, it is necessary to attach shoulder belts to relatively thin-formed sections, or even skin panels, of semimonocoque construction to achieve a satisfactory geometric configuration of the belts when in use. In most cases, attachment points need reinforcement. Attachments to welded tube and wood frame construction present a special problem in selecting the attachment point and the hardware for attachment of shoulder belts.

**Bulkhead attachments**. It is necessary that a bulkhead be a structural bulkhead rather than a cabin partition to offer a suitable structural attachment for a shoulder harness. The reinforcement hat stiffener on the aft side of the bulkhead, and the intercostal doubler on the forward side, illustrates one means of distributing restraint load to the bulkhead in two directions with a minimum of added weight. Although not as effective, the added hat stiffener and intercostal doubler can be installed on reverse sides of the bulkhead when the bulkhead stiffeners are on the aft side of the bulkhead.

**Wing carry-through and belt frame attachments**. Wing carry-through structure and belt frames offer reasonably substantial structure for attaching the upper end of a shoulder harness. Reinforcement of a belt frame should be considered in the same manner. Tapered reinforcements can offer similar fore and aft stability to the local attachment structure as well as load distribution to skin panels. Again, the goal is to provide local structural stability and load distribution to minimize local stress concentrations.

**Stringer attachments**. Direct attachment of a shoulder harness to body stringers is discouraged, because stringers are intended to carry tension loads only and it is difficult to reinforce the stringer to support bending stresses likely to be introduced by restraint loads. Intercostals between belt frames offer the best approach to attaching a shoulder harness between belt frames.

**Floor attachments**. Special precautions are necessary in attaching a shoulder harness to the floor behind a seat. Seat back strength is critical to performance of the shoulder harness, and will introduce additional loads to the remainder of the seat. These aspects need evaluation before proceeding with attaching the shoulder harness to the floor behind a seat. Recall, also, that a dual shoulder harness is needed for this installation, and the seat back needs to be near average mid shoulder height (about 25 inches above cushion) to minimize spinal compression loads. Two aspects should be considered in designing these attachments:

1. **Reinforcement.** The shoulder harness attachments at the floor may consist of an eyebolt or a connector plate; however, simple attachment to the floor panel is usually insufficient to support restraint loads. If a floor beam or other primary floor support structure is not available at the point necessary for attaching the shoulder harness, the addition of an intercostal between floor beams is warranted for connection of the eyebolt or connector plate. The intercostal will provide a beam to carry the local vertical restraint loads at the shoulder harness attachment.

2. **Retractor Mounting**. Recalling that most retractor frames are designed to transfer restraint loads through shear of the attachment fasteners, it may be necessary to install a vertically oriented connector plate, which is anchored to a floor beam or an intercostal. The vertical plate may also be needed if the bolt-on end fitting is used on the shoulder harness assembly.

It is recognized, however, that compromises are necessary in some aircraft due to the absence of sufficient structure at the ideal attachment points. Factors of hardware, geometric ramifications, strength and attachment techniques are presented to assist in making intelligent decisions in selecting and installing a shoulder harness-safety belt system. A checklist of factors to consider follows:

## Shoulder Harness-Safety Belt Checklist

1. Width of webbing in contact with occupant, nominally 2.0 inches or more.
2. Minimize webbing length for less webbing stretch.
3. Flexible cable in lieu of guy wire cable.
4. Buckle release force should be 12 pounds or less in the unloaded condition.
5. Single buckle for release and escape.
6. Webbing properly looped on length adjusters.
7. Tilt lock adjusters lock at 30 degrees or more.
8. Emergency locking retractors (inertia reels) engage at 0.75 to 1.5 G's.
9. Automatic locking and emergency locking retractors mounted to provide straight line entry and exit angle of webbing very important if webbing guide not present).
10. Retractor mounts designed to resist restraint loads by shear of the retractor counting bolts.
11. Webbing wrapped on retractor spool does not interfere with retractor locking.
12. Retractor spring tension sufficient to overcome webbing drag over seats and webbing guides for webbing retraction and stowage.
13. Quick disconnect end fittings safety pinned and protected from keeper damage.
14. Attachment position of safety belt permits a belt angle of 45 to 55 degrees for all seat positions.
15. Webbing guides position dual shoulder belts at middle of occupant's shoulder.
16. Lower attachment of single diagonal shoulder belt positioned to the side of occupant's hip.
17. Upper attachment of single diagonal shoulder belt provides belt angle across the torso and over the approximate middle of the shoulder for various sizes of occupant and various seat positions.

18. Elevation angle of the shoulder belt(s) extending behind the occupant is between -5 and +30 degrees from the longitudinal to avoid spinal compression loads and/or amplified forces in shoulder belts.

# Seats and Tracks

Inspect all seats and seat tracks for security of attachment, condition, and function of adjusting mechanisms. Floor carpets should be removed to permit inspection of the floor and associated structures to which seat and seat tracks are attached. This is the appropriate time to remove floor access covers and inspect floor substructure, controls, etc., below the floor.

In accordance with the appropriate compliance time requirement, which may be an AD, accomplish the following to your aircraft service manual:

1.  Measure each hole in the seat track(s) for excessive wear. When checking these holes for wear an allowance of 0.020 inches below the edge of the normal surface is permitted for the required measurement.
    a.  If the wear dimension across any hole exceeds 0.36 inches but does not exceed 0.42 inches, continue to measure each hole every 100 hours Time In Service (TIS) for excessive wear.
    b.  If the wear dimension across any hole exceeds 0.42 inches, prior to further flight, replace the seat track.

2.  Visually inspect the seat rail holes for dirt and any debris, which may preclude engagement of the seat pin(s). Prior to further flight, remove any such material.

3.  Lift up on the forward edge of each seat to eliminate all vertical play. In this position, measure the depth of engagement of each seat pin. If the engagement of any pin is less than 0.15 inches, prior to further flight, replace or repair necessary components to achieve a seat pin engagement of 0.15 inches or greater. If the track is worn, this dimension is measured from the worn surface, not the manufactured surface.

4.  Visually inspect seat rollers for flat spots. Assure all rollers and washers, which are meant to rotate, turn freely on their axle bolts (or bushings if installed). Prior to further flight, replace rollers having flat spots and any worn washers. If there is any binding between the bores of the rollers, washers, and axle bolts (or bushings if installed), prior to further flight, remove, clean, and reinstall these parts.

## *NOTE*
*Check the aircraft maintenance manual, as the measurements may be different than stated.*

# Windshields

Inspect all windows, windshield, and canopies for cracks, cleanliness, freedom of operation, and general condition. If the aircraft is pressurized, even minor flaws in windows, their attachments, and operating mechanisms can be critical. If there is any question, acquire the services of a certified mechanic or repair station.

The windshield should exhibit optical properties equivalent to those specified in **MIL-P-25374B for plastic windows, and MIL-G-25871B for glass or glass-plastic windows**. These documents contain information on laminate construction, optical uniformity, luminous transmittance, physical properties, environmental exposure, etc.

**Acrylic plastics** are known by the trade names of Lucite or Plexiglas and by the British as Perspex and meet the military specifications of **MIL-P-5425** for regular acrylic, **MIL-P-8184** for craze-resistant acrylic. Acrylic is a "Life time" and rated to a load factor of 1.5 (applied after the failure of the critical ply) reference section 23.571.

**Cellulose acetate** was used in the past but since it is dimensionally unstable and turns yellow after it has been installed for a time, it has just about passed from the scene and is not considered an acceptable substitute for acrylic. Life limited windows.

**Replacement Panels.** Use material equivalent to that originally used by the manufacturer of the aircraft for replacement panels. There are many types of transparent plastics on the market. Their properties vary greatly, particularly in regard to expansion characteristics, brittleness under low temperatures, resistance to discoloration when exposed to sunlight, surface checking, etc. Information on these properties is in MIL-HDBK-17A, Plastics for Flight Vehicles, Part II--Transparent Glazing Materials, available from the Government Printing Office (GPO). These properties are considered by aircraft manufacturers in selecting materials to be used in their designs and the use of substitutes having different characteristics may result in subsequent difficulties.

**Polymerizable Cements.** Polymerizable cements are those in which a catalyst is added to already thick monomerpolymer syrup to promote rapid hardening. Cement PS-30 and Weld-On 40 is polymerizable cements of this type. They are suitable for cementing all types of PLEXIGLAS acrylic cast sheet and parts molded from PLEXIGLAS molding pellets.

**Repair of Plastics.** Replace, rather than repair extensively damaged transparent plastic, whenever possible, since even a carefully patched part is not the equal of a new section, either optically or structurally. At the first sign of crack development on non-pressurized aircraft, drill a small hole with a # 30 or a 1/8-inch drill at the extreme ends of the cracks. This serves to localize the cracks and to prevent further splitting by distributing the strain over a large area. If the cracks are small, stopping them with drilled holes will usually suffice until replacement or more permanent repairs can be made. Repairs are permissible; however, they are not to be located in the pilot's line of vision during landing or normal flight. Check you manufacture maintenance manual and service bulletins for guidance.

**Permanent Repairs.** Windshields or side windows with small cracks that affect only the appearance rather than the airworthiness of a sheet, may be repaired by first stop drilling the ends of the crack with a # 30 or a 1/8-inch drill. Then use a hypodermic syringe and needle to fill the crack with polymerizable cement such as PS-30 or Weld-On 40, and allow capillary action to fill the crack completely. Soak the end of a 1/8-inch acrylic rod in cement to form a cushion and insert it in the stop-drilled hole. Allow the repair to dry for about 30 minutes, and then trim the rod off flush with the sheet. Again, this is for non-pressurized aircraft.

# Cabin Windows

During operation at altitude, aircraft passengers and control cabin spaces may be pressurized. In the event either a passenger or control cabin window "blows out" while pressurized, the aircraft will experience an "explosive" or sudden decompression. This occurrence could result in a catastrophic accident and underscores the importance of adequate maintenance inspection program for the aircraft cabin windows. This discussion on cabin windows will briefly highlight maintenance inspections. However, there are other windows such as inspection windows, toilet windows, etc. The manufacturer maintenance manual should be consulted for applicable details.

## Inspection. Examine each window for:

1. Scratches, cracks, delaminations, discoloration of panes, and chipping.
2. Binding of sliding windows, positive locking and locking mechanism release, seal deterioration, wear of bushings and guides.
3. Loose or missing window frame fasteners.
4. Rain repellency of windows.
5. Crazing (surface cracks).

# Scratched Windows

**Inner pane scratched.** Inner pane scratches may contribute to a window failure under cabin pressure and heat.

**Outer pane scratched.** Scratches on the outer pane reduce pane strength under normal cabin pressurization conditions. Any scratch causes stress concentration.

**Cracked panes.** Any window with a cracked pane should be replaced.

**Inner pane cracked.** This pane takes pressurization load and the airplane should not be pressurized if this pane is cracked.

**Outer pane cracked.** Cracks that extend toward the center of the pane or span the pane usually become progressively worse and the pane should be replaced at the first opportunity.

**Cracking of vinyl** usually occurs in the upper aft corner of the No. 1 windshields. It is a fail-safe, bird-proof core. The window should be replaced at the first opportunity.

**Delamination.** A delamination is the separation of either pane of glass from the vinyl core. When minor delamination occurs between the inner or outer pane and the vinyl core, the airplane could be flown pressurized. An electrically heated window need not be replaced due to delaminations unless the visibility is restricted or lack of window heating, or the pane is scorched.

**Chipping.** Chips on the laminated surface of the glass are layers or flakes of glass broken from a surface by excessive stresses. Presence of glass chips on laminated surface should be reason enough for window replacement if airplane is to be pressurized.

**Arcing.** Arcing will produce hot spots with possible eventual result of a cracked pane.

**Deterioration of seals.** Replace the seals.

# Criteria for Window Inspections

1. Optical and visibility criterion should be established by the operator based on the Manufacturer's maintenance manuals. For certain aircraft where no manufacture data exists AC 43.13 may be used as guidance.
2. A crack is a fissure perpendicular to the surface, which extends completely through the pane. Airplane should not be pressurized with a cracked pane.
3. Crazing is a series of small fissures perpendicular to the surface but not extending through pane. Improper pane installation or exposure to certain liquids can cause crazing. Check the manufacture limitations.
4. Surface crazing is permissible within certain limits if not a routed edge.
5. Routed radius crazing of a pane is more serious than in the overall surface. Since routed crazing requires pane removal to monitor the extent of crazing, the pane may as well be replaced.
6. Delamination is a separation of adjacent layers of laminate parallel to pane surface. Manufacturer's maintenance manuals provide recommended delamination limits and should be consulted.
7. Scratches in routed radius will be impossible to see, unless windowpane is removed.
    a. Scratches are most likely found on the exterior surface of the pane, which is exposed to weather and washing and accompanying foreign bodies, which inevitably get on that surface.
    b. Scratches are easily detected by visual examination and are critical if they exceed certain limits. Manufacturer's maintenance manuals provide recommended limits on scratch, depth and length and should be consulted.

# Window Crazing

Both basic forms of acrylics used in aircraft transparencies are affected by crazing. Crazing is a network of fine cracks that extend over the surface of the plastic sheet (it is not confined to acrylic materials) and are often difficult to discern. These fine cracks tend to be perpendicular to the surface, very narrow, and are usually less than 0.025mm (.001 inches) in depth. Crazing is induced by prolonged exposure to surface tensile stresses above a critical level or by exposure to organic fluids and vapors.

1. Stress crazing may be derived from: residual stresses caused by poor forming practice; residual surface stresses induced by machining, polishing, or gouging; and prolonged loading inducing relatively high tensile stresses at a surface.

2. Stress crazing has a severe effect on the mechanical properties of acrylics; however, the effects are reduced in stretched materials.

3. Stress crazing affects the transparency of acrylics. Generally, stretched acrylic panels should be replaced due to loss of transparency from stress crazing before significant structural degradation occurs.

# Windshield Optical Distortions

Since windows do accumulate minute scratches as part of everyday life (the kind you can't feel with a fingernail but can really see when flying into the sun), the products that fill fine scratches are great for regular use. If scratches still appear when flying toward the sun, the abrasive variety and some elbow grease are called for. This type of cleaner should be used occasionally only as needed. Most manufacturers of abrasive cleaners recommend following up with a scratch-filling product as a second step.

So what happens when you have scratches that you can't take care of with the above methods and perhaps you can feel with a fingernail? You have to get more aggressive. The danger, though, is in getting too aggressive.

Practically speaking, the only way to remove a scratch from clear acrylic is to remove material from around the scratch down to the greatest depth of the scratch, then polishing the window back to clarity. There are two problems with this process. First, polishing back to clarity can be a difficult process especially if you started with a coarser than necessary abrasive. Second, it is very easy to induce an annoying and possibly dangerous optical distortion if you have not worked evenly in a large enough area.

Keep in mind that some scratches are best left alone because sometimes the cure is worse than the ailment. But if you decide to proceed, the morals of the story are to have the patience to work with only the finest abrasive necessary to remove the scratch, and to work in a large enough area to prevent optical distortions. Also, be sure to practice on scrap material before you tackle a windshield or window.

The 3M Company, Meguiars, Micro-Surface (Micro-Mesh), and others all supply kits that will do this job with lots of your help. The kits consist of many progressively finer abrasive sheets or creams that are used in sequence to remove defects and to polish back to clarity. Another product, is the Satinal pad made by Transelco. This one time-use pad is dipped in water and makes a 5-micron slurry that will remove fine scratches and polish back to clarity in one step. For deeper scratches, it can be used in conjunction with 600, 1500, or 2000 grit-wet sandpaper. Again, it would be best to practice on scrap material. By now, you have figured out this can be a lot of work, and you're right.

Another consideration, especially on light aircraft, is the feasibility of trying to repair some windows. The windshield on the Cessna 150, for instance, is .125 (or 1/8") thick, and some Piper Cherokee rear windows are only .080 (or 5/64") thick. So when you start to remove material, you have to be aware of what you will have left structurally. Keep in mind that most repairable windows, such as those found on pressurized airliners, have published specifications for minimum allowable thickness. Most light aircraft have no such specification in most cases. Sometimes, labor spent on a repair attempt would probably be better spent installing a new window.

Another word of caution. If you are working on a homebuilt with polycarbonate, or "Lexan," windows, there is no good way to remove scratches. Polycarbonate is so soft that any attempt to remove material by abrasion will do more harm that good. There are hard-coated varieties of polycarbonate that are less scratchable, but trying to repair a scratch in these will only remove the hard coating. Your only option will be to fill minor scratches with a scratch-filling polish or replace the window.

# Cabin Inspection General

Some of the area's that are over looked in the cabin on inspections and later become a area of concern as follows:

## Gust Locks
Inspect gust locks for condition. Ensure that they release completely and cannot inadvertently engage.

## Cable rubbing bulkhead
If inspection reveals that cables or control rods have been chafing against some portion of the structure, they should be realigned. If further inspection reveals the cables or control rods to be worn beyond an acceptable limit, they should be replaced.

## Bellcrank checkpoints
Inspect all controls linkages for proper functioning and general condition. Check cables for frayed strands and proper tension. Examine pulleys and fairleads for misalignment, breakage, or looseness. Inspect bellcranks and torque tubes for alignment, cracks, freedom of movement, and proper safetying. Determine that the pulleys and fairleads, through which the control cables pass, are clean and that the surrounding structure does not interfere with their movement. Operate the controls to be sure there is no lost motion, binding, or chafing.

## Emergency exit checkpoints
Whenever a panel is removed for interior inspection, check the condition of all panel fasteners. Check the opening edges and the panel for cracks. All accessories should be inspected for security and, if movable parts are involved, for freedom of movement. Always check all emergency exit door seals. I have seen several installed improperly with the seals torn or cut. Open all emergency doors and inspect the seals.

## Door Locks
Inspect cabin and cockpit entrance doors and emergency exits for general condition. Check them for ease of operation and for security of attachment. If the aircraft cabin is pressurized, ensure that the door and window seals are intact and in place. Determine that emergency exit placards are clearly legible.

Ensure that the doors and emergency exits can be opened from inside the aircraft, and can be positively locked to prevent inadvertent opening during flight.

Examine baggage compartment for general condition. Inspect floor for defects. Check door hinges and locks for condition and satisfactory operation.

# Chapter 18

## STRUCTURES

# General Inspection Tips

The primary structure of the aircraft is designed to provide resistance to variable forces imposed while in operation by dispensing the forces through a structural pattern of "force flow" to the primary structural members of the wing and fuselage. External indications of failure, such as distorted skin, tilted or sheared rivets, and torn, dented, cracked, or corroded skin are usually obvious. Wrinkled skin, oil cans, and tilted rivets, adjacent to the obviously failed area often indicate secondary damage caused by transmission of stress from the failed area. Misalignment of doors and panels may indicate distortion of internal structure. Internal structural damage, although not always apparent, may be found by closely examining the exterior surface. For example:

1. Buckled skin between rivets at the end of a stiffener or stringer could mean that the last attaching rivet has failed, or that the stiffener or stringer is buckled in the area of the skin buckle. When a detailed inspection of the failed area is to be performed, functional parts should be actuated to determine if the failure has caused binding.

2. Deep diagonal skin buckles located over a frame, former, or rib could mean the member is distorted. When doubt exits concerning internal condition, the area in question should be opened and carefully inspected.

Fatigue Cracks. Detailed repair instructions are provided in manufacturer's service bulletins and manuals.

# Station Numbers

A numbering system is used on assemblies for aircraft to locate stations such as fuselage flames. Fuselage Frame-Station 185 indicates that the frame is 185 inches from the datum of the aircraft. The measurement is usually taken from the nose or zero station, but in some instances it may be taken from the firewall or some other point chosen by the manufacturer.

The same station numbering system is used for wing and stabilizer flames. The measurement is taken from the centerline or zero station of the aircraft.

# Areas Subject To Fatigue Cracks

1. Wing to fuselage attach fittings at center spar.
2. Horizontal stabilizer and tail stub front spar attach fittings.
3. Fuselage nose skin plating.
4. Main crew/cargo entrance door latch plates.
5. Rear fuselage frame and transverse floor beams.

# Rivets

Loose or sheared aluminum rivets may be identified by the presence of black oxide, which is caused to form rapidly by working of the rivet in its hole. This oxide will seep out from under the rivet head to stain the surrounding surface. Pressure applied to the skin adjacent to the rivet head will help verify the loosened condition of a rivet. Replacing rivets with screws is not an acceptable practice and would require a FAA form 337 major alteration in accordance with material substation. Reference Part 21 section 21.303.

Bending is a force or combination of forces that will cause a rigid member to curve or bow away from a straight line. Overloads, which cause bending, are usually the result of abnormal landing and flight loads, or improper ground handling of the aircraft. Bent components will result from the following practices: stepping or pushing on lift or other struts; lifting the aircraft by the stabilizer; jacking or placing supports under longerons; overloading cabin or baggage compartments; or exceeding turn limitations of the nose steering mechanism. On fabric-covered airplanes, a bent member can often be detected by looseness or wrinkling of the fabric. Wood or metal skin may become wrinkled, cracked, or distorted.

# Inspection Fuselage

Before starting the inspection, be certain that all plates, access doors and fairings have been opened or removed from the areas to be inspected. When opening inspection plates and cowling, take note of any oil or other foreign material accumulation, which may offer evidence of fluid leakage or other abnormal condition that should be corrected. Make note of these items, and then thoroughly clean all areas to be inspected in accordance with Part 43 Appendix D(a).

Examine the interior fuselage structure through access doors and inspection openings. Look for bent longerons or braces, cracked tubing or bulkheads, loose bolts or rivets, and missing safety wire or cotter pins. Carefully inspect the airframe structure using a magnifying glass at the wing, strut, and landing gear attachment fittings. Look for distortion, cracks, poor welds, or elongated bolt holes. Determine that the entire structure is free from corrosion, rust, deterioration, and other defects.

Inspect the aircraft structure to which the landing gear is attached for distortion, cracks, and general condition. Be sure that all bolts and rivets are intact and secure.

Inspect movable surfaces (ailerons, flaps, and trim tabs) for proper operation. Check for loose or pulled rivets, distortion, and loose fabric or skin attachment. Examine hinges and horns for security of attachment, breaks, bends, loose or worn pins, proper lubrication, and safetying.

At all times during inspection, be alert for evidence of rust, corrosion, cracked or broken welds, loose rivets or bolts.

Movable control surfaces such as elevators, rudders and trim tabs should be examined for damage or defects, loose rivets, loose fabric. Or skin distortion, and unsatisfactory glue joints. Inspect hinges and horns for security of attachment, breaks, bends, chafing, loose or worn pins, proper lubrication, and safetying.

# Fire Walls

Verify that a firewall meets the requirements of Part 27 section 27.1185 effectively separates any fuel tank from any engine. To minimize hazards of heat transfer to a fuel tank through a firewall during an engine compartment fire, verify that at least one-half inch of clear airspace exists between the tank and the firewall.

Carbon Monoxide leaks also can be performed on firewalls. Wait until night or put the aircraft in a dark hangar. Climb into the cockpit and have a friend shine a bright flood light close to the firewall. If light leaks into the cockpit, carbon monoxide can seep in. Mark it and seal it.

Inspect firewall for distortion, cracks, missing rivets or improper installed rivets. Pay peculiar attention where the engine mounts attach to the firewall. Cracks are not allowed and if found a repair is required per the manufactures repair instructions.

The following minimum thickness materials are considered acceptable for use in firewalls or shrouds for non-structural/non load-carrying applications, without being subjected to additional fire tests:

1. Stainless steel sheet, 0.015 inch thick.
2. Mild steel sheet protected against corrosion, 0.018 inch thick.
3. Titanium sheet, 0.016 inch thick.
4. Monel metal sheet, 0.018 inch thick.
5. Steel or copper base alloy firewall fittings/fasteners.

### *NOTE*

*Distortion of thin sheet materials and the subsequent gapping at lab joints or between rivets is difficult to predict; therefore, testing of the simulated installation is necessary to prove the integrity of the design. However, rivet pitches of 2 inches or less on non load-carrying titanium firewalls of 0.020 inch or steel firewalls of .018 inch are acceptable without further testing.*

# Visual Inspection

Visual inspection is the most widely used technique and is an effective method for the detection and evaluation of corrosion. Visual inspection employs the eyes to look directly at an aircraft surface, or at a low angle of incidence to detect corrosion. Using the sense of touch of the hand is also an effective inspection method for the detection of hidden well-developed corrosion. Other tools used during the visual inspection are mirrors, borescopes, optical micrometers, and depth gauges. The following shows the type of corrosion damage detectable using the visual inspection method: chipped, missing, and lifted paint; dished and popped rivets; skin bulges or lifted surfaces; corrosion products.

**Repair Of Aluminum Alloy Sheet Metal**. After extensive corrosion removal, the following procedures should be followed:

1. If water can be trapped in blended areas, chemical conversion coat and fill the blended area with structural adhesive or sealant to the same level and contour as the original skin. When areas are small enough that structural strength has not been significantly decreased; no other work is required prior to applying the protective finish.

2. When corrosion removal exceeds the limits of the structural repair manual, contact a cognizant engineer or the aircraft manufacturer for repair instructions.

3. Where exterior doublers are allowed, it is necessary to seal and insulate them adequately to prevent further corrosion.

4. Doublers should be made from alclad, when available, and the sheet should be anodized (preferred) or chemical conversion coated after all cutting, drilling, and countersinking has been accomplished.

5. All rivet holes should be drilled, countersunk, surface treated and primed prior to installation of the doubler.

6. Apply a suitable sealant compound in the area to be covered by the doubler. Apply sufficient thickness of sealing compound to fill all voids in the area being repaired.

7. Install rivets wet with sealant. Sufficient sealant should be squeezed out into holes so that all fasteners, as well as all edges of the repair plate, will be sealed against entrance of moisture.

8. Remove all excess sealant after fasteners are installed. Apply a fillet sealant bead around the edge of the repair. After the sealant has cured apply the protective paint finish to the reworked area.

# Corrosion Removal Around Countersunk Fasteners

Intergranular corrosion in aluminum alloys often originates at countersunk areas where steel fasteners are used. Removal of corrosion in a countersink is impossible to accomplish with the fastener in place.

When corrosion is found around a fixed fastener head, the fastener must be removed to ensure corrosion removal. It is imperative that all corrosion be removed to prevent further corrosion and loss of structural strength. To reduce the reoccurrence of corrosion, the panel should receive a chemical conversion coating, be primed, and have the fasteners installed wet with sealant.

Each time removable steel fasteners are removed from access panels; they should be inspected for material condition including the condition of the plating. If mechanical or plating damage is evident, replace the fastener. Upon installation, one of the following fastener installation methods should be followed:

a. Brush a corrosion preventive compound on the substructure around and in the fastener hole, start the fastener, apply a bead of sealant to the fastener countersink, and set and torque the fastener within the working time of the sealant (this is the preferred method).

b. Apply the corrosion preventive compound to the substructure and fastener, set and torque the fastener; or.

c. Apply a coating of primer to the fastener, and while wet with primer set and torque the fastener.

# Lap Seams

Some older aircraft have developed delaminations in cold bonded joints. Corrosion between the delaminated surfaces is caused by moisture intrusion along the edge of the mating parts or around fasteners securing the mating parts together. Localized bulging of the skin or internal structural component, usually around the fasteners, is the first indication of a corrosion problem.

Skin cracks or dished or missing fastener heads may also indicate severe corrosion in bonded joints. Corrosion, which occurs between skins, doublers, and stringers or frames, will produce local bulging or pulled rivets. Corrosion that occurs between the skins and doublers or tear straps away from backup structure such as stringer or frame will not produce local bulging. An external low frequency eddy current inspection may be used to determine the extent of corrosion in the skin. Lap joints should be opened with wedges to determine the full extent of corrosion damage. Internal visual inspection should be used to detect delaminated doublers or tear straps. A penetrating water displacement corrosion inhibitor should be applied to laying surfaces after corrosion removal and repair.

# Gear Doors

Inspect gear doors frequently for cracks, deformation, proper rigging, and general condition. Gear door hinges are especially susceptible to progressive cracking, which can ultimately result in complete failure, allowing the door to move and cause possible jamming of the gear. This condition could also result in the loss of the door during flight. In addition, check for proper safetying of the hinge pins and for distorted, sheared, loose, or cracked hinge rivets. Inspect the wheel wells for improper location or routing of components and related tubing or wiring. This could interfere with the travel of the gear door actuating mechanisms.

Excessive motion between normally close-fitting landing gear components may indicate wear, cracks, or improper adjustment. If a crack exists, it will generally be indicated by dirt or metallic particles, which tend to outline the fault. Seepage of rust inhibiting oils, used to coat internal surfaces of steel tubes, also assists in the early detection of cracks. In addition, a sooty, oily residue around bolts, rivets, and pins are a good indication of looseness or wear.

Excessive motion between normally close-fitting landing gear components may indicate wear, cracks, or improper adjustment. If a crack exists, it will generally be indicated by dirt or metallic particles, which tend to outline the fault. Seepage of rust inhibiting oils, used to coat internal surfaces of steel tubes, also assists in the early detection of cracks. In addition, a sooty, oily residue around bolts, rivets, and pins are a good indication of looseness or wear.

# Special Inspections

The aircraft logbook is the record in which all data concerning the particular aircraft is recorded. Information accumulated in this log can be used to determine the aircraft condition, date of inspections, and time on aircraft (and engines). It is a history of all significant events which have occurred to the airframe, its components and accessories and it provides a means of *indicating compliance* with the FAA Airworthiness Directives and manufacturers' service bulletins. During the service life of an aircraft, occasions may arise when a landing is made in an overweight condition or during a portion of the flight severe turbulence is encountered. Also, for a variety of reasons, rough landings are experienced.

Any time an aircraft has experienced a hard or overweight landing, it is recommended that a special structural inspection, which includes the landing gear, be performed. Typical areas which require special attention are landing gear support trusses for cracked welds, sheared bolts and rivets, and buckled structures; wheels and tires for cracks and cuts; and upper and lower wing surfaces for wrinkles, deformation, and loose or sheared rivets. If any damage is found, a detailed inspection is recommended. Most aircraft manual has a section that deals with special inspection and hard landing is covered in this manual.

The stress induced in a structure by a hard or overweight landing depends both on the gross weight at touchdown and the severity of impact (rate of sink). It is difficult to estimate vertical velocity at the time of impact, and whether a landing has been sufficiently severe to result in structural damage. With this in view, a special inspection should be performed after:

1. A landing is made at a weight known to exceed the design landing weight, or
2. A rough landing regardless of the landing weight.
3. Wrinkled wing skin is a sign of an excessive load, which may have been imposed during a landing. Another indication easily detected is fuel leaks and/or fuel stains along riveted seams.
4. Other possible damage locations are spar webs, bulkheads, nacelle skin and attachments, wing and fuselage stringers.

If these areas do not indicate adverse effects, probably no serious damage has occurred. A more extensive inspection and alignment is necessary if damage is noted.

If your aircraft is on an Approved Aircraft Inspection Program it provides a means for a certificate holder to incorporate specific inspection requirements into an inspection program. The program can be used to control repetitive Airworthiness Directives (ADs) and special inspections resulting from Mechanical Reliability Reports (MRR's) or other service experience.

Special inspections should be conducted as deemed appropriate by each operator, based on airplane maintenance experience. Any discrepancies found should be repaired per the aircraft maintenance manuals.

# Engine Mounts

Some engine mounts are heat-treated and **may not** be repaired by welding unless normalized and reheat-treated to their previous strength values. When cracks or inferior welds are found in such units, replacement or repair by the manufacturer or authorized repair facility is necessary. Nonheat-treated engine mounts may be repaired by welding if the work is **performed in accordance with the manufacturer's instructions** and is done by a person authorized in CFR Part 43.

Examine the entire engine mount structure with a magnifying glass, especially at welds. Look for evidence of cracks or failure and inferior welds. Ensure that all attachment bolts are tight and properly safetied. In the interest of safety, it is a recommendation that the technicians inspect the engine mounts for corrosion and repair or replace them, as necessary.

There has been a continuing problem with corrosion on portions of the engine mounts, which are exposed to heat from adjacent exhaust stacks. Cessna has issued Single Engine Service Letter No. SE76-22 dated November 15, 1976, which suggests that very high temperature enamel be applied to the areas of the engine mounts, which are in close proximity to the exhaust stacks. Cessna P/N CES1054-812S identifies this enamel.

Although the service letter specifically mentions the Model A185 and A188 series airplanes with the 300 hp engines, it is recommended the enamel be used on any airplane where corrosion of the engine mounts is accelerated by elevated temperatures. Check the service manual first or call the Cessna Technical support line at (316) 517-5800 for additional information. This only applies to Cessna aircraft. If you use it on a different Type Certificated aircraft it may require a field approval.

Service experience has revealed that an aging airplane needs more care and special attention during the maintenance processes and, at times, requires more frequent inspection of structural components for damage due to environmental deterioration, accidental damage, and fatigue. Typical areas requiring more frequent inspection, and key to continuing the useful life of an airplane are structural points that are safety of flight such as: Engine mounts as called out in **AC 91-60**.

To provide for a safe operation, a program called "continued airworthiness" should or has been developed by the manufacturer and used by owners/operators where virtually every component comprising an airplane is involved in some form of preservation, inspection, maintenance, preventive maintenance, overhaul, repair, and/or replacement activity. And not when it breaks.

# Factor of Safety Explained in Shop Terms

If the engineer's stress analysis for an airplane designed with a load factor of six (6 to 1) shows that a certain part must carry a normal load of 500 pounds he or she designs that part to be capable of carrying 3000 pounds.

The proportion between the 500 pounds normal load that the part must carry and the 3000 pounds it is capable of carrying is the **LOAD FACTOR**. Load Factor in most cases is 6 to 1, but will vary with different airplanes size, speed, and category.

The analysis of a part can be done by following the example below:

**NORMAL LOAD** is the air load on the structure due to weight in normal flight or 500 pounds.
**LIMIT LOAD FACTOR** due to recovery from dives, air-gusts, etc., is required by Federal Aviation Administration (FAA)) to be 4 to 1, that is (4 X 500 pounds)= 2000 pounds.

The CAA and CFR's require in most cases a **MINIMUM ULTIMATE FACTOR OF SAFETY** of 1.5, that is (4 X 1.5)=6 or (2000 pounds X 1.5)=3000 pounds.

An engineer have the utmost respect for **"factor of safety"** and designs parts to this strength or more, as the case demands. If a part designed has greater strength than the requirement factor of safety, the excess strength is called **"margin of safety."**

## *NOTE*

*The responsibility of maintaining the designed safety of parts will rest with the mechanic who builds or repairs the aircraft. The design safety is lost by scratches, nicks, cracks, insufficient edge distance for rivets, faulty rivets, rivet spacing, dull drills, bend radii too small, reforming flanges, drill or chuck cutting the bulb on extruded sections, etc.*

# Static Strength

A static load can be thought of as a single gradually applied load. Load factor ("G" or "N") is the ratio of the load (L) on the aircraft to the weight (W) of the aircraft. Load is the total force acting on the airplane. Limit Load Factor (LLF) is the maximum load factor authorized for operations. Limit Load (LL) is constant for all weights above design gross weight. The limit load factor is reduced if gross weight is increased. But, the LLF cannot be increased if the gross weight is decreased below the design gross weight. Engine mounts and other structural member are designed for the nominal LLF.

*Ultimate Load* (UL) is: "ultimate loads are obtained by multiplying the limit loads by the ultimate factor of safety. Failure shall not occur at the ultimate load. The ultimate factor of safety shall be 1.50" for all certified aircraft. **ULD = 1.50 x LLF**

The manufacture of the aircraft was required to conduct many categories of tests to assure that the airplane met the specifications/regulations including "structural" flight tests. These tests verified the structural limit loads to the extremes of the design envelope. Loads beyond the positive and negative limit loads were imposed in static ground tests to verify the design ultimate strength capabilities of the airframe.

It should be kept in mind that the tests were conducted upon new airplanes also that these airplanes undoubtedly were constructed with more care than the average production model. No corrosion of fatigue problems existed for these test airplanes. Older fleet airplanes may have reduced capability to withstand high load factors. Treat them with caution.

During unsymmetrical maneuvers, such as a rolling pullout, the wing that is rising will have more lift on it, and thus a greater load factor, than the down going wing. If an accelerometer were located in the centerline of the aircraft it would measure the average load factor. If the pilot reads 5 G's in the cockpit, the rising wing will be subject to 7 G's, and the down going wing would be subject to 3 G's. This is why the down going wing is limited by torsion in that the up aileron travels further than the down aileron and thus applies more torsion to the wing structure. As referenced in Fundamentals of Aircraft Material Factors by Charles E. Dole.

# Rivet Bearing Failure

The most common type of riveted joint used in aircraft construction is called the *lab joint*. The single lap joint is two sheets with a single rivet though them and a double lap joint is two sheets sandwiched by a third sheet and a single rivet though them.

There are four ways that a riveted joint can fail:

1. Bearing failure.
2. Tearing (tension) failure of the plate.
3. Shear tear out of the plate.
4. Rivet shear.

*Bearing Failure.* Unlike the other riveted joint failures, bearing failures occurs without actual separation of the joint. This type of failure results in the elongation of the rivet hole. If the rivet material is harder than the plate material a tension load will cause the plate material toward the edge of the plate to be crushed. The hole will then be elliptical in shape and the rivet will be loose in the hole. The joint will then be unsatisfactory and will have failed. The compressive stress caused by the harder river acting on the softer plate is called the bearing stress, (f br). The allowable bearing stresses of metals can be found in engineering handbooks like MIL-HDBK-5.

*Tension Failure.* If analysis shows that a rivet will shear, the logical solution would be to use a larger diameter river. But, this will increase the dimension, d, and may reduce the material in he plate to the point that tearing failure will occur. Another solution would be to use a rivet made of a material with a higher ultimate shear stress. This new material will be harder than the plate and could cause, bearing failure.

*Shear Tear Our.* Shear tear out (edge tear out) occurs when the rivet holes are drilled to close to the edge of the plate. A good rule of thumb is that the distance from the center of the hole to the edge of the plate should be at least 1.75 diameter. Reference MIL-HDBK-5 section 8.

*Rivet Shear.* If a rivet is in single shear fails, the broken area, A, will be the cross section area of the rivet, ($\pi r2$). A rivet that is in double shear has two shear areas that resist the shear forces. If shear failure occurs, the broken area is twice as large as in single shear, thus the shear stress is half that of the single shear fastener.

River holes are slightly larger than the diameter of the rivets. The strength of a riveted joint is based upon the expanded diameter of the rivet. The acceptable drill size for rivets may be found in Metallic Materials and Elements for Flight Vehicle Structure (MIL-HDBK-5).

Before you wash your aircraft look for smoking rivets. These are rivets with a black ring around them, which means they are loose and need to be replaced. Washing the aircraft removes all signs of smoking rivets so when inspecting an aircraft look before it is washed.

# Chapter 19

## HYDRAULICS SYSTEMS

# General Systems

Work performed by liquids is called "hydraulic" whereas work performed by air is called "pneumatic". A "closed" system would see the liquid continuously in a "loop", or being re-used over and over, such as in an aircraft hydraulic system. Hydraulic systems offer a tremendous mechanical advantage such that they are able to raise and lower landing gear. Other uses include engine valve lifters, shock absorbers, nose wheel shimmy dampers, anti-skid systems and control surface actuators.

Hydraulic fluid is very special because it allows maximum flow rate with minimum friction and serves as a lubricant for the working parts of the system. Also, it doesn't tend to foam, it's non-corrosive, and it's compatible with synthetic seals. The mineral-based MIL-H-5606 fluid used in virtually all light aircraft can be identified by its red dye. This type of hydraulic fluid is compatible with neoprene seals and hoses; no other fluid should be used in its place. Its big disadvantage: it is flammable and caution must be taken while pouring and storing it. Larger aircraft use a nonflammable; synthetic fluid MIL-H-8446-commonly referred to as Skydrol. It is pale purple (sometimes amber or light green depending on its grade) and is formulated for the higher operating pressures and temperatures of larger and faster aircraft. Skydrol is very susceptible to water contamination, corrodes shielding off of electrical wires, dissolves most aircraft paint finishes and will dissolve the seals used with mineral-based fluid systems.

Although some aircraft manufacturers make greater use of hydraulic systems than others do, the hydraulic system of the average modern aircraft performs many functions. Among the units commonly operated by hydraulic systems are landing gear, wing flaps, speed and wheel brakes, and flight control surfaces.

Hydraulic systems have many advantages as a power source for operating various aircraft units. Hydraulic systems combine the advantages of lightweight, ease of installation, simplification of inspection, and minimum maintenance requirements. Hydraulic operations are also almost 100% efficient, with only a negligible loss due to fluid friction.

All hydraulic systems are essentially the same, regardless of their function. Regardless of application, each hydraulic system has a minimum number of components, and some type of hydraulic fluid.

# Filters

Filters are an important part of the lubrication system, since they remove foreign particles that may be in the oil. This is particularly important in gas turbines, as very high engine speeds are attained, and the antifriction types of ball and roller bearings would become damaged quite rapidly if lubricated with contaminated oil. Also, there are usually a number of drilled or core passages leading to various points of lubrication. Since these passages are usually rather small, they are easily clogged. Filters have a life so change them regularly its cheap preventive maintenance. By checking the aircraft records you should find which filters have been changed or the lack of.

Whenever it is suspected that a hydraulic system has become contaminated, or the system has been operated at temperatures in excess of the specified maximum, a check of the system should be made. The filters in most hydraulic systems are designed to remove most foreign particles that are visible to the naked eye. Hydraulic liquid, which appears clean to the naked eye, may be contaminated to the point that it is unfit for use.

During heavy use the filter will unload if the flow is not kept at a steady rate. A system that has a spike period where the hydraulic pressure rises above the normal rate and flow increases will unload any filter allowing dirt and contamination to flow thru the filter.

# Hydraulic Fluid

Air and dirt in hydraulic systems are the most frequent causes of faulty operation. Air causes faulty release, irregular pressure, and noisy operation. Dirt and grit affects valve operation and produces leakage by cutting the various packings throughout the system.

When replenishing hydraulic fluid, **NEVER** mix dissimilar hydraulic fluids. This "mixing'" can result in complete system failure. Avoid spilling fluid when servicing hydraulic systems since some of these fluids severely damage paints and electrical insulation material.

One of the biggest problems in hydraulic systems is when a technician services the reservoir. They usually have an open can of hydraulic fluid, pour it in right along with all the dirt, and grime on top on the can. Or they will use a rag and wipe the top off leaving the lent from the rag and it entries the hydraulic system. Something most technicians forget or do not know is how to open a can of hydraulic fluid. Some will use screwdriver and punch holes in the top leaving small bits of metal in the fluid. The manufactures will suggest using a can opener approved for their products and are usually given out free when asked for. Knowing who has serviced the hydraulic system will tell a lot about the condition of the hydraulic components and it's cleanliness.

In April 1995, a FAA study concluded that the existing standard, NAS 1638, was adequate for classifying the particulate contamination levels for aircraft hydraulic fluid. At the FAA's request, an industry task force formed by the Society of Automotive Engineers (SAE) Committee A-6 studied the fluid contamination issues. The industry task force concluded that:

1. Flight control servoactuators had demonstrated operation at contamination levels up to NAS 1638 class 17 and higher.

2. An in-service limit of NAS 1638 class 9 prescribed by the majority of current airframe manufacturers was conservative, adequate, and the maximum recommended limit. The task force also studied chemical contamination effects and provided in-service limits for fluid properties such as specific gravity, moisture content, viscosity, and chlorine content.

This study was only on large commercial aircraft and not on part 135 or General Aviation aircraft, which seem to have the problems. To find out more on hydraulic fluids you can read SAE AIR-1362 - Physical Properties of Hydraulic Fluids.

The FAA has identified an existing industry standard, NAS 1638, that defines fluid cleanliness levels as Classes 00 to 12; has defined NAS 1638 class 9, as the in-service limit, verified that the manufacturers already recommend these limits in their maintenance manuals including a sampling interval, and helped develop an SAE ARP document for sampling and testing techniques. The intent of the safety recommendation has no regulatory corrective action is deemed necessary.

# Hydraulic Pumps

Most hydraulic systems use a hydraulic pump/motor that turns in one direction only. The fluid is directed to the up or down side of the actuators by means of manually controlled shuttle valves (i.e., landing gear and flap selector valves). The drawbacks of this system are the O-rings (seals) used on the various parts of the selector valves. Over a period of time the O-rings will become worn or nicked. This will prevent the pump from building up pressure due to internal leakage in the system. When this occurs, the pump will start to cycle more often.

It's important to check the aircraft records for pump changes. If a pump has been overhauled or repaired it should come with FAA Form 8130-3 Airworthiness Approval Tag with a Return to Service statement. On the 8130-3 Form should be a work order number. If the Work Order is not with the 8130 tag contact the Repair Station that issued the 8130 tag and request copies on the Work Order. Remember Repair stations only have to keep work order record for 2 years then they will or can destroy them.

# O-rings

Two dimensions define the size of an O-ring: it's inside diameter (ID) and its cross-sectional diameter (CS). O-rings are color coded per SAE ARP-1832 - Color Identification for O-Ring Seals.

Prevention of seal failures through proper design, material selection and maintenance certainly minimizes the risk of failure. Attention to the condition of replaced seals, as well as the equipment performance over time, will result in improved process reliability, reduced operating costs and a safer work environment.

O-ring seals often fail prematurely in applications because of improper design or compound selection. Examples of common failure modes. By correctly identifying the failure mode, changes in the design or seal material can lead to improved seal performance. From the end-user's point of view, a seal can fail in three (3) general ways:

1. Leaking
2. Contamination
3. Change in Appearance

One major factor in possible seal failure is the extreme and harsh environment in which seals are expected to perform. The sealing environment can consist of virtually anything from inert gases at room temperatures to aggressive chemicals at very high temperatures. The sealing environment may result in chemical degradation or swelling of the sealing components. Elevated temperatures may cause seal degradation, swelling or out gassing. And the pressure or more often, the vacuum environments can cause out gassing and weight loss. Contributing factors to seal failure in the sealing environment include:

1. *Chemical*— the type of chemical(s) in service
2. *Thermal*— the operating ranges of the seal (also any thermal cycling)
3. *Pressure/Vacuum*— the range of pressures or vacuum levels in the process

Analysis of the seal application is crucial to the understanding of possible failure. Component suppliers and equipment manufacturers perform most seal design. The designs are refined as experience is gained. As quickly as process technology changes, however, the experience gained with seal design may not be relevant to the latest process technology. Vacuum applications have historically relied on high levels of compression and gland fill to reduce permeation and trapped gases. These techniques, when applied to new materials, or at higher operating temperatures, can result in premature seal failure. The seal design and application can provide information about the cause of failure:

1. **Static Seals**— axial and radial, confined or unconfined
2. **Dynamic Seals**— axial (open-close) or radial (reciprocating or rotary)
3. **Sealing Gland Dimensions**—
   a. Shape (square, trapezoidal, etc.).
   b. Compression.
   c. Gland fill.
   d. Stretch.
4. **Installation Procedures**— stretch

# Common Seal Failures

## Abrasion

Description: The seal or parts of the seal exhibit a flat surface parallel to the direction or motion. Loose particles and scrapes may be found on the seal surface.

Contributing Factors: Rough sealing surfaces. Excessive temperature. Process environment containing abrasive particles. Dynamic motion. Poor elastomer surface finish.

Suggested Solutions: Use recommended gland surface finish. Consider internally lubed elastomers. Eliminate abrasive components.

## Compression Set

Description: The seal exhibits a flat-sided cross-section, the flat sides corresponding to the mating seal surfaces.

Contributing Factors: Excessive compression. Excessive temperature. Incompletely cured elastomer. Elastomer with high compression set. Excessive volume swell in chemical.

Suggested Solutions: Low compression set elastomer. Proper gland design for the specific elastomer. Confirm material compatibility.

## Chemical Degradation

Description: The seal may exhibit many signs of degradation including blisters, cracks, voids or discoloration. In some cases, the degradation is observable only by measurement of physical properties.

Contributing Factors: Contributing Factors: Incompatibility with the chemical and/or thermal environment.

Suggested Solutions: Selection of more chemically resistant elastomer.

## Explosive Decompression

Description: The seal exhibits blisters, pits or pocks on its surface. Absorption of gas at high pressure and the subsequent rapid decrease in pressure. The absorbed gas blisters and ruptures the elastomer surface as the pressure is rapidly removed.

Contributing Factors: Rapid pressure changes. Low-modulus/hardness elastomer.

Suggested Solutions: Higher-modulus/hardness elastomer. Slower decompression (release of pressure).

## Extrusion

Description: The seal develops ragged edges (generally on the low-pressure side), which appear tattered.

Contributing Factors: Excessive clearances. Excessive pressure. Low-modulus/hardness elastomer. Excessive gland fill. Irregular clearance gaps. Sharp gland edges. Improper sizing.

Suggested Solutions: Decrease clearances. Higher-modulus/hard-ness elastomer. Proper gland design. Use of polymer backup rings.

## Installation Damage

Description: The seal or parts of the seal may exhibit small cuts, nicks or gashes.

Contributing Factors: Sharp edges on glands or components. Improper sizing of elastomer. Low-modulus/hardness elastomer. Elastomer surface contamination.

Suggested Solutions: Remove all sharp edges. Proper gland design. Proper elastomer sizing. Higher-modulus/hardness elastomer.

## Out Gassing/Extraction

Description: This failure is often very difficult to detect from examination of the seal. The seal may exhibit a decrease in cross-sectional size.

Contributing Factors: Improper or improperly cured elastomer. High vacuum levels. Low hardness/plasticized elastomer.

Suggested Solutions: Avoid plasticized elastomers. Ensure all seals are properly post-cured to minimize outgassing.

## Over Compression

Description: The seal exhibits parallel flat surfaces (corresponding to the contact areas) and may develop circumferential splits within the flattened surfaces.

Contributing Factors: Improper design—failure to account for thermal or chemical volume changes, or excessive compression.

Suggested Solutions: Gland design should take into account material responses to chemical and thermal environments.

## Plasma Degradation

Description: The seal often exhibits discoloration, as well as powdered residue on the surface and possible erosion of elastomer in the exposed areas.

Contributing Factors: Chemical reactivity of the plasma. Ion bombardment (sputtering). Electron bombardment (heating). Improper gland design. Incompatible seal material.

Suggested Solutions: Plasma-compatible elastomer and compound. Minimize exposed area. Examine gland design.

## Spiral Failure

Description: The seal exhibits cuts or marks, which spiral around its circumference.

Contributing Factors: Difficult or tight installation (static). Slow reciprocating speed. Low-modulus/hardness elastomer. Irregular O-ring surface finish (including excessive parting line). Excessive gland width. Irregular or rough gland surface finish. Inadequate lubrication.

Suggested Solutions: Correct installation procedures. Higher-modulus elastomer. Internally lubed elastomers. Proper gland design. Gland surface finish of 8–16 microinch RMS. Possible use of polymer backup rings.

## Thermal Degradation

Description: The seal may exhibit radial cracks located on the highest temperature surfaces. In addition, certain elastomers may exhibit signs of softening—a shiny surface as a result of excessive temperatures.

Contributing Factors: Elastomer thermal properties. Excessive temperature excursions or cycling.

Suggested Solutions: Selection of an elastomer with improved thermal stability. Evaluation of the possibility of cooling sealing surfaces.

## Storage of replacement seals

1.  Store O-ring seals where temperature does not exceed 120° F.

2.  Keep seals packaged to avoid exposure to ambient air and light, particularly sunlight.

3.  During inspection, consider the following to determine whether seal replacement is necessary.

    a.  How much fluid is permitted to seep past the seals? In some installations minor seepage is normal. Refer to the manufacturer's maintenance information.
    b.  What effect does the leak have on the operation of the system? Know the system.
    c.  Does the leak of fluid create a hazard or affect surrounding installations? A check of the system fluid and knowledge of previous fluid replenishment is helpful.
    d.  Will the system function safely without depleting the reservoirs until the next inspection?

# Do's and Don'ts that apply to O-ring seals

1.  Correct all leaks from static seal installations.
2.  Don't retighten packing gland nuts; retightening will, in most cases, increase rather than decrease the leak.
3.  Never reuse O-ring seals because they tend to swell from exposure to fluids, and become set from being under pressure. They may have minor cuts or abrasions that are not readily discernible by visual inspection.
4.  Avoid using tools that might damage the seal or the sealing surface.
5.  Do not depend upon color-coding. Coding may vary with manufacturer.
6.  Be sure that part number is correct
7.  Retain replacement seals in their package until ready for use. This provides proper identification and protects the seal from damage and contamination.
8.  Assure that the sealing surfaces are clean and free of nicks or scratches before installing seal.
9.  Protect the seal from any sharp surfaces that it may pass over during installation. Use an installation bullet or cover the sharp surfaces with tape.
10. Lubricate the seal so it will slide into place smoothly.
11. Be sure the seal has not twisted during installation.

# Flexible Hoses

Flexible hose is used in aircraft plumbing to connect moving parts with stationary parts in locations subject to vibration or where a great amount of flexibility is needed. It can also serve as a connector in metal tubing systems. There are two major companies that make hoses for most aircraft Stratoflex and Aeroquip. Attached to each hose will be a metal band with the manufacture, which is the builder, part number, serial number, PMA number, etc. These requirements are spelled out in Part 21 and Part 45 of the Code of Federal Regulations.

If you are inspecting an aircraft and the manufacture calls out either Stratoflex or Aeroquip make sure the manufactures part is installed. Many times you may find a different manufacture hoses installed this is contrary to the manufactures guidance is will void the airworthiness certificate for the aircraft, making the aircraft unairworthy.

# Rubber Hose

Flexible rubber hose consists of a seamless synthetic rubber inner tube covered with layers of cotton braid and wire braid, and an outer layer of rubber-impregnated cotton braid. This type of hose is suitable for use in fuel, oil, coolant, and hydraulic systems. The types of hose are normally classified by the amount of pressure they are designed to withstand under normal operating conditions.

1.  Low pressure, any pressure below 250 p.s.i. Fabric braids reinforcement.

2.  Medium pressure, pressures up to 3,000 p.s.i. One wire braid reinforcement. Smaller sizes carry pressure up to 3,000 p.s.i. Larger sizes carry pressure up to 1,500 p.s.i.

3.  High-pressure (all sizes up to 3,000 p.s.i. -operating pressures).

Identification markings consisting of lines, letters, and numbers that are printed on the hose. These code markings show such information as hose size, manufacturer, and date of manufacture, pressure, and temperature limits. Code marking assist in replacing a hose with one of the same specification or a recommended substitute. Hose suitable for use with phosphate ester base hydraulic fluid will be marked "Skydrol use". In some instances several types of hose may be suitable for the same use. Therefore, in order to make the correct hose selection always refers to the maintenance or parts manual for the particular airplane.

There are two main hose manufactures Aeroquip and Stratoflex. Their product lines cannot be interchanged. The use of non-Stratoflex parts in the repair or manufacturing of Stratoflex hose is **prohibited** by the Stratoflex Company. When replacement of a flexible line (hose) is necessary, replacement should use the same type, size, part number, and length of hose as the line/hose to be replaced. This is outlined in the Technical Standard Order (TSO) for process specification for procedures as explained in AC 43.13-1B.

Both manufactures use MIL-H or SAE AS hose for their hose assemblies, but the hose assemble are manufactured to that's company's process specification. This specification is a roadmap how to produce a particular hose step by step. If your aircraft comes with Aeroquip hoses then they have to be replaced with Aeroquip hoses unless the manufacture manual allows the use of Stratoflex hoses and vice verse.

If you are inspecting an aircraft and notice two different types hoses manufacture part numbers one of them is more than likely the wrong hose assemble. If the owner has a Field Approval FAA Form 337 that allows it's use then it is a good part, if not then it is a bad part and should be changed.

FAA Technical Standard Orders (TSO) is the performance specification standards for aircraft parts, materials, etc. For example, aircraft tires are TSO approved; seat belts are also TSO approved items. Hose assemblies that are certified under the Technical Standard Order System, meet the requirements of section 21.303, Paragraph B, Subpart 3.

# Aircraft Hose Identification Band

Hose assemblies are tagged with a stainless steel band with the following information etched onto the band.

1.  Hose part number.

2. Manufacture.
3. FAA TSO C53a approval number.
4. Pressure tested and quarter and date.
5. Plant Code (Which company made the part under the PMA).
6. Date of manufacture.

# Hose Terms

**Assembly length** Hoses assembly length is measured from end of nipple to end of nipple, or flare to flare. This is the same as connection length (the distance between connections). Length is stated in inches and 1/8 inch. Example 0244 is 24 inches and 4/8 of an inch.

**Blisters** – a raised spot on the surface of the hose - usually containing air - sometimes referred to as voids or bubbles.

**Blow Down** - a term used to define rapid decompression of a pneumatic hose. This can result in the collapse of the inner tube caused by entrapped air in the hose structure trying to return to the inside of the tube.

**Carcass** the fabric, cords and/or metal reinforcing section of the hose, as distinguished from the inner tube and cover.

**Collapse** a term used to indicate the closing of the inside diameter of the hose due to kinking, vacuum, or other form of abuse.

**Effusion** the flow of gas under pressure through a rubber layer.

**Installation Tip** if you have a bundle of hoses that you must install and don't know where each hose is supposed to go then its best to start with the shortest hose and work your way to the longest. This way you won't end up with a hose that is too short.

**Wire Throw-Out** in braided hose, a broken end or ends in the wire reinforcements protruding from the surface of the braid.

**Length Changes** allow enough slack in the hose line to provide for changes in length when pressure is applied. The hose will change in length from -2% to -4%.

**O.D.** Outside diameter.

**Pin Pricked Cover** hose whose cover has perforations to permit the effusion of gas to the atmosphere.

**Proof pressure** the pressure applied to a hose assembly to ensure proper installation of fittings. This pressure is usually twice the operating pressure of the hose. To qualify, the hose assembly must contain this pressure without leaking for a specified period of time.

**Safety factor** safety factor - the difference between minimum burst pressure and the maximum operating pressure - usually four to one.

**Compound twist angle** when both fittings on a hose are angled fittings and the fittings go off in different directions, the angular relationship between fittings is termed the compound twist angle. The number of degrees between the fittings determines twist angle. For compound twist angles, hold the hose upright with the lower fitting on the center of this page and the upper fitting facing you. The direction of the lower fitting faces is the compound angle of the hose.

**Fireproof sleeve** is silicon covered which acts as a fire retardant, an insulator and a chafe protector. Installed by inserting the hose into the sleeve prior to hose fitting assembly.

# Identification of Fluid Lines

Fluid lines in aircraft are often identified by markers made up of color-codes, words, and geometric symbols. These markers identify each line's function, content, and primary hazard, as well as the direction of fluid flow.

In most instances, fluid lines are marked with 1-inch tape or decals. On lines 4 inches in diameter (or larger), lines in oily environment, hot lines, and on some cold lines, steel tags may be used in place of tape or decals. Paint is used on lines in engine compartments, where there is the possibility of tapes, decals, or tags being drawn into the engine induction system.

The aircraft and engine manufacturers are responsible for the original installation of identification markers, but the aviation mechanic is responsible for their replacement when it becomes necessary.

Generally, tapes and decals are placed on both ends of a line and at least once in each compartment through which the line runs. In addition, identification markers are placed immediately adjacent to each valve, regulator, filter, or other accessory within a line. Where paint or tags are used, location requirements are the same as for tapes and decals.

# Flexible Hose Inspection

Hose and hose assemblies should be checked for deterioration at each inspection period. Leakage, separation of the cover or braid from the inner tube, cracks, hardening, lack of flexibility, and excessive "cold flow" is apparent signs of deterioration and reason for replacement. The term **"cold flow"** describes the deep, permanent impressions in the hose produced by the pressure of hose clamps or supports.

# Proof-test After Assembly

All flexible hose must be proof-tested after assembly by plugging or capping one end of the hose and applying pressure to the inside of the hose assembly. The proof-test medium may be a liquid or a gas. For example, hydraulic, fuel, and oil lines are generally tested using hydraulic oil or water, whereas air or instrument lines are tested with dry, oil-free air or nitrogen. When testing with a liquid, all trapped air is bled from the assembly prior to tightening the cap or plug. Hose tests, using a gas, are conducted underwater. In all cases follow the hose manufacturer's instructions for proof-test pressure and fluid to be used when testing a specific hose assembly.

Place the hose assembly in a horizontal position and observe for leakage while maintaining the test pressure. Proof-test pressures should be maintained for at least 30 seconds. For the above mentioned is why you should have your hoses repaired or new purchased from a Repair Station that specializes in hoses. Repair stations have all the required data and hose test equipment your local mechanic may not have. At a certificated repair station your hose assembly will come with a FAA Form 8130-3 Airworthiness Approval Tag for Return to Service.

Some mechanic's will want to repair a leaking or burst hydraulic hose in accordance with AC 43.13. This repair may be acceptable for some hoses. However mechanic (A&P) still has to perform pressure a test to the manufacture standards. This will require a mechanic to have the tools, equipment and data to perform the pressure test to certify the hose as an airworthy part. Check the aircraft records for hose repairs and return to service entries and times.

# Installation of Flexible Hose Assemblies

Flexible hose must not be twisted on installation, since this reduces the life of the hose considerably and may also loosen the fittings. Twisting of the hose can be determined from the identification stripe running along its length. This stripe should not spiral around the hose.

Flexible hose should be protected from chafing by wrapping it with tape, but only where necessary.

The minimum bend radius for flexible hose varies according to size and construction of the hose and the pressure under which the hose is to operate. Bends that are too sharp will reduce the bursting pressure of flexible hose considerably below its rated value. Reference AC 43.13.

Flexible hose should be installed so that it will be subject to a minimum of flexing during operation. Although hose must be supported at least every 24 inches, closer supports are desirable. A flexible hose must never be stretched tightly between two fittings. From 5 percent to 8 percent of its total length must be allowed for freedom of movement under pressure. When under pressure, flexible hose contracts in length and expands in diameter.

Protect all flexible hose from excessive temperatures, either by locating the lines so they will not be affected or by installing shrouds around them.

# Repair of Metal Tube Lines

Scratches or nicks no deeper than 10 percent of the wall thickness in aluminum alloy tubing may be repaired, if they are not in the heel of a bend. Replace lines with severe die marks, seams, or splits in the tube. Any crack or deformity in a flare is also unacceptable and is cause for rejection. A dent of less than 20 percent of the tube diameter is not objectionable, unless it is in the heel of a bend. Dents can be removed by drawing a bullet of proper size through the tube by means of a length of cable. A severely damaged line should be replaced.

If you are working on aircraft that have a 4,000-PSI working system the above rule of thumb may not be advisable. Always check the manufacturer maintenance manual for correct limits and tolerances.

# Chapter 20

## OXYGEN SYSTEM

# Plastic Oxygen Lines

The following policy was extracted from a FAA memorandum dated December 27, 1983, to provide guidance regarding the use of flexible plastic tubing for oxygen distribution lines. While this guidance was generated for Part 23 airplanes, it is equally applicable for Part 25 airplanes.

1.  The FAA has determined that the use of plastic lines for an oxygen distribution system that is operating under continuous pressure is not acceptable for certification in Part 23 airplanes.

2.  Lines constructed of combustible materials, including nylon, polyvinylchloride (PVC) and Teflon may be used in oxygen lines, which are pressurized only when cabin depressurization occurs. The following precautions should be taken when using such lines in the oxygen system.
    a.  Swaged metal type end fittings should be used to prevent leakage from cold flow.
    b.  Lines should be protected from abrasion by use of a reinforcing sleeving of fabric braid.
    c.  Precautions should be taken to route such lines away from areas where they might be subjected to elevated temperatures, electrical arcing (relays and switches) and flammable fluids.

Tubing in the fuselage for high or low-pressure oxygen systems that are located behind liners or in the walls of the fuselage are typically made of rigid stainless steel (for high pressure) or aluminum (for low pressure). Synthetic flexible lines connecting the oxygen mask to the oxygen distribution system have been accepted. Swaged metal end fitted PVC tubing, covered with a synthetic braid (for abrasion resistance and strength), and should be used between the aluminum low-pressure distribution line and the passenger service unit manifold of many large transports. These tubes and aluminum line do not contain oxygen until a depressurization occurs. Then, the pressure is low and for a short duration. These hoses must meet the interior burn requirements.

Synthetic lines such as plastic or nylon cannot be recommended for oxygen high or low pressure lines that will be exposed to a continuous pressure (i.e., as opposed to pressurized when needed). These materials can cold flow. Care must be taken in the selection of the fitting design for exposures of even short duration.

In addition to cold flow, polyethylene and nylon will lose strength with increasing temperature. These materials are much more susceptible to combustion in the presence of oxygen than either stainless steel or aluminum. For these reasons, the FAA considers polyethylene or nylon tubing inappropriate and unsafe for oxygen lines that are subjected to continuous oxygen pressure.

# Oxygen Systems Servicing

Certain precautions should be observed whenever aircraft oxygen systems are to be serviced.

1.  Before servicing any aircraft with oxygen, consult the specific aircraft service manual to determine the type of equipment required and procedures to be used.

2.  Oxygen system servicing should be accomplished only when the aircraft is located outside of hangars.

3.  Personal cleanliness and good housekeeping are imperative when working with oxygen. Oxygen under pressure and petroleum products creates spontaneous results when they are brought in contact

with each other. Service people should be certain to wash oil and grease (including lip salves, hair oil, etc.), and dirt from their hands before working around oxygen equipment. It is also essential that clothing and tools are free of oil, grease, and dirt.

4.   Aircraft with permanently installed oxygen tanks usually require two persons to accomplish servicing of the system. One man should be stationed at the service equipment control valves, and the other stationed where he can observe the aircraft system pressure gauges.

# Tubing Routing and Mounting

There should be at least 2 inches of clearance between the oxygen system and flexible moving parts of the aircraft. There should be at least a ½-inch clearance between the oxygen system and rigid parts of the aircraft. The oxygen system tubing, fittings, and equipment should be separated at least 6 inches from all electrical wiring, heat conduits, and heat emitting equipment in the rotorcraft. Insulation should be provided on adjacent hot ducts, conduits, or equipment to prevent heating of the oxygen system. In routing the tubing, the general policy should be to keep total length to a minimum. Allow for expansion, contraction, vibration, and component replacement. All tubing should be mounted to prevent vibration and chafing. This should be accomplished by the proper use of rubberized or cushion clips installed at 24-inch intervals (copper) or 36-inch intervals (aluminum) and as close to the bends as possible. The tubing, where passing through or supported by the rotorcraft structure, should have adequate protection against chafing by the use of flexible grommets or clips. The tubing should not strike against the rotorcraft structure during vibration and shock encountered during normal use of the rotorcraft. The above information can and should apply to fixed wing aircraft.

**System Cleanliness.**  The completed installation shall be free of oil, grease, fuels, water, dust, dirt, objectionable odors, or any other foreign matter, both internally and externally prior to introducing oxygen in the system.

**Closures.**  Lines which are required to be disconnected, due to the location of the converter within the aircraft during aircraft maintenance checks or overhaul, should be capped to prevent materials which are incompatible with oxygen from entering the system when the system integrity is broken. Caps, which introduce moisture and tapes that leave adhesive deposits shall not be used for these purposes. All openings of lines and fittings shall be kept securely capped until closed within the installation.

**Degreasing.**  All components of the oxygen system should be procured for oxygen service use in an "oxygen clean" condition. Parts of the oxygen system, such as tubing, not specifically covered by cleaning procedures should be degreased using a vapor phase trichloroethane degreaser. Ultrasonics may be used in conjunction with vapor phase degreasing for the cleaning of components.

**Purging.**  The system should be purged with hot, dry 99.5 percent pure oxygen gas in accordance with the manufacturer recommendations after:

1.   Initial assembly of the oxygen system.

2.   After system closure whenever the oxygen system pressures have been depleted to zero, or the system has been left open to atmospheric conditions for a period of time or is opened for repairs.

# Oxygen System Maintenance

Remove from service any cylinders that show signs of abuse, dents, bulges, cracks, distortion, damaged thread, or defects, which might render them unsafe. When replacing an oxygen cylinder, be certain that the replacement cylinder is of the same size and weight as the one removed.

Replace or repair any cylinder mounting brackets that show signs of wear. Visible cracks may be welded in accordance with manufacturer's standards. Replace the cylinder straps or clamps that show wear or abuse.

Install lines, fittings, and equipment above and at least 6 inches away from fuel, oil, and hydraulic systems. Use deflector plates where necessary to keep hydraulic fluids away from the lines, fittings, and equipment.

**Maintenance and Replacement**. All parts of the oxygen system should be installed to permit ready removal and replacement without the use of special tools. All tubing connections and fittings should be readily accessible for leak testing with a leak test compound formulated for leak testing oxygen systems and for tightening of fittings without removal of surrounding parts.

# High Pressure Cylinders

Many installations utilize hospital type cylinders rather than aviation type cylinders. A concern with the hospital type cylinders is the yoke and the hard plastic washer that is commonly used with these cylinders. It is very difficult to properly attach these yokes since the aircraft and rotorcraft provides a high vibration environment and no positive lock is provided. Leaks are a continuous problem with this configuration. Yokes are available for these bottles that provide for a positive lock. Improved washers that provide for a good elastomeric seal and include a metal ring to limit crushing the washer are also available. If the hospital type bottles are to be used, only the modified yokes and improved seals should be considered for future installations. The preferred cylinder is the aviation type cylinder with the integral shut-off valve and regulator. All cylinders should be DOT approved.

Standard-weight cylinders must be hydrostatic tested at the end of each 5-year period (10 years if it meets the requirements in 49 CFR 173.34 e, 16). This is a Department of Transportation (DOT) requirement. These cylinders carry an ICC or DOT 3AA 1800 classification and are suitable for the use intended.

Lightweight cylinders must be hydrostatic tested every 3 years, and must be retired from service after 24 years or 4,380 pressurizations, whichever occurs first. These cylinders carry an ICC or DOT 3 HT 1850 classification and must be stamped with the approval after being inspected. (Reference 49 CFR 173.34 e, 15).

## CAUTION
*Use only aviation breathing oxygen when having the oxygen bottle charged.*

Any lines that pass through potential fire zones should be stainless steel.

**High Pressure**. Use of high-pressure lines may be necessitated by the use of a pressure regulator that is remote from the cylinder. The intent is to locate the regulator as close as physically possible to the cylinder, and to minimize the use of fittings. Lines of 6-inch lengths are encouraged with 18-inch lengths being the maximum in unusual circumstances. Lines made of stainless steel are recommended.

**Low Pressure.** Although lines may only be subjected to low pressures, if they are located behind upholstery or for any reason are not 100 percent visible during normal operation, they should be solid metal lines or high pressure flexible lines such as Aeroquip 300 series hose or Stratoflex 124 or 170 series hose assemblies. The so-called "green lines" should only be used in locations that are 100 percent visible during normal operation. This would restrict their use to the run between the mask and the bulkhead disconnects in the aircraft cabin.

Synthetic lines such as plastic, nylon, or rubber cannot be recommended for applications that will be exposed to continuous pressure (i.e., as opposed to pressurized when needed). These materials can cold flow.

# Lines and Fittings

**High Pressure**. Intercylinder connections are made with regular flared or flareless tube fittings with stainless steel. Usually fittings are of the same material as the lines. Mild steel or aluminum alloy fittings with stainless steel lines are discouraged. Titanium fittings should never be used because of a possible chemical reaction and resulting fire. An example of a series of fittings that has been accepted is the "SS" series Swagelok tube fittings (flareless).

**Low Pressure**. Fittings for metallic low-pressure lines are flared or flareless, similar to high-pressure lines. Line assemblies should be terminated with "B" nuts in a similar manner to a manufactured terminating connection. Universal adapters (AN 807) or friction nipples used in conjunction with hose clamps are not accepted for use in pressurized oxygen systems.

**Shut-off Valve**. Each system should contain a shutoff valve that is located as close as practical to the high-pressure cylinder(s), and it should be assessable to a flightcrew member. High-pressure cylinders should use slow opening/closing system shut-off valves. Where the regulator is part of the cylinder, and low-pressure oxygen is controlled, the emphasis on slow acting valves is not as significant, and use of a flow fuse may be possible. Use of a flow fuse must be supported by a system fault analysis and testing to show maximum flow will not result in nuisance trips, and reliable trips will be provided for malfunction conditions resulting in excess flow.

**Regulators**. The regulator should be mounted as close as possible to the cylinders. If nonaviation qualified regulators are to be considered, their service history should be reviewed and careful consideration should be given to the manufacturer's environmental qualification. Radio Technical Commission for Aeronautics Document D0-160 is a recognized and accepted standard for environmental considerations. As a minimum, consideration should be given to operation during altitude, temperature, and vibration extremes.

**Placards**. Appropriate, durable placards should be provided with the installed system. Emphasis should be placed on any precautions that are appropriate during filling of the system and so forth.

Replace any oxygen line that is chafed, rusted, corroded, dented, cracked, or kinked. Clean oxygen system fittings showing signs of rusting or corrosion in the threaded area. To accomplish this, use a cleaner recommended by manufacturers of oxygen equipment. Replace lines and fittings that cannot be cleaned.

## *Note*

***Do not allow oil, grease, flammable solvent, or other combustibles such as lint or dust to come in contact with threads or any parts that will be exposed to pressurized oxygen.***

It is advisable to purge the oxygen system any time work has been accomplished on any of the lines and fittings. Use dry nitrogen or dry air for purging the system. All open lines should be capped immediately after purging.

When oxygen is being lost from a system through leakage, a sequence of steps may be necessary to locate the opening. Leakage may often be detected by listening for the distinct hissing sound of escaping gas. If this check proves negative, it will be necessary to soap-test all lines and connections with a castile soap and water solution or specially compounded leak-test material. Make the solution thick enough to adhere to the contours of the fittings. At the completion of the leakage test, remove all traces of the soap and water.

# Chapter 21

## HOW TO OPERATE YOUR AIRCRAFT

## Pre-Flight

The worst thing a person can do is use an aircraft for flight instruction. This is usually a lease back situation where the owner of an aircraft will lease his treasure to a flying club or school for flight instruction. The flying school will usually maintain and perform all the maintenance and the owner will as the lease states pay for parts lots of parts in most cases. Below you will find a list of stuff to assist you in operating your aircraft without causing too much undue destruction of the equipment.

First of all preflight. Who does them anyway? This is when the aircraft is supposed to be inspected prior to flight by the pilot who is about to bet his/her life on the machine. It is not the time to make up for the fact that you or the instructor showed up late. A preflight is somewhat different but is often confused with a "walk around" which is something completely different. To be truthful about it, most pilots have absolutely no idea at all what they are actually supposed to be looking for on a preflight inspection. About the only thing that most pilots would find is if a wing is missing. To compensate for that, spend some time and look at everything on the airplane very closely. A good place to start is the pilot-operating handbook (POH), the Airplane Flight Manual (AFM), or the Type Certificate Date Sheet (TCDS) for aircraft with placards only.

## Control Wheel Lock

Always install the control wheel lock after a flight. If there is no control wheel lock on the airplane, use the seatbelts. Flight Control surfaces suffer more abuse on the ground when there is not a control wheel lock installed that they would in flight. The surface hinges are all metal to metal and unnecessary "wear and tear" on an airplane that's not even airborne in no way to operate an airplane.

## Fuel Level

When checking the fuel level in the tanks, stand on the inboard part of the upper wing access step as close to the fuselage as your shoes will go and use the hand hold "assist handles" to support your weight as you climb up to put your weight on the wing strut strip (on high wing aircraft). **NOTE** putting your hard shoe heal against a wing strut may damage it and it will fail in flight. **DO NOT** dent the strut with your shoe. If you stand on the outboard edge of the step, there a greater leverage outward on the step, it'll eventually crack or tear out of the fuselage, which requires many hours of expensive sheet metal work. You'll notice that most fuelers usually use a latter. If you can carry a latter in the aircraft.

## Scratch Windshield

Do not scratch the "windshield" when checking the fuel. You'll certainly scratch the windshield if you jump up on the step with the fuel strainer in your hand or your back pocket. Put the fuel strainer in a box or plastic bag in the back of the airplane when you are done using it to check fuel. Don't walk around with the fuel strainer.

The fuel strainer does not go in the back of the seat pouch. It and the fuel it contains will destroy the upholstery.

Don't put stuff on the dashboard/glareshield that'll scratch the "glass" which is really plastic. In a real airplane that has a real windshield made of real glass, this is not a problem. Anything, which is tougher than the plastic, will certainly scratch it.

# Engine Leaning

Do not over-lean the mixture. It'll destroy the engine. It'll crack cylinders. It'll burn the electrodes right off the spark plugs, which could lead to the loss of the engine inflight. If you "know" how to lean the mixture make sure you know how to "correctly" lean the mixture. A little "wasted" fuel or some fouled plugs are not a major concern especially in comparison.

# Doors

Some entrances of the doors are "over center." They lock you out of the airplane whey they are slammed. This is because the inside handles falls forward into the "lock" position when the door is closed from the outside. You can usually open the door on the other side of the airplane in most cases. Never yank or pull on the door handle.

Do not slam the door in an effort to close the door. It ruins the door, the door lock mechanism and the door hinges. If there wasn't an actual problem, slamming the door really hard a few times, there will be. It's a completely different design than the doors on you motor vehicle. Aviation from all I've seen has all been method over muscle. There is never a reason to have to slam a door.

**How doors are supposed to operate,** how to close a door. Go to full open with the outside door handle until it locks outward in the full open position. This normally happens when the door is first open. This arms the door to close. The doors will not close "peacefully" until this happens regardless of how hard it's slammed. The handle must be out and the door armed to closed. Gently pull the door inward, a certain door pin sensor on the door will hit the door jam and suddenly release the handle which was locked outward in the full open position, and the door handle will now go the closed inward retract position.

**How to close a door that won't close.** If the door does not close normally one of the two things is wrong.

1.  The door was not armed to close (outside door handle not in the out open position).

2.  The door pin sensor on the door does not properly contact the door jam so it never releases the door handle to close.

In the first case, first arm the door to close (outside door handle open and out) then push on the door pin sensor, while holding the handle, to get the handle to release just a little bit. With the handle released just a little bit, push or pull the door to close then allow the handle to close.

# Trash

There should be a cardboard box in he back of each airplane. Put all the trash in this box. Technically there shouldn't be any trash left in the airplane. It's supposed to be removed with other personal item, but if it's placed in the cardboard box in the back it's easy to remove. There should be no dirty oily trash behind the seat or on the floor. Oil has certain characteristic action around oxygen bottles (FIRE).

# Towbars

When using a towbar, most towbars are for steering the nose wheel only, not for pulling the airplane. If used incorrectly, a towbar can come loose, and it would hurt.

# Oil Record

Record all oil added. If the airplane is burning oil or leaking oil, the numbers will tell you. It's generally considered to be easier than trying to find a place to land. All the bellies on the airplane should be cleaned… well most airplanes. If an airplane starts to leak anything you should notice it on the preflight or post flight check visual inspection. The oil leak should be noted on a discrepancy sheet and the oil stains removed before the next flight.

# Dip Stick

Do not over-torque or tighten the oil dipstick. The easiest way to make the engine leak oil is to do exactly that, over-torque the dipstick. The filler tube is made of plastic on most aircraft. It cracks at the base of the tube on the engine case (block for non-aviation types), and out comes the oil, right from the engine case.

# Parking Brakes

When not to set the parking brake. If you did not pay tie down fees your aircraft may be towed with the parking brake set and will damage stuff. If wheel chocks are available use them.

How to set the park brake. The park brake lever handle is not to be used to apply the brakes. It is used to set the brakes after they are applied with the brake pedals. This means that you need to be inside the airplane and with your feet on the pedals to set the bakes. Trying to use the handle to set brakes ruins the handle.

# Brakes

Brakes, despite common mass misconception, there are not for taxiing, turning expect on certain model aircraft, or for holding centerline as you go barreling down the runway. They are really useful in case of an aborted takeoff when you'll actually need to stop. Hot brakes don't work very well. Please try not to ride the brakes. The nose gear is for steering. The brakes are for stopping.

The "short" runway is a few thousand feet. There is no need to make the first taxiway unless you want the mechanic to make money changing brake pads.

# Hard Landings

If you land excessively hard (exceeding what is proper, normal or reasonable) or you hit or drag the tail, someone needs to know. The airplane requires a hard landing inspection per the maintenance manual. Not telling someone may endanger the life or lives of the next pilot. On training aircraft stuff happens.

# Break In Oil

Most airplanes use something called "Red Label" W100. This is engine oil used for break-in procedures and different oil is used after break-in. Beware, W100 is break-in oil and 100 are normal oil in most cases. If you don't know ask mechanic what oil to use. Most pilots I have met come with an attitude they know everything, and will not admit they do not know something. A pilot with this attitude will do something stupid and blame someone else. When in doubt ask the mechanic they are trained professionals and not knuckle draggers.

# Ammeter Works

The way to confirm that the ammeter works is probably not working is by dropping the flaps and the suddenly reversing the flap motor. It spikes the motor. The Starting Engine procedure calls for "Starter-Check Disengaged" which is to see that the ammeter is somewhere in the positive, but is not pegged positive. Point being that after engine start, the ammeter should be somewhere in the positive side recharging the battery, which was just used to turn the starter. The pointer on the positive side means the alternator is working and feeding electrons into the electrical system. The negative pointer means that the battery is feeding electrons into the electrical system (bad thing to happen). In other words, after engine start look to confirm "oil pressure" and ammeter in the positive, but not pegged position. If the ammeter is in the positive position the alternator is working. Turning on the taxi and landing lights on simultaneously will also cause the needle to deflect. Why is it a bad thing if the ammeter pegs positive after engine start up? It means that all of a sudden you now have two alternators. WAIT...where did this second alternator come from? No ... there was no extra alternator installed during you last 100 hour or annual inspection. It used to be your starter, and is driven by the engine, it turn into an alternator and instead of using electricity it produces it electricity. What has happened is the starter is stuck engaged during starting and has not disengaged. This is called a "Hung Start," and on turbine engines this is a very bad thing.

# Interior Lights

After a night flight remember to turn off all the interior and integral instrument lights, in other word all the lights. As a part of the normal pre-flight it is a good habit to turn the little knobees counterclockwise to confirm that all the lights are off. There is no other way to tell if the lights are off or on in the daytime. The lights are useless in the daytime and it is a pain at the end of daylight not to have the lights when you need them at night. There is a light switch on most airplanes overhead that's placard "Dome Both Post." This switch should be left in the "Dome" position. The dome is that single overhead red light. The post lights are those zillion tiny post lights on the instrument panel next to the instruments.

# Stuff

Lastly, if there is anything, even minor stuff, that's wrong or concerns you with the airplane let someone know and write a squawk. Maintenance folk's love squawks that's how they make a living and keep you living.

# Section 22

## TOOLS

# The Proper Tool

The "get a bigger hammer" syndrome is the classic reference to tool abuse or overuse. But hammers, though misused more often than they should be, rarely make their presence felt in the wrong places as often as giant slip-joint pliers do. These large water pump and vise-grip pliers are usually listed as required tools and do work effectively on more situations than almost any other type of tool.

However, they are far from do-all tools and can lead to safety problems if misused, particularly if used on smaller nuts. The main problem is that a healthy grab on a tight nut leaves telltale, damaging tool marks that can progress into gouges if the pliers jaws slip before the required torque is reached.

One instance where use of the wrong tool can lead to operational aircraft problems is the use of water pump pliers on oxygen supply pressure regulator assemblies. When the teeth of the oversize pliers bite these nuts, they become chewed up with gouges and rounded flats. Deep gouges can adversely affect the structural integrity of nuts, and oxygen regulator leaks can result. In this particular case, the job can best be done using a 1 1/8-inch wrench firmly applied to seat this nut or compression fitting. In a pinch, an adjustable wrench may be used as a substitute; do not use pliers.

# Torque Wrenches

We use torque wrenches to ensure proper preloading of various types of fasteners. However, are we really accomplishing what we set out to do? We know how to use torque wrenches, and we can figure "indicated torque" from "actual torque" when using different extensions and/or adapters, but a question remains concerning the accuracy of the basic torque wrench itself. Some of us buy torque wrenches without any thought of checking the calibration before using them.

The Standard Aviation Maintenance Handbook, Number EA-2R2-0, published by International Aviation Publishers, states: "Proper torque may be obtained by using an accurate, recently calibrated torque wrench." FAA Advisory Circular (AC) 43.13-1B, Acceptable Methods, Techniques, and Practices - Aircraft Inspection and Repair, chapter 7, and states: "Calibrate the torque wrench at least once a year." The Snap-On Tools catalog states: "Periodic calibration is necessary to maintain accuracy."

I contacted three tool manufacturers: Utica Tools; Consolidated Devices, Inc.; and Snap-On Tools to discuss the calibration of their equipment. All three manufacturers referenced the National Standards.

The American National Standards Institute (ANSI) standards require a torque wrench to maintain accuracy through 5000 cycles. The Federal Standard FED.STD. GGG-W-868 requires a torque wrench to maintain accuracy for three cycles at 20, 40, 60, 80, and 100 percent of the indicator scale. The American Society of Mechanical Engineers (ASME) document B107.14M and the International Standards Organization (ISO) document 6789 require accuracy for three cycles at 20, 60, and 100 percent of the scale.

Torque wrench calibration is subjective and you must establish it considering the nature of application, frequency of use, condition, and time. This does not mean you can send a torque wrench for calibration after you use it 5000 cycles. There are many other factors to consider. If you drop a torque wrench, expose it to vibration, or if it meets with other detrimental conditions, this may affect the calibrated accuracy. Most "standard organizations" recommend that a torque wrench be calibrated at least once a year, and perform an in-house check using a torque tester at 3-month intervals. It is important to remember the torque tester also requires periodic calibration. If you do not have access to a torque tester and you drop a torque wrench, you should calibrate the torque wrench before you use it again. When you calibrate your torque wrench, you should receive a report that you can use to track its level of accuracy from one calibration date to the next. You can use this information to adjust the frequency of calibration. Remember that calibration may take 2 weeks or more and is required by Title 49 CFR Part 43.

# Equipment Calibration

In my monthly newsletter dated June 2001 issue, I touch on torque wrench calibration. A reader has asked me to expand on the topic to cover gauges and other tools. His question was if he buy's a new torque wrench when does the calibration start. Answer, one year from the last calibration date as shown on the qualification sheet provided with the tool. Remember not all torque wrench's even new ones come with calibration certifications. The certified torque wrench will cost you more than a non-certificated wrench. Ask the seller to provide you with a new calibration certification when you pick up your new toy/tool.

**Certification**--implies that a certificate is in existence, which certifies or states a qualification.

### Test Equipment Calibration Standards

The test equipment calibration standards must be derived from and traceable to one of the following:

1. The National Institute of Standards and Technology (NIST).

2. Standards established by the test equipment manufacturer.

3. If foreign-manufactured test equipment, the standards of the country, where it was manufactured, if approved by the Administrator.

The technician must make sure that the test equipment used for maintenance is the equipment called for by the manufacturer or equivalent. Before acceptance, a comparison should be made between the specifications of the test equipment recommended by the manufacturer and those proposed by the repair facility. The test equipment must be capable of performing all normal tests and checking all parameters of the equipment under test. The level of accuracy should be equal to or better than that recommended by the manufacturer. For a description of avionics test equipment used for troubleshooting, refer to the equipment or aircraft manufacturing instruction manual.

To preclude acceptance of nonconforming articles, or rejections due to improperly controlled tools and gauges, a quality control system should incorporate a schedule for inspection and calibration, to certified national measurement standards, of all inspection tools, gauges, and testing equipment, as well as production jigs, fixtures, templates, etc., which are depended upon as media for inspection. An acceptable schedule would have the inspection intervals established on the basis that such tools and gauges would be inspected prior to their becoming inaccurate or requiring adjustment, replacement, or repair.

A record keeping system would ensure that each piece of equipment or container is checked prior to first usage and at the proper periodic interval, and marked to indicate the date that the next inspection is due, and is removed from inspection and shop areas or conspicuously identified to prohibit usage after expiration of the inspection due date.

**Special Equipment or Instrumentation.** Climb performance tests require an airspeed indicator, sensitive altimeter, and total air temperature indicator with a known recovery factor. For reciprocating engine-powered airplanes, an induction air temperature gauge, engine tachometer, manifold pressure gauge and cylinder head temperature indicator may be appropriate. For turbine-powered airplanes, indicators of power parameters, such as torque meter, EGT, N1, N2, and propeller r.p.m. may be appropriate. A fuel counter and/or fuel flowmeter is useful. **All instruments should be calibrated, and the calibration data should be included with the test records.** In addition, a stopwatch and appropriate data recording board and forms are required.

Other Methods. Other methods of airspeed calibration are described in NASA Reference Publication 1046, "Measurement of Aircraft Speed and Altitude," by W. Gracey, May 1980.

The FAA's policy requiring standards used to calibrate inspection and test equipment, to meet a test accuracy ratio of 4:1 or greater, has been derived from private industry, government, and international specifications (e.g., American National Standard for Calibration (ANSI) ANSI/NCSL Z540-1-1994, Military Standard MIL-STD-45662A dated 1 August 1988, International Standard ISO 10012-1, corrected and reprinted 1993-05-01). All of these publications are readily available. These publications provide specifications and rules for which all Calibration Laboratories must adhere to, so calibration/verification results are consistent, credible, and traceable to the National Institute of Standards & Technology. (i.e., **correct calibration to a standard derived from the *National Bureau of Standards*).** The following is a summarization, taken from the aforementioned publications and address some of the issues:

Calibration laboratories shall have documented instructions on the use and operation of all relevant equipment, on the handling and preparation of items, and for calibration/verification, where the absence of such instructions could jeopardize the calibration/verifications. All instructions, standards, manuals and reference data relevant to the work of the laboratory shall be maintained up-to-date and readily available to the staff. In the absence of manufacture specifications for the measuring and test equipment being calibrated or verified, then, the collective uncertainty of the measurement standards shall not exceed 25% of the accuracy of the acceptable tolerance (4:1).

# Test Equipment Calibration

Test equipment such as meters, torque wrenches, static, and transponder test equipment should be checked at least once a year.

National Institute of Standards and Technology traceability can be verified by reviewing test equipment calibration records for references to National Institute of Standards and Technology test report numbers. These numbers **certify traceability** of the equipment used in calibration.

If a repair station/mechanic uses a standard for performing calibration, that calibration standard cannot be used to perform maintenance. The calibration intervals for test equipment will vary with the type of equipment, environment, and use. **The accepted industry practice for calibration intervals is usually one year.** Considerations for acceptance of the intervals include the following:

1. Manufacturer's recommendation for the type of equipment.

2. Repair facilities past calibration history, as applicable.

If the manufacturer's manual does not describe a test procedure, the repair station/mechanic must coordinate with the manufacturer to develop the necessary procedures, prior to any use of the equipment.

# Crimp on Terminal Lugs and Splices

The crimp (Pre-insulated crimp type) on terminal lugs and splices must be installed using a high quality ratchet type-crimping tool. Hand, portable, and stationary power tools are available for crimping terminal lugs. These tools crimp the barrel to the conductor, and simultaneously from the insulation support to the wire insulation.

Crimp tools must be carefully inspected:

1. Insure that the full cycle ratchet mechanism is tamper-proof so that it cannot be disengaged prior to or during the crimp cycle.

2. If the tool does not function or faults are found, reject the tool and send the tool to be repaired.

3. Only the manufacturer or an approved calibration laboratory makes the tool calibration and adjustments.

4. Suitable gages of the Go/No Go type are available and shall be used prior to any crimping operation and whenever possible during operation to ensure crimp dimensions.

For further information refer to **MIL-C-22520** Crimping Tools, Hand or Power Actuated, Wire Termination, and Tool Kits. This specification covers in detail the general requirements for crimp tools, inspection gages and tool kits.

# Equivalent Tools

Repair stations, air carriers and mechanics must make a determination of acceptability for equivalency of special equipment and/or tools used in maintaining aircraft and their associated components. Part 43 section 43.13(b) states "Each person maintaining or altering, or performing preventive maintenance, shall do that work in such a manner and use materials of such a quality, that the condition of the aircraft, airframe, aircraft engine, propeller, or appliance worked on **will be at least equal to its original or properly altered condition** (with regard to aerodynamic function, structural strength, resistance to vibration and deterioration, and other qualities affecting airworthiness).

The term equivalency means recommended equivalent to that recommended by the Original Equipment Manufacture (OEM) for the purpose of performing specifics tests or making required measurements to determine the airworthiness of an article. To determine equivalency, you should compare the required test operations or specifications and the technical data of the special equipment or test apparatus may look different, be made of different materials, be a different color, etc. However, as long as the tool is functionally equivalent for the specific test application the tool may be used in most cases.

A finding of equivalency can only be made based on an evaluation of a technical data file. Additionally, demonstrating functionality of special equipment or test apparatus may sometimes be required. This file should also describe any special manufacturing processes that are used in the controlling processes, including gauges and recording equipment.

Some tools have been manufactured by a method known as reverse engineering. Reverse engineering alone without data; drawings, testing, or reports may not adequately produce a tool or fixture functionally equivalent to an OEM's requirements.

Most of the test apparatus used for making airworthiness decisions are generic in nature and designed to make measurements that are not unique to a specific manufacturer's product or process. Equipment that is not "special" in nature only needs to be designed and calibrated to make measurements with the specific manufacturer's tolerances to be considered equivalent for those tests or measurements.

With recent technological advances, highly specialized test equipment or test apparatus is frequently required. Use of such equipment supports the continued airworthiness of aircraft systems and components to the manufacturer's specifications and tolerances.

Determining the equivalency of equipment and/or apparatus is the primary responsibility of the repair station, air carrier, mechanic, and not the FAA. The basis of equivalency for equipment or apparatus for products being maintained must meet the manufacturer's standards and specifications for tolerances and accuracy.

## Note

*An Aircraft Engineering Division AIR-100 memorandum dated December 21. 1999, states, "Designated Engineering Representatives (DER) MAY NOT approve or determine equivalency of tooling and test equipment." The FAA and DER may only make an Acceptance of functional equivalency for special equipment of functional equivalency for special equipment or test apparatus. It is important to emphasize that the burden of demonstrating equivalence is borne by the repair station, air carrier or mechanic and not the FAA.*

Standard industry practice would dictate that any special equipment or test apparatus that is used to make a critical airworthiness decisions or that requires calibration or inspection be given a unique part number and serial number to identify it with the repair station, air carrier or mechanic inventory system.

# CHAPTER 23

## ALTERATIONS AND MAJOR REPAIRS

# Approving Major Repairs and Major Alterations

First lets discuss the meaning of major alterations and major repairs. What is a Field Approval? A Field Approval is the granting, by an FAA airworthiness inspector, of FAA "approval" for a major repair or major alteration. The approval is given only after conducting a physical inspection and/or after reviewing data. A checklist is provided in the Appendix section.

There are three different kinds of Field Approvals for which the local FAA inspector can sign off:

1.  **EXAMINATION OF DATA** only: This is the most common form of Field Approval. The mechanic or repairman submits "acceptable" data to the local FAA office for approval. The "approved data" can be used to perform a major repair or major alteration. Once the data has been approved under this procedure it can be used only for that one aircraft (described in Block 1 of FAA Form 337). However, if you want to do the exact same repair or alteration to another like make or model aircraft you can use the original Form 337 as the basis for obtaining a new Field Approval for the second aircraft.

2.  **PHYSICAL INSPECTION,** demonstration or testing of the repair or alteration: This is rarely done except in cases where technicians find unapproved engine or components installed on aircraft, which apparently have been installed for some time. Since the aircraft has flown successfully for many hours, and FAA inspector can, if satisfied with the installation, approve the installation. He does so by signing a new Form 337.

3.  **EXAMINATION OF DATA** only for duplication on identical make and model aircraft by the original modifier: This is a procedure that saves the maintenance technician and the FAA a lot of time. For example, one technician wants to install duplicate avionics packages on as many Cessna 501s as possible; or maybe he wants to install duplicate installations of tundra tires on Beech 18s. The technician can submit the data to be approved along with a request that the data approval be extended to other identical aircraft. The FAA inspector, if satisfied, signs Block 3 that grants duplication of the data for the original Form 337. When the technician finishes a duplicate alteration on other aircraft, he sends the FAA a regular Form 337, properly filled out listing the "approved data" on the back and making references to the Field Approval. To avoid problems, attach a duplicate copy of the original Field Approval Form 337. With a recent to change to FAA Handbook 8300.10 this practice has been stopped for multi field approvals for FSDO Inspectors.

# What is a Field Approval

A Field Approval is not a regulation, it is a policy. Because it is a procedure and not a rule, a mechanic is not automatically entitled to a Field Approval even if he submits a "perfect" FAA Form 337 to the FAA.

Why? Because the authority to grant a Field Approval and the great burden of responsibility that goes with signing Block 3 of the Form 337 has been delegated only to the local FAA district office airworthiness inspector. The responsibility for data approval is so monumental that no one, not even the FAA administrator, may force the inspector to approve a major repair or major alteration against his or her better judgment. Since it is the inspector who makes the final decision and is held accountable by the FAA for that decision, most inspectors are overly cautious when it comes to signing off a Field Approval.

**Major alteration:** An alteration not listed in the aircraft, aircraft engine, or propeller specifications that also fits one or more of the following:

1. Might appreciably affect airworthiness by changing weight, balance, structural strength, performance, powerplant operation, or flight characteristics.
2. Is not done according to accepted practices or cannot be done by elementary operations.

**Major repair:** A repair that fits one or more of the following:

1. Might appreciably affect airworthiness by changing weight, balance, structural strength, performance, powerplant operation, or flight characteristics if improperly done.
2. Is not done according to accepted practices or cannot be done by elementary operations.

**Minor alteration:** Any alteration that is not classified as a major alteration.

**Minor repair:** Any repair that is not classified as a major repair.

**Field approval:** An approval by an authorized Airworthiness Aviation Safety Inspector (ASI) of a major repair or major alteration that is accomplished by one or more of the following, as appropriate:

1. Examination of data only - one aircraft.
2. Physical inspection, demonstration, testing, etc. - one aircraft.
3. Examination of data only - duplication of identical aircraft.

**Data:** Information that supports and/or describes the alteration or repair, including the following:

1. Drawings, sketches, and/or photographs.
2. Stress analysis.
3. Service Bulletins.
4. Engineering Orders.
5. Operating limitations.

**Approved data:** Data that can be used to substantiate major repairs/major alterations, derived from the following:

1. Type Certificate Data Sheets (TCDS).
2. Supplemental Type Certificate (STC) data provided that it specifically applies to the item being repaired/altered.
3. Airworthiness Directives (AD).
4. Airframe, engine, and propeller manufacturer's "FAA-approved" maintenance manuals or instructions.
5. Appliance manufacturer's manuals or instruction, unless specifically not approved by the Administrator or resulting in an alteration to the airframe, engine, and/or propeller FAA Form 337 [Front, Back, Info], Major Repair or Alteration, when the specified data has been previously approved and will be used as a basis for a field approval CAA Form 337, dated prior to 10/1/55 FAA Form 337[Front, Back, Info], used to approve multiple usage only, by the original modifier.
6. Structural Repair Manuals (SRM), only as a source of approved data for a major repair, when it is an FAA-approved document. Data that is contained in an SRM that is not FAA-approved can be used on a case-by-case basis if prior FAA approval is granted for that repair.
7. Parts Manufacturer Authorization (PMA), is considered approved data for the part only, an STC may be required for the actual installation.
8. Technical Delegation Option Authorization produced FAA-approved data.
9. Designated Standard Order Authorization (TSOA).

10. Engineering Representative (DER) approved data, only within authorized limitations.
11. Designated Alteration Station (DAS) FAA approved Repair data, under SFAR 36, for the holder's aircraft only.
12. Foreign bulletins, for use on U.S.-certificated foreign aircraft, when approved by the foreign authority.
13. Data describing an article or appliance used in an alteration, which is FAA-approved under a TSO.
14. As such, the conditions and tests required for TSO approval of an article are minimum performance standards. The article may be stalled only if further evaluation by the operator (applicant) documents an acceptable installation, which may be approved by the Administrator.
15. Data in the form of (TCA) Appliance Type Approval issued by the Minister of Transport Canada for those parts or appliances for which there is no current TSO available. The TCA certificate is included within the installation manual provided with the appliance and includes the dates of issuance and an environmental qualification statement.
16. Data describing a part or appliance used in an alteration, which is FAA-approved under a Parts Manufacturer Approval (PMA). (An STC may be required to obtain a PMA as a means of assessing airworthiness and/or performance of the part.)

**NOTE**
*AC 43.13, as amended, may be used as approved data, only if the following three prerequisites are met:*

*1. The user has determined that it is appropriate to the product being repaired/altered.*
*2. The user has determined that it is directly applicable to the repair/alteration being made.*
*3. The user has determined that it is not contrary to manufacturer's data.*

Many alterations are actually major design changes and may require a STC. Previously unapproved major changes to structural strength, reliability, and operational characteristics affect the airworthiness of the product and therefore require engineering approval. Typical major alterations in this category include the following:

1. Increase in gross weight and/or changes in center of gravity range.

2. Installation, changes, or relocation of equipment and systems that may adversely affect the structural integrity, flight, or ground handling characteristics of the aircraft.

3. Any change (alteration) of movable control surfaces that may adversely disturb the dynamic and static balance, alter the contour, or make any difference (plus or minus) in the weight distribution.

4. Change in control surface travel outside approved limits, control system mechanical advantage, location of control system component parts, or direction of motion of controls.

5. Changes in basic dimensions or external configuration of the aircraft, such as wing and tail platform or incidence angles, canopy, cowlings, contour or radii, or location of wing and tail fairings.

6. Changes to landing gear, such as internal parts of shock struts, length, geometry of members, or brakes and brake systems.

7. Any change to manifolding, engine cowling, and/or baffling that may adversely affect the flow of cooling air.

8. Changes to primary structure that may adversely affect strength or flutter and vibration characteristics.

9. Changes to systems that may adversely affect aircraft airworthiness, such as:

    a. Relocation of exterior fuel vents.
    b. Use of new type or different hydraulic components.
    c. Tube material and fittings not previously approved.

10. Changes to oil and fuel lines or systems that may adversely affect their operation, such as:

a. New types of hose and/or hose fittings.
b. Changes in fuel dump valves.
c. New fuel cell sealants.
d. New fuel or oil line materials.
e. New fuel or oil system components.

11. Any change to the basic engine or propeller design controls, operating limitations, and/or unapproved changes to engine adjustments and settings having an affect on power output.

12. Changes in a fixed fire extinguisher or detector system that may adversely affect the system effectiveness or reliability, such as:

a. Relocation of discharge nozzle or detector units.
b. Use of new or different detector components in new circuit arrangements.
c. Decreasing amount or different type of extinguishing agent.

13. Changes that do not meet the minimum standards established in a Technical Standard Order (TSO) under which a particular aircraft component or appliance is manufactured.

**NOTE**
*"Meet the minimum standards established in a Technical Standard Order" means that the equipment does not have to have TSO approval, but only needs to meet the requirements set by the TSO.*

14. Modifications to approved type (TSO) radio communications and navigational equipment that may adversely affect reliability or airworthiness, such as:

a. Changes that deviate from the vacuum tube or semiconductor manufacturer's operating limitations. Any changes to IF frequency Extension of receiver frequency range above or below the manufacturer's extreme design limits Major changes to the basic design of low approach aids. Changes that deviate from the design environmental performance.

15. Changes to aircraft structure or cabin interior of aircraft that may adversely affect evacuation of occupants in any manner.

Engineering assistance and advice must be requested when working in areas that include:

1. Use of synthetic covering material.
2. Substitution of parts.
3. Processes on which insufficient information is available.
4. New chrome plating applications.
5. New titanium applications.
6. Ceramic coatings.
7. New magnesium applications.
8. Use of synthetic resin glues.
9. New stripping or plating coatings.
10. New welding or brazing techniques.
11. Welding of certain types of propeller or engine parts.
12. Application of TSO's to specific installations.
13. Alternative means for complying with AD's.
14. Any change to a required aircraft instrument system.
15. Any other complex special process that if not properly performed could have an adverse effect on the integrity of the product.

# What is not a Major Alteration?

Not all alterations are major for example on the Type Certificate Data Sheets (TCDS) it may list several engines or propellers that can be install on a certain aircraft. As long as that engine or propeller is listed on the TCDS it is considered a minor and only requires a maintenance record (log book) entry. Also, if a piece of equipment is listed on the equipment list as optional it is still a minor alteration. And again only a record entry is required.

# Incomplete and/or Piecemeal Installations

Incomplete or piecemeal installation field approvals are intended to approve partial major modifications on aircraft that will be operated for an unspecified period of time. Aircraft having an incomplete equipment installation may be released for service only if the following has been accomplished:

1. The alteration data has been FAA-approved.
2. The incomplete/piecemeal alteration has been determined to not affect the safe operation of the aircraft.
3. The equipment installed remains deactivated and has placards affixed to prevent use.
4. The weight and balance reflects the incomplete installation.
5. The maintenance records have been completed and signed for the work that was actually accomplished.

# Avionic Alterations

When you permanently install an avionic component or system on a certificated aircraft you are altering the airframe and not the powerplant, propeller, or appliance. So on block 4 of FAA form 337, please mark "Airframe Alteration".

In instances where Advisory Circular AC 43.13 provides specific procedures which are appropriate to the repair and/or alteration being performed, it is incumbent upon the person authorized by CFR Part 43 to ensure that the AC 43.13 criteria being used is complied with and that a detailed reference is quoted an the FAA Form 337. That quote should include the specific page, paragraph, and/or figures of AC 43.13 used to perform that repair and/or alteration. The specific references to page and paragraph negates the necessity to write out detailed information; however, there is one exception, any placards placed in the aircraft should be quoted within block 8 of the 337. Where an Advisory Circular does not provide enough detail, written descriptions and/or drawings should be included within or attached to the 337. Remember, using any Advisory Circular, as approved data is appropriate only if that data is directly pertinent to the repair and/or alteration and if it is not contrary to manufacturer data.

The basic, steps to obtain a field approval

1. Contact the FAA inspector who will be approving the data and discuss the proposed repair and/or alteration.
2. The inspector will then evaluate the data and advise the applicant to proceed with the repair and/or alteration.
3. Perform the repair and/or alteration.
4. Block 6 of an original and one copy of the FAA Form 337 is completed and the 337 submitted to the FSDO (block 7 remains blank).

5. The FAA inspector's approval (following a conformity inspection, if required) will be made in block 3.
6. Approval for return to service will be accomplished by the person authorized in FAR 43 through the Completion of block 7 and resubmitted.

Multiple Avionics equipment/system listing on FAA form 337s: When multiple avionic systems/components are installed, those system/components which do not require "field approval" should be listed on a separate 337 from those systems/components which do require field approved. The exception is to not separate integrated systems/equipment.

# Special Circumstances Involving FAA Field Approval

The process for obtaining a field approval for navigation systems such as GPS, Loran-C, Multi-sensor, etc. and Cockpit Voice Recorders (CVR) can be time intensive. This is usually due to the system's installation complexity and/or the completion of required flight-tests, AFM Supplements, conformity inspections, etc. In order to lessen any operational burden on the aircraft- operator/owner, we recommend that initial approval in such cases be through the submittance of a 337, which limits the operation of the aircraft or system, to which can be approved by a person so authorized in CFR Part 43. For instance, a GPS system could be initially approved as limited to VFR with, a follow-up field approval for IFR. Though this entails two separate FAA Form 337s, it will sustain the airworthiness of the installation and the aircraft.

# Alteration Recordation Requirements

Remember, each major alteration will require two record entries. First, Section 43.9 states in part "each person who alters an aircraft, airframe, aircraft engine, propeller, appliance, or component part shall make an entry in the maintenance record of that equipment, and second. Major repairs and alterations shall be entered on a form, and the form disposed of, in the manner prescribed in 49 CFR 43 Part 43 Appendix B, by the person performing the work".

Data approval issued for one aircraft is applicable to only the aircraft described in Block 1 of FAA Form 337. This data cannot be used automatically as approved data for other aircraft. The data may be used only with the approval of the local office as the basis for obtaining approval on other aircraft.

Data approval issued for duplication of identical aircraft may be used as approved data only when the identical alteration is performed on an aircraft of identical make, model, and series by the original modifier. This will rarely be the case as most aircraft are never out fitted the same even if same make and model.

When the alteration has been performed by persons other than the original modifier, this data may be used as the basis for obtaining approval on other aircraft.

# Helpful Hints for Field Approvals

First, do not cut metal, splice wire or install equipment until you receive the approval. The only thing worse than not getting a Field Approval is telling your customer the expensive equipment you installed in his aircraft has to be removed.

Determine if the repair or alteration is major as defined by CFR 1. If it is major, go to the next step. Do not set unreasonable goals. Allow a reasonable time, at least 30 days for the Field Approval. Research all sources for "approved data" to make the repair or alterations. Find out what kind of data the inspector wants to see. Then assemble it in a reasonable and understandable format. The data must be current, accurate and must support as well as describe the alteration or repair. Data can be in the form of drawings, sketches or photographs. References to AC 43.13 and 2A. manufacturer's maintenance manuals, kits, bulletins, and service letters may be helpful.

A cover letter for the Form 337 describing in detail how you are going to accomplish the repair or alteration is also helpful. Vague or useless technical references are unprofessional and should be avoided because it destroys your credibility.

With your research completed, send the FAA inspector duplicate copies of the Form 337 along with the data you want approved. If you did your homework carefully and followed these helpful hints, you will have an excellent chance of getting your repair or alteration approved on the first attempt. If you do not, find out what is wrong and try again.

## Don't forget the ICA's

The purpose of the Instruction for Continued Airworthiness (ICA) is to provide instructions on how to maintain aircraft, which are altered, and appliances, which are installed in accordance with a field, approved major alteration. The ICA checklist is a guide for both the applicant who creates the ICA and the FAA Flight Standards inspector who accepts the ICA. The ICA developed in accordance with this guidance constitutes methods, techniques and practices "acceptable" to the Administrator.

# Alteration Approval

Alteration approval, issued for one aircraft, is applicable only to the aircraft described in Block 1 of FAA Form 337 This alteration cannot automatically be applied to other aircraft. This alteration may be used only with the approval of the local office as the basis for performing alterations on another aircraft.

# Recording Data Deviation

An alteration that uses data, which does not differ appreciable from previously approved data, does not require new or additional approval. Minor variations, which have no bearing on safety, are acceptable without formal approval and without submission of a formal application by the applicant. However, the deviation should be recorded on the FAA Form 337.

# Antenna's

When penetrating a pressurized compartment contact the local FSDO for guidance and special requirements.

On unpressurized cabins numerous aircraft models have been approved for the installation of communication and navigation antennas. What is required as follows?

1. A review of the individual aircraft Maintenance manuals will confirm if the proposed antenna location is previously approved.
2. When replacing a previously approved antenna with the same type model antenna, at the same location, all that is required is a maintenance entry.
3. If the replacement antenna is not the same model but has the same footprint and drag load, a maintenance entry is required.

4. When mounting an antenna in a new location that requires drilling holes to accommodate the change in footprint submit a field approval.

Other items frequently missing from block 8 of FAA form 337 that will be required as follows:

1. Adequate description of the work performed in relation to the major repair/alteration.
2. Electrical load analysis statement.
3. Annotation of appropriate VFR requirements pertaining to navigation systems contained in AC 20-121A, AC 20-129, AC 20-130, etc.
4. Annotation of appropriate IFR requirements pertaining to navigation systems contained in AC 20-121A, AC 20-129, AC 20-130, etc.
5. Annotation for updating of Weight and Balance and/or Equipment List.
6. A specific reference to "Data Approved by (or Acceptable to) the FAA." (i.e. STC, previous FAA field approval, 'Manufacturer's instructions, AC 43.13 references, etc,) documented.
7. Attached copies of substantiating documents as indicated immediately above (i.e. STC Certificate).
8. Annotation or. Attachment of a Certifying Statement by a flight test pilot (i.e. for CVR tape evaluation flights, navigation system flight tests, etc.).
9. Adequate references to Advisory Circular 43.13, specific to page, paragraph, and/or figures.

# What is a Supplemental Type Certificate?

A supplemental type certificate (STC) is a type certificate issued when an applicant has received FAA approval to modify an aircraft from its original design. The supplemental type certificate, which incorporates by reference the related type certificate, approves not only the modification but also how that modification affects the original design.

### How do you get your own supplemental type certificate?

For information regarding the supplemental type certificate application process, you may contact the FAA aircraft certification offices (ACOs) in your geographic area. You may also find it helpful to review related orders and advisory circulars, in particular, FAA Order 8110.4, "Type Certification," and AC 21-40, "Application Guide for Obtaining a Supplemental Type Certificate."

For complex design modifications, the Aircraft Certification Office may ask that you follow the "Original Design Approval Process."

### You've found a supplemental type certificate that you want to install on your airplane. What do you do now?

You must contact the supplemental type certificate holder to seek written permission. The supplemental type certificate and its related information all drawings, data, and specifications are the property of the supplemental type certificate holder. The FAA will not release this information without authorization from the owner.

### You can't find the supplemental type certificate holder. What do you do now?

If the mail you sent was returned "undeliverable" and there is no phone listing for the holder, please contact the issuing FAA office. Supplemental type certificates are approved and issued through FAA aircraft certification offices (ACOs), which serve the geographic area of the supplemental type certificate owner's residence. The ACO's can be found of the FAA web site or contact you local FSDO.

### How do you find what supplemental type certificate's have been done through FAA Forms 337 in your aircraft?

All FAA Forms 337 are mailed to FAA's Aircraft Registration's branch and in individual folders by registration number. You may visit FAA aircraft registry's website at http://registry.faa.gov/ or contact them at:

FAA
Aircraft Registration Branch, AFS-750
P O Box 25504
Oklahoma City OK 73125
Phone: (405) 954-3116

# Completion of FAA Form 337

FAA Form 337, Major Repair and Alteration (Airframe, Powerplant, Propeller, or Appliance) serve two purposes. One is to provide owners and operators a record of major repairs and major alterations indicating details and approval. The other purpose is to provide the FAA with a copy for the aircraft records. Who is responsible for the FAA Form 337 and disposition?

1. The person who performed or supervised the major repair or major alteration prepares the original FAA Form 337 (two copies). The holder of an IA then further processes the forms when they are presented for approval.
2. Instructions for the completion of FAA Form 337 information appears in AC 43.9-1E, Instructions for Completion of FAA Form 337, Major Repair and Alteration (Airframe, Powerplant, Propeller, or Appliance).
3. Disposition of FAA Form 337:
   a. The holder of an IA who has found a major alteration or a major repair to be in conformity with FAA-approved data should review the FAA Form 337 for completeness and accuracy, and complete item in block 7.
   b. The person performing a major repair or major alteration shall in accordance with 14 CFR Part 43:
      1. Give a signed copy of FAA Form 337 to the aircraft owner.
      2. Make the proper entry in the maintenance records.
      3. Forward the **duplicate original copy** to the local FAA FSDO within 48 hours, after return to service.
   c. The holder of an IA should ensure that the duplicate copy is an exact and legible reproduction of the original. The signatures should not be carbon copies but original signatures written in ink.
   d. If the FAA Form 337 information is completed for extended-range fuel tanks installed within the passenger compartment or a baggage compartment. The person who performs the work and the person authorized to approve the work by Part 43 section 43.7 shall execute FAA Form 337 info in at least triplicate, as required by 14 CFR Part 43, appendix B. One (1) copy of the FAA Form 337 shall be placed on board the aircraft as specified in section 91.417 of the rules. The remaining forms shall be distributed as previously noted.
   e. If FAA Form 337 has been completed for engines, propellers, spare parts or components, both copies of the form, with the approval portion completed, should be attached to the part or component until it is installed on an aircraft.
      1. The mechanic who makes the installation will, in accordance with 14 CFR Part 43, section 43.9(a)(4), complete both copies **(originals)** of FAA Form 337 by filling in blocks 1 and 2 and sign for the installation in the aircraft records, making reference to the FAA Form 337 in the record entry.

      2. Give a copy **(original)** to the owner and forward a copy **(original)** to the FAA FSDO for the area where the installing mechanic is operating.

# CAR's and CAM's

Certifications requirements are located in title 14 CFR's, or the predecessor to them, Civil Air Regulations (CAR). The two objectives of aircraft certification are to encourage and foster the development of civil aviation, and to ensure aviation safety. One method used by the Federal Aviation Administration (FAA) to fulfill these objectives is the aircraft certification system through which aircraft design and modification must be approved. Title 14 of the Code of Federal Regulations and the Civil Air Regulations define the minimum required safety standards for FAA certification. By demonstrating compliance with these regulations, an aircraft modifier may obtain the necessary FAA approval for a modification.

Advisory Circular 20-33 is to advise the public that such policy information as is contained in Civil Aeronautics Manuals (CAMs) 1, 3, 4a, 4b, 5, 6, 7, 9, 13, and 14, may be used in conjunction with specific sections of the Code of Federal Regulations which correspond with the sections of the Civil Air Regulations to which the policies are applicable, upon recodification effective February 1, 1965. CAM 8 may be used in conjunction with CFR 21.25, CFR 21.185, and CFR 21.187 for restricted category certification of small agricultural airplanes only.

Civil Aeronautics Manual policies provide detailed technical information on acceptable methods of complying with the regulations. Such policies are for the guidance of the public and are not mandatory.

Interested persons upon recodification should not discard CAMs covering the certification of products, because the rules contained therein, and accompanying policies, will continue to apply to products, which have been certificated thereunder.

If you have an aircraft manufactured before March 1, 1979 your aircraft is most likely a CAR built aircraft and only has to meet the CAR requirements. If your aircraft was built after March 1, 1979 they have to meet the requirement are in Part 23. The CAR's and CAM are now on the FAA web site at www.faa.gov/.

For example all aircraft are manufactured with a lap safety belt installed. CAR 3 aircraft only require a lap belt and not a shoulder harness. Some CAR 3 aircraft were manufactured with a shoulder harness, which is listed on the equipment list. If shoulder harnesses are not on the equipment list installed by the manufacture then there should be a FAA Form 337 for an alteration and record entry in the airframe record for the installation. All CFR Part 23 aircraft come with a shoulder harness installed from the manufacture. Remember the cut off date is March 1, 1979, if your aircraft was manufactured before that date it is a CAR 3 after it is a CFR 23 aircraft. Look at your Airworthiness Certificate it will give you a date in the bottom left corner; this is the date your aircraft was manufactured.

In the Appendix section is a short CAR checklist for reference only.

# APPENDEX

# Web Sites

### Advisory Circular Checklist
http://www.faa.gov/aba/html_policies/ac00_2.html
http://www.faa.gov/avr/afs/acs/ac-idx.htm (AFS only)

### Aircraft Maintenance (Field Approval Process Improvement Team Report)
HTTP://www.faa.gov/avr/afs/index.htm

### Alaska Region Alterations Home Page
*http://www.alaska.faa.gov/flt_std/Aws/Alterat.htm#Start*

### ATOS Home Page
http://www.faa.gov/avr/afs/atos/

### CAR's and CAM's
http://isweb.tasc.dot.gov/library/nsvcs.htm
http://www.faa.gov/fsdo/awsp/

### FAA Directives
http://www.faa.gov/aba/apf/directives/index.htm

### FAA History
http://www.faa.gov/docs/b-chron.doc

### CFR's
http://www.faa.gov/avr/AFS/CFRS/CFR_idx.htm

### Fed. Register's Web Page (NPRM's)
http://www.access.gpo.gov/su_docs/aces/aces140.html
http://www.access.gpo.gov/su_docs/

### Forms
http://www.opm.gov/forms/
http://feds.faa.gov

### General Aviation Maintenance Home Page (Field Approvals)
http://www.aea200.ea.faa.gov/ea01/airworthiness/airworthiness.htm

### Handbook Bulletins
http://www.faa.gov/avr/afs/bulletin.htm

### Handbooks, Safety Inspector's (Orders)
http://www.faa.gov/avr/afs/faa/home.html

### Industry Available Certificate Site
http://www.avweb.com/toc/database.html

### JAR's / JAA Home Page
http://www.jaa.nl/jar/jar.html

### MEL Policy Letters (1st address Draft & Final)
http://www.opspecs.com/MELPOLHUB.htm
http://www.opspecs.com/MELPolicyTalks/

**MEL Policy Letters by ATA Subject Areas**
http://www.opspecs.com/MELPolicyTalks/disc4_toc.htm

**NPRM**
http://www.faa.gov/avr/arm/nprm/nprm.htm

**Operations Specifications Hub, MMELS**
http://www.opspecs.com/

**Page for AFS**
http://www.faa.gov/abc/directiveschecklist/

**TCDS Home Page Type Certificate Data Sheets**
    **(TCDS) (STC's) & (TSO's)**
**(CFR Database Current and Historical Regulatory Documents)**
http://www.faa.gov/avr/air/airhome.htm
http://www.airweb.faa.gov/Regulatory_and_Guidance_library/rgHTML.nsf/htmlmedia/Make_Mo
    del_Selection.html

**Title 49 USC (Supplement 3 (49USC44713)**
http://www.access.gpo.gov/congress/cong013.html
http://www.access.gpo.gov/uscode/uscmain.html (direct)

**MIL-Specifications and Standards**
http://www.dodssp.daps.mil/
http://assist.daps.dla.mil/quicksearch/

# Engine Trend Monitoring

**INSTRUCTIONS:** Form is to be filled out by both the pilot and mechanic prior to or during Inspection interval. Asterisk (*) items are pilot functions.

DATE_____ OPERATOR_____
"N" NUMBER_____ S/N _____
MODEL NUMBER_____ MFG._____
TOTAL TIME_____ TYPE OF OIL USED_____
TOTAL TIME SINCE OVERHAUL _____ HOBBS/TACH_____

## AREA #1 ENGINE CASE COMPONENTS:

OIL ANALYSIS:

DATE TAKEN_____            LABORATORY_____
SILICON_____
ALUMINUM_____
IRON_____
TIN _____
CHROMIUM_____
COPPER_____

*OIL PRESSURE @ CRUISE RPM_____
*OIL TEMPERATURE @ CRUISE RPM_____
*STATIC RPM (FIXED PITCH)_____       TAKE OFF RPM(CONT. PITCH)_____
*MANIFOLD PRESSURE @ TAKEOFF_____

OIL FILTER CONDITION:
OK____
MAGNETIC PARTICLES_____ QUANTITY_____
NONMAGNETIC PARTICLES_____
OIL SCREEN CONDITION:
OK____
MAGNETIC PARTICLES_____ QUANTITY_____
NONMAGNETIC PARTICLES_____ QUANTITY_____
OIL CONSUMPTION_____ QTS PER_____ HOUR (S)

## AREA #2 CYLINDER/PISTON ASSEMBLIES:

*CYLINDER HEAD TEMP @ CRUISE_____ ALT _____
*EGT @ CRUISE _____ ALT _____

ENGINE COMPRESSION RESULTS:

#1 _____
#2 _____
#3 _____
#4 _____
#5 _____
#6 _____
#7 _____
#8 _____

SPARK PLUG CONDITION: 1 = good 2 = worn 3 = oil fouled 4 = carbon fouled
#1 CYLINDER TOP_____
      BOTTOM_____
#2 CYLINDER TOP_____
      BOTTOM_____
#3 CYLINDER TOP_____
      BOTTOM_____
#4 CYLINDER TOP_____
      BOTTOM_____
#5 CYLINDER TOP_____
      BOTTOM_____
#6 CYLINDER TOP_____
      BOTTOM_____
#7 CYLINDER TOP_____
      BOTTOM_____
#8 CYLINDER TOP_____
      BOTTOM_____

*FUEL CONSUMPTION GALLONS PER HOUR @ CRUISE_____

*OUTSIDE AIR TEMPERATURE_____

**AREA #3 ACCESSORIES**:
*MAGNETO DROP @ 1500/1700 RPM_____ Right _____ Left

*VACUUM GAUGE _____ @ 2100 RPM
*ELECTRICAL GAUGE_____ AMPS/VOLTS @ 2100 RPM

AIR FILTER CONDITION (1 = OK 2 = DIRTY)_____

# Small Airplane Certification Compliance Program

## RELATED REGULATIONS AND DOCUMENTS

Regulations: Title 14, Code of Regulations (CFR), Part 23:

| | |
|---|---|
| Section 23.45 | Performance-General. |
| Section 23.51 | Takeoff. |
| Section 23.65 | Climb: All engines operating. |
| Section 23.75 | Landing. |
| Section 23.77 | Balked landing. |
| Section 23.145 | Longitudinal controls. |
| Section 23.161 | Trim. |
| Section 23.175 | Demonstration of static longitudinal stability. |
| Section 23.177 | Static directional and lateral stability. |
| Section 23.201 | Wings level stall. |
| Section 23.203 | Turning flight and accelerated stalls. |
| Section 23.207 | Stall warning. |
| Section 23.221 | Spinning. |
| Section 23.561 | Emergency Landing Conditions-General. |
| Section 23.562 | Emergency landing dynamic conditions. |
| Section 23.605 | Fabrication methods. |
| Section 23.629 | Flutter. |
| Section 23.641 | Proof of strength. |
| Section 23.677 | Trim systems. |
| Section 23.723 | Shock absorption tests. |
| Section 23.725 | Limit drop tests. |
| Section 23.726 | Ground load dynamic tests. |
| Section 23.727 | Reserve energy absorption drop test. |
| Section 23.735 | Brakes. |
| Section 23.853 | Compartment interiors. |
| Section 23.865 | Fire protection of flight controls, engine mounts, and other flight structure. |
| Section 23.867 | Lightning protection of structure. |
| Section 23.954 | Fuel system lightning protection. |
| Section 23.965 | Fuel tank tests. |
| Section 23.1301 | Function and installation. |
| Section 23.1309 | Equipment, systems, and installations. |
| Section 23.1337 | Powerplant instruments. |
| Section 23.1431 | Electronic equipment. |
| Section 23.1581 | Airplane Flight Manual and Approved Manual Material-General. |
| Section 23.1585 | Operating procedures. |
| Section 23.1587 | Performance information. |

# COMPLIANCE CHECKLIST" TO CAR
# PART 3
### AS AMENDED TO NOVEMBER 1, 1949

**Subpart B\Flight Requirements**
**Weight Range and Center of Gravity**

* Indicates topics identified by NTSB Safety Recommendation A-95-13

# AIRCRAFT PURCHASE/SALES AGREEMENT

## DISCLAIMER

Please modify this agreement to suit your particular situation. However, Denny Pollard cannot and will not provide any assurance that the agreement is suitable for your situation and we will not provide any warranty or guaranty as to it's accuracy, or legal validity. You are electing to use the agreement by assuming any risk as to its legal correctness, validity, or consequences. Contact an Aviation Attorney for guidance and clarification.

AN AGREEMENT made and executed this _____ day of _____, by and between _____(hereinafter "buyer"), and _____ (hereafter "Seller").

WITNESSETH: In consideration of $_____, and other good and valuable considerations, the receipt of which is hereby acknowledged, the Parties hereby mutually agree as follows, to wit:

1. Seller agrees to sell to Buyer and Buyer agrees to purchase from Seller the following Aircraft:

Aircraft Make_____

Aircraft Model _____

Aircraft Year _____

Aircraft Registration Number _____

Aircraft Serial Number _____

Aircraft shall be equipped as follow:

_____

_____

_____

_____

_____

_____

_____

_____

_____

Seller warrants that the damage history to the aircraft is as follows:

_____

_____

_____

_____

_____

_____

Seller also warrants that the aircraft logbooks are complete and begin with the date of manufacture of the aircraft to the present or alternatively the logbooks are incomplete and begin on _____ and end on _____.

Seller warrants that Seller owns legal title to the above Aircraft and that title will be assigned to Buyer free and clear of any liens, claims, or encumbrances. Seller acknowledges that presently this airplane is (is not) encumbered to _____. Upon delivery of the Aircraft and payment of the balance of the purchase price in accordance with this Agreement, Seller shall execute a bill of sale granting good and marketable title to said Aircraft free and clear of all claims and encumbrances.

2. It is agreed that the purchase price of the Aircraft is _____ ($_____) which sum is due on delivery of the Aircraft. Cash, cashier's check, certified checks, or wire transfer shall pay any money paid pursuant to this Agreement.

3. (Optional) it is agreed that within _____ business days after the execution of this Agreement, an escrow shall be maintained with an escrow agent mutually agreeable to both parties. All funds, including the earnest money deposit, and the following documents pertaining to this transaction, shall be deposited with the escrow agent: (a) Bill of Sale for the Aircraft executed by the Seller to the Buyer; and (b) Application for Registration of the Aircraft to the Buyer. The fees

for the escrow service shall be paid by _____. The buyer shall pay a deposit of _____ Dollars ($_____) in to the escrow account immediately upon the establishment of the escrow. The deposit is non-refundable unless otherwise stipulated in this agreement. The deposit shall be credited to the purchase price of the Aircraft.

4. (Optional) Buyer shall pay Seller the sum of $_____ which sum shall be credited to the purchase price of the airplane. In the event that the airplane fails a pre-purchase inspection, in the sole discretion of the Buyer, the deposit shall be immediately refunded to Buyer, subject to the terms of this agreement. If buyer refuses for any reason to complete the purchase, other than a failure of pre-purchase inspection or a title search, Buyer's earnest money deposit shall be forfeited.

5. Subsequent to the execution of this Agreement and the payment of the earnest money deposit into escrow, or to the Seller as the case may be, the Buyer shall have the right to perform a pre-purchase inspection upon the Aircraft. The pre-purchase inspection mechanic shall be the Buyer's exclusive decision, so long as the mechanic possesses a current Airframe and Powerplant mechanic certificates issued by the Federal Aviation Administration. The pre-purchase inspection shall be performed at _____ Airport.

If the Buyer does not have the pre-purchase inspection performed within _____ (_____) days after the execution of this Agreement, Buyer shall have waived his right to such inspection. Upon completion of the pre-purchase inspection and a failure of the inspection, in the sole and exclusive discretion of Buyer, the Buyer shall have _____ (_____) days to notify Seller that Buyer will not purchase the Aircraft. If Buyer elects not to purchase the Aircraft, the Buyer shall notify Seller of this decision. Upon receipt of the notice of rejection, Seller shall immediately return all payments made by Buyer.

Upon completion of the pre-purchase inspection, Buyer shall present to the Seller any list of discrepancies. The Seller shall have _____ (_____) business days to review the discrepancies and to notify the Buyer of Seller's decision: (a) to pay to have the discrepancies repaired at Seller's expense and to complete the sale; or (b) to decline to pay the costs of repairs and to terminate the Agreement. If Seller declines to pay the cost of repairs, Seller shall refund, or have refunded the Buyer's deposit and shall reimburse the Buyer for the cost of the pre-purchase inspection.

6. It is agreed that the Aircraft and its logbooks shall be delivered on _____(date) at _____Airport. Payment in full is a condition of delivery. Title and risk of loss or damage to the Aircraft shall pass to Buyer at the moment of delivery. The Aircraft will be delivered to Buyer in its present condition, normal wear and tear excepted, with a valid FAA Certificate of Airworthiness.

Seller warrants that: (a) the Aircraft is in airworthy condition; (b) the Aircraft has a current annual inspection; (c) the Aircraft has a currently effective Standard air worthiness certificate issued by the Federal Aviation Administration; (d) all of the Aircraft's logbooks are accurate and current; (e) all applicable Airworthiness Directives have been complied with; (f) _____.

7. If the Aircraft is destroyed, or in Seller's opinion damaged beyond repair, Seller shall notify Buyer immediately and this Agreement shall be terminated and the Seller shall return all payments to Buyer and Seller will be relieved of any obligation to replace or repair the Aircraft. Seller will not be responsible or deemed to be in default for delays in performance of the Agreement due to reasonable causes beyond Seller's control.

8. If, for any reason, the Buyer is unable to pay the price of the Aircraft, as specified in this Agreement, the Seller shall return all documents to the Buyer except for the deposit which shall be retained as liquidated damages.

9. The Buyer shall pay any sales or use tax imposed by any state or local government, which results from the sale of the Aircraft.

10. All notices and requests required or authorized pursuant to this Agreement shall be in writing by certified mail, return receipt requested.

11.This agreement is a contract executed pursuant to the laws of the State of _____.

12. In the event any action is filed in relation to this Agreement, each party shall be responsible for his own attorney's fees.

13. This Agreement constitutes the entire Agreement between the parties. No statements, promises, or inducements made by any party to this agreement or any agent or any agent or employees of either party, which are not contained in this written contract, shall be valid or binding. This Agreement may not be enlarged, modified, or altered unless in writing signed by the parties.

IN WITNESS WHEREOF, the parties hereto have executed this Agreement the date and year first above written.

| | |
|---|---|
| Seller | Buyer |

# EXPERIMENTAL AIRCRAFT CERTIFICATION

*This is only a guide and should not be considered FAA approved data for certification as Orders, Regulations, and Aircraft Advisories change.*

Reference: 14 CFR 21.191(g), Order 8130.2F Para 146 and AC 20-27

## General Requirements

### Eligibility

1. Evidence that the aircraft was fabricated and assembled by an individual or group of individuals.
   Yes ___ No ___
2. Project undertaken for educational or recreational purposes.
   Yes ___ No ___
3. Aircraft complies with acceptable aeronautical standards and practices.
   Yes ___ No ___
4. Did someone else build the aircraft than owner?
   Yes ___ No ___
5. Did owner build more that 50% of fabrication and assembly operations?  Order 8130.2F Para 146(2)(c)
   Yes ___ No ___
6. Applicant submits a notarized FAA form 8139-12, Eligibility Statement, certifying for question number 5.
   Yes ___ No ___
7. Evidence is available to support question number 5.
   Yes ___ No ___

## Design and Construction

1. Was aircraft built completely from prefabricated parts or kits?
   Yes ___ No ___
2. Were used or salvaged major assemblies (e.g. wings, fuselage, Empennage, etc.) from type-certificated aircraft used.  Reference Order 8130.2F Para 146(b)(2)
   Yes ___ No ___

## NOTE

*No credit for fabrication and assembly will be given to the builder.*

## Kit Evaluation

*The FAA does not certify aircraft kits or approve kit manufacturers.  Evaluation must not be construed as meaning the kit is FAA "certified," "Certificated." or "approved".*

## FAA Requirements Order 8130.2F Para 146(e)(6)

1. FAA provided builder with the applicable forms and guidance.
   Yes ___ No ___
2. Builder submitted to the FAA three-view sketch, drawing, or photograph of purposed aircraft project and a tentative completion date.
   Yes ___ No ___
3. District office when requested, should provide the builder with the following:

   a. Aircraft Registration Application, Form 8050-1
   Yes ___ No ___
   b. Application for Airworthiness Certificate, Form 8130-6
   Yes ___ No ___
   c. Eligibility Statement-Amateur-Built Aircraft, Form 8130-12
   Yes ___ No ___

## Weight and Balance  Order 8130.2F Para 146(6)(f) and Section 91.9

1. Has applicant weighted the aircraft IAW procedures to determine?

    a. Forward most C.G loading                                           Yes ___ No ___
    b. Aft most C.G loading                                              Yes ___ No ___
    c. Center of gravity limits.                                       Yes ___ No ___
    d. Location of Datum                                            Yes ___ No ___
    e. Is ballast used, amount and location?                    Yes ___ No ___

2. The weight and balance report, including load limits for crew, oil, fuel, and baggage, should be in the aircraft.
                                                                   Yes ___ No ___
3. Did the FAA certify the weight and balance date is accurate for that aircraft.    Yes ___ No ___

# Airworthiness Certification Phase I

Reference Order 8130.2F Para 153

1. The aircraft should be completed in every respect.                      Yes ___ No ___
2. Applicant has submitted all required documentation.      **See above**    Yes ___ No ___
3. If applicant will not provide statement of eligibility ***STOP CERTIFICATION***, aircraft cannot be certificated as amateur-build until satisfactory evidence is provided.                Yes ___ No ___

# Aircraft Certification Phase II

**Record Inspection** Reference Order 8130.2F

## The FAA representative shall:

1. Obtain applicants Form 8130-6                                            Yes ___ No ___
2. Obtain applicants program letter identifying the aircraft and purpose        Yes ___ No ___
3. Registration requirements of CFR 47 have been met.                   Yes ___ No ___
4. Aircraft Markings IAW CFR 45.                                       Yes ___ No ___
5. FAA checks Aircraft Registry for any denial letters.                  Yes ___ No ___
6. Review aircraft records for required maintenance, inspections etc.        Yes ___ No ___
7. Arrange to review any inspection or technical date needed to establish conformity to type design. Yes ___ No ___
8. Test flights issued on FAA Form 8130-7 Special Airworthiness Certificate      Yes ___ No ___
9. Any relevant AD's have been complied with.  Reference AC 39-7        Yes ___ No ___
10. Required documentation's and records have been provided, flight manual, equipment list, maintenance records, and manuals as required.              Yes ___ No ___

## Aircraft Inspection

**FAA shall inspect and determine that:**  Order 8130.2F Para 147(b) and (c)

1. The aircraft is eligible by make and model, specification, TCDS, listing, as applicable.    Yes ___ No ___
2. Identification plate meets the requirements CFR 45.11                Yes ___ No ___

3. Information on Identification plate is correct matches information on FAA Form 8130-6 and IAW CFR 45.13
   Yes ___ No ___
4. Aircraft nationality and registration marks are IAW CFR 45, Subpart C.   Yes ___ No ___
5. Flight control system operates properly.   Yes ___ No ___
6. Engine(s), propeller(s) and associated instruments operate per the manufacture's instructions.   Yes ___ No ___
7. Pitot static system and associated instruments operate properly.   Yes ___ No ___
8. Instruments are marked IAW flight manual or other data.   Yes ___ No ___
9. All modification have been inspected and recorded and are in a safe condition for operations.   Yes ___ No ___
10. Emergency locator transmitter (ELT) is installed. AC-43.13-2A   Yes ___ No ___
11. Records indicate what whom, and date of inspection inspected.   Yes ___ No ___
12. Are the applicable placards, listings and markings installed per CFR 91.9.   Yes ___ No ___

# Required placards

1. Display (**EXPERIMENTAL**) IAW CFR 45 section 45.23   Yes ___ No ___
2. Passenger Notice at least 3/8 inch high:   **THIS AIRCRAFT DOES NOT COMPLY WITH FEDERAL SAFETY REGULATIONS FOR STANDARD AIRCRAFT.** Order 8130.2F Para 147(C)(7)
   Yes ___ No ___

# Certificate Issuance Order 8130.2F Para 147(d)

1. Issue FAA Form 8130 -7 Special Airworthiness Certificate. 8130.2F Para 191   Yes ___ No ___
2. Issue Operating limitations for aircraft Phase 1, CFR 91 section 91.319(b)   Yes ___ No ___
3. Issue Operating limitations for aircraft Phase and or Phase 2   Yes ___ No ___

## NOTE
*CFR 91.319(e) the FAA may prescribe any additional limitations in Phase 1 or 2 deemed necessary in the interest of safety. Order 8130.2F Para 153(a)*

4. FAA Inspection Recorded in Aircraft Records. Order 8130.2F Para 267(7)(d)   Yes ___ No ___

   a. Inspector's logbook statement. Order 8130.2F Para 267(7)(d)
      **"I find that the aircraft meets the requirements for the certification requested and have issued a Special Airworthiness Certificate dated _____.**

      **The next inspection is due _____."**
      Signed: *Inspector Name*, Aviation Safety Inspector, and WP-27

# Flight Test Areas Order 8130.2F Para 152

CFR part 91 section 91.319(b) requires that an unproven aircraft be assigned a flight test area. The area is prescribed IAW part 91 Section 91.305.

All testing must and will be in the assigned flight test areas to prove operating characteristic or design features. The time frame an amateur-built aircraft is assigned to a flight test area following any major change will be for a minimum of 5 hours. Order 8130.2F Para 152(d)

# Repairman Certificate

1. Issue as required Per Order 8300.10 Chapter 25 after completion of Phase I, 8130.2F Para 153   Yes ___ No ___

# Pre-Inspection Run Up
## Checklist

The following items should be checked and recorded during taxi and run up:

1. Ignition switch safety check
2. Com/transceiver check
3. Clock/timer/chronometer
4. Hour meter operation
5. Outside air temp
6. Atis identifier/barometric setting
7. Altimeter indicated altitude compared with field elevation
8. Brakes/parking brake
9. Ground steering
10. Wheel balance
11. Oil pressure idle/cruise
12. Oil temperature
13. Cylinder head temperature(s)
14. Fuel pressure/flow, idle/cruise
15. Primary alternator/generator (DC & AC)
16. Standby/#2 alternator generator (DC & AC)
17. Primary/standby voltage regulator
18. Magneto operation/drops
19. Propeller response
20. Vacuum/gyro air pressures, primary/stand-by#2
21. Engine controls
22. Throttle, mixture, prop, carburetor heat/alternate air, cowl flap(s), turbo
23. Carburetor air temperature
24. Hydraulic pressure
25. Tach calibration check
26. Exhaust gas temperature(s) Turbine inlet temperature
27. Compressor discharge temperature
28. Static power, max rpm/manifold press/fuel pressure/flow
29. Crankcase pressure, cowl flaps open, closed (at full static power)
30. Idle mixture rise/idle rpm/cut-off
31. Flight director/gyro horizon
32. Horizontal situation indicator/direction gyro
33. Turn coordinator/turn & bank
34. Compass/remote indicating compass
35. De-ice
36. Surface, windshield, prop de-ice
37. Propeller feather/un-feathering

With all the above out of the way and recorded it is time to taxi back to the hanger and start the compression checks.

# Ramp Inspection/100-Hour/Annual Checklist (GA)

## Part 23 & CAR 3 Aircraft

**REFERENCE DATA:**

8130.2, CAR-3, CFR 21 Certification, CFR 23 Airworthiness Standards, CFR 43 Maintenance, CFR 45 Markings, CFR 47 Registered properly, CFR 91 Pilot Responsibility, CFR 36 Noise, CFR 33 engines, CFR 39 AD's, CFR 145 Repair Stations and AC 43.13-1B & 2A Major Repair and Alterations, Manufacture Maintenance Manuals.

---

### INTERPRETATION OF THE TERM "AIRWORTHY"

**1)** The aircraft must conform to its type certificate.

　　**a.** When aircraft configuration and the components installed are consistent with drawings, specifications, and other data that are part of the type certificate (T/C), and include any supplemental T/C and field approval alterations incorporated into the aircraft.

**2)** The aircraft must be in condition for safe operation.

　　a. Aircraft relative to wear and deterioration i.e., corrosion, fluid leaks, tire wear, window delimitation/crazing.

**NOTE:** *If one or both of these conditions is not met, the aircraft would be considered unairworthy.* **Order 8130.2F para 9**

---

**NOTE:** This is only a guide and should not be considered FAA approved data for 100 hour or annual inspection checklist. Consult CFR 43 subpart D, for scope and detail of items to be included for 100 hour or annual inspections.

---

## Airman Attitude

| | | | |
|---|---|---|---|
| 1) Has Constructive attitude toward Compliance | Order 2150.3A par. 205 | Yes ☐ No ☐ N/A ☐ |
| 2) Verify A&P/IA certificate number and picture ID | CFR 65.91 | Yes ☐ No ☐ N/A ☐ |
| 3) Verify Pilots certificate number and picture ID | CFR 61.3 | Yes ☐ No ☐ N/A ☐ |

## Data

| | | | |
|---|---|---|---|
| 1) FAA-approved maintenance manuals available | CFR 43.13. | Yes ☐ No ☐ N/A ☐ |
| 2) Alterations IAW approved STC/TSO/PMA/Field approval or other FAA data, (337's) | CFR 21.97/101/113 | Yes ☐ No ☐ N/A ☐ |
| 3) Instructions for Continued Airworthiness | CFR 21.31, 21.50, 23.1529 | Yes ☐ No ☐ N/A ☐ |
| 4) Type Certificate Data Sheet (TCDS) | CFR 21.41/ CAR 3.15 | Yes ☐ No ☐ N/A ☐ |
| 5) Aircraft Flight Manual / Pilot Operating Hand book | CFR 21.5/CAR 3.72 | Yes ☐ No ☐ N/A ☐ |
| 6) Data plate aircraft | CFR 45.13 | Yes ☐ No ☐ N/A ☐ |
| 7) Data plate aircraft MFG before March 7, 1988 Make/model & S/N CFR 45.11(d) | | Yes ☐ No ☐ N/A ☐ |
| 8) Data plate engine on engine make and model/serial number CFR45.11 & 21.182 | | Yes ☐ No ☐ N/A ☐ |
| 9) Data plates critical components | CAR 3.18 CFR 45.15 | Yes ☐ No ☐ N/A ☐ |
| 10) Data plates Life Limited Parts | CFR 45.16 | Yes ☐ No ☐ N/A ☐ |

# Records

1) Registration current and in aircraft · CFR 91.9 / CAR 3.792 · Yes ☐ No ☐ N/A ☐
2) Airworthiness Certificate in aircraft dated and signed · CFR 91.203(a) & 21.175 · Yes ☐ No ☐ N/A ☐
3) Annual Inspection Total time_____ Description of work accomplished _____Date completed_____ and
   A&P/IA Signature _____ · CFR 43.11 & 91.417 · Yes ☐ No ☐ N/A ☐
4) All AD's, recorded in maintenance records and check recurring AD's
   a. Airframe · CFR 39 & 91.417 · Yes ☐ No ☐ N/A ☐
   b. Engine · CFR 39 & 91.417 · Yes ☐ No ☐ N/A ☐
   c. Propeller · CFR 39 & 91.417 · Yes ☐ No ☐ N/A ☐
   d. Appliances     Check for a list of items · CFR 39 & 91.417 · Yes ☐ No ☐ N/A ☐
5) Reduce Vertical Separation Minimums (RVSM) with Letter of Authorization (LOA)
   · CFR 91.706 · Yes ☐ No ☐ N/A ☐
6) Last **Annual** inspection completed: date _____ · CFR 43.11 & 91.417
   a. CFR 65.91 IA Name _____ Certification No._____ · Yes ☐ No ☐ N/A ☐
   b. 145 Repair station sign off date Repair Station number _____ · Yes ☐ No ☐ N/A ☐
7) Last **Progressive** Inspection phase signed of date · CFR 91.409(d) · Yes ☐ No ☐ N/A ☐
   a. Phase inspection dated and signed by A&P/IA · CFR 91.409(d)(1) · Yes ☐ No ☐ N/A ☐
   b. 145 Repair station number _____ · CFR 145.5/107/201/204 · Yes ☐ No ☐ N/A ☐
8) Last **100-hour** inspection date _____ Total time _____ · CFR 91.405(b)
   a. 145 Repair station number _____ · CFR 145.5/107/201/204 · Yes ☐ No ☐ N/A ☐
   b. A&P sign off date _____ Certification No, _____ CFR 43.15, 65.85, 91.409 · Yes ☐ No ☐ N/A ☐
   c. A&P/IA Signature _____ · CFR 43.11 & 91.417 · Yes ☐ No ☐ N/A ☐
9) Equipment list current and in aircraft     CAR-3.73 and CFR 23.29 & 91.9 · Yes ☐ No ☐ N/A ☐
10) Equipment list up-dated to match conformity of aircraft CAR 3.777 CFR 91.9 · Yes ☐ No ☐ N/A ☐
11) Status of Life Limited parts **Effective April 15, 2002** · CFR 43.10 · Yes ☐ No ☐ N/A ☐
12) Current approved flight manual **after 03-1-1979** in aircraft CFR 21.5/23.1581, 91.9 Yes ☐ No ☐ N/A ☐
13) Current flight manual POH **before 03-1-1979** in aircraft Yes ☐ No ☐ Revision number/date _____
    Limitations and placards · CAR 3.778 CFR 21.5/23.1581, 91.9 Yes ☐ No ☐ N/A ☐
14) Current weight & balance report dated & signed CAR 3.71, **23.1519**, 23.1581, 91.9 Yes ☐ No ☐ N/A ☐
15) Identification data plate secured to aircraft fuselage exterior · CFR 45.11 · Yes ☐ No ☐ N/A ☐
16) If applicable, check the MEL to determine that : · CFR 91.213 · Yes ☐ No ☐ N/A ☐
    a. Issued by N-number and serial number to the aircraft operator · Yes ☐ No ☐ N/A ☐
    b. A Letter of Authorization from a district office; check deferred items for placards and dates
       · Yes ☐ No ☐ N/A ☐
17) Maintenance Records for each Engine, Propeller, Airframe and Appliances in accordance with
    · CFR 91.417 · Yes ☐ No ☐ N/A ☐
18) **ATC transponder** date ___ **24 calendar months** check. CFR 91.413 & 23.1301 · Yes ☐ No ☐ N/A ☐
19) **ELT** TSO-C91a /TS0-C126 **every 12 months** check date 06/21/1985 CFR 91.207 Yes ☐ No ☐ N/A ☐
20) **Altimeter test every 24 months**.     CFR 91.411and CFR 43 Appendix E · Yes ☐ No ☐ N/A ☐
21) **Pitot static transponder test every 24 months** CAR 3.665 CFR 43 Appendix F · Yes ☐ No ☐ N/A ☐
22) Deferred items under Part 91.213 for Day VFR · CFR 91.213 · Yes ☐ No ☐ N/A ☐
    a. Is the item placarded · Yes ☐ No ☐ N/A ☐
    b. Is there a maintenance record entry · Yes ☐ No ☐ N/A ☐
    c. Is the item disabled or removed · Yes ☐ No ☐ N/A ☐

# Cockpit Inspection

1) Instrument & placards are correctly located per POH/AFM & TCDS · CFR 23.1541-1567/ CAR 3.755
   · CFR 91.31 · Yes ☐ No ☐ N/A ☐
2) INOP placards · CFR 91.213 · Yes ☐ No ☐ N/A ☐
   a. INOP instruments disabled or removed by an A&P · CFR 91.213 · Yes ☐ No ☐ N/A ☐
   b. Equipment list up-dated · CFR 91.213 · Yes ☐ No ☐ N/A ☐

| | | | |
|---|---|---|---|
| c. Maintenance record entry | CFR 91.213 | Yes ☐ No ☐ N/A ☐ |
| d. Weight and balance record updated | CFR 91.9 | Yes ☐ No ☐ N/A ☐ |
| e. Minimum Equipment List (MEL) for aircraft | CFR 91.213(a)(1) | Yes ☐ No ☐ N/A ☐ |
| 3) Vacuum indicating system, **Life limited** pump | CFR 23.1301 | Yes ☐ No ☐ N/A ☐ |
| 4) Compass card Yes ☐ No ☐ Readable | CAR 3,385 CFR 23.1547 & 25.1547 | Yes ☐ No ☐ N/A ☐ |
| 5) Additional instruments not on equipment list or Form 337 | CAR 3.661CFR 21.113 | Yes ☐ No ☐ N/A ☐ |
| 6) Type of clock installed original analog or digital working | AC 20-94 | Yes ☐ No ☐ N/A ☐ |
| 7) Nav Radio P/N 1 _____, P/N 2 _____ matches equipment list | | Yes ☐ No ☐ N/A ☐ |
| 8) Conforms to Type Certificate (TC) per POH/AFM see item (5,6) | | Yes ☐ No ☐ N/A ☐ |
| 9) Cockpit fuel smell | CAR 3.440 / CFR 23.863 | Yes ☐ No ☐ N/A ☐ |
| 10) Data plate information matches registration | CFR 45.11/13 & 47.3 | Yes ☐ No ☐ N/A ☐ |
| 11) Intercom jack, how many any extra ____and required Form 337 | | Yes ☐ No ☐ N/A ☐ |
| 12) Fire extinguisher gage    Green ☐ Red ☐ | CFR 23.1199 | Yes ☐ No ☐ N/A ☐ |
| 13) Fire Extinguishing Agent **commuter category** installed | CFR 23.1197 | Yes ☐ No ☐ N/A ☐ |
| 14) Fire extinguisher easy access to pilot | CFR 23.851 | Yes ☐ No ☐ N/A ☐ |
| 15) Oxygen equipment and supply lines condition | CFR 23.1441thru1453 | Yes ☐ No ☐ N/A ☐ |
| 16) Oxygen bottle if required Green ☐ Red ☐ | CFR 23.1441 | Yes ☐ No ☐ N/A ☐ |
| Hydro AA 5 years HT 3 year retire at 24 years | AC 43.13-1b para 9-51 | Yes ☐ No ☐ N/A ☐ |
| 17) Instrument filter covers installed | | Yes ☐ No ☐ N/A ☐ |
| 18) Yoke chain safety wired, loose or corrosion present | CFR 43.13 | Yes ☐ No ☐ N/A ☐ |
| 19) Cockpit control knob shape correct type | CAR 3.384 CFR 23.781 | Yes ☐ No ☐ N/A ☐ |
| 20) Flap, gear, knobs installed | CAR 3.384 CFR 23.781 | Yes ☐ No ☐ N/A ☐ |
| 21) Electrical wiring more **than ½ inch slack** | AC 43.13-1B para 11-118 | Yes ☐ No ☐ N/A ☐ |
| 22) Electrical wiring clamps/marking as required | AC 43.13-1B sec. 11 | Yes ☐ No ☐ N/A ☐ |
| 23) Tie-wraps items of mass in the cabin | CFR 23.561 | Yes ☐ No ☐ N/A ☐ |
| 25) Loose wires under dash not clamped | CFR 23.1351 | Yes ☐ No ☐ N/A ☐ |
| 26) Fuel selector moves to all positions and placarded | CAR 3.364 CFR 23.951 | Yes ☐ No ☐ N/A ☐ |
| 27) Brake master cylinder leaking R/H ☐ L/H ☐ | CRF 43.13 | Yes ☐ No ☐ N/A ☐ |
| 28) Thoroughly clean the aircraft and aircraft engine | CFR 43App D | Yes ☐ No ☐ N/A ☐ |
| 29) Cargo tie downs or nets if installed | CFR 91.525 | Yes ☐ No ☐ N/A ☐ |
| 30) General, uncleanness and loose equipment that might foul the controls, apparent and obvious defects and insecurity of attachment. | CRF 43App D | Yes ☐ No ☐ N/A ☐ |
| 31) Stall warning system horn works | CAR 3.120 CFR 23.1323 | Yes ☐ No ☐ N/A ☐ |
| 32) Windshield STC for one piece | CFR 43 Appendix A | Yes ☐ No ☐ N/A ☐ |
| 33) Windows tinted | TCDS/Equipment list | Yes ☐ No ☐ N/A ☐ |
| 34) Sun visor installation or STC with form 337 | CFR 43.13 | Yes ☐ No ☐ N/A ☐ |
| 35) Windshield and windows conditions | CAR 3.382 CFR 23.775 | Yes ☐ No ☐ N/A ☐ |
| 36) Windscreen clear ☐ scratches ☐ cracks ☐ crazing ☐ | | |
| Reference CFR23.775 AC 43.13-1b and MIL-P-5425 | | Yes ☐ No ☐ N/A ☐ |
| 37) Windows stopped drilled, cracked, or crazed CAR 3.382 CFR 23.775, and AC 43.13-1B Chapter 3 paragraph 318 (a)(2), and MIL-P-5425 | | Yes ☐ No ☐ N/A ☐ |

# Instruments                                          CFR 91.205

## Flight Instruments minimum required

| | | |
|---|---|---|
| 1) An Airspeed indicator | CAR 3.655CFR 23.1303 | Yes ☐ No ☐ N/A ☐ |
| 2) An Altimeter indicator | CAR 3.655 CFR 23.1303 | Yes ☐ No ☐ N/A ☐ |
| 3) Direction indicator | CAR-3.666 CFR 23.1303 | Yes ☐ No ☐ N/A ☐ |

## Minimum Instruments Required Visual-flight rules (day)

| | | |
|---|---|---|
| 1) Air speed indicator | CAR 3.655 CFR 91.205(b) | Yes ☐ No ☐ N/A ☐ |
| 2) Altimeter | CAR 3.655 CFR 91.205(b) | Yes ☐ No ☐ N/A ☐ |
| 3) Magnetic direction indicator | CAR 3.655 CFR 91.205(b) | Yes ☐ No ☐ N/A ☐ |
| 4) Tachometer for each engine | CAR 3.655 CFR 91.205(b) | Yes ☐ No ☐ N/A ☐ |
| 5) Oil pressure gauge for each engine using pressure system | CAR 3.655 CFR 91.205(b) | Yes ☐ No ☐ N/A ☐ |
| 6) Manifold pressure gauge for each altitude engine | CAR 3.672 CFR 91.205(b) | Yes ☐ No ☐ N/A ☐ |

7) Fuel gauge indicating the quantity of fuel in each tank     CFR 91.205(b)    Yes ☐ No ☐ N/A ☐
8) Landing gear position indicator, if retractable     CFR 91.205(b)    Yes ☐ No ☐ N/A ☐

## Minimum Instrument for Instrument flight rules

1) Two-way radio communications and navigation equipment    CFR 91.205(c)    Yes ☐ No ☐ N/A ☐
2) Gyroscopic rate-of-turn indicator    CAR 3.668 CFR 91.205(c)    Yes ☐ No ☐ N/A ☐
3) Slip-skid indicator    CFR 91.205(c)    Yes ☐ No ☐ N/A ☐
4) Sensitive altimeter adjustable for barometric pressure    CFR 91.205(c)    Yes ☐ No ☐ N/A ☐
5) Clock displaying hours, minutes, and seconds with sweeping second hand pointer or digital presentation    CFR 91.205(c)    Yes ☐ No ☐ N/A ☐
6) Generator or alternator of adequate capacity    CFR 91.205(c)    Yes ☐ No ☐ N/A ☐
7) Gyroscopic pitch and bank indicator (artificial horizon)    CFR 91.205(c)    Yes ☐ No ☐ N/A ☐
8) Gyroscopic direction indicator (directional gyro)    CFR 91.205(c)    Yes ☐ No ☐ N/A ☐

## Powerplant Instrument (all aircraft)    CAR –3 Subpart F and Part 23

1) Fuel quantity indicator per tank    CAR 3.672 CFR 23.1305(a) Yes ☐ No ☐ N/A ☐
2) Oil pressure indicator for each engine    CAR 3.674 CFR 23.1305(a) Yes ☐ No ☐ N/A ☐
3) Oil temperature indicator for each engine    CFR 23.1305(a)    Yes ☐ No ☐ N/A ☐
4) Oil quantity measuring device for each engine    CAR 3.674 CFR 23.1305(a) Yes ☐ No ☐ N/A ☐
5) Fire warning indicator if required by    CFR 23.1205    Yes ☐ No ☐ N/A ☐
6) Tachometer indicator for each engine    CFR 23.1305(b)    Yes ☐ No ☐ N/A ☐
7) Cylinder head indicator for each engine    CFR 23.1305(b)    Yes ☐ No ☐ N/A ☐
    a. Cowl flaps installed    C    AR 3.675 CFR 23.1305(b)    Yes ☐ No ☐ N/A ☐
    b. Commuter category aircraft    CFR 23.1305(b)    Yes ☐ No ☐ N/A ☐
8) Manifold pressure indicator for each engine and for each engine with an controllable pitch propeller    CFR 23.1305(b)    Yes ☐ No ☐ N/A ☐

## Instrument Arrangement    CAR 3.661    CFR 23.1321

1) Attitude indicator on panel top center position    CFR 23.1321    Yes ☐ No ☐ N/A ☐
2) Airspeed indicator adjacent to and directly to left of the instrument in the top center position.    CFR 23.1321    Yes ☐ No ☐ N/A ☐
3) Altitude indicator adjacent to and directly to right of the instrument in the top center position.    CFR 23.1321    Yes ☐ No ☐ N/A ☐
4) Magnetic direction indicator placard must state whether the calibration was made with radio receivers **on or off**    CFR 23.1547    Yes ☐ No ☐ N/A ☐
5) Magnetic direction indicator more than **10 degrees** off    CFR 23.1547    Yes ☐ No ☐ N/A ☐

## Instrument Markings    CAR 3.755    CFR 23.1543

1) Marking on cover glass must be in alignment with face    CFR 23.1543    Yes ☐ No ☐ N/A ☐
2) Each arc and line must be clearly visible to pilot    CFR 23.1543    Yes ☐ No ☐ N/A ☐
3) All related instruments must be calibrated in compatible units    CFR 23.1543    Yes ☐ No ☐ N/A ☐

## Electrical System    CAR 3.694    CFR 23.1367

1) Switches
    a. Able to carry rated current    CAR 3.682 CFR 23.1367    Yes ☐ No ☐ N/A ☐
    b. Enough distance or insulating material between current carrying parts and the housing so that vibration will not cause shorting    CAR 3.681 CFR 23.1367    Yes ☐ No ☐ N/A ☐
    c. Labeled as to operation and circuit controlled    CFR 23.1367    Yes ☐ No ☐ N/A ☐
2) Circuit Breakers/Fuses
    a. Circuit protection    CAR 3.690 CFR 23.1357    Yes ☐ No ☐ N/A ☐
    b. Each resettable circuit trip free cannot be overridden    CFR 23.1357    Yes ☐ No ☐ N/A ☐
    c. Fuses readily available and spare    CAR 3.692 CFR 23.1357    Yes ☐ No ☐ N/A ☐
    d. Breakers labeled and rating    CAR 3.691 CFR 23.1357    Yes ☐ No ☐ N/A ☐
3) Master Switch
    a. Wired to disconnect each electrical power source from the distribution systems    CAR 3.688 CFR 23.1361    Yes ☐ No ☐ N/A ☐

    b.   Switch is easily discernible and accessible to crew     CAR 3.695 CFR 23.1361   Yes ☐ No ☐ N/A ☐

4)  Wiring inspection                          CAR 3.681 CFR 23.1351 and AC43.13 chapter 11
    a.   Chafed or frayed wires                            Yes ☐ No ☐ N/A ☐
    b.   Insulation penetration                            Yes ☐ No ☐ N/A ☐
    c.   Outer insulation cracking                        Yes ☐ No ☐ N/A ☐
    d.   Damage or exposed wires                       Yes ☐ No ☐ N/A ☐
    e.   Evidence of over heating                       Yes ☐ No ☐ N/A ☐
    f.   Evidence of arcing                              Yes ☐ No ☐ N/A ☐
    g.   Evidence of chemical contamination              Yes ☐ No ☐ N/A ☐

5)  Wire Marking                               CFR 23.1351 and AC43.13 chapter 11
    a.   Gage, circuit, and gage size                      Yes ☐ No ☐ N/A ☐
    b.   Marked 15 inched maximum intervals           Yes ☐ No ☐ N/A ☐

6)  Grounding Points                     CFR 23.1351 AC 43.13 chapter 11, AC 25-16 and AC 25-10
    a.   Tightness of nuts (torque)                     Yes ☐ No ☐ N/A ☐
    b.   Cleanliness of attach points                   Yes ☐ No ☐ N/A ☐
    c.   Corrosion                                  Yes ☐ No ☐ N/A ☐

7)  Sleeving and Conduits                CFR 23.1351 AC 43.13 chapter 11, AC 25-16 and AC 25-10
    a.   Damages outer surfaces (kinks, holes, flats spots, etc.)   Yes ☐ No ☐ N/A ☐
    b.   Wear                                     Yes ☐ No ☐ N/A ☐
    c.   Adequate drain holes                         Yes ☐ No ☐ N/A ☐

8)  Clamping Points                       CFR 23.1351 AC 43.13 chapter 11, AC 25-16 and AC 25-10
    a.   Improper installation                        Yes ☐ No ☐ N/A ☐
    b.   Clamp/wire damage                         Yes ☐ No ☐ N/A ☐
    c.   Clamp cushion migration                    Yes ☐ No ☐ N/A ☐
    d.   Loose wires                              Yes ☐ No ☐ N/A ☐

## Equipment / Furnishings

1)  Equipment installed functions properly         CAR 3.622 CFR 23.1301(d) Yes ☐ No ☐ N/A ☐
2)  Flight manual correct for aircraft                   TCDS       Yes ☐ No ☐ N/A ☐
3)  Trim tab indicator readable and functions properly        CFR 43.13    Yes ☐ No ☐ N/A ☐
4)  Emergency brake handle installed                  CFR 21.31    Yes ☐ No ☐ N/A ☐
5)  Batteries proper installation, & charging       CAR 3.683 CFR 23.1353    Yes ☐ No ☐ N/A ☐
6)  Battery vented overboard  CAR 3.683 CFR 23.1353 & AC 43.13-1B PARA 11-22   Yes ☐ No ☐ N/A ☐
7)  Battery NiCad gage for thermal run away            CFR 23.1353    Yes ☐ No ☐ N/A ☐
8)  Thermal/Noise insulation                      CFR 23.853    Yes ☐ No ☐ N/A ☐
9)  Relief tube, corrosion areas                      CFR 43.13    Yes ☐ No ☐ N/A ☐
10) New interior material Certs.        CAR-3.388 and CFR 23.853/25.853 Yes ☐ No ☐ N/A ☐
11) Interior replaced Yes ☐ No ☐ New ☐ Have Burn Certifications     Yes ☐ No ☐ N/A ☐
12) Seat covers, sheep skin material Certs.     CAR-3.388 and CFR 23.853   Yes ☐ No ☐ N/A ☐
13) Seat covers (automotive) require burn certification      CFR 23.853   Yes ☐ No ☐ N/A ☐
14) Worn seat material CFR 25.853 for a CAR-3.388 aircraft Part 91 & 23.853, AC 43.13-1B Para 9-61
                                                           Yes ☐ No ☐ N/A ☐
15) Has interior been altered or material substituted     CFR 21.303/43.11   Yes ☐ No ☐ N/A ☐
16) Seat back locks broke                 CAR 3.390 CFR 23.785   Yes ☐ No ☐ N/A ☐
17) Seat rails holes elongated Yes ☐ No ☐ Check AD.     CFR 39    Yes ☐ No ☐ N/A ☐
18) Seating configuration, how many seats allowed          TCDS    Yes ☐ No ☐ N/A ☐
19) Head rest missing and not on equipment list          CFR 91.9    Yes ☐ No ☐ N/A ☐
20) Seat belts for stitching, cuts, or frayed       CFR 91.107 & 23.785   Yes ☐ No ☐ N/A ☐
21) Seat belts proper storage and marking      CAR 3.715 TSO-22 & 23.785   Yes ☐ No ☐ N/A ☐
22) Seat Belts Plastic locking ring missing, FWD ☐ AFT ☐     CFR 45.14    Yes ☐ No ☐ N/A ☐
23) Seat belt secured when not is use               CFR 23.785(d)   Yes ☐ No ☐ N/A ☐
24) TSO C-22 marking on seat belts CAR 3.390/715 CFR 45.15 CFR 91.205(b)(13,14)  Yes ☐ No ☐ N/A ☐
25) **Shoulder harness required after July 18, 1978**        CFR 23.785(g)(1)   Yes ☐ No ☐ N/A ☐
26) **Shoulder harness required after Sept. 16, 1992(PAX) helicopter**     Yes ☐ No ☐ N/A ☐
27) Cabin divider(s) / Curtains / Door(s)               CFR 23.853   Yes ☐ No ☐ N/A ☐
28) Heating system / AD's / decay test          CAR 3.388 CFR 23.859   Yes ☐ No ☐ N/A ☐

| | | | | | |
|---|---|---|---|---|---|
| 29) Cabin cooling (air conditioning), Ck / | CAR 3.393 CFR 23.831 | Yes ☐ | No ☐ | N/A ☐ |
| 30) Outflow / Safety / Dump valve(s)condition | CAR 3.394 CFR 23.843 | Yes ☐ | No ☐ | N/A ☐ |
| 31) Pressurization seals /boots /gaskets condition | CAR 3.396 CFR 23.831 | Yes ☐ | No ☐ | N/A ☐ |
| 32) Glare shield painted flat black | CFR 23.773 | Yes ☐ | No ☐ | N/A ☐ |
| 33) Door latches lock | CFR 23.783 | Yes ☐ | No ☐ | N/A ☐ |
|    a. Door sprung | CAR 3.389 CFR 23.783 | Yes ☐ | No ☐ | N/A ☐ |
|    b. Door Seals worn | CAR 3.387 CFR 23.783 | Yes ☐ | No ☐ | N/A ☐ |
|    c. Door slide track lock broken | CAR 3.387 CFR 23.783 | Yes ☐ | No ☐ | N/A ☐ |

## Misc. Fuselage

| | | | | | |
|---|---|---|---|---|---|
| 1) Cabin pressure controller service compressor 24 months | CAR 3.395 CFR 23.843 | Yes ☐ | No ☐ | N/A ☐ |
| 2) Pressurization seals /boots /gaskets, voids, and cracks | CFR 23.843 | Yes ☐ | No ☐ | N/A ☐ |
| 3) Antenna installation doubles per | AC43.13 2A, CFR 23.571/572 | Yes ☐ | No ☐ | N/A ☐ |
| 4) Corrosion on antenna's | CAR 3.395 CFR 23.609 | Yes ☐ | No ☐ | N/A ☐ |
| 5) Fabric covered aircraft condition good ☐ poor ☐ | AC 43.13-1B Chapter 2 | Yes ☐ | No ☐ | N/A ☐ |
| 6) Emergency exit placards | CAR 3.768 CFR 23.1557(d) | Yes ☐ | No ☐ | N/A ☐ |
| 7) Any addition mirrors installed on wings requires Form 337 | CFR 43Appen.A | Yes ☐ | No ☐ | N/A ☐ |
| 8) Condition of paint, is corrosion present **NOT** allowed | CAR 3.295 CFR 23.609 | Yes ☐ | No ☐ | N/A ☐ |

## Aircraft exterior inspection

| | | | | | |
|---|---|---|---|---|---|
| 1) Wash and clean all oil, grease and dirt from aircraft | CFR 43 Appendix D | Yes ☐ | No ☐ | N/A ☐ |
| 2) Nationality and registration marks per CFR 45.29 Check 3 inch marking per date Jan. 1,1983 and repaint. Over 30 years 2 or12 inch | CFR 45.22(b) | Yes ☐ | No ☐ | N/A ☐ |
| 3) Rotating beacon installation proper doublers **Required after 08-11-71** CFR 23.1401 | | Yes ☐ | No ☐ | N/A ☐ |
| 4) Anticollision light system installed CAR 3.705 CFR 91.209(b) / CFR 23.1401 | | Yes ☐ | No ☐ | N/A ☐ |
| 5) Anticollision light installed after 03/11/1996 Red or white CFR 91.206(b)(11) | | Yes ☐ | No ☐ | N/A ☐ |
| 6) AFT nav light proper color **white** CAR 3.702 CFR 23.1385-1399 | | Yes ☐ | No ☐ | N/A ☐ |
| 7) Panel seams miss match, extra paint in front of static port | CFR 23.1325 | Yes ☐ | No ☐ | N/A ☐ |
| 8) Static ports paint in hole or other things L/H ☐ R/H ☐ CAR 3.665 CFR 23.1325 | | Yes ☐ | No ☐ | N/A ☐ |
| 9) Static vent painted over L/H ☐ R/H ☐ CAR 3.665 CFR 23.1325 | | Yes ☐ | No ☐ | N/A ☐ |
| 10) Pitot heat indicator amber light | CFR 23.1326 | Yes ☐ | No ☐ | N/A ☐ |
| 11) Pitot heat element operational | CFR 23.1326 | Yes ☐ | No ☐ | N/A ☐ |
| 12) Pitot tube worn around hole Yes ☐ No ☐ Not plugged | | Yes ☐ | No ☐ | N/A ☐ |
|    a. Air Speed Last inspection date _____ | CFR 23.1325 | | | |
| 13) Static wicks missing | | | | |
|    a. Right wing | CFR 23.867 | Yes ☐ | No ☐ | N/A ☐ |
|    b. Left wing | CFR 23.867 | Yes ☐ | No ☐ | N/A ☐ |
|    c. Right elevator | CFR 23.867 | Yes ☐ | No ☐ | N/A ☐ |
|    d. Left elevator | CFR 23.867 | Yes ☐ | No ☐ | N/A ☐ |
|    e. Rudder | CFR 23.867 | Yes ☐ | No ☐ | N/A ☐ |

## Landing Gear CAR-3 and Part 23

| | | | | | |
|---|---|---|---|---|---|
| 1) Correct tire and wheel for the aircraft | CAR 3.362 CFR 23.733 | Yes ☐ | No ☐ | N/A ☐ |
| 2) Tire service Main ____ R ☐ L ☐ Nose Tire ☐ | CAR 3.362 CFR 23.733 | Yes ☐ | No ☐ | N/A ☐ |
| 3) Tires condition wear, cuts, or weather cracking L/H ☐ R/H ☐ NLG ☐ | AC 43.13 para 9-14 | Yes ☐ | No ☐ | N/A ☐ |
| 4) Landing Gear struts leaking L/H ☐ R/H ☐ NLG ☐ | AC 43.13 par 9-2/4 | Yes ☐ | No ☐ | N/A ☐ |
| 5) Landing gear struts extension L/H _____ R/H _____ AC43.13 para 9-2/4 | | Yes ☐ | No ☐ | N/A ☐ |
| 6) Landing gear fairing condition L/H ___R/H___ Nose __CFR 23.607, CFR 23.1193 | | Yes ☐ | No ☐ | N/A ☐ |
| 7) Fairing cracked ☐, Hardware missing ☐. | CFR 23.607/1193 | Yes ☐ | No ☐ | N/A ☐ |
| 8) Landing gear fairings missing, check equipment list and W&B | CFR 21.29 | Yes ☐ | No ☐ | N/A ☐ |
| 9) Steering shimmy dampener leaking, won't track | CFR 23.745 | Yes ☐ | No ☐ | N/A ☐ |
| 10) Brake pads worn. L/H ☐ R/H ☐ **0.100 in-thickness min.** CAR 3.363 CFR23.735 | | Yes ☐ | No ☐ | N/A ☐ |

11) Brake lines condition, frayed, corrosion on fittings L/H ☐ R/H ☐   CFR 23.735    Yes ☐ No ☐ N/A ☐
12) Brake rotor corrosion, warped, or under size L/H ☐ RH ☐   CFR 23.735    Yes ☐ No ☐ N/A ☐
13) MLG strut / axle / torque links L/H condition   CFR 23.721    Yes ☐ No ☐ N/A ☐
14) MLG strut / axle / torque links R/H condition   CFR 23.721    Yes ☐ No ☐ N/A ☐
15) NLG strut / axle / torque links L/H condition   CFR 23.721    Yes ☐ No ☐ N/A ☐
16) MLG L/H door actuating system / Hoses condition   CFR 23.1435    Yes ☐ No ☐ N/A ☐
17) MLG R/H door actuating system / Hoses condition   CFR 23.1435    Yes ☐ No ☐ N/A ☐
18) NLG door actuating system / Hoses condition   CFR 23.1435    Yes ☐ No ☐ N/A ☐
19) MLG L/H Landing gear actuator switch(s) condition   CFR 23.729    Yes ☐ No ☐ N/A ☐
20) MLG R/H Landing gear actuator switch(s) condition   CFR 23.729    Yes ☐ No ☐ N/A ☐
21) Repack wheel bearing   CRR 43 Appendix D    Yes ☐ No ☐ N/A ☐
22) Wheel nut cotter pin proper length and installed correctly   AC 43.13-1-B    Yes ☐ No ☐ N/A ☐
23) NLG Landing gear actuator switch(s) condition   CFR 23.729    Yes ☐ No ☐ N/A ☐
24) Land gear strut chrome damaged – reference manufacture maintenance manual    Yes ☐ No ☐ N/A ☐
25) Landing light covers cracked, missing hardware L/H ☐ R/H ☐   CFR 23.729    Yes ☐ No ☐ N/A ☐
26) Position / Warning / Safety squat switch or (WOW) switch   CFR 23.729    Yes ☐ No ☐ N/A ☐
27) Emergency extension / blow down   CAR 3.358 CFR 23.729    Yes ☐ No ☐ N/A ☐
28) Gear Emergency operation does it work   CAR 3.357 CFR 23.729    Yes ☐ No ☐ N/A ☐
29) Landing Gear Retract/Extension System   CAR 3.356 CFR 23.729    Yes ☐ No ☐ N/A ☐
30) Main landing gear locking mechanism for operation   CRR 43 Appendix D    Yes ☐ No ☐ N/A ☐
31) Main gear trunnions strut bushings for wear   L/H ☐ R/H ☐ CFR 43.13    Yes ☐ No ☐ N/A ☐
32) Main gear bungee cord condition L/H ☐ R/H ☐ Manufacture manual    Yes ☐ No ☐ N/A ☐
33) Main landing & nose gear lubrication while on jacks L/H ☐ R/H ☐ CFR 43.13    Yes ☐ No ☐ N/A ☐
34) Lube type of grease used per manufacture _____   CFR 43.16    Yes ☐ No ☐ N/A ☐
35) Floats and skis for security and defects   CRR 43 Appendix D    Yes ☐ No ☐ N/A ☐

## Landing Gear     Specification     Actual

| | Specification | | | Actual | | |
|---|---|---|---|---|---|---|
| **Actuator cushion** | Up _____ | Down _____ | | Up _____ Down _____ | | |
| Down lock over center | N __ | L __ | R __ | N __ | L __ | R __ |
| Down Lock clearance | N __ | L __ | R __ | N __ | L __ | R __ |
| Up lock clearance | N __ | L __ | R __ | N __ | L __ | R __ |

## Hydraulic System

1) Hydraulic Distribution / Hoses condition/life limit   CAR 3.726 CFR 23.1435    Yes ☐ No ☐ N/A ☐
2) Hydraulic pressure relief valve   CFR 23.1435    Yes ☐ No ☐ N/A ☐
3) Hydraulic accumulator charge   CAR 3.728 CFR 23.1435    Yes ☐ No ☐ N/A ☐
4) Hydraulic reservoir / venting   CFR 23.1435    Yes ☐ No ☐ N/A ☐
5) Hydraulic filter change life limit   CFR 23.1435    Yes ☐ No ☐ N/A ☐
6) Hydraulic electric motor brushes and condition   CFR 23.1351    Yes ☐ No ☐ N/A ☐

## Flight Control/Wing

1) Wing attach fittings for cracks, elongated bolt holes L/H CAR 3.317 CFR 23.572    Yes ☐ No ☐ N/A ☐
2) Wing attach fittings for cracks, elongated bolt holes R/H CAR 3.317 CFR 23.572    Yes ☐ No ☐ N/A ☐
3) **Wing L/H** dents, cracks, Loose rivets, Corrosion, nav light **red**   CFR 23.603/1385 Yes ☐ No ☐ N/A ☐
4) L/H wing Fuel vent direction **check AD's** FWD ☐ AFT ☐   CFR 23.975    Yes ☐ No ☐ N/A ☐
5) **Wing R/H** dents, cracks, Loose rivets, Corrosion, nav light **green**   CAR 3.295 CFR 23.603/1385
   Yes ☐ No ☐ N/A ☐
6) R/H Fuel vent direction   FWD ☐ AFT ☐ CFR 23.975    Yes ☐ No ☐ N/A ☐
7) **Flaps L/H** cracks _____, loose hardware _____, Properly installed _____.    Stop drill cracks
  CAR 3.339 CFR 23.655/697    Yes ☐ No ☐ N/A ☐
8) **Flaps R/H** cracks _____, loose hardware _____, Properly installed _____.    Stop drill cracks
  CAR 3.339 CFR 23.655/697    Yes ☐ No ☐ N/A ☐
9) **Aileron R/H** cracks ___, Loose hardware ___, Properly installed    Yes ☐ No ☐ N/A ☐
  Cable rigging loose Annual/100 hour inspection   CAR 3.337 CFR 23.655/685/689    Yes ☐ No ☐ N/A ☐

10) **Aileron  L/H** cracks ___, Loose hardware ____, Properly installed   CAR 3.294       Yes ☐ No ☐ N/A ☐
   Cable rigging loose Annual/100 hour inspection      CAR 3.337 CFR 23.655/685/689       Yes ☐ No ☐ N/A ☐
11) Deicer boots condition worn, holes, debonded, type CAR .7127 CFR 23.1416/1419       Yes ☐ No ☐ N/A ☐
12) **Rudder** moves up & down, bearing loose, cracks, repairs CAR 3.332 CFR 23.685       Yes ☐ No ☐ N/A ☐
13) Rudder / trim tab attach fittings condition, loose       CAR 3.337 CFR 23.685       Yes ☐ No ☐ N/A ☐
14) **Lubrication**, systems lube per manufactures recommendations       CFR 43.13       Yes ☐ No ☐ N/A ☐
15) Electrical bonding straps broken or frayed       CAR 3.337-1 CFR 23.867       Yes ☐ No ☐ N/A ☐
16) **Horizontal Stab L/H** cracks ☐, Loose rivets ☐, Hardware installation and safetied ☐, Stop drill cracks CFR
   23.572 Stops ☐       CFR 23.675       Yes ☐ No ☐ N/A ☐
17) **Horizontal Stab R/H** cracks ☐ Loose rivets ☐ Hardware installation and safetied       ☐ Stop drill cracks CFR 23.572,
   Stops ☐___       CFR 23.675       Yes ☐ No ☐ N/A ☐
18) Stopped drilled holes in elevator without doublers R/H ☐       CFR 23.572       Yes ☐ No ☐ N/A ☐
19) Stopped drilled holes in elevator without doublers L/H ☐       CFR 23.572       Yes ☐ No ☐ N/A ☐
20) Elevator trim control system rigging       CAR 3.337 CFR 23.659       Yes ☐ No ☐ N/A ☐
21) Elevator trim indicator control works       CAR 3.337 CFR 23.677(a)       Yes ☐ No ☐ N/A ☐
22) Elevator / trim tab attach fittings L/H       CAR 3.337 CFR 23.572       Yes ☐ No ☐ N/A ☐
23) Elevator / trim tab attach fittings R/H       CAR 3.337 CFR 23.572       Yes ☐ No ☐ N/A ☐
24) Elevator trim / servo tab structure       L/H       CAR 3.337 CFR 23.572       Yes ☐ No ☐ N/A ☐
25) Elevator trim / servo tab structure       R/H       CAR 3.337 CFR 23.572       Yes ☐ No ☐ N/A ☐
26) Control surface attach fittings condition       CAR 3.328 CFR 23.572       Yes ☐ No ☐ N/A ☐
27) Control surface balancing all primary controls after repair or paint       CAR 3.159 CFR 23.659
   Yes ☐ No ☐ N/A ☐
28) STOL devices / control system condition       CFR 23.572       Yes ☐ No ☐ N/A ☐
29) Boundary layer control / vortex generators, cracks and condition       CFR 23.572       Yes ☐ No ☐ N/A ☐
30) Flight Control Surface Travels / Cable Tension       CAR 3.345 CFR 23.143       Yes ☐ No ☐ N/A ☐
31) Gust lock, condition, worn holes       CAR 3.341 CFR 23.572       Yes ☐ No ☐ N/A ☐
32) Autopilot trim indicator annual/100 hour check rigging       CAR 3.343 CFR 23.143       Yes ☐ No ☐ N/A ☐
33) Autopilot system condition       CFR 23.143       Yes ☐ No ☐ N/A ☐
34) Yaw damper condition       CAR 3.347 CFR 23.143       Yes ☐ No ☐ N/A ☐
35) Electric trim rigging and condition       CAR 3.343 CFR 23.143       Yes ☐ No ☐ N/A ☐
36) Flight control pulleys worn, broken, or frozen up       CAR 3.345 CFR 23.689       Yes ☐ No ☐ N/A ☐
37) Flight control cables broken strands/rust  Reference AC43.13       CFR 23.689       Yes ☐ No ☐ N/A ☐
38) Flight control Surface Travel/Cable Tension       CAR 3.345 CFR 23.391 to 23.459       Yes ☐ No ☐ N/A ☐

| **Travel Spec Actual** | **Tension Spec** | **Actual** | |
|---|---|---|---|
| Control Column | _____ | _____ | _____ |
| **Aileron** | _____ | _____ | _____ |
| Aileron Trim Tab(s) | _____ | _____ | _____ |
| Rudder | _____ | _____ | _____ |
| Rudder Trim Tab | _____ | _____ | _____ |
| Elevator/Stabilator | _____ | _____ | _____ |
| Elev / Stab Tab(s) | _____ | _____ | _____ |
| Flap | _____ | _____ | _____ |
| Moveable Stabilizer | _____ | _____ | _____ |
| Rudder Pedals | _____ | _____ | _____ |

## Engine Inspection

**Reference CAR Subpart E, CFR 23 Subpart E Powerplant, and 43 Appendix D**

1) Thoroughly clean the engine       CFR 43 App. D   Yes ☐ No ☐ N/A ☐
2) Perform engine static run       CFR 33.26/43.15 Yes ☐ No ☐ N/A ☐
3) Perform engine idle run r.p.m. check       CFR 33.26/43.15 Yes ☐ No ☐ N/A ☐
4) Perform mag drop check       CFR 33.37       Yes ☐ No ☐ N/A ☐
5) Mag "P" lead wires not cracked or broken       CFR 33.28       Yes ☐ No ☐ N/A ☐
6) Shut down engine and check for engine oil and fuel leaks       CFR 33.25       Yes ☐ No ☐ N/A ☐
7) Engine Data plate installed       CAR 3.670 CFR 45.13       Yes ☐ No ☐ N/A ☐

| | | | | |
|---|---|---|---|---|
| a. L/H engine Make Model/Series matches TCDS | CFR 45.13 | Yes ☐ | No ☐ | N/A ☐ |
| b. R/H engine Make Model/Series matches TCDS | CFR 45.13 | Yes ☐ | No ☐ | N/A ☐ |
| 8) Certification basic of components installed 337's | CFR 45.15 | Yes ☐ | No ☐ | N/A ☐ |
| 9) Instruments CFR 23.1305 instruments | | Yes ☐ | No ☐ | N/A ☐ |
| a. Engine | CFR 23.1301 | Yes ☐ | No ☐ | N/A ☐ |
| a. Cylinder head temperature | CFR 43.15 | Yes ☐ | No ☐ | N/A ☐ |
| b. Oil temperature check | CFR 43.15 | Yes ☐ | No ☐ | N/A ☐ |
| b. Accessories | CFR 23.1301 | Yes ☐ | No ☐ | N/A ☐ |
| 10) Engine cowl loose/missing hardware Location _____ | CAR 3.625 CFR 23.1193 | Yes ☐ | No ☐ | N/A ☐ |
| 11) Firewall bent, cracked, or missing fasteners | CAR 3.623 CFR 23.1191 | Yes ☐ | No ☐ | N/A ☐ |
| 12) Firewall wire and hose grommets condition | CAR 3.623 CFR 23.1191(c) | Yes ☐ | No ☐ | N/A ☐ |
| 13) Firewall has corrosion | CAR 3.624 CFR 23.1191(e) | Yes ☐ | No ☐ | N/A ☐ |
| 14) Engine mount structure for cracks, dents, etc. | CFR 23.23 | Yes ☐ | No ☐ | N/A ☐ |
| 15) Retorque cylinder base nuts and case half per manufacture recommendations | | Yes ☐ | No ☐ | N/A ☐ |
| 16) Engine shock mount cracks, worn, hardware condition | CFR 33.33 | Yes ☐ | No ☐ | N/A ☐ |
| 17) Flex tubing condition weather cracking, worn, etc. | CAR 3.638 CFR 23.1183 | Yes ☐ | No ☐ | N/A ☐ |
| 18) Engine oil leaking Location _____ | CAR 3.638 CFR 23.1183 | Yes ☐ | No ☐ | N/A ☐ |
| 19) STC for Bracket air filter if installed & Form 337 | CFR 21.111/1091 | Yes ☐ | No ☐ | N/A ☐ |
| 20) Air Filter dirty/foreign particles | CAR 3.605 CFR 23.1107 | Yes ☐ | No ☐ | N/A ☐ |
| 21) Condition of baffle seals and installation Good ☐ Poor ☐ Substituted type of baffle material ☐ | | | | |
| | CAR 3.625 CFR 33.15/17/21 & CFR 23.1043 | Yes ☐ | No ☐ | N/A ☐ |
| 22) Wire chafing, fuel lines, no wires clamped under them | CAR 3.681 AC 43.13-1B | Yes ☐ | No ☐ | N/A ☐ |
| 23) Electrical wire Slack between supports **Max1/2 inch** | AC 43.13-1B fig.11.9 | Yes ☐ | No ☐ | N/A ☐ |
| 24) Engine/Electric fuel pump condition wires, mounting Good/worn | CFR 23 | Yes ☐ | No ☐ | N/A ☐ |
| 25) Ignition harness condition Good ____ Worn ____ | CFR 23 | Yes ☐ | No ☐ | N/A ☐ |
| 26) Clean and gap spark plugs per engine manufactures recommendations | | Yes ☐ | No ☐ | N/A ☐ |
| 27) Rotate spark plugs per manufacture recommendation (One gasket required) | | Yes ☐ | No ☐ | N/A ☐ |
| 28) Starter ring broken teeth | CFR 23 | Yes ☐ | No ☐ | N/A ☐ |
| 29) Alternator/generator drive belts condition worn, cracked, broke | CFR 23 | Yes ☐ | No ☐ | N/A ☐ |
| 30) Cylinders cracked fins, rocker cover leaking   1__ 2__ 3__ 4__ 5__ 6__ | | Yes ☐ | No ☐ | N/A ☐ |
| 31) Cylinders barrel cracked (Chrome)   1__ 2__ 3__ 4__ 5__ 6__ | | Yes ☐ | No ☐ | N/A ☐ |
| 32) Cylinders check records for times & certifications 1__ 2__ 3__ 4__ 5__ 6__ | | Yes ☐ | No ☐ | N/A ☐ |
| 33) Exhaust stacks cracks, defects, installation   1__ 2__ 3__ 4__ 5__ 6__ | | | | |
| | CAR 3.615 CFR 23.1121 and CFR 33.21 | Yes ☐ | No ☐ | N/A ☐ |
| 34) Muffler cracked, location _____, **Recurring AD's** | CAR 3.617 CFR 23.1121 | Yes ☐ | No ☐ | N/A ☐ |
| 35) Muffler leak test to 2 psi internal pressure | AC 43.13-1b para 8-49 (d) | Yes ☐ | No ☐ | N/A ☐ |
| 36) Rocker cover or push rods leaking oil past seals | | Yes ☐ | No ☐ | N/A ☐ |
| 37) Preheater shroud condition cracks, vibration | CAR 3.617 CFR 23.1101 | Yes ☐ | No ☐ | N/A ☐ |
| 38) Carburetor heat box condition of holes | CAR 3.617 CFR 23. | Yes ☐ | No ☐ | N/A ☐ |
| a. Proper hardware screws and nuts | CFR 23. | Yes ☐ | No ☐ | N/A ☐ |
| 39) Engine controls properly safetying ☐ travel ☐ AC 43.13-1B para 7-122 thru 127 | | Yes ☐ | No ☐ | N/A ☐ |
| 40) Engine case nuts torqued and right side up | CFR 43 Appendix D (d)(2) | Yes ☐ | No ☐ | N/A ☐ |
| 41) Crankcase for cracks, leaks and security of seam bolts | CFR 33. | Yes ☐ | No ☐ | N/A ☐ |
| 42) Engine mounts for corrosion, cracks **NONE Allowed** | CFR 23.363 | Yes ☐ | No ☐ | N/A ☐ |
| 43) Cowl flap control and operational limitations | CAR 3.625 CFR 23.1047 | Yes ☐ | No ☐ | N/A ☐ |
| 44) Cowl flap check for cracks | CFR 43.13 | Yes ☐ | No ☐ | N/A ☐ |
| 45) Alternate/ Ram air / Carb heat | CAR 3.606 CFR 23.1093 | Yes ☐ | No ☐ | N/A ☐ |
| 46) Turbo Waste gate (Non automatic) | CFR 23.1091 | Yes ☐ | No ☐ | N/A ☐ |
| 47) Vacuum pump lines, clamps condition  Good ☐ Worn ☐ | CFR 23 | Yes ☐ | No ☐ | N/A ☐ |
| 48) Supercharger overall condition  Good ☐ Bad ☐ | CFR 23.1109 | Yes ☐ | No ☐ | N/A ☐ |
| 49) Electrical wiring cracked, burned, broken | CAR 3.693 CRR 23.1163(b) | Yes ☐ | No ☐ | N/A ☐ |
| 50) Oil filter opening placard | CAR 3.767 CFR 23.1557(c)(2) | Yes ☐ | No ☐ | N/A ☐ |
| 51) Drain oil | CFR 43 Appendix D | Yes ☐ | No ☐ | N/A ☐ |
| 52) Clean oil screen | CFR 43 Appendix D | Yes ☐ | No ☐ | N/A ☐ |
| 53) Replace oil filter | CFR 43 Appendix D | Yes ☐ | No ☐ | N/A ☐ |
| 54) Check filter for metal particles in accordance with manufacture CFR 43.15, 23.1019 | | Yes ☐ | No ☐ | N/A ☐ |
| 55) Oil drain plug/valve condition and positive locking | CAR 3.574 CFR 23.1021 | Yes ☐ | No ☐ | N/A ☐ |

| | | | | |
|---|---|---|---|---|
| 56) | Oil radiator supporting structure for security | CAR 3.572 CFR 23.1023 | Yes ☐ No ☐ N/A ☐ |
| 57) | Oil tanks condition and free of vibration | CAR 3.563 CFR 23.1013 | Yes ☐ No ☐ N/A ☐ |
| 58) | Hose inspection/replacement manufacture limits | CFR 43.10 | Yes ☐ No ☐ N/A ☐ |
| 59) | Mechanic has a master orifice for differential compression tester (MFG requirement) | | Yes ☐ No ☐ N/A ☐ |
| 60) | Differential Compression Test, 80psi /60 psi cylinder | | |
| | CFR 43 Appendix D and AC 43.13-1B paragraph 8-14 | | Yes ☐ No ☐ N/A ☐ |

1 ____ 2 ____ 3 ____ 4 ___ 5 ___ 6 ___ If **25%** difference check cylinder for problems.

## Fuel System    CAR-3 Subpart E and Part 23

| | | | |
|---|---|---|---|
| 1) | Remove cowling and clean engine of all oil and dirt | CRR 43 Appendix D | Yes ☐ No ☐ N/A ☐ |
| 2) | Injection fuel lines **Recurring AD** if required every 100 hours | CFR 39 | Yes ☐ No ☐ N/A ☐ |
| 3) | Fuel bowl leaking | CAR 3.431 CFR 23.999 | Yes ☐ No ☐ N/A ☐ |
| 4) | Fuel quantity sensor / transmitter condition | CFR 23.955 | Yes ☐ No ☐ N/A ☐ |
| 5) | Fuel boost / Aux. pump(s) bypass condition | CAR 3.449 CFR 23.955 | Yes ☐ No ☐ N/A ☐ |
| 6) | Fuel lines vibration/clamped    CAR 3.550 CFR 23.993 & AC 43.13-1B para 8-31 | | Yes ☐ No ☐ N/A ☐ |
| 7) | Carburetor security, throttle arm/bushing loose | CAR 3.551 CFR 23.994 | Yes ☐ No ☐ N/A ☐ |
| 8) | Mixture control linkage condition | CAR 3.630 CFR 23.1147 | Yes ☐ No ☐ N/A ☐ |
| 9) | Throttle control binding condition | CAR 3.628 CFR 23.1143 | Yes ☐ No ☐ N/A ☐ |
| 10) | Engine primer leaking | CAR 3.442 CFR 23.1141 | Yes ☐ No ☐ N/A ☐ |
| 11) | Remove and clean carburetor screen | | Yes ☐ No ☐ N/A ☐ |
| 12) | Induction System Screens condition | CAR 3.448 CFR 23.1107 | Yes ☐ No ☐ N/A ☐ |
| 13) | Fuel pump condition and AD requirement | CFR 23.991 | Yes ☐ No ☐ N/A ☐ |
| 14) | Fuel system lines and fittings conditions | CAR 3.550 CFR 23.993 | Yes ☐ No ☐ N/A ☐ |
| 15) | Fuel system drains, lock shut and drains properly | CFR 23.999 | Yes ☐ No ☐ N/A ☐ |
| 16) | Clean and inspect fuel tank strainer condition | CFR 23.977 | Yes ☐ No ☐ N/A ☐ |
| 17) | Filler cap must have electrical bonding (chain on cap) | CFR 23.973 | Yes ☐ No ☐ N/A ☐ |
| 18) | Fuel placards **L/H wing** Yes ☐ No ☐ **R/H wing** CAR 3.761 CFR 23.1557(c) | | Yes ☐ No ☐ N/A ☐ |
| 19) | Fuel tank caps seal condition, tight seal, flat, cracked CAR 3.445 CFR 23.973(c) | | Yes ☐ No ☐ N/A ☐ |
| 20) | Fuel tank sump drained of water | CAR 3.444 CFR 23.971 | Yes ☐ No ☐ N/A ☐ |
| 21) | Fuel tank condition for cracks, vibration, leaks | CFR 23.963 | Yes ☐ No ☐ N/A ☐ |
| 22) | Fuel line and hose condition left/right side | CFR 23.993 | Yes ☐ No ☐ N/A ☐ |
| 23) | Fuel drain valve positive locking | CAR 3.551 CFR 23.999 | Yes ☐ No ☐ N/A ☐ |
| 24) | Fuel strainer or filter condition | CAR 3.448 CFR 23.997 | Yes ☐ No ☐ N/A ☐ |
| 25) | Blistering of sealant in a fuel cell caused by corrosion | CFR 23.963(c) | Yes ☐ No ☐ N/A ☐ |
| 26) | Fuel nonmetallic liners leaks | CAR 3.442-1 CFR 23.965((d) | Yes ☐ No ☐ N/A ☐ |
| 27) | Unusable fuel supply check reference TCDS | CAR 3.440 CFR 23.959 | Yes ☐ No ☐ N/A ☐ |
| 28) | Fuel gauge reads zero when fuel tank is empty | CAR 3.440 CFR 23.1337(b) | Yes ☐ No ☐ N/A ☐ |

## Propeller Inspection

| | | | |
|---|---|---|---|
| Propeller Part number and serial number | | **CFR 45.11** | Yes ☐ No ☐ N/A ☐ |

Part number #_____ Serial Number #_____

| | | | |
|---|---|---|---|
| 1. | Is there a propeller maintenance record (log book) | CFR 43.2(a) | Yes ☐ No ☐ N/A ☐ |
| 2. | If no propeller log book sign 100-hour off in airframe record | CFR 43.11 | Yes ☐ No ☐ N/A ☐ |
| 3. | Propeller seal leaking | CFR23.907 | Yes ☐ No ☐ N/A ☐ |
| 4. | Propeller for nicks, cracks, and damage | AC 43.13-2B para 8-73 | Yes ☐ No ☐ N/A ☐ |
| 5. | File marks after dressing propeller **NOT** allowed | CFR 43.13 | Yes ☐ No ☐ N/A ☐ |
| 6. | Mechanic record entry after dressing nicks | CFR 43.9 | Yes ☐ No ☐ N/A ☐ |
| 7. | Propeller spinner had doubler added to repair cracks **Not ALLOWED** CFR 23.907 | | Yes ☐ No ☐ N/A ☐ |
| 8. | Propeller spinner(s) cracks ___, **NO cracks allowed** nuts safety wired __ Missing screws from spinner None allowed ____ Reference Service Letters if cracked: | | |
| | a. McCauley 1992-14C -part **must be replaced** | | Yes ☐ No ☐ N/A ☐ |
| | b. Hartzell HC-SL-61-91 **Requires a Field Approval** | | Yes ☐ No ☐ N/A ☐ |
| | c. Sensenich **See aircraft maintenance manuals** | | Yes ☐ No ☐ N/A ☐ |
| 9. | Propeller grinding when rotating | AC 43.13-1B para 8-2(c )(2) | Yes ☐ No ☐ N/A ☐ |

10. Corrosion pitting on blades or hub **None Allowed**  CFR A35.3  Yes ☐ No ☐ N/A ☐
11. Paint on propeller blades, type per manufacture manual  CAR 3.295 CFR 23.609  Yes ☐ No ☐ N/A ☐
12. If repainted after rework type of paint applied lacquer base or polyurethane enamel and was it recorded in the propeller maintenance record  CFR 43.5  Yes ☐ No ☐ N/A ☐
13. STC for different propeller than original  per TCDS  CFR 21.111  Yes ☐ No ☐ N/A ☐
14. STC propeller check engine gages for new limitations  CFR A35.4  Yes ☐ No ☐ N/A ☐
15. Is the propeller the right diameter / width  CAR 3.416 CFR 23.45  Yes ☐ No ☐ N/A ☐
16. Propeller ground clearance  CAR 3.422 CFR 23.925  Yes ☐ No ☐ N/A ☐
17. Has the propeller tips been altered (rounded or square)  CFR 43Append A  Yes ☐ No ☐ N/A ☐
18. Are their repairs in the propeller maintenance records  CFR 43.9  Yes ☐ No ☐ N/A ☐
19. Has the shot peen been removed after reworked at hub  CFR 43.9  Yes ☐ No ☐ N/A ☐
20. Has the hub seal been replaced (service life)  CFR 43.9  Yes ☐ No ☐ N/A ☐
21. Prop Hub is oil/grease filled and/or leaking  CFR 35.3  Yes ☐ No ☐ N/A ☐
22. When was the last hub overhaul  CFR 35.3  Yes ☐ No ☐ N/A ☐
23. Pitting corrosion on Hub **NONE ALLOWED**  CFR 35.3  Yes ☐ No ☐ N/A ☐
24. Hub, blade clamps, and pitch change mechanisms should be inspected for corrosion **NONE ALLOWED**  CFR A35.3  Yes ☐ No ☐ N/A ☐
25. Were new propeller bolts installed  CFR A35.3  Yes ☐ No ☐ N/A ☐
26. Were new nuts used on the propeller bolts  CFR A35.3  Yes ☐ No ☐ N/A ☐
27. New cotter pins installed in retaining nuts per Manufacture  CFR A35.4  Yes ☐ No ☐ N/A ☐
28. Is the spinner shimmed to the spinner bracket if required  CFR A35.3  Yes ☐ No ☐ N/A ☐
29. Pitch change counterweights on blade clamps should be inspected for security, safety  CFR A35.3  Yes ☐ No ☐ N/A ☐
30. Adequate counterweight clearance within the spinner  CFR 23.925  Yes ☐ No ☐ N/A ☐
31. Are the propeller blades in track  CFR 23.925  Yes ☐ No ☐ N/A ☐
32. De-icer boots for signs of deterioration and security  CFR 23.929  Yes ☐ No ☐ N/A ☐
33. Propeller **total time** is recorded in propeller record  CFR 91.417(2)  Yes ☐ No ☐ N/A ☐
34. Propeller vibration rate  CAR 3.431 CFR 23.907  Yes ☐ No ☐ N/A ☐
35. Propeller clearance to ground and gear  CAR 3.417 CFR 23.925  Yes ☐ No ☐ N/A ☐
36. Check blade play and blade track.  CFR 43.13  Yes ☐ No ☐ N/A ☐
37. Lubricate the propeller assembly.  Refer to Hartzell Service Letter HC-SL-61-184 for procedure.  (If you have a Hartzell)  CFR 43.13  Yes ☐ No ☐ N/A ☐
38. Propeller backing plate made of composite check propeller hub for pitting corrosion  Yes ☐ No ☐ N/A ☐

## Avionics Installed

Type of Avionics:  List by part number and serial number.  CAR 3.721
ALTIMETERS  Yes ☐ No ☐ N/A ☐
ENCODING  Yes ☐ No ☐ N/A ☐
Mfg: ACK Model: ACK 30  Yes ☐ No ☐ N/A ☐
Type of Avionics: AUDIO PANEL  Yes ☐ No ☐ N/A ☐
Mfg: KING Model: KMA 20  Yes ☐ No ☐ N/A ☐
Type of Avionics: COLLISION AVOIDANCE SYSTEMS  Yes ☐ No ☐ N/A ☐
Mfg: RYAN INTERNATIONAL CORPORATION Model: ATS 7000  Yes ☐ No ☐ N/A ☐
Type of Avionics: GPS  Yes ☐ No ☐ N/A ☐
Mfg: KING Model: KLN 90  Yes ☐ No ☐ N/A ☐
Type of Avionics: RNAV  Yes ☐ No ☐ N/A ☐
Mfg: KING Model: KNS 80  Yes ☐ No ☐ N/A ☐
Type of Avionics: LOC  Yes ☐ No ☐ N/A ☐
Mfg: KING Model: KI 208  Yes ☐ No ☐ N/A ☐
Type of Avionics: NAV-COMM  Yes ☐ No ☐ N/A ☐
Mfg: KING Model: KX 170 B Channels: 720  Yes ☐ No ☐ N/A ☐
Type of Avionics: COMM  Yes ☐ No ☐ N/A ☐
Mfg: KING Model: KY 197 Channels: 720  Yes ☐ No ☐ N/A ☐
Type of Avionics: TRANSPONDERS  Yes ☐ No ☐ N/A ☐
Mfg: KING Model: KT 76A  Yes ☐ No ☐ N/A ☐
Type of Avionics: STORMSCOPE  Yes ☐ No ☐ N/A ☐

| | | |
|---|---|---|
| Mfg: 3 M Model: WX 1000+ | | Yes ☐ No ☐ N/A ☐ |
| Type of Avionics: GS | | Yes ☐ No ☐ N/A ☐ |
| Mfg: KING Model: KI 201 | | Yes ☐ No ☐ N/A ☐ |
| Type of Avionics: AUTOPILOTS | | Yes ☐ No ☐ N/A ☐ |
| Mfg: S-TEC Model: SYSTEM 60 PSS | | Yes ☐ No ☐ N/A ☐ |
| Mfg: CENTURY Model: CENTURY II B | | Yes ☐ No ☐ N/A ☐ |

## De-Icing Systems

| | | |
|---|---|---|
| Known Ice System: | CFR 23.1416` | Yes ☐ No ☐ N/A ☐ |
| Ice Lights work and condition | CFR 23.1416 | Yes ☐ No ☐ N/A ☐ |
| Prop De-Ice condition | CFR 23.1416 | Yes ☐ No ☐ N/A ☐ |
| De-Ice Type: | CFR 23.1416 | Yes ☐ No ☐ N/A ☐ |
| Wing Tail Boots condition | CAR 3.712 CFR 23.1416 | Yes ☐ No ☐ N/A ☐ |
| Boots Condition: | CAR 3.712 CFR 23.1416 | Yes ☐ No ☐ N/A ☐ |
| Windshield De-Ice condition | CFR 23.1416 | Yes ☐ No ☐ N/A ☐ |
| Windshield Wipers condition | CFR 23.1416 | Yes ☐ No ☐ N/A ☐ |
| Jet Intake De-Ice condition | CFR 23.1416 | Yes ☐ No ☐ N/A ☐ |
| Pitot Heat condition | CFR 23.1416 | Yes ☐ No ☐ N/A ☐ |

## Additional Equipment

| | | |
|---|---|---|
| Dual Controls: | CFR 23.777 | Yes ☐ No ☐ N/A ☐ |
| Type: Yoke. | CFR 23.777 | Yes ☐ No ☐ N/A ☐ |
| Stall Warning System works | CFR 23.703 | Yes ☐ No ☐ N/A ☐ |
| Stick Shaker works | CFR 23.672 | Yes ☐ No ☐ N/A ☐ |
| Rotating Beacon works | CAR 3.703 CFR 23.1401 | Yes ☐ No ☐ N/A ☐ |
| Strobe Light works | CFR 23.1401 | Yes ☐ No ☐ N/A ☐ |
| Taxi Lights works | CAR 3.655 CFR 23.1383 | Yes ☐ No ☐ N/A ☐ |
| Navigation Light works | CAR 3.661 CFR 23.1389 | Yes ☐ No ☐ N/A ☐ |
| Long Range Fuel | CFR 23.959 | Yes ☐ No ☐ N/A ☐ |
| Aux Fuel Qty works | CFR 23.955 | Yes ☐ No ☐ N/A ☐ |
| Single Point Refuel condition | CFR 23.953 | Yes ☐ No ☐ N/A ☐ |
| Lavatory condition | CFR 23.1561 | Yes ☐ No ☐ N/A ☐ |
| Galley condition | CFR 23.1561 | Yes ☐ No ☐ N/A ☐ |
| Cabinetry condition | CFR 23.1561 | Yes ☐ No ☐ N/A ☐ |
| Other Equipment condition | CAR 3.725 CFR 23.1561 | Yes ☐ No ☐ N/A ☐ |
| Intercom System works | CFR 23.1561 | Yes ☐ No ☐ N/A ☐ |
| Entertainment equipment CD player check for alteration form | CFR 43 App. A | Yes ☐ No ☐ N/A ☐ |
| Gap seal kit installed | CFR 43 App. A | Yes ☐ No ☐ N/A ☐ |
| Brackett Aero Filter STC installed | CFR 43 App. A | Yes ☐ No ☐ N/A ☐ |

## Special Inspections

| | | | Hours | Months | Years |
|---|---|---|---|---|---|
| 1. | Airworthiness Directives AD's | CFR 39 | ☐ | ☐ | ☐ |
| 2. | Engine fuel and oil lines | | ☐ | ☐ | ☐ |
| 3. | Brake lines | | ☐ | ☐ | ☐ |
| 4. | Air filter engine | | ☐ | ☐ | ☐ |
| 5. | Air filter instruments | | ☐ | ☐ | ☐ |
| 6. | Wing structural areas | | ☐ | ☐ | ☐ |
| 7. | Hard and over weight landings | | ☐ | ☐ | ☐ |
| 8. | Lighting strike damage | | ☐ | ☐ | ☐ |
| 9. | Hail damage | | ☐ | ☐ | ☐ |
| 10. | Severe Turbulence Inspection | | ☐ | ☐ | ☐ |
| 11. | Corrosion damage Inspection | | ☐ | ☐ | ☐ |
| 12. | Radio Equipment | | ☐ | ☐ | ☐ |

| 13. | Emergency Locater Transmitter (ELT) | CFR 91.207 | ☐ | ☐ | ☐ |
| 14. | Pitot Static | CFR 91.411 | ☐ | ☐ | ☐ |
| 15. | Transponder | CFR 91.411 | ☐ | ☐ | ☐ |
| 16. | Rigging checks | CFR 43 App. D | ☐ | ☐ | ☐ |
| 17. | New Weight and balance aircraft for compensation / hire | | ☐ | ☐ | ☐ |
| 18. | Magneto 200, 500 and etc. coil, contacts, etc. Inspection | | ☐ | ☐ | ☐ |
| 19. | Rigging Inspection | | ☐ | ☐ | ☐ |
| 20. | Oxygen bottles Inspection (Hydrostat) | | ☐ | ☐ | ☐ |
| 21. | Lubrication Inspection | | ☐ | ☐ | ☐ |
| 22. | Hose Inspection Fuel and Hydraulic | | ☐ | ☐ | ☐ |
| 23. | Compass magnetic direction (calibration) | CFR 23.1327 | ☐ | ☐ | ☐ |
| 24. | Airspeed indicator inspections | CFR 23.1323 | ☐ | ☐ | ☐ |
| 25. | Remove the rocker box covers and check for freedom of valve rockers | | ☐ | ☐ | ☐ |

## <u>Misc., Items</u> Aircraft Inspection

Below are some of the reported items found on New and Low Time aircraft, which should stress the importance of performing a thorough inspection:

| | Yes | No | N/A |
|---|---|---|---|
| Aileron control cable not over pulley; | ☐ | ☐ | ☐ |
| Aileron cable improperly installed in bell crank/cable retaining pin was not installed; | ☐ | ☐ | ☐ |
| Bolts loose on the vertical and horizontal stabilizer fin attachments; | ☐ | ☐ | ☐ |
| Broken and cracked electrical terminals; | ☐ | ☐ | ☐ |
| Control cable turnbuckles not saftied; | ☐ | ☐ | ☐ |
| Flap follow-up cable chafing on brake line; | ☐ | ☐ | ☐ |
| Foreign items in fuel cells/tanks; | ☐ | ☐ | ☐ |
| Fuel lines twisted, bent, kinked, obstructing flow; | ☐ | ☐ | ☐ |
| Fuel lines chafing - inadequate clamping | ☐ | ☐ | ☐ |
| Incorrect propeller bolts installed; | ☐ | ☐ | ☐ |
| Jam nuts drilled but no safety wire installed; | ☐ | ☐ | ☐ |
| Lock clips missing from control cable turnbuckles; | ☐ | ☐ | ☐ |
| Loose rivets in horizontal stabilizer leading edge; | ☐ | ☐ | ☐ |
| Main wheel tires do not clear wheel bays; | ☐ | ☐ | ☐ |
| Numerous drill chuck marks in aft face of pressure bulkhead. | ☐ | ☐ | ☐ |
| Oil lines leaking at connections; | ☐ | ☐ | ☐ |
| Primer line "T" fitting not installed; | ☐ | ☐ | ☐ |
| Propeller blade retention ferrules under torqued; | ☐ | ☐ | ☐ |
| Elevator trim cable wrapped around primary rudder control cable; | ☐ | ☐ | ☐ |
| Rivet holes drilled but rivets not installed, different areas; | ☐ | ☐ | ☐ |
| Rudder cable bell crank attach bolts loose; | ☐ | ☐ | ☐ |
| Rudder cable bolts fitted upside down; and | ☐ | ☐ | ☐ |
| Unreliable fuel quantity indications. | ☐ | ☐ | ☐ |

# Life limits CFR 43.10
This checklist is not exhaustive and does not supersede Manufacture's publications and is up-dated periodically!

| Calendar/ Hourly Life limited Items: | Years. | Hours. |
|---|---|---|
| **Airframe** | | |
| Gyro air filters, central | 5 | 500 |
| Non-Teflon fuel, oil, and hydraulic hoses | 15 | 3000 |
| Teflon fuel, oil, and hydraulic hoses | 20 | 4000 |
| Seat belt / shoulder harness webbing | 20 | |
| Stabilizer attach bolts | 25 | 6000 |
| Wing bolts | 25 | 6000 |
| **Engine** | | |
| Engine shock mounts | 15 | TBO |
| Non-Teflon fuel, oil, and hydraulic hoses | 8 | TBO |
| Teflon fuel, oil, and hydraulic hoses | 15 | TBO |
| Continental Engines | 2000 SL 98-9 | |

| Special Inspection Items: | Years. | Hours. |
|---|---|---|
| **Airframe** | | |
| Gyro air pump carbon vanes | 6 | 500 |
| Electric hydraulic pump motor | 15 | 500-1500 |
| Electro mechanical gear actuator | 15 | 3000 |
| Gear actuator motor brushes | 2 | 250 |
| Gear motor internal inspection / lubrication | 15 | 3000 |
| Flight control trim actuator(s) | 15 | 4500 |
| Electrical flap actuators/motors | 20 | 4000 |
| Stabilizer mounting bolts torque inspection | 5 | |
| Wing attach bolts torque inspection | 5 | |
| **Propeller** | | |
| Fixed pitch propeller recondition | 6 | 2000 |
| Mounting hardware | 20 | 2000 |
| Constant speed propeller overhaul | 6 | 2400 |
| Prop governor reseal | 15 | 1500 |
| Governor (Woodward) | 5 | 2400 |
| Accumulators | 5 | 1800 |
| **Engine** | | |
| Alternator | | 500 |
| Gear drive alternator internal inspection | 5 | 300 |
| Belt driven alternator internal inspection | 5 | 500 |
| Internal magneto inspection | 5 | 500 |
| Valve inspection/dry lash clearance | 15 | TBO |
| Cam / cam follower inspection (TCM engines) | 15 | mid life |
| Bendix fuel injector servo overhaul | 20 | TBO |
| Pressure carburetor overhaul | 20 | TBO |
| Primer nozzles cleaned and spray pattern | 5 | |
| Continental unmetered fuel pressure check | 2 | 400 |
| Diaphragm fuel pumps overhaul | 20 | TBO |
| Internal starter inspection | 5 | mid-life |
| Turbocharger oil inlet check valve(s) | 10 | 1000 |
| Turbocharger oil scavenge check valves(s) | 10 | 1000 |
| Hydraulic waste gate actuator(s) resealing | 10 | 1000 |

This is only a guide and should not be considered FAA approved data for life limits. Consult the manufacture recommendations, type certificate data sheets (TCDS), AD's, or the limitations section of FAA-approved airplane or rotorcraft flight manuals.

# Proposed Alteration Checklist

1. Description of alteration: _____
   _____
   _____

2. Make/Model: _____ Serial Number: _____
3. Type Certificate Data Sheet: _____

4. Certification basic:    CAR 3, 4a, 4b, 6, 7, or 8 _____
                          CFR.23, 25, 27, 29, 31, 33, or 35 _____

5. Will this Alteration effect the following:
   a.  Weight and balance                                                     Yes ☐ No ☐
   b.  Balance                                                                Yes ☐ No ☐
   c.  Structural Strength                                                    Yes ☐ No ☐
   d.  Performance                                                            Yes ☐ No ☐
   e.  Powerplant operation                                                   Yes ☐ No ☐
   f.  Flight Characteristics                                                 Yes ☐ No ☐
   g.  Occupants/cargo                                                        Yes ☐ No ☐
   h.  Fire protection                                                        Yes ☐ No ☐
   i.  Capability with other repair/alterations                              Yes ☐ No ☐
   j.  Flight manual supplement                                               Yes ☐ No ☐
   j.  Engine mounts                                                          Yes ☐ No ☐
   k.  Engine cooling/baffling                                                Yes ☐ No ☐
   l.  Flight Performance                                                     Yes ☐ No ☐
   m.  Landing gear                                                           Yes ☐ No ☐
   n.  Wings                                                                  Yes ☐ No ☐
   o.  Control Systems                                                        Yes ☐ No ☐
   p.  Tail surfaces                                                          Yes ☐ No ☐
   q.  Fuselage                                                               Yes ☐ No ☐
   6.  The user has determined that it is appropriate to the product being repaired/altered   Yes ☐ No ☐
   7.  The user has determined that it is directly applicable to the repair/alteration being made   Yes ☐ No ☐
   8.  The user has determined that it is not contrary to manufacturer's data   Yes ☐ No ☐
   9.  Will this action have any other effect on airworthiness?               Yes ☐ No ☐
   10. Will this action be accomplished by methods other than elementary operations?   Yes ☐ No ☐
   11. Will this action have a major effect on the product's type certificate?   Yes ☐ No ☐
   12. By definition of CFR 1 and CFR 43, Appendix A, is this a major repair?   Yes ☐ No ☐
   13. Review aircraft records for previous alterations and repairs that may have an affect on the
       proposed alteration or repair                                          Yes ☐ No ☐

Will this action effect the product's TSO (Tech Std. Order)? Ref: CFR Part 21 Subpart O   Yes ☐ NO ☐ N/A ☐
If "YES", obtain manufacturer's approval proceeding.

## Step 1:
Reference AC 43.9-1 Instructions for Completion of FAA Form 337           Yes ☐ No ☐

Make sure Block 8 is filled out with the 16 steps for the ICA or mark the bottom of Block 8 and attach your ICA with
supporting documents such as:

1.  Detailed description of the proposed alteration or repair             Yes ☐ No ☐
2.  Detailed design standards such as methods, sketches, drawings, stress analyses, photographs,
    electrical load analyses, etc.                                        Yes ☐ No ☐

3.  Testing procedures or methods to meet certification and/or operating rules, such as flammability, carbon monoxide, and noise requirements                                    Yes ☐ No ☐
4.  Detailed design standards, to ensure that the operator has considered all applicable design standards and has analyses to substantiate the findings in this regard.  The standards must consider at least the following:
    a.  The certification basis (fail safe, damage tolerance, etc.)                     Yes ☐ No ☐
    b.  The structural requirements that may be affected by the alteration or repair     Yes ☐ No ☐
    c.  Any hazards that may affect the aircraft or its occupants                        Yes ☐ No ☐
    d.  Weight and balance computations                                                  Yes ☐ No ☐
    e.  Operating limitations                                                            Yes ☐ No ☐
    f.  Any other factors affecting safety or airworthiness                              Yes ☐ No ☐

Evaluate the Proposal to Determine Compatibility With the Current Aircraft Configuration.  Make a preliminary evaluation of the proposed alteration and an inspection of the aircraft, as required.  Accomplish at least the following, as applicable:

1.  Review aircraft records for previous alterations and repairs that may have an affect on the proposed alteration or repair.                                                                        Yes ☐ No ☐
2.  Review maintenance and inspection procedures to determine that the alteration or repair is referenced                                                               Yes ☐ No ☐
3.  Inspect aircraft for the following:
    a.  Previous alterations or repairs that may not have been recorded.  Compatibility of previous alterations or repairs with intended alterations or repairs.                       Yes ☐ No ☐

## _Do NOT proceed with the alteration or repairs prior to receiving FAA approval._

## Step 2:

Submit **two** original Form 337 to the local Flight Standard District Office (FSDO), with the following blocks left **blank**:

1.  Block 3 is for FAA only                                                              Yes ☐ No ☐
2.  Block 6 is conformity statement                                                      Yes ☐ No ☐
3.  Block 7 is approval for return to service                                            Yes ☐ No ☐

## Step 3:

1.  Make sure you get the name and telephone number of the Inspector who will be evaluating your data for approval.
                                              Maintenance Inspector      Yes ☐ No ☐
                                              Avionics Inspector         Yes ☐ No ☐

2.  Give the FAA inspector your name and telephone number to be reached at              Yes ☐ No ☐
3.  Does your Form 337 require ACO engineering assistance, contact Inspector            Yes ☐ No ☐
4.  If you have not received your Form 337 back it two weeks contact Inspector          Yes ☐ No ☐
5.  Do **NOT** make promises to the owner when to expect completion                     Yes ☐ No ☐

## Step 4:

1.  Start work when you have Block 3 signed and dated by the FAA.                        Yes ☐ No ☐
2.  Maintenance and inspections performed must be recorded in accordance with FAR Sections 43.9
                                                                                        Yes ☐ No ☐
3.  Send completed copy of Form 337 with Block 6 and 7 signed and dated to the local Flight Standard District Office after work is completed.                                             Yes ☐ No ☐
4.  Provide owner with original copy or Form 337                                         Yes ☐ No ☐

# Required Data

**Data:** Information that supports and/or describes the alteration or repair, including the following:

| | |
|---|---|
| Drawings, sketches, and/or photographs | Yes ☐ No ☐ |
| Stress analysis | Yes ☐ No ☐ |
| Service Bulletins | Yes ☐ No ☐ |
| Engineering Orders | Yes ☐ No ☐ |
| Operating limitations | Yes ☐ No ☐ |

**Approved data:** Data that can be used to substantiate major repairs/major alterations, derived from the following:

1. Type Certificate Data Sheets    Yes ☐ No ☐
2. Supplemental Type Certificate (STC) data, provided that it specifically applies to the item being repaired/altered    Yes ☐ No ☐
3. Airworthiness Directives (AD)    Yes ☐ No ☐
4. Airframe, engine, and propeller manufacturer's "FAA-approved" maintenance manuals or instructions
5. Appliance manufacturer's manuals or instruction, unless specifically not approved by the Administrator or resulting in an alteration to the airframe, engine, and/or propeller    Yes ☐ No ☐
6. FAA Form 337 [ Front, Back, Info ], Major Repair or Alteration, when the specified data has been previously approved and will be used as a basis for a field approval    Yes ☐ No ☐
7. CAA Form 337, dated prior to 10/1/55    Yes ☐ No ☐
8. FAA Form 337[ Front, Back, Info ], used to approve multiple usage only, by the original modifier Yes ☐ No ☐
9. Structural Repair Manuals (SRM), only as a source of approved data for a major repair, when it is an FAA-approved document. Data that is contained in an SRM that is not FAA-approved, can be used on a case-by-case basis if prior FAA approval is granted for that repair.    Yes ☐ No ☐
10. Parts Manufacturer Authorization (PMA), is considered approved data for the part only, an STC may be required for the actual installation    Yes ☐ No ☐
11. Technical Standard Order Authorization (TSOA)    Yes ☐ No ☐
12. Delegation Option Authorization produced FAA-approved data    Yes ☐ No ☐
13. Designated Engineering Representative (DER) approved data, only within authorized limitations Yes ☐ No ☐
14. Designated Alteration Station (DAS) FAA approved    Yes ☐ No ☐
15. Repair data, under SFAR 36, for the holder's aircraft only    Yes ☐ No ☐
16. Foreign bulletins, for use on U.S.-certificated foreign aircraft, when approved by the foreign authority    Yes ☐ No ☐
17. Data describing an article or appliance used in an alteration, which is FAA-approved under a TSO. As such, the conditions and tests required for TSO approval of an article are minimum performance standards. The article may be stalled only if further evaluation by the operator (applicant) documents an acceptable installation, which may be approved by the Administrator.    Yes ☐ No ☐
18. Data in the form of (TCA) Appliance Type Approval issued by the Minister of Transport Canada for those parts or appliances for which there is no current TSO available. The TCA certificate is included within the installation manual provided with the appliance and includes the dates of issuance and an environmental qualification statement.    Yes ☐ No ☐
19. Data describing a part or appliance used in an alteration, which is FAA-approved under a Parts Manufacturer Approval (PMA). (An STC may be required to obtain a PMA as a means of assessing airworthiness and/or performance of the part.)    Yes ☐ No ☐

# Acceptable Data

This data may also be used as a basis to gain FAA data approval for major repairs.

1. AC 43.13-1 and 2, Acceptable Methods, Techniques, and Practices (Aircraft Inspection and Repair), may be used directly as approved data (**for repairs only**) without further approval only when there is no manufacturer repair or maintenance instructions that address the repair and the user has determined that it is

   a. **Appropriate to the product being repaired;**      Yes ☐ No ☐
   b. **Directly applicable to the repair being made; and**      Yes ☐ No ☐
   c. **Not contrary to manufacturer's data.**      Yes ☐ No ☐

2. FAA FIELD APPROVAL (FAA FORM 337) issued for duplication of identical aircraft may be used as approved data only when the identical alteration is performed on an aircraft of identical make, model, and series by the original modifier. FAA Form 337's info. Approved in 1955 or earlier may be used as approved data.      Yes ☐ No ☐

3. Manufactures technical manuals, (e.g. bulletins, kits, etc.)      Yes ☐ No ☐

# ACO Assistance for Alterations/Repairs

**Engineering assistance and advice must be requested when working in areas that include:**

1. Use of synthetic covering material      Yes ☐ No ☐
2. Substitution of parts      Yes ☐ No ☐
3. Processes on which insufficient information is available      Yes ☐ No ☐
4. New chrome plating applications      Yes ☐ No ☐
5. New titanium applications      Yes ☐ No ☐
6. Ceramic coatings      Yes ☐ No ☐
7. New magnesium applications      Yes ☐ No ☐
8. Use of synthetic resin glues      Yes ☐ No ☐
9. New stripping or plating coatings      Yes ☐ No ☐
10. New welding or brazing techniques      Yes ☐ No ☐
11. Welding of certain types of propeller or engine parts      Yes ☐ No ☐
12. Application of TSO's to specific installations      Yes ☐ No ☐
13. Alternative means for complying with AD's      Yes ☐ No ☐
14. Any change to a required aircraft instrument system      Yes ☐ No ☐
15. Any other complex special process that if not properly performed could have an adverse effect on the integrity of the product.      Yes ☐ No ☐
16. Alterations requiring a flight manual supplement or operations limitations changes must be coordinated with the Aircraft Certification Office.      Yes ☐ No ☐
17. Any alteration or repair that may have changed the aircraft flight characteristics appreciably or substantially affected its operation in flight, will be operationally checked in accordance with CFR Section 91.407 and the results recorded on the aircraft records.      Yes ☐ No ☐

An alteration or repair requiring either an operational flight test to show compliance with the regulations, or a change to a flight manual or operations limitations must be coordinated with the appropriate engineering office. Yes ☐ No ☐

# Importing Aircraft
## Checklist

**Reference: Order 8130.2 Chapter 6 Para 241**

Under the procedure of CFR 21.19 imported aircraft with a Type Certificate are entitled to a U.S. airworthiness certificate (standard or special) if the CAA of the country of manufacture certifies, and the FAA finds, that the aircraft conforms to its approved TC and is found to be in a condition for safe operation.

AC 21-23
CFR 21 Subpart H
CFR 36, 39, 45, 49, and 91
**Requirements for Airworthiness Certification**

## Standard Airworthiness Certificate FAA Form 8130-6

| | | |
|---|---|---|
| 1. | Form 8130-6 completed and signed prior to submitting | Yes ☐ No ☐ |
| 2. | Form 8130-6 check block 11 Import___ CFR 21.183.c | Yes ☐ No ☐ |
| 3. | Application made by owner | Yes ☐ No ☐ |
| 4. | Agent must have a letter of authorization 8130.2 para 242 | Yes ☐ No ☐ |
| 5. | Has a completed C of A Check Certification Office. | Yes ☐ No ☐ |
| 6. | Contact aircraft registry A/W has not been previously denied | Yes ☐ No ☐ |
| 7. | Form 8130-1 Application for export 8130.2 para 220 | Yes ☐ No ☐ |
| 8. | Form 8130-4 Export certificate of airworthiness | Yes ☐ No ☐ |
| 9. | Proof of ownership | Yes ☐ No ☐ |
| 10. | Did the aircraft require a special flight permit to be brought in | Yes ☐ No ☐ |
| 11. | 100 hour inspection complete Reference 8130.21 para 60 | Yes ☐ No ☐ |

## Registration Requirements:

| | | |
|---|---|---|
| 1. | Registration application completed | Yes ☐ No ☐ |
| 2. | Registration application submitted Part 47 hard copy in A/C | Yes ☐ No ☐ |
| 3. | Nationality/markings applied CFR 45, subpart C | Yes ☐ No ☐ |
| 4. | Aircraft title | Yes ☐ No ☐ |
| 5. | Security documents CFR 49 | Yes ☐ No ☐ |
| 6. | Is the registered owner a U.S. citizen | Yes ☐ No ☐ |

### NOTE
### *The FAA can't issue an exemption for the above requirements.*

| | | |
|---|---|---|
| 7. | Evidence of de-registration from the exporting state _____ | Yes ☐ No ☐ |
| 8. | U.S. registration required _____ CFR 47 | Yes ☐ No ☐ |
| 9. | Is the registered owner a corporation | Yes ☐ No ☐ |
| 10. | Does the registered owner hold a alien registration card | Yes ☐ No ☐ |

## Aircraft Inspection Requirements

## Product Identification

| | | |
|---|---|---|
| 1. | 100 hour inspection requirement completed CFR 21.183 (c)(d)(2) | Yes ☐ No ☐ |

2. Aircraft data plate ___ CFR 21.182 and meets requirements of CFR 45. Subpart B    Yes ☐ No ☐
3. Engine data plate affixed to engine.    Yes ☐ No ☐
4. Data plates fire proof CFR 45.13    Yes ☐ No ☐
5. Information etched, stamped engraved CFR 45.13    Yes ☐ No ☐
6. Data plate secured not to be defaced    Yes ☐ No ☐
7. Data plate location rear most entrance door or fuselage surface near the tail    Yes ☐ No ☐
8. Propellers data plate places on a non -critical part    Yes ☐ No ☐
9. Appliances data plate CFR 21.502    Yes ☐ No ☐
10. Parts spares acceptance CFR 21.502 and subpart O    Yes ☐ No ☐
11. Materials spares acceptance CFR 21.502 and subpart O    Yes ☐ No ☐
12. Life limited parts must have maintenance records CFR 91.417    Yes ☐ No ☐

# DATA PLATE information:

Reference CFR 45 Subpart B

1. Builder name Airframe ____ Engine ___    Yes ☐ No ☐
2. Model designation    Yes ☐ No ☐
3. Builders serial number serial number _____    Yes ☐ No ☐
4. Type certificate number if any TC number _____    Yes ☐ No ☐
5. Product certificate number if any TC number _____    Yes ☐ No ☐
6. Engine establish the rating _____    Yes ☐ No ☐
7. Jan. 1, 1984 exhaust emission requirements older    Yes ☐ No ☐

# Noise Requirement:

Reference:
CFR 21.93(b), 21.183(e) or 21.185(d)
CFR 36, SCFR 41, or CFR 91 subpart I as applicable

1. Classification in change in type design    Yes ☐ No ☐
2. Aircraft conforms to original TC shows evidence    CFR 21.183 (c) (d) (1)    Yes ☐ No ☐
3. Proper fuel venting    Yes ☐ No ☐

# Approved Flight Manual

1. Has approved flight manual English language    CFR 91.9    Yes ☐ No ☐
2. Has approved markings in English    Yes ☐ No ☐
3. Placards in English    Yes ☐ No ☐
4. Up-dated weight and balance    Yes ☐ No ☐
5. Equipment List    Yes ☐ No ☐

# Logbooks and Maintenance Records
Reference CFR 91 section 91.417 and CFR 39

1. Aircraft accompanied by logbooks    Yes ☐ No ☐
2. Required inspections accomplished (annual)    Yes ☐ No ☐
3. AD's compliance airframe    Yes ☐ No ☐
4. AD's compliance engine    Yes ☐ No ☐
5. AD's compliance propeller    Yes ☐ No ☐ N/A ☐
6. AD's compliance rotor    Yes ☐ No ☐ N/A ☐
7. AD's compliance appliance    Yes ☐ No ☐ N/A ☐

8. AD's compliance life limited     Yes ☐ No ☐ N/A ☐
9. Applicant can identify repairs/modification     Yes ☐ No ☐ N/A ☐
10. Any alterations were accomplished in accordance with an approved STC or other FAA-approved data.
    Yes ☐ No ☐ N/A ☐

## If aircraft meets the requirements for certification request:

1. Make a aircraft logbook entry per Order 8130.2 para 237 (8)(d)     Yes ☐ No ☐
2. Complete section 5 and 8 of Form 8130-6 per 8130.2 para 267(7)(d     Yes ☐ No ☐
3. Issue FAA form 8100-2 Standard Airworthiness Certificate per 8130.2 para 238     Yes ☐ No ☐

**Airframe Maintenance record entry per 3130.2 para 237 (8)(d) as follows:**

## FAA Inspectors Record entry

"I find that the aircraft meets the requirements for the certification requested and issued a (Standard)(Special) Airworthiness Certificated dated _____. The next inspection is due _____."

Signed: John Doe, Aviation Safety Inspector, WP-00.

# Definitions

**Airworthiness:** Section 603(c) of the FAA Act of 1958 and CFR 21.183 (a), (b), (d), and (e), both set two conditions necessary for issuance of an airworthiness certificate: ❶ the aircraft must conform to the type design (certificate); and ❷ it is in a condition for safe operation. The above conditions also appear on the front of the standard airworthiness certificate, FAA Form 8100-2.

**Discussion:** Regarding condition ❶, conformity to type design is considered attained when the required and proper components are installed and they are consistent with the drawings, specifications and other data that are a part of the type certificates and approved alterations. (Cf. CFR 21.31)

**Condition ❷** refers to the condition of the aircraft with relation to wear and deterioration - conditions such as skin corrosion, window delamination or crazing, fluid leaks, tire wear, etc.

**Airworthy:** An aircraft can be considered airworthy when the Administrator finds it conforms to the specifications of its type certificate, and it is in a condition for safe operation. If one or both of these conditions are not met, the aircraft would not be considered airworthy.

**Aeronautical product:** means any civil aircraft or airframe, aircraft engine, propeller, appliance, component, or part to be installed thereon.

**Code of Federal Regulations (CFR):** Laws passed by Congress and administrated by the Federal Aviation Administration.

**Direct Drive Engines:** are those piston-powered engines where the propeller is bolted on the end of the crankshaft and the prop turns at the same speed as the crankshaft.

**Geared Engines:** are usually the higher powered, more complex engines using a reduction gear on the nose of the aircraft, and with the prop attached to it. As a result, the prop will turn somewhat slower than the crankshaft, resulting in a lower prop noise level. When the engine is geared, we precede the engine designation with a "G." Thus a geared, opposed (O) normally aspirated Lycoming engine with a 480 cubic inch displacement of the cylinders would be designated a GO-480 model.

**Inspection:** The routine performance of inspection tasks at prescribed intervals. The inspection must ensure the airworthiness of an aircraft up to and including its **overhaul or life-limits**.

**Maintenance:** Means the performance of inspection, overhaul, repair, preservation, and the replacement of parts, materials, appliances, or components of a product to assure the continued airworthiness of that product, including the performance of approved modifications.

**Modification:** means making a change to the type design.

**Normally Aspirated Engine:** is one that is not turbocharged or supercharged. If the airplane has a manifold pressure gauge, at full takeoff power at sea level on a standard day it would indicate a MP reading of approximately 29" of Hg. Takeoff power at 5,000 ft. density altitude airport would read about 24" MP. The normally aspirated engine uses atmospheric pressure and is thereby altitude limited.

**Preventive Maintenance:** is simple or minor preservation operations or replacement of small standard parts not involving complex assembly operations.

**Progressive Maintenance:** This is a continuous maintenance program whereby the required FAA and manufacturer inspections are accomplished during the most convenient time, while keeping the aircraft in a state of continuous airworthiness. Several General Aviation airframe manufacturers have established sound Progressive Maintenance programs with FAA approval. Owners and operators are reminded that certain FAA requirements must be met before a Progressive Maintenance program can be used. These requirements are contained in the Code of Federal Regulations,

Part 43, "Maintenance, Preventive Maintenance, Rebuilding and Alteration," and Part 91.409, "General Operating and Flight Rules."

The Progressive Maintenance program has had more appeal where planes for hire are involved (i. e., commuter, air taxi, flight instruction), rather than those privately owned

**Scheduled (Routine) Maintenance:** The performance of maintenance tasks at prescribed intervals.

**Structural Inspection**: A detailed inspection of the airframe structure that may require special inspection techniques to determine the continuous integrity of the airframe and its related.

**Scheduled Maintenance.** Maintenance tasks performed at prescribed intervals are considered scheduled maintenance. Some of these tasks are performed concurrently with inspection tasks and may be included on the same work form. Work forms that include maintenance instructions must be provided for a record of the accomplishment of these tasks.

   (a)   Scheduled tasks include replacement of **life-limited** items and components requiring periodic overhaul, special nondestructive inspections (such as X-rays), checks or tests for on-condition items, lubrications, and weighing aircraft.

**Service Bulletins:** The FAA states that whenever an aircraft or engine manufacturer determines, through service experience, that his product may be improved by some modification, or that the service life of his product may be extended by some particular maintenance or repair, he may issue a service bulletin. The latter will tell what the trouble is and how to remedy it. The service bulletin usually addresses those items that affect safety of flight

**Supercharged Engines:** as manufactured by Textron Lycoming used a compressor wheel to pack air into the cylinders; but the compressor is driven by the crankshaft through an intricate gearing system, which takes considerable horsepower from the engine to operate. In comparison with a turbocharged engine, it is a medium altitude powerplant.

**Turbocharged Engines:** as manufactured by Lycoming simply consist of a turbocharger unit with a small turbine wheel attached by a common shaft to a compressor wheel, and utilizes the engine exhaust gas by directing it over the turbine wheel to drive the compressor. The horsepower loss in operating the turbocharger is negligible. Turbocharging can provide greater utility to the piston engine by providing sea-level horsepower, in some models, as high as 20,000 feet; or it can be used to add horsepower to the engine particularly for takeoff. The faster the engine runs, the more air the turbocharger can pack into the cylinder to compensate for the thin air of altitude, or to increase the horsepower. Although this definition is somewhat over-simplified, it is a basic definition of turbocharging of General Aviation power plants.

**Unscheduled:** (Non-Routine) Maintenance: The performance of maintenance tasks when mechanical irregularities occur. These irregularities are categorized as to whether or not they occur during flight time.

**Visually Accessible:** For the purpose of this book, means that a section, area, parts, system, etc., of the aircraft, can be viewed by the opening of a hatch/door or the removal of an inspection plate. It does not mean the removal of equipment, components, or the disassembly of any part of the aircraft that cannot be performed by simple means.

# Index

## A

A&P, 8, 9, 19, 20, 21, 23, 29

A&P mechanic, 3, 8, 9, 19, 20, 21, 22, 23, 28, 29, 30, 32, 34, 36, 37, 38, 39, 67, 84, 142, 146, 174

Accident history, 34

Administrative, 46

Advisory circular, 8, 66, 71, 125, 142, 193, 196, 198, 200

Aileron, **120**, 164

Agreements, 5, 6, 11 136

Aircraft Flight Manual (AFM), 12, 13, 14, 16, 144, 145, 147, 180, 194

Aircraft owner, 8, 21, 28, 31, 46, 59, 60, 75, 76, 121, 125, 197

Aircraft records, 1, 6, 7, 8, 9, 11, 15, **26**, 27, 34, 36, 44, 62, 63, 94, 166, 168, 174, 197

Aircraft Registry, 7, 77, 197

Aircraft Title, 7, 8

Aircraft mechanic, 2, 20, 94, 101

Airworthy, 1 4, 9, 11, 23, 26, 27, 28, 45, 47, **64**, 128, 174, 208, 214, 133

Airworthiness, 1, 2, 3, 5, 6, 8, 11, 12, 16, 17, 18, 19, 20, 21, 22, 26, 27, 29, 31, 35, 37, 39, 40, 44, 47, 49, 53, 55, 57, 58, 62, 63, 64, 65, 66, 75, 93, 94, 97, 99, 100, **125**, 126, 128, **132**, 133, 139, 140, 147, 151, 163, 168, 187, 188, 190, 191, 194, 195, 200, 233

Airworthiness Certificate, 5, 6, 8, 11, 12, 19, 22, 24, 27, 37, 46, 58, 60, **62**, 63, 64, 65, 66, 121, 126, 132, 137, 172, 198, 233

Airworthiness Directive (AD), 1, 5, 9, 12, 16, 17, 17, 24, 26, 27, 32, 33, 40, 41, **42**, 43, **46**, 49, 53, 63, 89, 162, 163, 190

Airworthiness Inspector, 6, 189

Alterations, 5, 6, 11, 12, 14, 15, 17, 20, 21, 22, 23, 24, 26, 27, 31, 37, **45**, 48, 75, 133, 142, 144, **189**, 190, 191, 193, 194, 195, 200

Alternators, 42, 49, 52, **112**, 183

Annual inspection, 2 3, 319, 20, 21, 22, 27, 28, 37, 40, **41**, 42, 43, **44**, 47, 80, 127, 128, 183, 214

Antennas, 43, 195

Approved date, 14, 22, 40, 52, 133, 134, 135, 139, 189, **190**, **191**, 193, 194, 195, 197

Approved part, 13, 75, 127, 133, **134**, 135, 138, 139

ATA codes, 49

Avionics, 2, 3, 50, 185, 189, 194

## B

Baffle seals, 9, 50, 70, 74, **75**, 191

Battery, 10, 30, 41, 49, 53, 111, 112, 113

Bearings, 30, 50, 68, 79, 80, 87, 88, 89, 96, 97, 98, 100, **101**, **102**, 103, 104, 105, 106, 107, 108, 117, 166

Bill of Sale, 11, 59, 60, 66, 207

Blades, 5, 9, 50, 57, 87, 88, 89, 90, 91, 94

Bolts, 51, 71, 72, 88, 89, 96, 97, 98, 100, 120, 135, 143, 150, 152, 153, 159, 162, 163

Brakes, 9, 10, 13, 30, 41, 96, 98, 99, 101, 166, **182**, 191

Bus, 111, 112, 113

## C

CAR-3, 94, 126, 127

Carburetor, 10, 52, 71, 81, 85

Calendar, 18, 19, 33, 35, 41, 43, 45, 46, 51

Calibration, 50, 71, 128, 140, 184, **185**, **186**, 187, 188, 213

Carcass, 99, 109, **173**

Carpet, 126, 153

Categories of aircraft, 62

Center of gravity (CG), 14, 15, 73, 120, 191

Cessna Aircraft Company, 6

Certification, 6, 14, 16, 24, 42, 44, 46, 49, 58, 61, **63**, **64**, 66, 70, 73, 94, 125, 126, 136, 147, 151, 176, 185, 196, 198, 214, 211

Certification basis, 126, 127, 148, 151

Certificate of Registration, 61

Change of Address, 60, 61

Civil Aeronautics Administration, 126

Civil Air Regulation, 125, 151, **198**

Circuit Breakers, 111, 113, 145, 147

Chord, 92

Chrome 93, 103, 192

Clocks, 22, 48, 147, 148, 213

Code of Federal Regulations, 1, 15, 21, 22, 26, 35, **120**, 120, 148, **198**, 233

Compression check, 10, 67, 70

Composite, 25

Computer, 25, 48, 56, 60, 66

Contract, 4, 5, 8, 9, 10, 11, 15, **24**, 47, 59, 60, 141

Control surface, 30, 49, 91, 120, 135, 159, 166, 180, 191

Cord, 49, 50

Corrosion, 27, 37, **38**, 49, 50p, 53, 54, 67, 74, 76, 86, 87, 88, 89, 94, 96, 97, 99, 100, 101, 103, 105, 106, 108, 111, **116**, **117**, 118, 119, 131, 140, 145, 150, 159, 160, 161, 163, 179

Cracks, 9, 29, 50, 53, 56, 70, 72, 75, 82, 83, 84, 85, 87, 89, 92, 93, 96, 97, 98, 100, 110, 123, 124, 131, 145, 153, 154, 155, 156, 157, 158, `59, 161, 162, 163, 164 169, 171, 174, 182

Crankcase, 10, 70, 74, 78, **79**, 80, 81, 84

Cylinders, 50, 57, 67, 70, 76, 76, 80, 82, 83, 84, 97, 99, 178, 179, 181

# References

A brief history of the federal aviation administration and its predecessor agencies. FAA website. [Online]. Available: http://www.faa.gov/apa/history/briefhistory.htm [2002, January 30]. Adamski, A.J., & Doyle, T.J. (1999). Introduction to the aviation regulatory process (4th ed.). Michigan: Hayden-McNeil Publishing, Inc. An overview of the federal aviation administration. FAA website. [Online]. Available: http://www.faa.gov/apa/history/overvue.htm [2002, January 30]. Assistant Administrator for Financial Services Office of Cost and Performance Management Standards and Information Division. (2001). Administrator's fact book. [Online]. Available: http://www.atctraining.faa.gov/factbook [2002, January 30]. Kane, R.M., (1999). Air transportation (13th ed.). Iowa: Kendall/Hunt Publishing Company. This is the FAA. FAA website [Online]. Available: http://faa.gov/eduacation/documents.other. thisisfaa/index.htm [2002, January 30]. Wells, A.T., (1997). Commercial aviation safety (2nd ed.). New York: McGraw-Hill. References A brief history of the federal aviation administration and its predecessor agencies. FAA website. [Online]. Available: http://www.faa.gov/apa/history/briefhistory.htm [2002, January 30]. Adamski, A.J., & Doyle, T.J. (1999). Introduction to the aviation regulatory process (4th ed.). Michigan: Hayden-McNeil Publishing, Inc. An overview of the federal aviation administration. FAA website. [Online]. Available: http://www.faa.gov/apa/history/overvue.htm [2002, January 30]. Assistant Administrator for Financial Services Office of Cost and Performance Management Standards and Information Division. (2001). Administrator's fact book. [Online]. Available: http://www.atctraining.faa.gov/factbook [2002, January 30]. Kane, R.M., (1999). Air transportation (13th ed.). Iowa: Kendall/Hunt Publishing Company. This is the FAA. FAA website [Online]. Available: http://faa.gov/eduacation/documents.other. this is faa/index.htm [2002, January 30]. Wells, A.T., (1997). Commercial aviation safety (2nd ed.). New York: McGraw-Hill. References Adamski, A. J., Doyle, T. J., Aviation Regulatory Process. (3rd ed.). (1995). Westland, MI: Hayden-McNeil Publishing, Inc. Federal Aviation Administration. (1998). Code of Federal Regulations and Aeronautical Information Manuel. New Castle, WA: ASA. Hertzler, J. V. (1997). New Record Keeping Requirement. Aviation Maintenance Regulatory Report. Retrieved March 10, 1999 from the World Wide Web: http://avtrak.com/publications/7-31.htm King, F. H. (1986). FAA Order 8130 Airworthiness Certification of Aircraft and Related Products [Online] www.faa.gov. FAA Order 8300.10 Airworthiness Inspectors Handbook. [Online] www.faa.gov. FAA-H-8083-1 Aircraft Weight and Balance Handbook. FAA Advisory Circulars [Online] www.faa.gov. FAA Federal Aviation Regulations [Online] www.faa.gov. Fundamentals of Aircraft Material Factors by Charles E. Dole. Metallic Materials and Elements for Flight Vehicle Structure (MIL-HDBK-5 &1 7). [Doc. No. 1993, 29 FR 5451, Apr. 23, 1964, as amended by Amdt. 43-14, 37 FR 14291, June 19, 1972; Amdt. 43-23, 47 FR 41086, Sept. 16, 1982; Amdt. 43-24, 49 FR 44602, Nov. 7, 1984; Amdt. 43-25, 51 FR 40703, Nov. 7, 1986; Amdt. 43-27, 52 FR 17277, May 6, 1987; Amdt. 43-34, 57 FR 41369, Sept. 9, 1992; Amdt. 43-36, 61 FR 19501, May 1, 1996]. MIL-W-22759C, MIL-C-85570, MIL-P-25374B, MIL-G-23827, MIL-C-81309, MIL-G-25871B, SAE Publication J1661, ASTM Publication D1682, ASTM Publication D5034 and D5035, Title 49 U.S. Code part 1-100, FAA Order 8130.2, FAA Order 8300.10 change 16, FAA Order 2150.3, TCM Service Bulletin SB89-9, TCM SB 96-11, Lycoming Service Bulletin 533 and 474B, Textron Lycoming Key Reprints, Lycoming service instruction No. 1111 and 240, Hartzell Service Letter HC-SL-61-91, McCauley Service Letter 1992-12C, Piper Service Bulletin 1044, T.O. 1-1A-14, Flight Standards Service Release No. 453, Federal Test Method Standard No. 191A, SAE ARP-1832, SAE Aerospace Standard (AS) 1055B, and SAE Aerospace Information Report (AIR) 1377A. Alternative Refrigerants, hhtp://www.epa.gov/doc/ozone/title6/sna[/macssubs. National Aerospace Standards (NAS), Army-Navy Aeronautical Standard (AN), Society of Automotive Engineers (SAE), SAE Sematec, Joint Electron Device Engineering Council, Joint Electron Tube Engineering Council, and American National Standards Institute (ANSI). Aeronautics Bulletin" (Bulletin 7-A) Civil Aeronautics Board "Civil Air Regulations" (CAR), Federal Specification P-S-1792, GGG-W-868l American Society of Mechanical Engineers (ASME) document B107.14M and the International Standards Organization (ISO) document 6789, NASA Reference Publication 1046, "Measurement of Aircraft Speed and Altitude," by W. Gracey, May 1980. American National Standard for Calibration (ANSI) ANSI/NCSL Z540-1-1994, Military Standard MIL-STD-45662A dated 1 August 1988, International Standard ISO 10012-1, corrected and reprinted 1993-05-01). Teledyne Continental Motor, Inc. McCauley propellers, Sensenich Propellers, Hartzell Propellers, Hamilton Standard Propellers, Aeroshell, Barden Precision Ball Bearing

Printed in the United States
By Bookmasters